BORDER THINKING ON THE EDGES OF THE WEST

Drawing on scholarly and life experience on, and over, the historically posited borders between "West" and "East," the work identifies, interrogates, and challenges a particular, enduring, violent inheritance – what it means to cross over a border – from the classical origins of Western political thought. The study has two parts. The first is an effort to work within the Western tradition to demonstrate its foundational and enduring, violent conception of crossing over borders. The second is a creative effort to explore and encourage a fundamentally different outlook towards borders and what it means to be on, at, or over them. The underlying social theoretical disposition of the work is a form of post-Orientalist hermeneutics; the textual subject matter of the two parts of the study is linked using Walter Benjamin's concept of the storyteller.

The underlying premise of the work is that the sense of violent possibility on the borders between "West" and "East" existed well before the more recent "age of imperialism" and even before there was a "West" or an "East" to speak of. That sense is constitutive of a political imagination about borders developed deep within the revered sources of Western culture. On the other hand, confronting the influence of such violent imaginaries requires truly novel modes of hermeneutical openness, hospitality and solidarity.

Seeking to offer a new understanding and opening in the study of borders, this work will provide a significant contribution to several areas including international relations theory, border studies and political theory.

Andrew Davison is Professor of Political Science at Vassar College, USA.

WORLDING BEYOND THE WEST
Series Editors:
Arlene B. Tickner, Universidad de los Andes, Bogotá, Ole Wæver, University of Copenhagen, David Blaney, Macalester College and Pinar Bilgin, Bilkent University

The *Worlding Beyond the West* series editorial board are:
Naeem Inayatullah (*Ithaca College, USA*), Himadeep Muppidi (*Vassar College, USA*), Mustapha Kamal Pasha (*University of Aberdeen, UK*), Sanjay Seth (*Goldsmiths, University of London, UK*), Quin Yaqing (*China Foreign Affairs University, China*), Navnita Chandra Behera (*Jamia Milia Islamia University, India*).

Historically, the field of International Relations has established its boundaries, issues, and theories based upon Western experience. This series aims to explore the role of geocultural factors in setting the concepts and epistemologies through which IR knowledge is produced. In particular, it seeks to identify alternatives for thinking about the "international" that are more in tune with local concerns and traditions outside the West.

1. INTERNATIONAL RELATIONS SCHOLARSHIP AROUND THE WORLD
Edited by Arlene B. Tickner and Ole Wæver

2. THINKING THE INTERNATIONAL DIFFERENTLY
Edited by Arlene B. Tickner and David L. Blaney

3. INTERNATIONAL RELATIONS IN FRANCE
Writing between discipline and state
Henrik Breitenbauch

4. CLAIMING THE INTERNATIONAL
Edited by Arlene B. Tickner and David L. Blaney

5. BORDER THINKING ON THE EDGES OF THE WEST
Crossing over the Hellespont
Andrew Davison

BORDER THINKING ON THE EDGES OF THE WEST

Crossing over the Hellespont

Andrew Davison

LONDON AND NEW YORK

First published 2014
by Routledge
2 Park Square, Milton Park, Abingdon, Oxfordshire OX14 4RN

and by Routledge
711 Third Avenue, New York, NY 10017

First issued in paperback 2016

Routledge is an imprint of the Taylor and Francis Group, an informa business

British Library Cataloguing in Publication Data
A catalogue record for this book is available from the British Library

Library of Congress Cataloging in Publication Data
Davison, Andrew, 1962–
   Border thinking on the edges of the West : crossing over the Hellespont / Andrew Davison.
      pages cm. – (Worlding beyond the West ; 5)
   Includes bibliographical references and index.
   1. Boundaries–Philosophy. 2. Border crossing–Philosophy. 3. East and West. I. Title.
   JC323.D38 2014
   320.1'2–dc23
               2013027600

ISBN 13: 978-1-138-28786-0 (pbk)
ISBN 13: 978-0-415-70979-8 (hbk)

Typeset in Times New Roman
by Taylor & Francis Books

Permissions

Rome and the Mediterranean: Books XXXI–XLV of the History of Rome from its Foundation by Livy, translated by Henry Bettenson, introduction by A.H. McDonald (Penguin Classics, 1976). Translation © Henry Bettenson, 1976. Introduction © A.H. McDonald, 1976. Reproduced by permission of Penguin Books Ltd.
The History of Alexander by Quintus Curtius Rufus, translated by John Yardley, introduction and notes by Waldemar Heckel (Penguin Classics, 1984). Translation © John Yardley, 1984. Introduction, notes and additional material © Waldemar Heckel, 1984. Reproduced by permission of Penguin Books Ltd.
I wish to thank Yaşar Kemal for his generosity in permitting me to convey extensive selections from *Ince Memed*, volumes 1–3, Istanbul: Yapı Kredi Yayınları. *Şu dünyada ne iyi insanlar var.*

CONTENTS

*Preface: working in, on, and beyond the imagination of the
West today*   vii
A note on the use of italics for foreign-language words   xvii
Abbreviations   xviii

Introduction   1

I   Synopsis   1

II   Part one: When words maintain their meanings and the world is
       an abode of war   2

III   Part two: On the fatal boundaries   4

IV   A link: Storytelling as counsel   7

V   Conclusion: Perhaps not crossing at all   11

PART ONE
When words maintain their meanings and the world is an abode of war   15

I   Conceptual stability in a sea of change   15

II   A hermeneutic, participatory approach   18

III   *"To cross thy stream, broad Hellespont!"*   24

IV   Crossing for empire, godliness, and glory   31

V   Crossing as war, part I   37

CONTENTS

VI   A note on liberation and glory   43

VII   Crossing as war, part II   46

VIII   Alternatives, part I: Crossing in flight   61

IX   Alternatives, part II: In praise of the Medizer   63

X   Crossing the Hellespont   81

XI   A tradition of meanings   84

PART TWO
On the fatal boundaries   91

I   Introduction   91

II   The village of Değirmenoluk   93

III   Vayvay   121

IV   Sakızlı   181

Conclusion: Perhaps not crossing at all   266

       Index   287

PREFACE

Working in, on, and beyond the imagination of the West today

You and I were walking along the river towards the railway bridge and we had a heated discussion in which you made a remark about "national character" that shocked me by its primitiveness. I then thought: what is the use of studying philosophy if all that it does for you is to enable you to talk with some plausibility about some abstruse questions of logic, etc., and if it does not improve your thinking about important questions of everyday life, if it does not make you more conscientious than any … journalist in the use of the dangerous phrases such people use for their own ends. You see, I know that it's difficult to think well about "certainty," "probability," "perception," etc. But it is, if possible still more difficult to think, or try to think, really honestly about your life and other people's lives. And the trouble is that thinking about these things is not thrilling, but often downright nasty. And when it's nasty it's most important. – Let me stop preaching. What I wanted to say was this: I'd very much like to see you again; but if we meet it would be wrong to avoid talking about serious non-philosophical things. Being timid I don't like clashes, and particularly not with people I like. But I'd rather have a clash than mere superficial talk.

Ludwig Wittgenstein[1]

What is entailed, both imaginatively and in practice, in *crossing over* the most symbolically meaningful borders in our experience? What is entailed in *being on*, or *going to*, "the other side"? What can someone who has traveled with the hope of conveying something understandable across borders – the original purpose of the Fulbright dissertation grant I was privileged to receive in the early 1990s – someone who, as a result, now lives across the divide, give back? I seek to resuscitate the memories of first encounters – places and spaces where we all seemingly first met, as collectivities, and in the process created powerful first impressions, many of which emerged and disappeared too quickly, some of which remain accessible through the study of history, literature, and other modes of artistic expression.

I began the thinking and research for *Border Thinking on the Edges of the West: Crossing Over the Hellespont* before the attacks on Washington and New York on September 11th, 2001, but my efforts were spurred on by the subsequent US invasions of Afghanistan and Iraq and the ongoing battle that the society I inhabit most of the year continues to wage against what it officially calls its "enemies" ("terrorists," "extremists," etc.). The work is now complete, and after concluding this preface, I will lower from the wall of my office, just above my desk to my right, a reprint of a sketch of General Louis-François Lejeune's famous painting *La Bataille d'Aboukir*. The sketch is entitled *Victoire d'Aboukir*, and depicts Napoleon's attack on Ottoman forces in July of 1799 at the Battle of Aboukir, on the Mediterranean coast of Egypt. The original painting is on display in the Palace at Versailles. I first saw the print at the French Army Museum in Paris in late September of 2001, during a visit to Europe that I had planned earlier that year as part of my sabbatical. My goal was to visit museums and monuments in several European cities to study Europe's aesthetic rendering, if you will, of its encounter with its Islamic neighbors. After the attacks on September 11th, 2001, the intellectual curiosities of my project reverberated with relevance in a way I could never have foreseen.

I had been studying several aspects of the West's relationship to Muslim societies for over a decade: in my work on secularism and modernity in Turkey; in my studies of the ideological foundations of US foreign policy in relation to Islamist resistance in the societies of the Persian/Arabian Gulf; and in a new project entitled, "Europe and its Boundaries," that I was about to co-direct with my colleague at Vassar, Himadeep Muppidi. We were in the process of articulating a new scholarly and pedagogical agenda that examined political modernity from both within and outside the conceptual borders of Europe. This project involved deep consideration of the interpretive and ethical dilemmas of "border" encounters. *Border Thinking on the Edges of the West* gathers and evolves my thinking on these issues by examining two prominent political imaginaries on what are prominently considered the cultural and civilizational boundaries of "the West." As a prelude to developing these reflections, I want to explain why I'll be lowering *Victoire d'Aboukir* from my office wall.

That fall of 2001, I visited tens of museums in Paris, Berlin, Madrid, Granada, Seville, Cordoba, Toledo, and Istanbul, from where I had set out. I had already been to the museums of London, Athens, and Rhodes the year before, and was also later to travel to Brussels with the participants in the project on Europe and its boundaries. My visits to the museums of Europe were like a refresher course on historical precedents for the US/NATO invasion of Afghanistan. Whatever the *casus belli*, the new war clearly reiterated the violence of the European imperial and colonial pasts. Western armies, promoting themselves as vigilant defenders of freedom, civilization, and forces for nothing but good, and, while "aiming only to hunt down terrorists," righteously expanding their global power by crossing into foreign lands and attacking and subduing all within sight. One could read about the roads that had been paved by European experience in Muriel E. Chamberlain's excellent *Formation of the European Empires, 1488–1920*, which I had in my pocket during my European travels. Or one could also visit the museums and see this history profoundly alive in the monuments, museum displays, and public sculptures and architecture of Europe.

Not surprisingly, my visits to naval and military museums were especially illuminating – museums like the Museo del Ejército in Madrid, the Alcázar in Toledo, and Musée de l'Armée in Paris where I saw *Victoire d'Aboukir*. I was struck by the elaborate and extensive displays and descriptions of colonial adventure and warfare, from rows upon rows of material and symbolic accoutrements of war to the actual spoils of conquest, large and small. The Algiers display in the Army Museum in Paris, for example, contains both a gold standard on which the principles "Liberté, Égalité, Vigilance, Discipline and Subordination" are embroidered and a constructed model of pre-conquest Algiers. Near the model, a small showcase displays a pair of girl's shoes brought back from Algeria to France.

I have spent over a decade looking above my desk at the scenes of *Victoire d'Aboukir*. The sketch portrays the all-out French assault on the Turkish garrison at Aboukir. The French had suffered a defeat in Aboukir Bay at the hands of the British a year earlier. Napoleon's campaigns in Syria and Palestine had been pushed back as well. Napoleon and a huge French fleet now arrive with zeal on the shores of Egypt for what will be a two-year occupation.

A clear sky takes up almost the entire top third of the sketch. Below it, the sea, a fortress at the end of a long peninsula on the shore, and a beach on which tens of well-ordered columns march against "les Turcs." Plumes of smoke rise from the ships and around the Turkish troops on the beaches. In the foreground, Napoleon sits atop his horse on a hill overlooking the beach. He is directing his troops towards a group of Turcs. Some of the latter appear to have been rounded up and subdued by the French, some continue to fight, in vain. The faces of several turbaned men who have fallen to the ground grimace with agony, fear, and despair. One man holding a dagger raises it just as a French soldier is about to pierce his chest with a bayonet. An old man crouches in fear behind a cactus on top of which a tent or some kind of cover has fallen.

Napoleon's horse is leaping in the air at full gallop out from an area with several palm trees, on the left side of the sketch, just in front of a hilltop fortress tower out of which the body of a dead Turc hangs, next to another who is exchanging fire with French soldiers below. His efforts, too, are in vain. The French are about to seize the tower.

Napoleon's fully erect posture, with one arm on the reins of his horse and the other pointed straight ahead, contrasts with that of a turbaned Turc who has fallen on the ground several meters away. Balancing his body with one arm on the ground, the Turc raises the other, palm open, above his head as if pleading to the rider on the horse above him to be rescued from his fate. To his side lie several sprawled bodies, Turcs and French. One, a Turc, covers the decapitated body of a French soldier. The latter's severed head lies next to a curved sword in the hand of the dead Turc. A wounded fighter is getting attention from the French. A camel kneels by a cactus, its fruit carts spilt beside it. To its side, a fallen palm tree lies across the ground.

With Napoleon's confident pose and the Turcs succumbing under his power, the French certainly have the look of control, of *victoire*. We know who wins this particular battle, one that will also be sculpted into the east side of the *Arc de Triomphe* in Paris within the next twenty years, wherein the names of General Lejcune and General Joachim Murat, the commander given credit for the victory by personally subduing his Turkish rival, will be engraved as well. In the bas-relief on the *Arc*, entitled *La Bataille d'Aboukir* and carved by Bernard Gabriel Seurre, we again see a scene of capitulation in the immediate context and aftermath of the violent encounter at Aboukir. Turcs surrender and submit to a military leader on horseback. A turbaned body lies below the horse, near or under its rear hoof. The horseman is most likely Napoleon. The rider could also be General Murat, since the scene resembles another famous painting of the bloody battle, Antoine Gros's *Murat at the Battle of Aboukir* (1806). In that painting, just as in the bas-relief on the Arch of Triumph, turbaned bodies lie sprawled on the ground, trampled under the hooves of the gallantly poised leader's horse.

This is what I observed in Europe's encounter with Islam in some of Europe's most treasured artistic spaces: Victorious Europeans attacking or triumphantly trampling over Muslims. The Art of Triumph, of glorious killing and enemy submission. Of course, insofar as much of this art aimed to "recapture" the historical record, it made a great deal of sense. "Between 1800 and 1812, no less than 70 paintings deal with the Egyptian campaign under the leadership of [the French Museums Director] Vivant Denon."[2] Similar efforts have been underway in the United States since the invasions of Afghanistan and Iraq, and, in Europe, well before Aboukir. Since the Crusades, the *Reconquista*, and the Ottoman sieges of Vienna, warfare against and resistance to the power of Muslim empires has been very much a part of Europe's historical self-understanding. It is the depth of the ongoing projection of this self-understanding that I learned about and wish to underscore. I seemed to encounter it everywhere I went.

In Granada, Spain, before entering the *Capilla Real*, the Royal Chapel designed to sanctify the place of Ferdinand and Isabella in the history of Christianity, guests are greeted by "The Capitulation of Granada," a huge wall hanging of Francisco Pradilla Ortiz's (1848–1921) famous painting depicting the surrender by the last Muslim ruler of Granada, Muhammad XII (Boabdil), to Ferdinand and Isabella. Inside the entombment chamber in the chapel, a carefully sculpted relief on the end of Ferdinand's marble coffin that visitors stroll by shows a rider, presumably Ferdinand, on a horse trampling over several turbaned bodies, at least two of which receive direct blows from its hooves.

In Seville, the symbolism of the tomb of Christopher Columbus in the Cathedral of Seville is less obvious, but no less poignant. The monument shows four pallbearers carrying Columbus's coffin. The bearers represent the four kingdoms of Spain at the time of the Reconquest and Columbus's voyage to the Americas – both in 1492. The two front figures support the coffin with one arm and hold a sepulcher in the other. The front right figure represents the Kingdom of León. It bears the red lion design of Alfonso VII of León (1105–57), a renowned local crusader against the Moors in his time. The sepulcher in his hand does not rest on the ground near his foot. Its sharpened end pierces a partially split pomegranate, the symbol of Andalusian Granada. The Spanish word for pomegranate is *granada*, and the fruit is still understood as the symbol of the city's past. The cover brochure, for example, of "El Archivo Histórico Municipal de Granada," which I picked up on a visit, shows the *Sello de Cera Ayuntamiento, 1493* – the partially split *granada*. Although this symbolism of the pierced *granada* escapes the attention of many visitors to the tomb, I learned of the connection from personnel in the cathedral, who pointed my attention to the *granada*. The message is profound. With Granada in possession, Columbus sought the conquest of the world, and that is what would eventually follow.

The art of these particular monuments came together in Brussels, in one of its many monuments to Europe's colonial self-understanding. The statue above the main entrance to the King of Spain Building (*Den Coninck Van Spaignien*) at the Grand Place – a "World Heritage" site – sports a triumphant bust of the king, surrounded by a wreath and various military insignia. Below, on both sides of the bust, roughly where the legs of the king might be, sit two full figures. To the king's left a Native American, and to his right a bearded and turbaned Moor. Both are loosely clad. Their hands are bound behind their backs, their heads tilted inward and, showing effects of coerced subordination, only slightly lifted towards the king. This is nothing but a monument to conquest, bondage, and enslavement.

More art and more ships arriving at sea, more columns of neatly ordered troops firing and slaying ahead, more disorderly, turbaned Moors vainly firing back in *Débarquement de l'armée Française en Afrique 14 Juin 1830*, a sketch from an old manuscript that caught my eye in a used bookstore in Paris. Even more troops, artillery, and plumes of smoke at the "Batalla de Wad-Ras en 1860," during Spain's invasion of Morocco. The painting hangs in the Sala de Africa in the Alcázar in Toledo.

There are other forms of art related to the encounter between Europe and Islam. Many paintings of the European Orientalists, for example, display less violent imagery. Perhaps the most famous, most complex, and most political works are those of Eugene Delacroix, some of which I had the chance to view in Paris. In paintings like *Algerian Women in their Apartments* (1834) or the many other European depictions of "the Orient" by Delacroix's contemporaries, one sees fascination with the beauty of the peoples, architecture, and lands over the border. Indeed, some of these paintings are truly beautiful works of art. However, when viewing a magnificent effort to depict scenes of life in a Muslim setting like *Algerian Women in their Apartments*, it is somehow difficult to escape the knowledge that European access to this beauty came on the heels of conquest. The privacy of the Algerian women in their apartments feels shattered by Delacroix's skillful brush, their homes invaded and subordinated to a power-laden European gaze. As the women sit in their apartments, one can almost hear the swishing and creaking of hundreds of naval ships arriving on the coast, see the thousands of troops hauling themselves and their artillery onto the shore, hear their commanders, bursts of fire, shouts and screams. You can almost smell the smoke that filled the air as the Europeans arrived. One can almost see everywhere, without even having to see it, the ultimate image to come: that of a proud leader riding high, having confidently and triumphantly slain, defeated, and subdued the enemy. European access to the beauty of Algiers required ambush and invasion.

Moreover, accompanying many of these masterful strokes of beauty is a culture of fear, suspicion, and hatred expressed through the artist's brush. Delacroix's *The Fanatics of Tangier* (1838) shows a political rally that Dela-croix is said to have personally witnessed. A priestly man on a horse carries a green banner. Contorted, bearded, turbaned and cloaked bodies seem to throw themselves around him in a wild frenzy. Contrast that image with *Victoire*'s neatly ordered columns. Similarly, Delacroix's *Massacre at Chios* (1824) aligns closely with this deep historical memory as it reverses it: At Chios, les Turcs are guilty of massacre. The painting shows the Turk as the mounted victor, standing above slaughtered and traumatized Greeks, women and children. The account of the violence is debated by historians. Dela-croix's painting was said, along with writings by Hugo and Byron, to have mobilized European sympathy for the Greeks in their battle for independence from Muslim rule. More cultural underpinnings, in the texts of the great poets. The horror of the violence against the European, which is simi-larly represented in the 1822 painting *Firing of the Turkish Fleet*, on display in Chios (and available for purchase as a postcard or poster at the Chios Nautical Museum) or in Theophilos Hatzimichael's *Death of Marcos Bot-saris* (1823) on display in the Theophilos Museum in Mytilene, contrasts with the triumphant glory of the violence against the Turc-Moor-Arab-Muslim. When the conquered is the European, it is terror; when it is the Muslim, it is glorious, even sacred. In the Museo de Bellas Artes in Valencia, Spain, a painting hung too high for me to read its caption shows a crusading fighter descending from the heavens through a storm of clouds. A bright red cross adorns his breastplate armor. The fighter also holds a sword in his hand above his head at the same angle as the cross. The cross and the handle of the sword make two crosses descending for battle towards Earth.

With war led mostly by Christians and Muslims erupting again in September of 2001, it was sometimes difficult during my trip to keep the historical contexts distinct. In their huge glass advertisement showcases, newsstands in Paris posted blow-up covers of weekly magazines that addressed the events of the present with images and concepts resonant of the past. A cover of *L'Express* shows a face, half covered by a black veil. Under it, the advertisement for the lead story: *Le fanatisme, ses mystères, son histoire, ses ressorts*. A similar poster of the latest edition of the *Le Nouvel Observateur* has a picture of turbaned Afghani fighters holding anti-aircraft missiles. Its heading: *Afghanistan, Pakistan, Asie Centrale: La Poudrière du Monde*. Both were published in the third week of September 2001. The cover images and art combined like the cross and the sword: similar images, similar messages. The outside world resembled the collection in the museum, the collection in the museum spoke to the outside world. In Europe's art of encounter, the bodies of the Muslim seem always to appear in battle and contained on the other end of Europe's sense of power.

This remarkable consistency occurs in Europe's most cherished spaces, but such art is not of course unique to the centers of Europe. One sees similar battle art on its edges, for example, in the modern Ottoman art of conquest and glory in Istanbul's Military Museum. There, the turbans reside, for the most part, on the heads of the victors. Similar Art of Triumph may be seen as well in Istanbul's public monuments, even some of its contemporary public art. The colorful wall mosaics placed in 1999 in the city's new subway stations to commemorate the 700th anniversary of the founding of the Ottoman Empire depict the Ottoman conquest of Constantinople in 1453. The mosaics show the Ottoman navy making its heroic preparations to sail upon the ancient city. Ships approach and armed soldiers scale and capture the walls of the city. One scene shows the victorious Fatih Sultan Memed – Sultan Memed the Conqueror – leading his army inside the gates of the city. The art depicts the glory of the arriving Turks and the submission of the Christians. There are no fallen bodies in the mosaic, but other paintings of these scenes as well as paintings of other historical encounters between the Muslim Turks and Christian European armies provide plenty of blood, horror, and glory, including the victorious leader atop his horse, like Napoleon, pointing forward. One could substitute Napoleon for a victorious sultan and reverse the various banners and bodies of Émile Jean-Horace Vernet's *Bonaparte at the Battle of Aboukir* and produce a copy of some of the art in Istanbul's Military Museum.

If the Art of Triumph is not limited to Europe's centers, it's also not particularly new in the history of the world either. The *Alexander Sarcophagus, circa 325–311 BC* in the Istanbul Archeological Museum that I visited just before setting out on my trip to Western Europe contains the same motifs as the Art of Triumph. "Alexander the Great," reads the caption of one postcard from the collection, "mounted on a horse and chasing a Persian soldier." "A mounted Persian charging a Greek; a Persian archer; a Persian lowering his dead friend," reads another. "A Greek commander charging a Persian who is falling from his horse." "A mounted Persian charging a fallen Greek and a Greek killing a Persian." More bodies under more hooves of more stampeding horses ridden by more soldiers, one of them perhaps Alexander. They thrust their weapons into the bodies of the turbaned others, some of whom already lay dead, mouths agape, sprawled on the ground beside or under the horses' hooves.

There is a strange parallel between the posture of two of these vanquished fighters, kneeling on the ground and trying to shield themselves from further blows, and the turbaned Turc in *Victoire d'Aboukir*. There is also a similar concordance between Alexander's triumphant charge and that of Napoleon. Alexander's arm is raised back at a ninety-degree angle, either to hurl more objects at the enemy or to spur on his horse which, with its front legs in the air like Napoleon's, is in full stride. The two fighters cringing in fear are about join others in death under the trampling hooves of the conquerors. Alexander's horse, like Napoleon's in the *Arc de Triomphe*, rides over a fallen body on the ground. Indeed, it is said that Napoleon had launched his invasion of Egypt partly to emulate Alexander's conquest of the world. In this sense, the Art of Triumph above my desk participates in a longer history of Europe's own proud encounters with others, stretching back to ancient battles between European and Asian powers. Many of those battles, I underscore, began or involved an important crossing over the Hellespont. For those of us on the other side of all these crossings, it has been one conqueror after another. One comes and goes, and then another.

With the historical depth of the violence of this encounter in mind, I embarked on the specific project that has led to *Border Thinking on the Edges of the West: Crossing Over the Hellespont*. I feel deeply grateful to many friends whose thoughtful company sustained and propelled this project. Thank you so much to Cevdet Akçay, Bruce Baum, Andrew Bush, Olga Bush, Ece Doğrucu, Dan Frank, Aapta Garg, Hannah Eidman, İgal Ers, Richard Friedenheim, Luke Harris, Anton Hart, Katie Hite, Mark Hoffman, Bill Hoynes, Gürol Irzık, Sibel Irzık, Brian Johnson, Tim Koechlin, Gün Kut, Şule Kut, Bill Lynn, Rick Matthews, Beth McCormick, Himadeep Muppidi, Nesrin Mutlu, Sam Opondo, Taha Parla, Joe Perl, Sahara Pradhan, Katherine Restuccia, Martin Sampson, Jonathan Schultz, Paul Soper, Ron Steiner, Britt Van Paepeghem, Greg White, and Steve Wolf. Steve, Paul, and Andy have been wise and most generous companions in thought from the beginning of the project, and Nesrin and İgal were there in these ways halfway through. I can't thank them enough. I am also deeply grateful to Sahara for extensive conversion and her patient and meticulous work with the manuscript during the final phases of the project.

I would also like to acknowledge the tremendous support provided by the editors of this series, Arlene B. Tickner, Ole Wæver, David Blaney, and Pinar

Bilgin; by Nicola Parkin, Peter Harris, and Dominic Corti of Routledge; and by Alison Neale. Similarly, I am deeply indebted to tens of students at Vassar College over the last decade – especially my interlocutors in the classes Seminar in Political Theory, Political Modernity in Turkey, and Diasporas: Borderline Jews (co-taught with Andrew Bush) – for their willingness to engage and reflect in unconventional ways upon questions of border life.

In what follows, I make every effort to engage the texts I examine in this study as much on their own terms as is humanly possible, and I openly acknowledge the extent to which my interpretations are significantly shaped by my deep unease with current political conditions, especially the ongoing violent encounters – both material and symbolic – between the United States and especially the Muslim societies and milieux (that is, including within the United States) in and over which it exercises its power. In relation to this work, I have viewed this unease somewhat as enabling much of the value-driven, passionate intellectual engagement that follows. My unease has also produced in me less a desire to celebrate naively the "alternatives" I have experienced over the conceptual borders of the West (where they are not "alternatives"; they just are), or to comfort myself falsely by condemning the violence I espy and feel within in a particular dimension of the Western political imagination. Instead, my unease has propelled me to listen with every ounce of interpretive energy I can muster to the voices and expressions of each disposition, each way of being in the world. In relation to the violent dispositions of conquest, I try to understand their grip upon – so as to begin to shed their influence over – our collective imagination and constitution. In relation to being outside that imagination, to resisting conquest and thinking – and living – borders between us differently, I seek to convey something about understanding and being in the world differently that I have learned and experienced as a result of the privilege of conversation I have enjoyed on the other side of the various Hellesponts in the Western imagination. There are many dilemmas and difficulties involved in this project. I discuss and grapple with them the best I can along the way.

For now, as my next movement within a different way of being, I will lower *Victoire d'Aboukir* from the wall of my office. For over a decade, it has reminded me almost daily of the needs to digest and transcend the cycle of mutual and reciprocal assault, to consider and reconsider the meaningfulness of "crossing" borders, and to contemplate alternative ways of crossing, including perhaps, as I shall discuss, not *crossing* at all. I will lower the print now because it represents, repeatedly, a concept and orientation towards others that I seek to purge from my constituted being. This is no easy task. The legacy is profoundly deep. I will probably fall short of this goal. Yet the imperial aura of subduing the other, the bayonet about to pierce the man's heart, the futile hope for rescue, the crouching in fear, the severed head ... like the daily news reports of never-ending slaughter from the current pursuits of glorious victory, they've all become entirely too distasteful, too *dis*honorable. Moreover, their effect on us needs to be something other than repetition, something to counter the inherited impulse *to cross* again. "We stand," writes Hamid Dabashi, "mere individuals, upon a heap of old, scattered, useless and yet dangerous memories. Whether they control us or we control them is the key criterion to any meaningful future."[3] If the grimaces of agony, fear, and despair, on the one hand, and the proud slayer of the other, on the other, say anything to me, it is that a real transformation in the direction of more hospitable solidarities and forms of mutual regard is necessary. In lowering the print, I am not eliminating, I cannot eliminate, the violence from memory. I am relocating myself in the history of the West, of the world. It's time.

In the midst of this work, fate took hold and I fell in love on the other side of the Hellespont, at the base of the Taurus Mountains. I wish I could express in words how much I have learned in being with Evrim Uyar-Davison and becoming part of her family. Some of what I feel comes to expression indirectly in what follows. The rest I wish to convey by dedicating this work to her and to our families, especially to Barbara Davison and Hatice Uyar, Maxwell Davison and Hüseyin Uyar.

To my mind, the conflicts of today and tomorrow are not between "West" and "East." They are and will be between two dispositions that only sometimes neatly map along geographical, "cultural" or "civilizational" axes: one predisposed to crossing over borders or entering unfamiliar spaces well armed and prepared to subdue and dominate all one encounters, and another prepared to inhabit relationships favoring just forms of social accompaniment and solidarity in the meaningful and life-affirming spaces of experience. In reality, the constellation of possibilities often equals more than two; things are often much messier than "either this or that." After years of study on this question, however, I'd like to suggest that sometimes the options are that simple. It is the work and self-scrutiny it takes to admit the simplicity of it that are difficult.

Notes

1 L. Wittgenstein, "Letter to N. Malcolm, 16.11.1944," in B. McGuinness (ed.) *Wittgenstein in Cambridge: Letters and Documents, 1911–1951*, London: Wiley and Blackwell, 2008, 370.
2 G.-G. Lemaires, *The Orient in Western Art*, Cologne: Könemann, 2001, 109.
3 H. Dabashi, *Theology of Discontent: The Ideological Foundation of the Islamic Revolution in Iran*, New York: New York University Press, 1993, 519.

A NOTE ON THE USE OF ITALICS
FOR FOREIGN-LANGUAGE WORDS

As discussed in the Introduction, this work employs a hermeneutical approach to issues of translation and dialogue. The non-italicized use of foreign-language terms in many parts of this work is purposeful.

ABBREVIATIONS

H	Herodotus, *The History*, David Grene (trans.), Chicago: The University of Chicago Press, 1987.
HA	Quintus Curtius Rufus, *The History of Alexander*, John Yardley (trans.), New York: Penguin Books, 1984.
İM1	*Yaşar Kemal, İnce Memed 1*, Istanbul: Yapı Kredi Yayınları, 2006 (1952).
İM2	Yaşar Kemal, *İnce Memed 2*, Istanbul: Yapı Kredi Yayınları, 2007 (1953).
İM3	*Yaşar Kemal, İnce Memed 3*, Istanbul: Yapı Kredi Yayınları, 2004 (1953).
İM4	Yaşar Kemal, *İnce Memed 4*, Istanbul: Yapı Kredi Yayınları, 2007 (1955).
PW	*The Landmark Thucydides: A Comprehensive Guide to the Peloponnesian War*, Robert Strassler (ed.), Richard Crawley (trans.), New York: Simon and Schuster, 1996.
RM	Livy, *Rome and the Mediterranean*, Henry Bettenson (trans.), New York: Penguin Books, 1976.

INTRODUCTION

Since these concepts are indispensable for unsettling the heritage to which they belong, we should be even less prone to renounce them. Within the closure, by an oblique and always perilous movement, constantly risking falling back within what is being deconstructed, it is necessary to surround the critical concepts with a careful and thorough discourse – to make the condition, the medium, and the limits of their effectiveness and to designate rigorously their intimate relationship to the machine whose deconstruction they permit; and, in the same process, designate the crevice through which the yet unnamable glimmer beyond the closure can be glimpsed.

Jacques Derrida[1]

Openness to voices, familiar or strange, may well have to be the first criterion of the shared self which transcends nation-states, communities, perhaps even cultures themselves. A direct, sharp awareness of man-made suffering, a genuine empirical feel for it, may be the second.

Ashis Nandy[2]

I
Synopsis

Drawing on scholarly and life experience on, and over, the historically posited borders between "West" and "East" and "Europe" and "Turkey," *Border Thinking on the Edges of the West: Crossing Over the Hellespont* offers an interpretive study of two paradigmatic political imaginaries concerning life on what "the West" constitutes as one of its most historically and mythologically significant borders, the shores of the Hellespont. The two major parts of the study are linked by a political and ethical initiative to identify, interrogate, and challenge the grip of a particular, enduring, and violent inheritance from the classical Greek-Macedonian-Roman origins of the Western political imagination.

Specifically, in Part One, "When words maintain their meanings and the world is an abode of war," I identify and describe the tradition of

1

constituting border crossing as essentially a violent practice that requires going well armed and prepared for both danger and plunder. I interpret the meanings, purposes, and practices associated with border crossing in classical thought as exemplifying an important instance of conceptual stability at the origins of the Western tradition, one that reaches into contemporary literature about the classical period as well as contemporary thinking and literature about the borders of "West" and "East."

In Part Two, "On the fatal boundaries," I converse with an alternative tradition and political imaginary found precisely where the Western border imaginary posits fear and death – across the Hellespont in the Taurus Mountains that the Romans once named and understood as "the fatal boundaries." Part Two is an effort to develop and demonstrate both the limits of the Western imaginary and a hermeneutically textured alternative to what it might mean to approach border spaces otherwise. In this regard it is written from across every Hellespont in the Western experience, where border spaces are teeming with abundant life, beauty, and the struggle for justice against conquest, not war and possible booty.

An underlying premise of this work is that the sense of violent *possibility* on the borders between "West" and "East" – at the real and metaphorical shores of the Hellespont – is neither very new nor accidental. These senti-ments are constitutive of a political imagination about border experiences found deep within the inherited sources of Western culture – well before the Crusades or the more recent "age of imperialism," even before there was "a West" or "an East" to speak of. The study thus first engages and describes a tradition of "pre"-"Western" thinking about the border spaces between what have come to be called "the West" and "the East," and then explores in depth one kind of creative, hermeneutical effort required to resist the ongo-ing influence of the inherited violent imagination. What follows in this Introduction is a more detailed summary of the goals and purposes of each part of the study.

II
Part one: When words maintain their meanings and the world is an abode of war

Part One illuminates in detail the meaning of crossing over a border in classical Greek and Roman historical understanding. Finding a fundamen-tally stable meaning across these historical periods, I demonstrate the need for an important refinement in the dominant and paradigmatic under-standing in the field of political theory that the movement from *polis* to empire entailed a fundamental shift in the constitutive languages of political life. I argue that at the borders of the *polis* and empire, as well as within imperial borders, "crossing over" consistently means going well armed and disposed towards violence, conquest, and the accumulation of riches. A corresponding, embedded understanding is that in addition to spoils, life on the other side of the border contains threats and dangers, and that subduing such threats and overcoming such dangers by crossing "to the end of the world" brings both fame and glory to those who cross over.

To show this consistent and deeply constitutive understanding from *polis* to empire, I provide an exhaustive, contextual, and hermeneutical reading of the explicit and implicit expressions of border crossing in the seminal historical texts of the era, especially: *The History* of Herodotus, *The Peloponnesian War* by Thucydides, Quintus Curtius Rufus' *The History of Alexander*, and major sections of Titus Livy's *Rome and the Mediterranean (Ab Urbe Condita)*. I elaborate upon the methodological rationale for the selection of these particular texts slightly more at the end of this Introduction and in greater detail in the early sections of Part One.

Because of the imaginary significance of the Hellespont in the Western tradition, from Homer and Ovid through Lord Byron, the study begins by engaging the meaning of "crossing the Hellespont" in the seminal historical texts as they narrate the historic crossings by the Persians, Greeks, Macedonians, Romans, and the armies of Antiochus III. *Crossing the Hellespont* is a common idiom in all the classical texts. I examine the embedded and contextual meanings of this idiom in each usage. The work then extends outward from the Hellespont, to the ends of the (known) world in both directions, east and west, to engage the meanings of additional border crossings in the context of the multiple epic conflicts narrated in the classical texts. In each usage and with only very rare exceptions (also discussed), the meanings and purposes of crossing over remain fundamentally the same, in each direction, from *polis* to empire, Athens to Rome, the borders of Greece and Persia to the shores of Sicily, and from the Hellespont to what the Romans termed the "fatal boundaries"[3] of the Taurus Mountains in Anatolia. To illuminate this fundamentally violent concept of border life, I provide contextualized accounts of the kinds of violence that were undertaken when one party or another crossed over to the other side.

As I discuss in the early parts of the study, I focus on the period in question because of its status in the political theoretical tradition as the exemplary historical period wherein the distinct character of the Western tradition as a tradition constituted by conceptual change took shape. I also show that this particular instance of conceptual stability reaches far into the present, specifically into contemporary political and historical literature about both the period in question and the imaginative significance of the Hellespont, literature that essentially repeats the meaning and usage of crossing over found in the classical texts. While there are counterexamples through time, I thus illustrate the enduring quality of the classical understanding of crossing over in the Western imagination. This consistency in meaning across time suggests that alongside significant conceptual innovation in the transition from *polis* to empire lies an equally tenacious human conceptual phenomenon – a phenomenon of permanent and persistent conceptual re-affirmation of longstanding meaning in the history of "the West." I thus suggest a slight shift in emphasis in "the West's" self-understanding as a tradition of conceptual innovation, one drawn from the era in which this dimension is understood to have taken shape. Innovation in "the West's" political conceptual capacities should be seen against this background of, and even in the context of, conceptual fixity. Moreover, my hope is that this exercise of disclosing, revealing, remembering, and highlighting the destructive and life-negating associations of border crossing, of embracing them for reflection and scrutiny,[4] allows us to challenge their demonstrable, lasting grip on us.

To this end, in the latter part of Part One, I scrutinize other border experiences accounted for within the classical texts in pursuit of alternative, less and/or non-violent ways of understanding borders and what it means to cross them. I argue that there exist significant moments of alternative possibility within these texts – in, for example, Herodotus' cross-cultural inquiries, Alexander's renowned empathetic practices towards those he and his armies conquered, and several subaltern figures within the texts. An example of the latter on which I reflect extensively is the figure of the Medizer, the said betrayer of Hellas who goes to "the other side." I consider these alternatives seriously but maintain that provocative as they are, they remain expressed and contained within the dominant discourse of crossing violently. They thus fail to offer or exemplify alternative ways of approaching, conceptualizing, understanding, thinking, and/or being on or with borders otherwise. Part Two is an effort to address this difficult task.

III
Part two: On the fatal boundaries

Part Two seeks to challenge the enduring classical Western violent understanding of crossing the Hellespont by presenting – relative to the meanings explored in Part One – an "other" and "counter" political imaginary about life on its boundaries – that is, on or over the other side of every "Hellespont" within its political imagination. Specifically, I converse with the languages of life on one of the borders central to the texts of the classical period – the "fatal" boundaries on the Taurus Mountains – where a different, living imaginary resides, one that resists the conception of it as a space of danger, threat, and death. In this part, moreover, I seek to display the fundamental, complex, and radical shift in consciousness and being required to approach all liminal spaces between "the West" and those on the other side of its borders in a more open and coeval fashion. This discussion is informed by non- and post-Orientalist hermeneutical theory,[5] contemporary ethical theories of hospitality,[6] my more recent scholarly work in the field of global or comparative hermeneutical political inquiry, and vast personal experience in professional and, through marriage, family milieux in Turkey, including in the Taurus Mountains, over the last fifteen years. I do not, however, meta-theoretically explicate my project in Part Two. I "do" it through a display of my learning and experience within languages across the Hellespont, on the "boundaries" that the West posits as "fatal," that is, as requiring preparation for danger and death.

My main focus is to convey, in an original, hermeneutical fashion, stories from a masterpiece of contemporary world literature written from the milieu of the Taurus Mountains: the four-volume epic *İnce Memed*, written by the acclaimed writer in Turkey, Yaşar Kemal (1923–). Yaşar Kemal grew up in the *Toroslar* (the Taurus range, in Turkish) and its *Çukurova* (Cilicia) plains below – the historic lands of many Anatolian peoples, where the Greeks and Persians clashed, Alexander marched, and the Romans battled. In the period under examination in Part One, these were the boundaries where armies feared to pass and "heroic" efforts were made to *cross* them, especially the Cilician Gates, the steep and narrow gorge that Alexander traversed against all odds. Most of the stories in Yaşar Kemal's magnificent *oeuvre*, including *İnce Memed*, are imaginative portraits of the people and environs of the area. These works are deeply informed by an awareness of the meaningful history of the *Toroslar* and, more significantly, they powerfully speak for a different conception of precisely those spaces that the Western political ima-ginary posits as *fatal. İnce Memed* is Yaşar Kemal's most acclaimed work. The stories within it portray existence on what "the West" understands as its "fatal boundaries" to be teeming with life, beauty, and the widely shared understanding that violence of the kind that is narrated and normalized in the classical Western texts – and which of course occurs in the stories of *İnce Memed* as well – must be fought, resisted, and, at some point, brought to an end. This imaginary – "counter" in relation to the classical tradition of understanding what lies across the Hellespont – is embodied in the character of İnce Memed as a creative expression of the steadfast humaneness con-stitutive of the people of the Taurus Mountains, precisely those whose world is seen within the dominant Western imagination as necessitating a violent and fearful encounter, not one of coeval regard and esteem.

There are certainly other ways to stimulate alternative reflection about "crossing over the Hellespont," such as accounts of alternative border phi-losophies, reviews of the many "Western" and/or "Eastern" intellectual sources over time that have challenged violent border discourses or presented entirely non-violent conceptions of life. Such work is ongoing in many dis-ciplines and is very useful. I have chosen to attempt a more unconventional approach, informed by contemporary literature on the political significance of thinking on and from borders between hierarchicalized and colonially ordered societies, premised upon the idea that dialogical engagement on and from such borders is one route to replacing colonial relations with more coeval forms of human regard. Seen from the perspective of the Western tradition, *İnce Memed* is a text from the borders. Bringing the imaginary contained within it to expression necessarily contrasts and contests "the West's" imagination of its border spaces, opening up a possibility for a fundamental reconceptualization both of "the border" and possible relations to, on, and across it.

This part of the study is further premised upon the idea that works of art like *İnce Memed*, the imaginative quality of which is purposefully grounded in lived language and experience, offer valuable sites for theoretical reflection on the nature of political life and existence. Literature, in particular, can work against inherited, hegemonic traditions by offering a repertoire of different voices, potentially opening readers up (through empathy, identification with characters or plots, and so on) to various forms of life other than their own (or perhaps repressed or subordinated within their own). Yaşar Kemal writes with vast life experience in the Taurus milieu, a profound awareness of its legendary significance, intense identification with its peoples, and mastery of its poetic and literary forms. As a youngster, he was an accomplished bard in the tradition of the seventeenth- and eighteenth-century oral poets, Karacaoğlan and Dadaloğlu; in school he dreamed of becoming a scholar of Eastern cultures; and after finishing university, he first worked as a journalist in the *Toroslar*, gathering stories, poems, and songs and reporting for one of Turkey's prominent newspapers, *Cumhuriyet*.[7] The first volume of *İnce Memed* was first published as a serialized installment for the paper.

> I didn't just fall out of the sky. I was born in a village in *Çukurova*; I lived life in a small town and was nourished by the natural environment within a plot of land, and I experienced the *Toroslar* and the Mediterranean … Even the *Iliad* mentions the inhabitants of Cilicia as participants in the Trojan War. I am proud of my land, and I am telling you about Cilicia to brag a little. The Cilicians came to the aid of Troy with their beautiful horses. Throughout its history my country has been famous for the beautiful horses that are raised there. When the Assyrians occupied Cilicia – during our captivity – every year we paid a tribute of 360 purebred horses. Do you realize where I come from? The *Çukurova* is the entire Mediterranean. My country is hemmed in by the *Toros* Mountains, which encircle it like a new moon fronting the Mediterranean before us. I am a man of the mountains, the plains, and the sea.[8]

In *İnce Memed*, Yaşar Kemal provides imaginative portraits of the villages and peoples of *Çukurova* and the *Toroslar*, and pages upon pages of descriptions of the plains and mountains.

Moreover, he has written with the explicit purpose of bringing the languages of the *Toroslar* and *Çukurova* into literary expression. Kemal has described the language of his stories as a creative fusion of several different languages, what he has called the "local speech" of *Çukurova* and the "speech of Istanbul," the urban center of contemporary literature in Turkey.[9] Within that milieu, Kemal pioneered the phenomenon of bringing the oral languages of village life in Turkey into written literature.

> I wanted to create a new kind of narrative, beginning with a whole new language. The oral literature that I knew did not lend itself well to the language of the written literature. I thought that particular Western narrative techniques were linked to the nature of those languages and civilizations, although some vestiges remained of the oral traditions that existed before the transition to written literature occurred. In contrast, in Anatolia, we were still living with the freshness and intensity of the oral traditions that had been forgotten in the West. In Anatolia, hundreds of bards and poets still traveled from village to village. However, the written language was conservative and closed to change; Turkish, a living language in the art of the bard, was nonetheless a dead language when institutionalized. My land belonged to a world in which a dead language reigned without competition.[10]

That *İnce Memed* is written from these linguistic borders is clear to the reader of these works in Turkish. Understanding some of the expressions and idioms requires familiarity with the languages of the Taurus milieu. Some of these are not even to be found in Turkish dictionaries, let alone Turkish–English dictionaries. Turkey's most famous linguist, Ali Püsküllüoğlu, sought to address this gap by producing the *Yaşar Kemal Sözlüğü – A Yaşar Kemal Dictionary* (1974)!

Thus, while there are significant differences between *İnce Memed* and the seminal texts analyzed in Part One, both bring the languages of experience of the peoples under consideration to expression in the widely familiar idioms of their day, and both provide sites for reflection upon the dominant political imaginaries of life. In these ways, the authors of all these works may be seen as what Walter Benjamin calls *storytellers*.

IV
A link: Storytelling as counsel

"Counsel is less an answer to a question than a proposal concerning the continuation of a story which is just unfolding," writes Benjamin in his essay "The Storyteller."[11] "In every case the storyteller is a man who has counsel for his readers," he writes. This is in part because the greatest of storytellers are those for whom the written tale, in drawing from "experience which has been passed on from mouth to mouth ... differs least from the speech of the many nameless storytellers" whose stories they convey. Significantly,

Benjamin considers Herodotus to be "the first storyteller of the Greeks," because he traveled to know the local tales and traditions of the many societies he visited.

However, Walter Benjamin laments: as familiar as the name of the story-teller "may be to us, the storyteller in his living immediacy is by no means a present force." Benjamin maintains that, "The art of storytelling is reaching its end because the epic side of truth, wisdom, is dying out." Rather than storytelling from in-depth travelers like Herodotus or "resident tillers of the soil" like Yaşar Kemal, we receive "information" and read, as individuated audiences, the works of solitary novelists. Benjamin gathers such phenomena under the rubric of "secular productive forces of history" that have denuded the art of storytelling of its perpetual wisdom in the form of counsel.

> Counsel woven into the fabric of real life is wisdom. The art of storytelling is reaching its end because the epic side of truth, wisdom, is dying out. This, however, is a process that has been going on for a long time. And nothing would be more fatuous than to want to see it merely a "symptom of decay," let alone a "modern" symptom. It is, rather, only a concomitant symptom of the secular productive forces of history, a concomitant that has quite gradually removed narrative from the realm of living speech and at the same time is making it possible to see a new beauty in what is vanishing.

Reaching back to Herodotus and forward to the tales of Yaşar Kemal, this study works to display, against these secular productive forces of history, how the languages of epic narratives remain embedded quite profoundly in the realm of living speech and, simultaneously, the beauty that Benjamin locates in the art of storytelling, especially in the form of counsel it provides for its readers. Such counsel "does not expend itself. It preserves and con-centrates its strength and is capable of releasing it even after a long time."

To exemplify the power of storytelling, Benjamin points to the story told by Herodotus of the conquered Egyptian King Psammenitus who stood "mute and motionless" and showed no emotion as the Persians paraded his own family members by him on the way to execution, but beat his fists against his head in tremendous grief at the sight of one of his elderly and impoverished servants going off to the same fate. Benjamin describes Montaigne's interpretation of the story of Psammenitus. Montaigne wondered why the king grieved openly when he saw his former servant.

> Montaigne answers: "Since he was already overfull of grief, it took only the smallest increase for it to burst through its dams." Thus Montaigne. But one could also say: The king is not moved by the fate of those of royal blood, for it is his own fate. Or: We are moved by much on the stage that does not move us in real life; to the king,

this servant is only an actor. Or: Great grief is pent up and breaks forth only with relaxation. Seeing the servant was the relaxation. Herodotus offers no explanations. His report is the driest. That is why this story from ancient Egypt is still capable after thousands of years of arousing astonishment and thoughtfulness. It resembles the seeds of a grain which have lain for centuries in the chambers of the pyramids shut up airtight and have retained their germinative power to this day.

It is similarly the underlying view of the present study that storytelling has a germinative power over our imaginations, for better and worse, and can indeed provide astonishingly inexhaustible and open counsel for our times.

Throughout both Parts One and Two, I therefore seek to occupy what Benjamin describes as the position of "a man listening to a story." That person "is in the company of the storyteller; even a man reading one [a storyteller] shares this companionship." I seek to do so in Part One with the first storyteller of the Greeks and those who followed him in his tradition, and I seek to do this in Part Two with Yaşar Kemal whose epic tales of İnce Memed speak, in poignant ways, back to the counsel provided in the stories of the classical storytellers. We have seen Benjamin's regard for Herodotus as a storyteller. That Yaşar Kemal ranks as what Benjamin describes as a "great storyteller" is beyond question as well. "The great storyteller will always be rooted in the people."

Border Thinking on the Edges of the West: Crossing Over the Hellespont is a product of sitting in the company of these great storytellers for over a decade. In the company of the classical historytellers, I have listened to their stories with an ear towards how they conceptualize hundreds of border crossings. I have listened and heard a kind of violence and hostility that I believe tragically remains alive in our speech and experience – all of us, "West" or "East," who have, in some sense, inherited the memory of these stories, for whom these stories constitute our, or part of our, tradition(s). "*Memory*," writes Benjamin, "creates the chain of tradition which passes a happening on from generation to generation," and these texts have been passed on, or their stories shared, around the world, certainly around the worlds that have inherited the impact of their key actors (the Persians, Greeks, Egyptians, Rome, etc.). As the story of the Egyptian king demonstrates, there is much counsel in the stories of the classics, but I seek to challenge one particular, dominant dimension of this counsel: the counsel that crossing over a border requires going prepared for violence. This wisdom – and this *is* considered wisdom on a huge scale, especially among "realists" in my profession of Political Science who view these texts as profound sources of guidance for state behavior in international relations.[12] The memory of this wisdom needs, I suggest, to be awakened in a different way, its tradition called into question and challenged.

I sit in Yaşar Kemal's company differently. I sit with him in the *Toroslar*, one of the borders across the Hellespont that various actors in the stories of the classical historians either feared to cross or crossed for greater glory. I listen and receive the gift of Kemal's stories teeming with life, hospitality, and the constant struggle for justice against violent conquest. That is, I sit in the company of Yaşar Kemal to illuminate the germinative power of a different epic account of humanity and to gain a glimpse of "the unnamable glimmer beyond the closure"[13] of the Western narrative of *crossing over*. Of course, as I have emphasized above, it is "different" or "alternative" only from the perspective of that narrative. For the people whose stories Kemal tells, it is their story, their form of life.

I do not attempt to present the entire story of İnce Memed, nor do I aspire to translate all that could be translated within the story. Instead of a one-to-one translation, I sit in Yaşar Kemal's (and the reader's) company and *convey* extensive but selected parts of the stories within each volume of İnce Memed that, when juxtaposed with the stories told in Part One, provoke thoughtfulness – in Walter Benjamin's sense above – about the flaws, indeed fatal flaws, of the inherited Western imaginary of *crossing* borders. This reflection gets provoked through the demonstrable existence of another narrative precisely where one is not, within the inherited Western tradition, expected to exist.

Only volumes one and two of İnce Memed have been translated and published in English, but I have not relied upon these translations. Outstanding works in many ways, some of the nuances of the "local speech" to which Kemal refers go missing from the text, which then appears as a more or less direct translation. This is not unusual in translations of Turkish literature, and the language of these works is especially difficult to translate, but these nuances may be brought to the surface in a creative hermeneutical effort, one that suspends the expectation that only the (literary) language into which a story is being translated should appear in what is called a translation.

My approach to (non-)translation, or conveying, is informed by the hermeneutical and ethicopolitical underpinnings of this study that emphasize exploring the difference between different discursive grammars by bringing to awareness the liminal space of difficult or impossible translation between languages in conversation. My efforts in Part Two thus amount to something other than a translated reproduction of İnce Memed in a second language. The intricate nuances of hermeneutical interpretation are important to this effort, particularly a radically open sense of what understanding may mean in conversational accompaniment: how it may include an openness to understanding what is difficult, opaque, inscrutable or resistant to translation as much as it may entail a fuller and seemingly more complete understanding of another's meanings. Hermeneutical understanding through conversation may even mean understanding that some things expressed in another language may not be understood (easily, at all, right away, etc.), even that there may be nothing "there" to be "understood." These forms of understanding are not *not* understanding. They become visible through a hermeneutic understanding of the limits of understanding, and they are ways of understanding otherwise or, in the important idiom of Hans-Georg Gadamer, *understanding differently* that may be experienced when, as a result of significant differences between languages in conversation, one naturally finds oneself experiencing something other than ease of translation. One may find oneself receiving another language that one understands oneself as not understanding. Bringing this liminal space between languages in conversation into awareness, rather than suppressing it, is one form of understanding (understanding of the condition of liminality), and it is something that can be displayed in what I am calling conveying. The image I am working with is as follows: I am sitting between Yaşar Kemal and the readers of this work, in the company of both. The storyteller tells his stories, I listen and convey to you, his other listeners.

V
Conclusion: Perhaps not crossing at all

In *Border Thinking on the Edges of the West*, then, I endeavor to display the differences between the narrative of crossing over analyzed in Part One and the life-world imaginary brought to expression in Part Two in order to provoke thoughtful and critical, re-reflective re-engagement with the inherited violent, classical imagination in favor of a different imagination of what exists on or over what it considers a border. The goal is not necessarily to understand the Other (e.g. Memed) as such, but, by receiving astonishingly different counsel, to make possible other understandings of the border and those on its "other" "sides." The effect of establishing a liminal space between crossing over and being otherwise suggests that other things can happen in the understanding one has of "the" "other" "side" and what it may mean to "go" there.

Ultimately, I seek through my retelling of the astonishing stories of İnce Memed to demonstrate the possibility of learning to be otherwise in relation to borders. Especially in writing otherwise – in style, form, rhythm and pulse – from one of what "the West" considers its fatal boundaries, I seek to expose the highly contingent and provincial (non-universal) character of the inherited Western understanding of crossing over, its destructive impact, and to move readers to be otherwise in relation to what it means to be at or on the Hellesponts of our lives. This work attempts, therefore, to provoke a different relation to all borders characterized within any tradition, in one form or another, as fatal.

By way of conclusion, I explore the implications of the juxtaposition of these stories for how we, as members of humanity whose memories have been shaped by these stories, live in a bordered world. I engage in these

11

reflections because for me, following Walter Benjamin, "the storyteller joins the ranks of the teachers and sages." In both sets of astonishing stories, the storytellers with whom I am in company are teachers and sages. Within their stories, they pose questions we have yet or may never know to pose, and what they provide are not single answers but continuations of the posing, of the story, and of the life that continues to unfold. If we are fortunate, if we pay attention, we may receive wisdom from them. As Benjamin concisely puts it, "The storyteller is the figure in which the righteous man" – the man or woman willing to receive the powerful wisdom of another – "encounters himself" (or herself).

It is important to underscore that I understand myself experientially to live in both traditions analyzed here, and thus that in this study I dwell within both in a deeply hermeneutical fashion, attempting to explore their constitutive webs of meaning concerning borders, to identify the valences of significant terms within those webs, and to show how they meaningfully constitute consciousness and existence within each respective tradition. In Part One, one could say that I express and, for the purposes of under-standing, embrace[14] the violence that I am aware of within my "home" tradition. Similarly, in Part Two, one could say that I express and embrace the meanings of another tradition within which I (have learned to) live – that of those on the other end of the power of those who have crossed over in a violent fashion. From within the narrative of crossing over, spaces between are considered "borders."

I believe that the juxtaposition between the kinds of violent power associated with crossing over borders examined in Part One and the life-affirming resistance to such violence depicted in Part Two allows us genuinely open reflection about the enduring validity of the Western tradition's conception of the border spaces at its edges, its Hellesponts. As stratified societies (as in "the West"), these spaces of course also contain violence. However, as is clearly the case with *İnce Memed*, the political imagination available within them is not limited to the exercise of coercive violence and, moreover, glori-fies not the expansion of power through violence but the affirmation of life through resistance to, and the end of, such violence. In this regard it offers a different heroic narrative in relation to the heroic narratives of the conquer-ing border crosser. As I show in Part One, a disposition of counter-violence is unavailable within both the dominant and subordinate (e.g. Medizer) dis-courses of the seminal texts of the founding Western experience, whereas it is eminently present, and properly valorized, within the seminal texts of the Taurus Mountains.

The effort to think borders otherwise is not new within contemporary Global and Border Studies. A central premise of global political thought is that borders need not be seen (only) as hedges against violence that they (ironically and tragically) fail to contain; they may be spaces of possibility where relations of esteem, regard, and solidarity may occur. With Yaşar

12

Kemal and the many İnce Memeds on what the West sees at its fatal boundaries, then, I write within this shared project, in the name of life, of beauty, and of esteem for peoples on all sides of any civilization's projected borders. The project of Part Two is to bring different potentialities for being-on/at-the-border to expression in a different fashion, and to do so in obvious and direct effort to contest the transcending grasp of the tradition of crossing over violently. The interlinguistic disposition displayed there reveals the existence of another world in the world, one foreign to the inherited imaginary but welcome to creative efforts to live and be constituted otherwise. In an increasingly interconnected world, I hope readers with similar migratory imaginations (achieved in a variety of ways, through travel or study or concern about the state of an antagonistic world) will value this effort, in addition to enjoying the stories that they will find there. Realists, on the other hand, are sure to charge *naïveté*.

The central goal of *Border Thinking on the Edges of the West*, then, is to interrogate enduring ways of conceiving of borders and to suggest new possibilities for "crossing" them, or for something entirely different, perhaps not *crossing* at all. I offer reflections on the limits of the inherited tradition of border crossing in the latter pages of Part One in order to stimulate reflection about different ways of approaching "fatal" boundaries, a discussion that I continue in the Conclusion. A fundamental premise of the entire work, written I believe into each and every utterance, is that re-situating and re-locating our constitutedness   our being, in this sense – in relation to enduring violent theoretical inheritances requires, in addition to openness to alternative traditions (Part Two), significant reflective engagement with the violent traditions that inhabit us (Part One).

To conclude the study, I explicate what I mean when I assert that a different disposition towards the borders of "the West" might require perhaps not crossing over at all. Specifically, I explore, in light of the wisdom found in the stories in Parts One and Two, what may happen in one's being when old, tired, destructive, and life-negating understandings are challenged through the kind of arduous and complicated dialogical effort attempted throughout the work by the more life-affirming understandings on and over the conceptual borders of the former understanding. There is no single, definitive answer to this question, but *Border Thinking on the Edges of the West* provokes its consideration, and I conclude by addressing it as it relates specifically to the wisdom of the two traditions explored in this study.

Notes

1 J. Derrida, *Of Grammatology*, Baltimore: Johns Hopkins University Press, 1976, 14.
2 A. Nandy, "Shamans, Savages, and the Wilderness: On the Audibility of Dissent and the Future of Civilizations," *Alternatives* vol. 14, 1998, 276.

3 Livy, *RM*, XXXVIII.45, 378.
4 R. Williams, *Keywords: A Vocabulary of Culture and Society*, Oxford: Oxford University Press, 1983, 24.
5 See, e.g., W. Mignolo, *Local Histories/Global Designs: Coloniality, Subaltern Knowledges and Border Thinking*, Princeton: Princeton University Press, 2000; H. Dabashi, *The World is My Home: A Hamid Dabashi Reader*, Piscataway, NJ: Transaction Publishers, 2010.
6 See, e.g., J. Derrida, *The Other Heading: Reflections on Today's Europe*, Bloomington: Indiana University Press, 1992; and E. Levinas, *The Cambridge Companion to Levinas*, S. Critchley and R. Bernasconi (eds), Cambridge: Cambridge University Press, 2002.
7 Y. Kemal, *Yaşar Kemal on his Life and Art*, Syracuse: Syracuse University Press, 1999, 64, 75, 89, 95–96.
8 Ibid., 85, 89.
9 Ibid., 59–60.
10 Ibid., 66.
11 W. Benjamin, "The Storyteller: Reflections on the Works of Nikolai Leskov," slought.org/files/downloads/events/SF_1331-Benjamin.pdf (accessed 10 November 2011).
12 See, e.g., V. Davis Hanson, "Introduction: Makers of Ancient Strategy, from the Persian Wars to the Fall of Rome," in V. Davis Hanson (ed.) *Makers of Ancient Strategy, from the Persian Wars to the Fall of Rome*, Princeton University Press, 2010, 1–10; and S. Jones, *In the Graveyard of Empires: America's War in Afghanistan*, New York: W.W. Norton & Co., 2009, 3–5. On Thucydides, who is frequently discussed in these circles, see D. Welch, "Why International Relations Theorists Should Stop Reading Thucydides," *Review of International Studies* vol. 29, 2003, 301–19; and D. Kagan, *Thucydides: The Reinvention of History*, New York: Penguin, Books, 2009, 232–34.
13 Derrida, *Of Grammatology*, 14.
14 By embrace, I mean to invoke the central imperative of hermeneutical interpretation: not to agree but to understand, and to come to such an understanding that whatever disagreements exist become almost impossible to maintain, not because one agrees – for one may strongly disagree with what one understands very well – but because one understands.

Part One

WHEN WORDS MAINTAIN THEIR MEANINGS AND THE WORLD IS AN ABODE OF WAR

What might it mean to distinguish between life-affirming and life-negating myths that comprise our dominant imaginations of political possibility, and, more importantly, to detach ourselves from the latter in favor of the possibilities of the former? Part of the answer lies in examining the meaningful content of practices within the highly regarded narrative and discursive spaces of revered and honored traditions, to identify and explore their grip on the constitutive meanings of the tradition, and to consider possibilities both inherent to or beyond them. How to write these possibilities as an insider-stranger – from within the tradition but with an awareness of an outside? These are the things they said. I believe this is what they meant. But, within my belief lies resistance, for I want to understand what it might mean to lose this very understanding.

I
Conceptual stability in a sea of change

Who of all mankind persuaded you to make war upon my land and to be my enemy rather than my friend?

The Persian ruler Cyrus[1]

So we cannot either of us retreat, but the struggle is on, for doing and suffering, that either everything here shall fall to the domination of the Greeks or everything there to the Persians. There is no middle ground for this enmity.

Xerxes[2]

Thus did fear guard the space between the two sides.

Herodotus[3]

15

It seems unlikely that the long struggle between East and West is going to end very soon. The battle lines drawn during the Persian wars more than twenty-three centuries ago are still, in the selfsame corner of the world, very much where they were then.

Anthony Pagden[4]

A *defining feature* of Western political thought, an almost first lesson learned about its essential character as a tradition, is its inherent capacity to encompass significant conceptual change over time.[5] Paradoxically, conceptual innovation is, in James Farr's words, the tradition's "truly constant" feature.[6] Changing political circumstances produce shifts in theoretical focus, altered political visions and perspectives, new framings of the meanings and goals of political life, and even radically different vocabularies and grammars for constituting political activity.

This essential pattern of change was set early in the life of the tradition. Aristotle identified dynamism and variety in constitutional forms and visions of the good life. More dramatically, words themselves "changed their ordinary meaning," wrote Thucydides, as the plague overturned the Athenian social order during the Peloponnesian war,[7] and further changes occurred with the displacement of the *polis*, first by the Macedonian and then by the Roman Empire. This shift in what Sheldon Wolin calls the spatial domain of theorizing politics produced significantly different visions of the very nature of political life:

> The [classical political] association was political because it dealt with subjects of common concern, and because all of the members were implicated in a common life. As Aristotle had remarked, it was quite possible to enclose the whole of the Peloponnese by a single wall, yet this would not create a *polis* ... Hence if the historical task of Greek political theory had been to discover and to define the nature of political life, it devolved upon Hellenistic and Roman thought to rediscover what meaning the political dimension of existence might have in an age of empire ... The megalopolis had displaced the *polis*, and in this new spatial dimension the old notion of the political association, as sustained by a friendship among familiars, appeared anachronistic. The concept of the political community had been overwhelmed by the sheer number and diversity of the participants.[8]

In the movement from *polis* to empire, Wolin writes, "new priorities appeared, emphases were redistributed, and the phenomena of political life were surveyed from an altered perspective."[9] This is the Western tradition. Its defining and impressive (though not necessarily unique) quality as exemplified right from its start is that words change their meanings. There are of

16

course "continuities"[10] as well, but the most central meanings of political life – citizenship, law, the state, and politics itself – come to vary with new political circumstances and challenges. The essence of the tradition over time is innovation, diversity, and change. A conceptual newness is always, in potential, in the making. Even *stability* will come to have different meanings.

My purpose here is not to displace this picture but to reflect hermeneutically once more on the passage from *polis* to empire and to suggest a slight readjustment in emphasis on a very particular, but not trivial, dimension of political thought during this period, one that I believe has powerful implications for conceptualizing the world, especially its putative division between West and East. Working from the borders and other liminal boundaries of *both polis* and empire, and focusing especially on borders associated with the boundaries between Europe and Asia, I want to suggest that a hermeneutical reading of the exemplary historical narratives of political experience of this particular era – primarily, though not exclusively, *The History* of Herodotus, *The Peloponnesian War* by Thucydides, Quintus Curtius Rufus' *The History of Alexander*, and selections from Titus Livy's *Rome and the Mediterranean* – suggests that a shared and stable set of understandings, a broadly shared world view, exists concerning a crucial dimension of political space, namely, borders and what it means, explicitly and implicitly, to "cross" them. Very specifically, *crossing over* a border, a river, a pass, and so forth has a particular and shared set of constitutive meanings, invokes a particular and shared set of relationships, and constitutes a particular and shared form of practice. It means (or, more accurately, far removed from the time, with the particular concerns of my interpretive horizon guiding me, and in both dialogue and translation, I read it as meaning; more below) engaging in war, aggression, imperial expansion, or one of a hundred or so other acts of war. This is not to say that exchanges over the border of a non-violent nature (e.g. diplomacy, trade, games, cultural sharing) do not exist. They do, as evidenced, for example, in shifting alliances over time between the Greeks and the Persians, the Isthmian Games,[11] or budding elite theories of human universalism in early Stoic philosophy. However, such relationships and transcendent philosophy notwithstanding, when stories related to *crossing over* borders are told in the classics, the meaning is consistently going armed for violent purposes. Spaces on the other side of liminal boundaries are abodes of war such that entering them means enlivening one's most aggressive instincts, demonstrating one's power, and meeting others on the other side with force and arms. This family of concepts around crossing over constitutes an almost preconstituted way of talking, thinking, imagining, valuing, and understanding a movement across a border into an unfamiliar, or simply another, place; an almost preemptive conceptual attack on the life on the other side of the border, configuring the other side as a space of violence, where one must enter well armed and ready to kill and plunder. *Crossing over* is a concept in the political topography of warfare.

I aim to identify and highlight this pattern both in general and with specific attention to what the inherited classics of the Western tradition constitute as one special liminal space between Europe and Asia – the small waterway known as the Hellespont (literally, Sea of Helle) where significant conflict between warring parties coming from both its shores has occurred and what the texts I examine produce as the division between worlds. Also known as the Dardanelles and the Çanakkale *Boğazı* (Straits), the Hellespont is the thirty-eight-mile long and approximately three mile-wide strait that runs between the Aegean and Marmara Seas. It is the "stormy seas" of this waterway across which, according to the Greek myth, Leander "safely crossed"[12] to unite with his lover Hero, and the British Lord Byron later swam to emulate Leander's famous journey. The straits get their ancient name from Helle, who fell into the sea in the story of the Golden Fleece. As such, the Hellespont was not only a key strategic passage in the history of human conflict; going from Sestos in the west or Abydos in the east also figures prominently in the mythopoetic imagination of Western civilization.

Notes

1 Said to the vanquished Lydian King Croesus after the latter invaded Persia thinking that the great kingdom whose destruction the oracle foretold would be the Persian, not his own. *H*, 1:87, 74.
2 *H*, 7:11, 473–74.
3 *H*, 8:132, 605.
4 A. Pagden, *Worlds at War: The 2,500-Year Struggle between East & West*, New York: Oxford University Press, 2008, 538.
5 S. Wolin, *Politics and Vision: Continuity and Innovation in Western Political Thought*, Princeton: Princeton University Press, 2004, 64.
6 J. Farr, "Understanding Conceptual Change Politically," in T. Ball, J. Farr, and R. Hanson (eds) *Political Innovation and Conceptual Change*, Cambridge: Cambridge University Press, 1989, 24.
7 *PW*, 3:82.4, 199.
8 Wolin, *Politics and Vision*, 64, 69, 70.
9 Ibid., 64.
10 Ibid., 22.
11 *RM*, XXXIII.32, 126.
12 Ovid, *Leander to Hero*, Perseus Digital Library, www.perseus.tufts.edu/hopper/text.jsp?doc=Perseus%3Atext%3A1999.02.0085%3Apoem%3D18 (accessed 1 June 2009).

II
A hermeneutic, participatory approach

To examine the meanings of crossing the Hellespont in classical thought, I turn to the seminal historical texts of early Western historical experience not simply because they provide accounts of the crucial events and outlooks of the time. I turn to them primarily because they are written in, and thus expressive of, the languages of those outlooks. In many cases, they tell the stories of the crossings as the stories were told to them. In this regard I approach these works as virtual interlocutors for a hermeneutical engagement of the meanings constitutive of the world they inhabited and whose seminal events they recorded.

The hermeneutical approach seeks to understand the constitutive meanings of the worlds of others through actual or metaphorical dialogue (and within permanent constraints and possibilities of linguistic difference and historical distance). The aim is to produce what Charles Taylor describes as languages of perspicuous contrast that give expression to the range of understandings and horizontal possibilities that emerge in conversation with those whose life practices one seeks to understand.[1] Thus, when I assert that crossing over *means* something particular in the classical histories, I mean to say that this meaning is in my understanding of the meaning and usage of the concept crossing over as it comes to me in conversation with these texts. In this regard, my reading is substantially presentist, but it is not facile. A conceptual pattern in the view of the world exists in these works; it exists across translations, and it is one that the thousands of readers of the classics encounter.[2] It may even exist in the original authorial intentions embedded in the texts, but whether or not it does is less a concern than that the pattern may be espied in the texts as we receive them.

My approach parallels the reconstructive or participatory approach offered by James Boyd White in his reading of *The Peloponnesian War*. White views the "central terms" and "ways of talking" in texts as giving expression both "to a particular world" and the world of which the text is a part.[3] The texts I examine invite such a reading because they purposefully offer a "place to stand, a place from which [readers] can observe and judge the character and events of the world";[4] The languages of texts thus may be seen as "resources" that "establish the possibilities of expression in a particular world," and virtual interlocutors to whom the following crucial questions may be posed:

> What world of shared meanings do these resources create, and what limits do they impose? What can be done by one who speaks the language and what cannot? ... How is the world of nature defined and presented in this language? ... What social universe is constituted in this discourse and how can it be understood?[5]

Scholars debate the historical accuracy and implications of each of the classical histories but they do not contest that the various authors purposefully sought to record and account for the extant outlooks on political life and space, or that the language in which they did so exemplifies the language of their time. In these ways, the texts I examine are what Fred Dallmayr calls exemplary voices[6] of their tradition and interlocutive sources for a hermeneutically shaped, metaphorical dialogue. It is significant that each narrative was constructed with explicit attention to the constitutive understandings of the time. "Through my entire history," writes Herodotus, "it is my underlying principle that it is what people severally have said to me, and what I have heard, that I must write down."[7] This is partly what made him, for Walter Benjamin, the first storyteller of the Greeks. Similarly, Thucydides, a participant in the Peloponnesian war, states that the "reports" of others played a significant role in constructing both the important speeches in his work as well as the narrative.[8] In this regard, these works appear to have been constructed partly with the goal of providing access to what is understood in hermeneutics as the subjective ("individual") and intersubjective (commonly shared and contested) meanings constitutive of political thought and experience.

This is not to say that the histories are themselves constructed on hermeneutical terms. Frequently, the historians speak in clearly objectivist terms. Each author, that is, appears to have seen his work as providing more or less complete knowledge of the crucial events and ways of life of the societies they discussed which would set the record straight for the future. Moreover, their narratives at times display language that appears at odds with the languages of many of the participants in their histories, especially when those participants belong to societies with which they were less familiar. For example, the seminal historical narratives routinely subordinate what the authors describe as "barbarians" – a term of inferiority within Hellenic discourse – to the functioning power of the historical discourses through simultaneous representation, erasure, and omission.[9] They also routinely silence alternative perspectives within the societies that comprise their central focus, and they express, either explicitly or implicitly, judgments concerning "worthy"[10] topics, proper politics, achievement, failure, and victory for one side or another.[11] These aspects of these works cannot be ignored, or set aside, and I shall address their importance as I proceed. Still, in this project, I am less interested in exploring the positivist, Orientalist, or colonial shortcomings of these works than in seeing them as exemplary voices of their time. That is, I take them less as historical authorities than as storytelling participants in the languages of their day. When Livy proclaimed, "Let us know our traditions,"[12] he made his history expressive of those traditions, not simply their record. Curtius Rufus' history of Alexander appears to proceed with similar purposes. It is missing its first, lost book and with it, perhaps, an explanation of the historian's methodology, but it is clearly part hagiography and part critique of Alexander written in the languages of Curtius Rufus' time. In sum, the classical histories are expressive of the understandings we seek to make sense of. They therefore constitute the primary sources for an interpretive reading of the constitutive beliefs and languages of political space from the *polis* to empire. For all their imbalances, omissions, marginalizations, and erasures, they offer participatory hermeneutical insight into the concepts that inform this project – as they may be understood today, through the horizons of the present concerns of this work, and in translation.

That the classical meanings of *crossing* and *crossing over* come to us today is evident in the way that these terms remain the language in and through which the events told in the classical sources are retold in contemporary history, with the same, or very nearly the same, meanings they had for the classical historians. Editorial commentaries offered by contemporary historians, as well as widely read scholarly and popular literature on the same events, repeat the essential conceptual matrix found in the classical texts, sometimes giving even more explicit military-related meaning than found in the original text. A brief illustration may be useful.

In what follows, I shall argue that in one of its patterned usages in the seminal texts, *crossing* is frequently associated, in very explicit terms, with army movements of one kind or another. This meaning is also evident when the parties are said to be doing other things than crossing over land, such as *sailing*, but where a *crossing* of some kind or another is said to be taking place. In such usages, *sailing* may be used with the same military-related meaning of *crossing*, but without any explicit mentioning of a *crossing*.[13] So, for example, Thucydides describes at one point how the Spartans "made all haste" to Mytilene.[14] The embedded meaning may be said to be the Spartans *crossed* to Mytilene, and this is precisely how Robert Strassler, the contemporary editor of *The Landmark Thucydides*, recasts Thucydides' observation in one of Strassler's many editorial summaries that accompany the main text. Strassler writes, "the Spartan fleet crosses over the Aegean to Asia."[15] Here Strassler astutely captures the uptake of one of central meanings of *crossing over* – a naval crossing – *and* he explicitly adds the accoutrement ("fleet") where it was absent in Thucydides. Strassler extrapolates correctly, because, as I shall suggest, embedded in the meaning of *crossing* is crossing *as* or *with* a naval fleet. Walter Heckel's contemporary reconstruction of the missing first book of Curtius Rufus follows a similar pattern. He reconstructs Alexander's "crossing into Asia" using fragments of that very expression from other classical authors, such as Diodorus Siculus and Arrian.[16] I shall elaborate on this matter in greater detail ahead, after we have gained an understanding of the dominant cluster of meaning within the classical texts. Here, we must appreciate the lasting power of the meaning of the original expression of *crossing*. "In 547 B.C.E, ... the famously wealthy Lydian king Croesus – 'as rich as Croesus,' as the saying goes – *crossed* the Halys and invaded Cappadocia" (emphasis added), writes Anthony Pagden in his *Worlds at War: The 2,500-Year Struggle between East & West*, written many centuries after the original sources from which he draws.[17] Herodotus' descriptions of the Persian Wars, Pagden continues, "begin with a *crossing* from Asia into Europe, *which means conveying an army* across the Hellespont ... " (emphases added).[18] Pagden conveys more or less the precise meaning of the text *in the same language of the original text*, and, significantly, he *uses* the terms in his own contemporary account with the same meaning. The ancient idiom seems to translate easily into the contemporary one. He continues: "Xerxes, seated on a white throne on a nearby hill, poured libations from a golden cup and prayed with his face toward the rising sun. The *crossing* now began. It lasted seven days and nights without a break" (emphasis added).[19] "Seven days in all it took the task force *to pass* from Asia to Europe" (emphasis added), paraphrases Tom Holland in his *Persian Fire: The First World Empire and the Battle for the West*. "The *army crossed* the eastern pontoon ... [Xerxes] was the very last man to make *the crossing*" (emphases added).[20] Holland describes this "crossing the Hellespont" in a related footnote as well.[21]

Contemporary usages that reiterate the classical meanings of *crossing* and *crossing over* suggest the existence of a widely shared and stable understanding, a tradition of thought, indeed what Michel Foucault, in his study of the subject from Greece to Rome, called "a truly general cultural phenomenon,"[22] concerning the meaning of these central concepts of political space and possible practices within it. To be clear: my reading of this tradition occurs within this tradition as well. The existence of a tradition of thought, that is, situates the reading I offer here within this tradition. It is not an objective explanation, or one that aspires to objectivity. I am conveying what is in my understanding of the understandings of these traditions within the hermeneutic circle continually drawn by the classical and contemporary languages of crossing borders. Another way of stating this is to underscore what Foucault asseverates in his study of Hellenic and Roman discourses on the subject: "the stake, the challenge of any history of thought, is precisely that of grasping when a cultural phenomenon of a determinate scale actually constitutes within the history of thought a decisive moment that is still significant for our modern mode of being."[23] I am writing within this, my, our, modern mode of being, seeking to establish this particular understanding of crossing over as still significant within us. My broader claims about conceptual stability in the passage from *polis* to empire should be read in this context. This is not an objective designation. I am writing about these languages from within their histories, not over them. What follows is my understanding having listened to what has been said by the exemplary voices of the tradition. They have spoken, and they continue to speak. What do they say? Let us, then, "cross" the Rubicon.

Notes

1 For a concise statement of this approach, see, e.g., my "Hermeneutics and the Politics of Secularism," in L. Cady and E. Shakman Hurd (eds) *Comparative Secularisms in a Global Age*, New York: Palgrave MacMillan, 2010, 25–40.

2 *Crossing* and *crossing over* are the English translations of several related Greek and Latin words from the original texts, especially διάβασις, *transitus, traicere,* and *transgredi.* Texts consulted: *Herodotus,* New York: Harper and Brothers, 1876–77; *Thucydides,* in four volumes, London: William Heinemann, 1917–21; *Livy,* in 13 volumes, London: William Heinemann, 1919–59; and *Quintus Curtius,* London: William Heinemann, 1946.

3 J. Boyd White, *When Words Lose their Meaning: Constitutions and Reconstitutions of Language, Character, and Community,* Chicago: The University of Chicago Press, 1984, 17.

4 Ibid.

5 Ibid., 7–12.

6 F. Dallmayr, *Dialogue Among Civilizations: Some Exemplary Voices,* New York: Palgrave Macmillan, 2003.

7 *H,* 2:123, 184–85.

8 *PW,* 1.22.1–3, 15.

9 See G. Prakash, "Subaltern Studies as Postcolonial Criticism," in C. Hall (ed.) *Cultures of Empire: A Reader,* Manchester University Press, 2000, 121–36.

10 Some leaders are "not worthy of mention" (*H,* 7:96, 500); "[I]t is not worth my while to describe the details of the wars waged by foreign nations against each other, since I am bearing a more than sufficient load in attempting a full record of the history of the Roman people" (*RM,* XLI.25, 495); "Many other pieces of information are transmitted concerning the Indians, but it did not seem worth holding up my narrative to report them" (*HA,* 8.9.37, 198).

11 Though an argument can be made that they did so not uncritically of their favorites and, within the scope and limits of their horizons, not always uncharitably towards those they held in less regard. Defending the objectivity and veracity of his account, Thucydides says, for example, that "the Athenians are no more accurate than the rest of the world in their accounts of their own tyrants and of the facts of their own history" (*PW,* 6.54.1, 390).

12 Quoted in A.H. McDonald, "Introduction," in Livy, *RM,* 7.

13 Note as well that what is translated as *crossing* in the new revised Crawley edition by Strassler ("forces … crossed the Ionian Gulf," *PW,* 7.33.3, 446), is translated as *sailing* in Forster Smith's translation ("sailed with all their forces across the Ionian Sea," *Thucydides,* volume 4, 61).

14 *PW,* 3.29, 172.

15 Ibid.

16 W. Heckel, "Summary of the Lost Books One and Two," in *HA,* 25.

17 A. Pagden, *Worlds at War: The 2,500-Year Struggle between East & West,* New York: Oxford University Press, 2008, 10.

18 Ibid., 21.

19 Ibid., 24.

20 T. Holland, *Persian Fire: The First World Empire and the Battle for the West,* New York: Anchor Books, 2005, 244.

21 Ibid.

22 M. Foucault, *The Hermeneutics of the Subject: Lectures at the Collège de France, 1981–1982,* New York: Palgrave MacMillan, 2005, 9.

23 Ibid.

III
"To cross thy stream, broad Hellespont!"[1]

Even before the poet Ovid made the Hellespont famous for swallowing up Leander and depriving him of Hero's "fragrant kisses," and certainly well before Lord Byron, self-declared "degenerate modern wretch," famously imitated Leander's swim in the nineteenth century, gaining both "glory" and a bad cold,[2] what Homer called the "riptide straits"[3] of the Hellespont had been the site of numerous, legendary crossings and the idea and image of crossing it had earned epic significance in the Western imagination. There crossed the Achaeans, the Achaemenid Persians, the Athenians, the Spartans, the Macedonians, the Seleucids, and the Romans. They rushed, one after another, to or across the Hellespont in the major imperial conflicts of the sixth through second centuries BCE. Coming from either direction, they claimed imperial rights of conquest or inheritance over the Ionian and Troad regions of western Anatolia, where peoples from the Aegean and Mediterranean seas to the west had established colonies many centuries earlier.[4] Those areas came under expanding Persian control in the sixth century, unleashing a series of revolts, wars, and imperial campaigns in which crossing the Hellespont consistently had central significance. In the seminal histories of each conflict, however, while the powers that cross the Hellespont change, the idea and character of their crossings remain fundamentally stable.

The Persian ruler Darius crossed with his army several times, first in retreat during Persia's first invasion of Europe in 513 BCE[5] that had been launched across the Bosphorus to the north,[6] and then twice in his efforts to avenge and punish the Athenians for their role in supporting the Ionian revolt from Persian rule from 499–494/3.[7] Enmities had begun to grow eight years before the revolt, when representatives of the Athenian ruler Cliesthenes had approached the Persian governor of Sardis, Artaphrenes, seeking an alliance. "Who are these people," Artaphrenes asked as he rejected their offer, "and where in the world do they live that they ask the Persians to become their allies?"[8] Another Athenian – Hippias, the son of the despot Pisistratus – approached Artaphrenes as well, scheming to take power back in Athens. Herodotus blames Hippias for much of the conflict that followed, for "he stirred everything up, slandering the Athenians to Artaphrenes and trying to manage it that the Athenians would become subjects of himself and Darius."[9] Learning of Hippias' plans, the Athenians "sent messengers to Sardis to urge the Persians not to listen to those who were banished from Athens," but Artaphrenes returned a stern warning: "if they would keep their skins safe, they should take back Hippias." When the Athenians heard this, they rejected the idea and "resolved to be openly at enmity with the Persians,"[10] and, "just at this moment, when they were thinking like this and were at odds with the Persians," the Athenians received the Ionian ruler at

Miletus, Aristogoras, who was seeking support for a revolt against Persia. Furious with the Persians, the Athenians agreed to assist Aristogoras by sending ships to support the Ionian revolt. For Herodotus, "these were the ships that were the beginning of evils for both Greeks and barbarians."[11]

The Ionian revolt failed, but Aristogoras attacked Sardis, burned "the temple of the native goddess Cybele, and it was this that the Persians took as their excuse later when they, in their turn, burned the temples of the Greeks."[12] At the end of the revolt, the Persian leader Darius learned of the Athenians and vowed revenge. "He took [a bow], fitted an arrow with it, and shot it into the sky, and as he sent it up he prayed, 'Zeus, grant me the chance of punishing the Athenians'."[13] To do so, Herodotus tells us, "the Persians *crossed* [διαβαντες] *the Hellespont* with ships and marched by land through Europe, making for Eretria and Athens."[14] Defeated by Athens at the Battle of Marathon (490), however, they fell short of this goal under Darius.

Seeking "vengeance and requital," Darius' son Xerxes vowed "to bridge the Hellespont and drive [his] army through Europe to Greece," proclaiming that "I ... will never stop till I have destroyed and burned Athens, since it was the people of Athens who of themselves began the wrongdoing against me and my father, first when they came to Sardis ... and burned the groves and holy places there [and], secondly, [what] they did to us when we landed in their country."[15] Xerxes' campaign in 480 did not, initially, go well either. A storm "smashed" the first bridge made of flax and papyrus rope for the crossing "and broke it all to pieces."[16] Herodotus reports that Xerxes was so "furious" that he "bade his men lay three hundred lashes on the Hellespont" and had them curse the water: "You bitter water ... King Xerxes will *cross* you," his men proclaimed, "whether you will it or not."[17] When a new bridge made of boats was finished, Xerxes wept in happiness at the sight of the "Hellespont covered with ships and all the shores and plains of Abydos full of men."[18] He "poured the libation from a golden cup and prayed to the sun that no chance should befall him such that it should check his conquest of Europe ... When he had finished his prayer, he threw the cup into the Hellespont and also a golden mixing bowl and a Persian sword ... When all this was done, they *crossed over* ... "[19]

Xerxes captured Athens, "setting the whole acropolis on fire," but, like his father, lost the war. Defeated at Salamis in 480, Xerxes bolted to the Hellespont which became again the scene of important battles and revolt.[20] The Athenians rushed there as well to destroy Xerxes' bridge. They found it already broken and, hoping to deal a final blow to Persian power, then "*crossed over* from Abydos ... and besieged Sestos."[21] Sestos and the other cities of the Chersonese were ruled by the Persian governor Artayctes, the grandson of the Persian general who had initially encouraged King Cyrus to expand the empire by seizing more land, and in so doing, take hold of western Anatolia where the Persians were facing revolt once again.[22] Herodotus ends *The History* by recounting Artayctes' rule and fate upon his capture by the Athenians. As a ruler, he had "perpetrated deeds of lawlessness upon"[23] the people – "collecting women even into the temple,"[24] "accumulating much property"[25] at their expense, and plundering the tomb of Protesilaus at Elaeus. Protesilaus was believed to "have been the first man of Agamemnon's army to set foot upon the soil of Asia when the Greeks sailed against Troy," and he was killed in the Trojan War.[26] To make Protesilaus' tomb his own property, Artayctes was said to have deceived his own superior Xerxes. When taken by the Athenians, Artayctes tried to bribe his way out of captivity, but the Athenian general Xanthippus (father of Pericles, who was famously to lead Athens in the Peloponnesian war) refused. Herodotus relates that "The people of Elaeus were begging for the man's destruction as a revenge due to Protesilaus, and the general's own inclinations were that way anyhow. So they brought him down to the shore where Xerxes *had bridged the strait [the Hellespont]* ... and they nailed him to boards and hanged him up; and his son they stoned to death before his eyes."[27] Thus partial vengeance by one of the parties to enmity across the Hellespont was had on its shores in the year 479.

Half a century later, the Hellespont again became the site for legendary conflict, in the twenty-first year of the Peloponnesian war when Athens faced and routed its Peloponnesian challengers, led by Sparta, in a naval battle in the heart of the waters of the Hellespont, just off the point of Cynossema at its narrowest section. Thucydides recounts this battle at the end of *The Peloponnesian War*. Reeling from major defeats in Sicily and Euboea and facing many challenges – political turmoil at home; an alliance between Sparta and Persia; and a revolution against its imperial rule in the coastal islands and cities of Ionia, including on the Hellespont at Abydos and Lampsacus[28] – the Athenians made Sestos "the center of defense of the whole Hellespont."[29] In battle, they took advantage of a moment of disorder when the Spartans thought victory was theirs[30] and, "without a blow," sent the Peloponnesians sailing for safety – not far, as Thucydides notes, "owing to the narrowness of the Hellespont."[31]

Like Herodotus' *History*, Thucydides' narrative ends on the shores of the Hellespont, with a discussion of the tumultuous aftermath of this battle. The Spartans returned to recover their losses and, breaking their short-lived alliance with the local Persian governor Tissaphernes, helped to expel some remaining Persian garrisons. Tissaphernes had not only failed to fulfill promises of aid. He had also negotiated a possible alliance with the Athenians – perhaps, as Thucydides suggests, to "wear out and paralyze" both parties.[32] Now, with Athens victorious and the Spartans turning against the king, Tissaphernes "made all sail for Ionia." In Thucydides' words, the Persian was "determined to rejoin [the Peloponnesians] in the Hellespont," because he worried that another rival satrap might befriend the Spartans "and, at less cost, perhaps succeed better against Athenians than he had done."[33]

Thucydides' narrative ends – before the conclusion of the war – with the image of a Persian leader making sacrifices on his way to the Hellespont in the hope of vanquishing the Athenians once and for all. On the shores of Hellespont, old enmities continued to simmer.

With renewed assistance from the Persians, Sparta eventually defeats Athens – in the Hellespont in 405 at the Battle of Aegospotami, north of Sestos, in which nearly the entire Athenian fleet in the Hellespont was captured. Persian control over the region resumed until 336, when the new power in Greece, Macedonia's Phillip II, sent his troops across the Hellespont, declaring war in retaliation for the earlier invasions of Darius and Xerxes. With Philip's untimely murder at the start of the campaign, the task fell to his son Alexander, known worldwide as Alexander the Great. In the words of the historians, he "took his army across [the Hellespont] to Abydos" in 334.[34]

As he crossed, Alexander made a series of sacrifices and ritual gestures that symbolically brought the many prior crossings – from the Trojan through the Greek, Persian, and Peloponnesian wars – into one story. At Elaeus he sacrificed to Protesilaus.[35] He also tossed a spear into the water and "half the way over he slaughtered a bull as an offering to Poseidon and poured wine from a golden cup into the sea to propitiate the Nereids."[36] Once across, he made sacrifices at Troy to the Goddess Minerva (Athena), and, before battle with the Persians, like his father, he proclaimed a desire for revenge: Addressing the Greeks among his troops he said "that these [the Persians] were the peoples who had inflicted wars upon Greece ... that these were the men who had demolished and burned their temples, stormed their cities, violated all the laws of god and men."[37] He later repeated these charges in a missive to Darius after the victorious Macedonian army had sent the Persian leader running. Alexander reminded Darius of the harm the Persians had inflicted upon Greece: "The Darius whose name you have assumed wrought utter destruction upon the Greek inhabitants of the Hellespontine coast and upon the Greek colonies of Ionia, and then *crossed* [*traiecit*] *the sea* with a mighty army, bringing the war to Macedonia and Greece."[38] Using the idiom of the ages, the contemporary scholar Robert Strassler identifies further significance in Alexander's achievements.

> Crossing the Hellespont in 334, Alexander completely destroyed Persian military power in a series of ... victories in just three years. By 331, when the last Great King, Darius III, died ignominiously in flight, Alexander ... began to rule over both Greece and Persia. Ten years later, when he died in Babylon, the independent *polis* was well on its way to oblivion, and the Hellenistic world was born.[39]

Thus, the movement from *polis* to empire occurs not simply with *the expansion of* Macedonian power. It occurs after, in the wake of, and *as a product*

27

of Alexander's *crossing the Hellespont.* Crossing over the Hellespont lies at the heart of the transition from *polis* to empire. According to Rufus, Alexander underscored the significance of this crossing as well. When his army arrived at the next body of water on their path – the River Granicus – Alexander was advised to proceed with caution. He was told that the army would face stiff opposition. Curtius Rufus reports that Alexander responded that, "having *crossed the Hellespont,* he would not be stopped by a mere trickle such as the Granicus."[40] Similarly, speaking to his troops later at the Persian capital of Persepolis, he exclaimed: "Just look! Beginning the war at the Hellespont, we have delivered Ionia from subjection to the insolent barbarian."[41]

If the new world of empire begins with Alexander's crossing over the Hellespont, competition within that world after his death more or less ceases at the Hellespont as well, over a century later, when Rome puts down challenges to its imperial rule by defeating Philip V of Macedonia (ruled 221–179) and Antiochus III of the Seleucid empire (ruled 222–187). Both were successor states to Alexander, and both had crossed the Hellespont hoping to expand their power. Livy describes how Rome's allies "Attalus [of Pergamon] and the Rhodians might have won the splendid title of 'Liberators of Greece' if they had pressed on against Philip" before Rome's full assault. "But by allowing him to *cross back to the Hellespont* and to increase his strength by the occupation of strategic points in Thrace, they kept war going and handed over to the Romans the glory of conducting it to a successful end."[42] Soon thereafter, Antiochus crossed the Hellespont to claim hereditary rights of repossession over the city of Lysimachia, founded at the beginning of the Chersonese isthmus by Lysimachus, one of Alexander's officers who had succeeded Alexander's rule over the Hellespontine region.[43] As many had done before him, Antiochus "left Ephesus with his fleet and sailed for the Hellespont," Livy writes, "ordering his land forces *to cross* from Abydos."[44]

Livy's *Rome and the Mediterranean* further illustrates how crossing the Hellespont remained an idiom of power during Rome's conquest of western Asia. Livy reports that Attalus of Pergamon delivered to Rome "the news that Antiochus had *crossed the Hellespont* with his army,"[45] and that during a discussion over possible war alliances, a representative of Antiochus "boasted" to the Achaen Council that "a countless host of cavalry was *crossing the Hellespont* ... the great king of all Asia and part of Europe ... was coming from the farthest bounds of the East to liberate Greece" from Roman domination.[46] However, the king was defeated in Greece by the Romans who then sailed "to the Hellespont"[47] to end Antiochus' challenge more definitively. Livy writes that the Roman commander Livius took his thirty ships with the "intention being to make the necessary preparations for the *crossing* of the army."[48] The Romans were surprised to meet no resistance at the coast and "realized that they had been conceded the *crossing into Asia,* an operation which they had supposed would entail heavy fighting." So, "they *crossed* to shores that were, one might say, in a state of peace, with no opposition" and "encamped there."[49]Antiochus sought peace, but the Romans rejected his offer,[50] saying, "You should have resisted us at the Hellespont"[51] and demanding "that it was not only from Ionia and Aeolis that the king's garrisons should be withdrawn; just as all Greece had been liberated, so all cities in Asia should be set free."[52] Soon thereafter, Rome decimated Antiochus' forces at the Battle of Magnesia, inland from the Aegean coast.

In the movement from *polis* to empire, historical figures and regimes change, constitutions shift and revolutions occur, but one thing remains more or less constant: the meaning of *crossing the Hellespont*. Further elaboration of this meaning follows, but at this point it may be said that *crossing the Hellespont* in these narratives means undertaking an imperial war expedition. Crossing relates directly to army maneuvers and deployments for invasion, frequently accompanied by prayer rituals of one kind or another, in the context of pursuing territorial expansion, requital, and domination of an inherited foe. Darius first crossed to expand his empire and then to punish the Athenians for their sending ships in support of the Ionian revolt. Xerxes did so with similar goals. Athens, Sparta, and the Persians sought to maintain or expand their imperial power by subduing each other and those who resisted them. Alexander renewed earlier desires for vengeance, but otherwise shared imperial aspirations with the others, as did Antiochus and Rome, which once more sought to punish (what it viewed as) an illegitimate crosser (invader). Even more fundamentally, *crossing* entails being in a hostile relationship with those on the other side of the border, who are seen as having wronged you or your relations, and who, as a result, must be subdued. Each crossing thus recalls the earliest exchanges of enmity between the Athenians and the Persians summed up powerfully in Xerxes' famous declaration: "We cannot either of us retreat," he said, "but the struggle is on, for doing and suffering, that either everything here shall fall to the domination of the Greeks or everything there to the Persians. There is no middle ground for this enmity."[53] *Doing* is *crossing the Hellespont,* and *suffering* is what follows. As Xerxes suggests (through Herodotus), the doing and suffering are bound up within the broader, shared practices of imperial domination.

Notes

1 Lord Byron, "Written after Swimming from Sestos to Abydos," *The Complete Poetical Works of Lord Byron*, New York: Macmillan, 1907, 293.
2 Ibid.
3 Homer, *The Iliad*, New York: Penguin, 1990, 2:957, 126.
4 Colonization of the Aegean Islands, the Ionian coast, southern Italy, Libya, southern France, the Thracian coast, the Sea of Marmara, and the Black Sea

began in the middle of the eighth century BCE and became the foundation later
for Athenian empire.

5   All subsequent dates are BCE unless otherwise noted.
6   *H*, 4:88–89, 313; 4:143, 331; 5:23, 365.
7   *H*, 6:43, 425; 7:1, 466.
8   *H*, 5:78, 389.
9   *H*, 5:96, 399.
10 *H*, 5:96, 400.
11 *H*, 5:97, 400. Unless otherwise noted, all emphases are mine.
12 *H*, 5:102, 402.
13 *H*, 5:105, 403.
14 *H*, 6:43, 425.
15 *H*, 7:8, 469.
16 *H*, 7:35, 482.
17 *H*, 7:35, 482.
18 *H*, 7:45, 486.
19 *H*, 7:54–55, 489.
20 *H*, 9:102ff.
21 *H*, 9:114, 662.
22 *H*, 9:122, 664.
23 *H*, 7.33, 482.
24 *H*, 7.33, 482.
25 *H*, 9:120, 663.
26 Arrian, *The Campaigns of Alexander*, New York: Penguin, 1976, 66. See Homer, *The Iliad*, 2:796–802, 122.
27 *H*, 9:120, 664.
28 *PW*, 8.62.1, 517.
29 *PW*, 8.62.3, 517.
30 *PW*, 8.105.2, 545.
31 *PW*, 8.106.1, 545.
32 *PW*, 8.57, 514, 8.87, 531.
33 *PW*, 8.109, 548.
34 Arrian quoted in *HA*, 22; see also, Arrian, *The Campaigns*, 70.
35 According to Arrian, Alexander hoped to "have better luck" (*The Campaigns*, 66).
36 Arrian, *The Campaigns*, 66. "There is a further tradition," Arrian adds, "that he built an alter on the spot where he left the shore of Europe and another where he landed on the other side of the strait, both of them dedicated to Zeus, the Lord of safe landings, Athena, and Heracles. Once ashore, he traveled inland to Troy and offered sacrifice to Athena, patron goddess of the city; here he made a gift of his armor to the temple, and took in exchange, from where they hung on the temple walls, some weapons which were still preserved from the Trojan War. They were supposed to have been carried before him by his bodyguard when he went into battle" (ibid.).
37 *HA*, 3.10.8–9, 41.
38 *HA*, 4.1.10, 50–51. He wrote as well of Xerxes' invasion and charged this Darius with hiring assassins to murder his father, adding this as one of the reasons for his own crossing.
39 Robert Strassler, "Epilogue," in R. Strassler (ed.) *The Landmark Thucydides: A Comprehensive Guide to the Peloponnesian War*, New York: Simon and Schuster, 1996, 554.
40 *HA*, 23.

41 *HA*, 6.3.3, 122. Later in his campaign, he also attempted to motivate them for more conquest by recalling "when we were sailing across the Hellespont" (*HA*, 9.2.24, 216).
42 *RM*, XXXI.15, 35.
43 *RM*, XXXIII.40, 133; XXXIV.59, 190.
44 *RM*, XXXIII.38, 132.
45 *RM*, XXXV.23, 214.
46 *RM*, XXXV.48, 228.
47 *RM*, XXXXVII.7–9, 285–86.
48 *RM*, XXXVII.9, 286.
49 *RM*, XXXVII.33, 311.
50 *RM*, XXVII.35, 313.
51 *RM*, XXVII.35, 314.
52 *RM*, XXXVII.35, 313.
53 *H*, 7:11, 473–74.

IV
Crossing for empire, godliness, and glory

These are imperial campaigns, one after another, grounded in the pursuit of vengeance, retribution, and territorial expansion. They seek victory that will allow them to dominate, subjugate, and subdue all peoples, that will bring them the reward of a world empire, and, with it, the status of exemplars of governance and/or earthly gods. These aims are not only those described in the language of the stories recounted in the histories; they are in the language of the actors within those stories. The crossers are not simply sailing from Europe to Asia or Asia to Europe. They are crossing the Hellespont to reach and conquer, as they understand it, the furthest limits of the other side. Thus they cross so as never to need to cross again, as "if a boundary," to borrow from Curtius Rufus, "could ever stand in the way of unbridled ambition."[1] Those crossing from the eastern direction already "regarded," as Herodotus says of the Persians, all of Asia as their own;[2] and those crossing from the west aimed for all of Greece – and much of Europe – to be theirs. Each hoped to expand its empire on its own side as well as on the other side. All of them referred to this in one form or another as a "world empire." In this regard, crossing literally meant conquering the world.

"If we subdue them," Xerxes proclaimed as he marched "to the furthest limits of that continent," "we shall show to all a Persian empire that has the same limit as Zeus's sky. For the sun will look down upon no country that has a border with ours, but I shall make them all *one* country ... " (emphasis in original).[3] "[T]here shall be no other army in the world to stand against us. So now," he put it in the shared idiom of the age, "let us ... *cross over*."[4] Similarly, Athens sought to eliminate threats to its empire – first by maintaining it under Pericles and then by extending it under his followers, especially Alcibiades, who embarked on the ill-fated Sicilian expedition. Even before of the outbreak of large-scale war, Athens *"crossed over"* – to Euboea, for example – to put down revolts to its empire.

Athens viewed its empire as acquired by right, not by violence[5] "because," as the Athenians tell the people of Melos, "through daring patriotism"[6] "we overthrew the Mede"[7] – that is, the Persians who had, in another idiom of the day, "come from the ends of the earth to the Peloponnesus."[8] As Pericles exhorted the Athenians to "hand down our power to our posterity unimpaired" during his famous funeral oration for fallen citizens, he urged them both to see "the power of Athens" and to "hold vengeance upon our enemies."[9] "I say that as a city, we are the school of Hellas; while I doubt if the world can produce a man, who where he has only himself to depend upon, is equal to so many emergencies, and graced by so happy a versatility as the Athenian."[10] The world has produced the Athenian exemplar. "The admiration of the present and succeeding ages will be ours, since we have not left our power without witness ... we have forced every sea and land to be the highway of our daring, and everywhere, whether for evil or for good, have left imperishable monuments behind us."[11] Winning the war means saving the empire and Athens' imperial reputation, so "what you are fighting against is not merely slavery as an exchange for independence, but also loss of empire and danger from the animosities incurred in its exercise."[12] Pericles believed Athens should maintain, not expand, its empire during the war, but after he dies expansionists like Alcibiades take over and, in Thucydides' famous expression, "grasp at something further":[13] They "sailed" to Sicily seeking – in Alcibiades' words – "to conquer ... the Sicilians, and after them the Italians also, and finally to assail the empire and city of Carthage."[14] The aim of the expedition to Sicily – for which it was necessary "to *cross* the Ionian Sea"[15] – was said to be to "liberate" it by "extending" Athens' empire to "rule the whole of the Hellenic world."[16] *Liberation* here is not simply ideological; it is the term in and through which these crossers express the condition of the ruled in a world empire that knows no bounds.

Alexander aimed for much more than that. He wanted the whole world "in" his "power" and "possession,"[17] even to open up a "second world"[18] in his imperial "expedition across Asia"[19] to what he, like Xerxes, called "the ends of the earth."[20] Not "content" with his "inheritance,"[21] he "set out to conquer," "subjugate,"[22] and "subdue not only the Persians but all races on earth,"[23] and to reach "the Ocean" "where the sun rises"[24] – "the sea which nature has decided should be the limit of human existence."[25] In short, in crossing over, he sought nothing less than "domination of the world."[26] Throughout the expedition, he proudly described his empire's "universal invincibility"[27] and, at near end, boasted of "having Asia in my possession from the Hellespont to the Red Sea."[28] Arriving at "the ends of the earth" – and of course seeing more – he proclaimed success in "establishing" "an empire comprising most of the world!"[29]

His successors Philip and Antiochus sought precisely this goal as well, in parts of Europe and Asia, before they fell to the Roman Empire.[30] In battle, victorious Rome projected and acquired the popular reputation of non-imperialist liberator,[31] but Livy reveals its other side. The Romans initially warned Antiochus to "keep within the confines of Asia" and "not *cross* to Europe";[32] later, though, they set their "eyes fixed on Asia" not only to liberate it but to have "sovereignty" and to "rule" over it.[33] Livy records the mobilizing rhetoric of a Roman commander before the battle of Thermopylae, the site whose significance as the place of Spartan martyrdom was well known. "You should keep this thought before your minds," the Roman general says,

> that you are fighting not simply for the freedom of Greece ... but to liberate from the Aetolians and from Antiochus a people formerly liberated from Philip; ... and afterwards you will open to Roman rule Asia and Syria and all the realms, with all their riches, as far as the rising of the sun. And after that, what will prevent our having the Ocean as the boundary of our empire from Gades to the Red Sea – the ocean which enfolds the entire world in its embrace? What will prevent the whole human race from reverencing the name of Rome next after the gods?[34]

Tiberius Gracchus echoed similar aspirations at the trial of Lucius Scipio, who was charged with misappropriating spoils for personal gain. Tiberius Gracchus argued that Lucius Scipio should not "be put in prison ... for [he] had crushed the richest king on earth; he had extended the empire of the Roman people to *the furthest boundaries of the world*;[35] [and] he had bound King Eumenes, the Rhodians" – Rome's *allies* – "and so many cities of Asia by obligations to the Roman people ... ";[36] Livy notes that this statement was met with applause. Rome freed Europe and Asia from the control of its enemies but not from its own power. As Antiochus put it, the Romans had become "masters of the whole world."[37]

As the Roman aspirations suggest, each of the imperial crossings was partly constituted in meaningful relation to the revered gods: As they crossed, each undertook rituals of worship, blessing, prayer, sacrifice, and dedication, offering reverence to the gods and simultaneously seeking such reverence. At the Hellespont, both Xerxes and Alexander "first prayed," made dedications, " ... and then *crossed over*."[38] Similarly, the Athenians offered "prayers customary before" "*crossing* to Sicily,"[39] and when the Spartans came to the frontiers for battle, they busily inspected what Thucydides calls the "sacrifices for *crossing*," sometimes reading the signs as inauspicious and turning back.[40] Alexander, the Romans, and Antiochus paid sacrificial heed to the Goddess Minerva: Alexander at the Hellespont where he also honored through prayers the memory of the first Greeks to

33

cross to Asia; the Romans at Phocaea and Troy (Ilium), where they were honored as descendants of the city.[41] Antiochus sacrificed at Ilium as well.[42]

Such customary gestures to the gods took place in part because these conflicts involved holy stakes. A central reason for war was offence taken at the destruction of sacred sites – the temples at Sardis and Athens, for example – or the sense of righteous retribution for having been harmed in the course of one invasion or another. Livy calls the desecration of sacred sites "acts of war" when he describes how the Romans "sacked the temples and carried off the statues" at Bacchium early in their invasion of Asia.[43] Reciprocal demolitions of temples, shrines, tombs, and monuments in Calcis and Athens were prominent as well in the prior wars between Philip and Rome, with each incident inciting more desire for vengeance.[44] After Philip reduced Athenian sacred sites to rubble, the Athenians "heaped curses and execrations on Philip, his family, and his realm, his forces on land and sea, and the whole race and name of the Macedonians"[45] – a response that recalls Darius' desire to punish the Athenians and Xerxes' determination to exact his father's revenge. The memory of these offenses, moreover, appears to be very long. In his exhortation to his troops, Alexander described the Persian invasions of Europe as "unholy wars"[46] that "violated all the laws of gods and men."[47] "The gods," he said, "support the better cause."[48]

Alexander's historic triumph epitomizes the aspirations for world domination of each crosser, the central reason greatness has been attached to his name. He successfully emulated "Father Liber's triumph on his victorious march through all the nations from the Hellespont right through to the ocean,"[49] and he carried out acts that were believed to be possible only by the gods: uniting worlds that have been "separated by nature," opening "a second world," and so forth. He came to be seen, to see himself, and to require others to see him as a god, the son of Jupiter[50] – an identity conferred upon him by those he conquered as well.[51] "I shall," he declared in triumph, "give distinction to places that have none; I shall open up to all the people of the world lands set far away by nature."[52] Renown and glory was "the end of their toil, to which they had devoted all their prayers," he told his troops.[53] *The History of Alexander* concludes with Curtius Rufus underscoring Alexander's success. Describing the homage paid to Alexander's body where it lay in Alexandria, Curtius Rufus writes, "every mark of respect continues to be paid to his memory and his name."[54] This is the final sentence of Curtius Rufus' history. It is what we, too, shall remember: Every mark of respect.

Every Hellespont crosser aimed for precisely this pinnacle of honor, an honor even more profound than the honorable death in battle that Alexander and the other crossers are said to have welcomed as well. An honorable death means honor in death, and where death is welcome eternal fame is prized. Having acquired the renown of world dominator and reached the known limits of the world, Alexander had no other destination, nowhere else to go, and thus nothing else to cross over, no additional earthly possession to acquire. What more power do the gods possess that he has not acquired by crossing? Like them, Alexander had the world "in" his "power."[55] Thus his death was much less a disappearance from life than a second reappearance, a second showing in his second world, in the status of "god." With every mark of respect continually given to his name – in many cities that bear it – Alexander crossed even the boundaries of afterlife for ordinary mortals. There could be no more sacred answer to the prayers of his subjects, no more righteous pursuit according to the laws of men and gods, than to cross over to death and remain alive forever in the hearts and minds of ordinary mortals. Each of the crossers crossed in spiritual company with the gods in pursuit of becoming earthly immortals. They sought to have the world know that they possessed everything under the sun by conquering the furthest limits of the earth. They crossed, that is, to arrive at a place, earthly and spiritually, where one could cross no more. These are some of the deeper intentions associated with crossing over in these texts, almost without variation.

With similar purposes for crossing activated in the same part of the world, these separate wars slowly appear to blend into one, one single conflict involving similar purposes. The participants in these conflicts are not unaware of these relationships: they feel, argue, and place themselves within the legacies of each lasting conflict. They understand that they are involved in an enduring struggle between enmities born long ago (as the later historians are aware that their histories are connected to the earlier ones). In defending their aims in Asia, for example, the Romans trace their roots to Troy, whose residents, Livy tells us, in turn honored them as their descendants.[56] Moreover, Rome defended its actions in Asia by backing what it calls the "colonial" efforts of the early Greeks who had settled Ionia "to increase the progeny of the most ancient of peoples, and to propagate their stock all over the world."[57] Rome, that is, places itself in the history of Greek colonization, and thus right in the heart of the enmities that grew from the first Ionian revolt after which Darius vowed and prayed for revenge. Wrath and a thirst for vengeance took Darius and Xerxes to Europe twice, giving the Athenians renown in the Hellas as the "saviors of Greece"[58] and an empire whose right they claimed for their courage and bravery. Holding on to their empire, the Athenians crushed revolts against their power with brutality and sought new glories in a greater empire, only to encounter the wrath of the invaded once more. "Let us engage in anger," said Gylippus, the Spartan commander of the Syracusans and their allies upon defeating the Athenians. "Nothing is more legitimate than to claim to satisfy the whole wrath of one's soul in punishing the aggressor and nothing is more sweet, as the proverb has it, than the vengeance upon an enemy, which it will be ours to take."[59] Passions for vengeance were burning strong as well when the Macedonians torched the palace of the Persian capital Persepolis. The torching was meant "to avenge Greece,"[60] just as the destruction of Antiochus was meant, by the

Romans, as an extension of the centuries-old Greek colonial project in Asia. Destruction is within the core of the meaning of crossing.

Notes

1 *HA*, 10.10.6, 256.
2 *H*, 1.4, 34.
3 *H*, 7:8, 468–69; 7:55, 489.
4 *H*, 7:53, 489.
5 *PW*, 1.75.2, 43; 5.89, 352.
6 *PW*, 1.7.4, 22.
7 *PW*, 5.89.1, 352.
8 The latter expression is that of the Corinthians in their speech at Sparta, *PW*, 1.69.5, 39.
9 *PW*, 2.43.1, 115; 2.42.4, 115. "Athenian power" is one of the concepts Thucydides offers as the cause of war (*PW*, 1.118.2, 65).
10 *PW*, 2.41.1, 114.
11 *PW*, 2.41.4, 114.
12 *PW*, 2.63.1, 125–26.
13 *PW*, 4.21.2–3, 234.
14 *PW*, 6.90.2, 413.
15 *PW*, 6.30.1, 377. "A wide sea *to cross* with their armament," says Hermocrates (6.34.4, 380).
16 *PW*, 6.18.3, 372; 6.90.3, 413. Note that for Thucydides, Athens needed a just and moderate leader like Bracias, or to listen to Nicias, who cautioned them not to "grasp at another empire" (*PW*, 6.10.5, 367), but it got Alcibiades and eventually its collapse.
17 *HA*, 9.6.20, 227.
18 *HA*, 9.6.20–21, 227.
19 *HA*, 9.1.3, 212.
20 *HA*, 9.1.26, 217.
21 *HA*, 9.6.19, 226.
22 *HA*, 6.3.3, 122.
23 *HA*, 3.10.5, 41.
24 *HA*, 9.1.22, 217.
25 Coenus to Alexander, before going to the Ganges, *HA*, 9.3.13, 219.
26 *HA*, 4.1.38, 53; 7.7.12–14, 165.
27 *HA*, 6.3.6, 122; 7.7.12, 165.
28 *HA*, 9.6.20, 227.
29 *HA*, 10.2.2.4, 243.
30 See, e.g., *RM*, XXXIII.38, 131.
31 *RM*, XXXI.31, 50; XXXIII.33, 127.
32 *RM*, XXXIV.59, 190.
33 *RM*, XXXVII.45, 322.
34 *RM*, XXXVI.17, 254–55.
35 "Beyond the Taurus mountains" to "the furthest corner of the earth" (*RM*, XXXVIII.59, 395; cf. e.g., XXXVIII.53, 388).
36 *RM*, XXXVIII.60, 396.
37 *RM*, XXXVII.45, 323.
38 *H*, 7:53, 489; *HA*, 27.
39 *PW*, 6.44.2, 386.

40 *PW*, 5.116.1, 357.
41 Arrian, *The Campaigns of Alexander*, New York: Penguin, 1976, 66; *RM*, XXXV.43, 254, XXXVII.37, 314.
42 *RM*, XXXV.43, 224.
43 *RM*, XXXVII.21, 299.
44 *RM*, XXXII, 23, 92.
45 *RM*, XXXI, 45, 64.
46 *HA*, 5.6.1, 105.
47 *HA*, 3.10.8–9, 41.
48 *HA*, 4.1.13, 51.
49 *HA*, 3.12.18, 46.
50 *HA*, 8.1.43, 179; 8.5.5–6, 197.
51 e.g., *HA*, 8.10.1, 198.
52 *HA*, 9.6.22, 227.
53 *HA*, 9.9.4, 233.
54 *HA*, 10.10.20, 257.
55 *HA*, 9.6.20, 227.
56 *RM*, XXXV.43, 254, XXXVII.37, 314.
57 *RM*, XXXIV.58, 190.
58 *H*, 7:139, 515.
59 *PW*, 7.68.1, 467.
60 *HA*, 5.7.4, 107.

V
Crossing as war, part I

It is a remarkable feature of nearly every usage of the concept of "crossing" or "crossing over" in these seminal historical texts of the Greek through Roman experience that the concept – whether associated or located at the Hellespont or not – is almost always accompanied in its usage by the explicit mention of some form of military- or battle-strategic meaning. Here, now, I speak especially within the discourses of the historians: come to a statement about crossing in their narratives and you will find an army and its movements somewhere in the vicinity. Often, you'll find it in the very same sentence.

More specifically, the great majority of its usages contain explicit references to military movements, maneuvers, and accoutrements, such that that which crosses, moves, sails, etc. across a border is most often an army on its way to, or already in, battle, with its supplies and servants. As movement of or related to the military, then, crossing "means," as Alexander is said to have put it in reference to a possible invasion of Scythia, "armed invasion"[1] or some similar form of maneuver related to military practices, including and especially the movement of forces[2] and equipment for war.[3] These practices include "marching,"[4] "advancing,"[5] "penetrating,"[6] "passing through,"[7] "occupying,"[8] "halting,"[9] "encamping,"[10] "establishing bases,"[11] "fortifying,"[12] "blockading,"[13] "reconnoitering,"[14] or making tactical shifts (with one's rear secure,[15] etc.) required for battle of one kind or another.[16]

The basic narrative pattern of associating crossing with war movements within the seminal histories is remarkably consistent in this regard.

Herodotus, for example, recounts that the Persian crossings were – "*army crossings*" – Darius' over the Bosphorus[17] and Xerxes' over the Hellespont. Notice the linkage between army and crossing. "Seven days and seven nights did his [Xerxes'] *army cross.*"[18] When Darius returned over the Hellespont, "he crossed, himself *along with his ships*" – read forces – "into Asia" while at the same time keeping "his general in Europe" to prosecute the war.[19] Herodotus states that when Xerxes crossed into Europe, it was "with the greatest *hosts of any army* we have heard of"[20] – he estimates 5,283,220 persons, almost half of them "*fighting* men"[21] – that is "*troops* that *crossed.*"[22] What crosses is a "*fighting force,*" those who "came with the army:" "This is the number of the whole of Xerxes' fighting force; but no one could give the exact number of the women who baked the bread or of the concubines, or the eunuchs, or the transport animals and baggage carrying cattle and Indian dogs that *came with the army* ... "[23] Thucydides similarly links crossing and military maneuvers. "Pericles *crossed over with an army* of Athenians to" Euboea,[24] and Athens "*crossed* to Sicily *with an armament* now consisting of *one hundred and thirty-four trireme*s in all (besides two Rhodian penteconters) of which one hundred were Athenian vessels – sixty men-*of-war*, and forty *troopships* ... five thousand and one hundred *hoplites* in all," plus allies, servants, archers, slingers, "light-armed exiles," suppliers, bakers, stonemasons, carpenters and their *tools for raising fortification*, plus "hundreds of other boats and merchant ships which followed the armament voluntarily for purposes of trade; all of which now left Corcyra and struck across the Ionian sea together."[25] The "*forces ... crossed* the Ionian Gulf *with all their armament* to the Iapygian promontory ... took on board ... darters ... persuaded their allies in Italy ... to send them three hundred darters and two triremes, and *with this reinforcement* coasted on ... "[26] During the Ionian revolts against Athens, the latter "*crossed over and encamped* at Miletus,"[27] the Chian general "*crossed over with his army* to Chios,"[28] and the "Athenian *armament* now *crossed over* from Lesbos to Chios."[29] For Curtius Rufus (for example), the Macedonian "*army crossed* the Caucasus"[30] and Alexander's prepared "to *cross* the river [Hydaspes] *with the rest of his troops* ... "[31] Similarly, Livy writes, "Titus Quinctius *crossed* ... and reached Corcyra *with 8,000 infantry and 800 horses*. From Corcyra he *crossed in a quinquereme* ... "[32] The consul's brother "entrusted ... with command of the sea coast ... *crossed* to Corcyra with two *quinqueremes.*"[33] Deciding on an alliance, Achaean supporters of an alliance with Rome describe the Romans as "men [who] have *crossed* the sea *with great fleets and armies* to bring you your freedom ... "[34] The Romans observe that Antiochus "had already *crossed with a huge fleet and a first-class army* ... "[35] Huge it was: After Antiochus sacrificed at Troy, "he set out *with forty decked ships and sixty open vessels, while 200 cargo-boats followed,* laden with all kinds of provisions, and other *equipment for war.* He set course first for the island of Imbros; and from there he *crossed to* Sciathos ..." Thus it fell from the lips of his representative to say that "a *countless host of cavalry* was *crossing the Hellespont.*"[36] After setbacks, the Romans defeat the Aetolians, who send a messenger to Antiochus with "instructions to muster his *land forces* again and *cross* to Greece ... his allies should not be left in the lurch; and he must not allow the Romans, relieved of all anxieties after they had wiped out the Aetolian people, to *cross into* Asia *with all their forces.*"[37] "Livius was already on his way from Canae to the Hellespont with *his own thirty ships and the seven quadriremes* that King Eumenes had brought with him, his intention being to make the necessary preparations for the *crossing of the army* ... "[38] These are just some examples.

The conceptual linkage between crossing and military might is so tight that the idea repeats itself in the historian's reports of what those invaded said was happening. The Syracuse leader Hermocrates, for example, sees the Athenians coming and says, "They have a wide sea to *cross with all their armament.*"[39] Similarly, in his condemnation of the Persians' invasions of Europe, Alexander described them as having "*crossed the sea with a mighty army,* bringing the war to Macedonia and Greece."[40] It is as if what appear to be four separate words in the expression are only one in meaningfulness: *crossing-with-an-army* (or armament, troops, naval ships, war equipment, etc.). The concepts *crossing* and *crossing over* appear, within these historical narratives, incomplete without their war and military-related attachment. This is the case whether or not there is mention of armies and their equipment. Crossing – including *crossing the Hellespont* – means invading, attacking, and making war. Thus, for example, Antiochus' "*crossing into* Europe" – which only takes place after "he decided that *his forces* were adequate" – and the Romans' "*crossing into* Asia" essentially, then, mean the same thing.[41] So does Roman speculation on Phillip's possible invasion of Rome: It is enough to say, "if Philip were to *cross over* to Italy."[42] The meaning – to make war upon – is clear. We also see all these meanings, explicit and implicit, in Livy's account of Hannibal's advice to Antiochus. Hannibal insisted that "the king ... should *cross* into Europe *with all the rest of his forces,* and keep his army in Greece, not *crossing* to Italy, but ready *to cross*; for that would be enough to give the appearance of aggressive intentions and give rise to rumors of invasion."[43] This vignette illustrates the exact meaning of *crossing,* since appearing ready *to cross* is to display aggressive intentions, to make the show of an invasion. When one is ready *to cross,* there is no additional need to detail the accompanying equipment for war. It may be assumed to be right there, in the reference to crossing.[44]

It is important to note that within the narratives, the various accoutrements accompanying the crossers – ships, supplies, etc. – are essentially instruments for war. This includes bridges. Insofar as bridges are usually described in these accounts as means for crossing, they are not simply paths to the other side. They are – and are understood as – means for making war.[45] Darius' and Xerxes' bridges were built, Herodotus says, for the *"army crossing."* Alexander *"bridged* the river [Euphrates], ordering *the cavalry* to *cross* first and *the phalanx* after them ... *"*[46] Where bridges, boats, bakers, horses, elephants, etc. are the instruments for war, those parts of the earth's surface that one must cross for war are seen as, in the words of Cobares (the servant strategist of Darius' ignominious killer and successor Bessus), "barriers to arms."[47] This was Cobares' view of rivers in particular. In this view, rivers are obstacles to crossing, barriers to the movement of the military. Their character as a constraint lasts, however, only so long as they are not bridged. Bridges, as means for crossing, are means for war so that when the bridge is completed, the military along with its supplies, etc. can *cross over.* At this point, rivers, which have ceased being obstacles (to crossing), have become pathways for crossing – for war. The world is an abode of war.

To cross, then, means to go or come, "prepared and equipped,"[48] for war, invasion, and conquest. Darius "crossed *and conquered* Thrace"; "So the two sides ... went eagerly *into battle*, with the islands and the Hellespont for the stakes of the game."[49] So did those who followed. "We sailed first to Sicily *to conquer* ... " said Alcibiades.[50] We are "men," the Romans asseverated, "who have *crossed* the sea *and waged war* on sea and land."[51] This is, if you will, the macro meaning of the concept. It conveys the movement – marching or sailing – of "fighting men" and their supplies "against"[52] one's "enemies"/"foes."[53] A further question remains: What additional meanings and practices accompany each crossing? Once one crosses as such, what occurs next – at what might be called the micro level of crossing – in the lands into which one has crossed?

Before conveying these meanings, I must note that the pattern for both the macro and micro meanings was set, in my understanding, in Herodotus' first explicit usage of the concept crossing in *The History*. He uses it as he sets the broader historical context for Persian claims over Asia, while recounting the Lydian King Croesus' daring judgment to attack the Persians based upon the oracle's statement that foretold the destruction of a great kingdom were he to do so. The great kingdom he destroyed was his own – such is the power of the oracle over human judgment – but before Croesus falls, Herodotus describes Croesus' invasion of Persia, when he "crossed" the River Halys, separating west and east Anatolia, *"with his army"* and attacked the Persians. Or, more precisely, when Thales of Miletus "brought his [Croesus'] *army* across for him."[54] Herodotus relays Croesus' reasons for crossing: "because [Croesus] longed for additional territory but mostly because he trusted the oracle" that foretold the destruction of a great kingdom; and because he wanted to take vengeance on Cyrus on behalf of Croesus' brother-in-law Astyages, king of Media, who "had been subjugated by Cyrus" (who was also Astyages' banished grandson).[55] Note the meanings:

territorial expansion under the guidance of the gods, destruction, and vengeance enacted upon a foe. These are the macro-level meanings we have examined thus far. After Croesus crossed, Herodotus writes, Croesus undertook additional activities that are related to the crossing by virtue of having been made possible by the crossing. I call these the micro-level meanings. Croesus' army, for example, *"destroyed* the farms of the Syrians, *captured* the city of the Pterians, and *made slaves* of the people, and he captured all the neighboring towns; moreover, he *drove* the Syrians from their homes, though," Herodotus hastens to observe, "they had done no harm to him."[56] In the first explicit usage in Herodotus, then, we see a full cluster of the embedded macro- and micro-level meanings of crossing over. It means engaging in an expansionist holy war to capture,[57] destroy, enslave, and expel people who have done the crosser no harm.

Notes

1 *HA*, 7.7.12, 165. "One river is in our way, crossing it means armed invasion of Europe."

2 e.g. "After scattering and routing the enemy, [Alexander] crossed the shattered fortifications and moved his forces towards the outcrop" (*HA*, 8.2.22, 181). Antiochus tries to have the Aetolians "seize hold of the top of the mountain found [at Thermopylae], so as to deny the Romans the chance of crossing by any mountain track" (*RM*, XXXVI.16, 253).

3 I provide illustrative passages in these citations for usages that are not illustrated the forthcoming discussion of the main text.

4 e.g. *H*, 4:89, 314; 7:50, 483; 7:56, 490; 8:33, 568; 8:51, 567; *PW*, 6.88.5; 9.1.8, 212; *RM*, XXXVI.33, 269; *HA*, 9.1.8, 212.

5 e.g. *H*, I:207, 126–27; *PW*, 3:106.1–3, 214; cf. having one's "progress impeded" (*HA*, 6.3.16, 123), or "not being stopped" (*HA*, 23).

6 e.g. *HA*, 4.1.27–29, 52–53.

7 e.g. *PW*, 7.29, 66.

8 e.g. the Persians at Delphi *"occupied* ... to plunder the shrine at Delphi and show its treasures to King Xerxes" (*H*, 8:35, 368); cf. also, the Athenians who occupy the holy site of Delium at Boeotia (*PW*, 4.97.3–4.98.2, 276–77).

9 e.g. *PW*, 4.91.1, 273.

10 e.g. *PW*, 8.25.1, 495; *HA*, 7.5.18, 159; *RM*, XXXIV.26, 165; XXVII.33, 311; XXXVII.38, 316.

11 e.g. "Alexander of Acarnania ... foresaw certain victory if the king crossed into Europe and established a base for war in some part of Greece" (*RM*, XXXV.18, 212); and Antiochus "crossed the River Phrygius and established his base" before the Battle of Magnesia (*RM*, XXXVII.37, 315).

12 e.g. *PW*, 8.14.3, 490; 8.38.2, 502; "established a garrison in their city" (*HA*, 9.8.10, 231).

13 e.g. *HA*, 9.4.5, 220.

14 "The consul had received information from Charopus of Epirus about the passes which the king [Philip] had occupied with his army; and after wintering in Corcyra he *crossed* to the mainland at the beginning of spring and proceeded to *move his army* towards the enemy. When he was some five miles from the king's camp, he left the legions in a *fortified* position while he himself *advanced* with

light armed troops *to reconnoiter*" (*RM*, XXXII.6, 73); cf. "informing" in *PW*, 3.3.5, 160.

15 "[T]here cities were keeping [Antiochus] in Asia: Zmyrna, Alexandria, Troas, and Lampascus. He had so far failed either to take them by assault or to lure them into friendship by terms of peace; and he was *unwilling to leave them in his rear* when he *crossed* into Greece" (*RM*, XXXV.42, 223).

16 As in a tactical shift in war deliberations, "When Quinctius found that he was having no effect at all on his allies by contending with them, he brought them round to agreement with his own design by pretending to cross over to their opinion" (*RM*, XXXIV.34, 175). Crossing as bringing others around to one's own design through pretence.

17 *H*, 4:88, 313.

18 *H*, 7:56, 490.

19 *H*, 4:143, 331.

20 "This was far the greatest host of any we have heard of; ... what nation did Xerxes not bring out of Asia against the Greeks?" (*H*, 7:20–21, 477–78).

21 *H*, 7:184–86, 534–36.

22 *H*, 7:55, 489.

23 *H*, 7:186, 536.

24 *PW*, 1.114.3.

25 *PW*, 6.43–44.1, 385–86.

26 *PW*, 7.33.3–5, 446–47.

27 *PW*, 8:25.1, 495.

28 *PW*, 8.32.2, 500.

29 *PW*, 8.38.2, 502.

30 *HA*, 7.3.21, 155.

31 *HA*, 8.13.22, 206.

32 *RM*, XXXII.9, 76.

33 *RM*, XXXII.16, 82.

34 *RM*, XXXI.21, 91.

35 *RM*, XXXIII.44, 135.

36 *RM*, XXXV.48, 228.

37 *RM*, XXXVI.26, 263.

38 *RM*, XXXVII.9, 286.

39 *PW*, 6.33.6, 380.

40 *HA*, 4.1.10, 50–51.

41 *RM*, XXXIII.31, 125; XXXVII, 26, 263; XXXVI.41, 274–75.

42 *RM*, XXXI.7, 28.

43 *RM*, XXXIV.61, 192.

44 For similar usages in other classical texts, see e.g. Xenophon, *The Persian Expedition*, Harmondsworth, Middlesex: Penguin, 1949, 21 and 249; *The Histories of Polybius*, Bloomington: Indiana University Press, 1962, Vol. 1, I.5, 5; Vol. 2, XVI.29, 195 and XXI.13, 270; Arrian, *The Campaigns of Alexander*, New York: Penguin, 1976, 68–69; Plutarch, *The Life of Alexander the Great*, New York: The Modern Library, 2004, 15–17.

45 This makes sense in material terms as well. My point here is to see their constitutive meanings, too.

46 *HA*, 4.9.12, 71; see also 8.10.2–4, 203.

47 *HA*, 7.4.15, 156.

48 To borrow from Livy, where Eumenes comes to Phocaea and finds "the Romans preparing and equipping for a naval battle" (*RM*, XXXVI.43, 277).

49 *H*, 9:102, 656.

50 *PW*, 6.90.3, 413. Cf. when Alcibiades *"crossed* over ... to Sparta ... and *inflamed* and *stirred* the Spartans" to *join the war* against Athens at Syracuse (*PW*, 6.88.10, 6:92, 412, 414). Also, Livy terms Antiochus' objective in crossing into Europe as "sustaining a war against Rome" (in addition "to seizing possession of Greece") (*RM*, XXXV.43, 254).

51 *RM*, XXXIV.32, 173.

52 *H*, 7:50, 488.

53 *H*, I:4, 34.

54 *H*, 1:75, 68–7.

55 *H*, 1:73, 66. Herodotus also describes Cyrus' failed "crossing" into the land of the Massagatae (*H*, 1:206–7, 126–27), Cambyses' "crossing the desert" "against Egypt" (3:1–4, 211–13), and how the fourteenth-century Egyptian King Sesostris "crossed from Asia to Europe and conquered the Scythians and Thracians" (2:103, 173). By the time we get to the Persian invasion of Europe in Book Four, the meaning of the concept has been set.

56 *H*, 1.76, 68.

57 Croesus "captured the city of the Pterians ... and neighboring towns" (*H*, 1:76, 68).

VI
A note on liberation and glory

Before describing the micro-level meanings in greater detail, it seems necessary to address a particular tension in these texts between the meaning of crossing over that I am suggesting and the purposes for crossing as reported in the testimony of many of the actors in the narratives. To summarize all of these expeditions in the language of war and conquest, as I have, is to make a claim about their character that is slightly at odds with the stated purposes, as far as we know them, of the historical actors who proclaimed their intentions to be liberation, not conquest. This applies especially to the language used by and in the historical accounts of the Athenians and the Romans. These parties saw themselves and were seen by many others as champions of freedom and rule by law against tyranny, "enslavement" and rule by kings.[1] The Athenians claim "the experience of" and "hunger for freedom" as their reasons for refusing to accede to the Persian demand to give earth and water to the king, something others in Europe had done during the Persian invasion.[2] With this constitutive self-understanding, the wars of Athens thus always have something to do with freedom, as they instruct, for example, the Camarinaens in a neighboring city of Syracuse. The Athenians claim that since Syracuse has its eyes on Camarina, they have come "as liberators" – "not to enslave but to prevent any from being enslaved."[3] Similarly, the Romans consistently declare their aims to be the "liberation" of "all Greek cities in Europe and Asia," as the terms of peace with Phillip declared: "All cities "should have their freedom and their own laws."[4] They describe themselves as having "crossed the sea and waged war ... to achieve this liberation,"[5] and they are seen by many as "fighting for the freedom of other men ... at the cost of hardship and peril to herself ... even prepared to cross the sea in order to prevent the establishment of unjust dominion in any quarter of the globe, and to ensure that right and justice, and the rule of law, should everywhere be supreme."[6]

The tribute the Romans collect, the presence of their garrisons in various cities, and exceptions to the condition of liberty in strategically located cities of Europe where they maintain the upper hand in governance lead some, like the Aetolians, to criticize Roman emancipatory claims as "empty words," an "illusory show of liberty."[7] The Aetolians call the situation instead "the state of subjection to the Roman nod"[8] and side with Antiochus as a restorer of liberty.[9] Livy asserts that this "criticism was not entirely baseless."[10]

Hence the question arises, given the present analysis of the aims of crossing as imperial conquest, are the Aetolians right in describing the Roman claims as empty? Are the emancipatory claims of the imperial powers to be treated as *ideological* illusions? Or, does our focus on the meanings associated with crossing over allow one to approach the emancipatory claims as something other than ideology?[11] I want to suggest that it does and to do so in a way that neither confirms nor legitimates the emancipatory claims.

We have seen that each crosser aims to reach the end of the known world and, in the process, to create a world empire. As the example of the Romans above shows, the populations liberated from one ruler do not necessarily achieve their freedom or independence from rule itself. Imperial rule, that is, is the end of rule by one power and the beginning of rule by another. At the same time, however, the Romans describe and consider the populations under their power as "liberated." This claim can be said to make sense if we understand liberation in relation to the glory-world-empire matrix of meanings of crossing over. In this context, liberation is relative to a perception of prior confinement, not simply under the tutelage of another regime, but within the limited borders of smaller states and/or opposing imperial powers. Liberated here entails freed to live, like all others within the world's empire, without the constraints of any known confines. It is not that the populations within the empire become politically free as such. Empire is not republicanism (states founded on violence for the purposes of the liberty of their citizens) writ large. It is that their political situation alters, along with that of the previously confined imperial power itself, from inhabiting a living space and political realm with definitive limits, to one that itself knows no borders because it aspires to encompass the entire (known/inhabited) world, one whose limits are, to borrow from Alexander, "the limits of human existence." Those who live within an imperial realm reaching from one end of the earth to another, are in this sense "liberated" – from borders! The polis is *gone*, and has been replaced by global empire.

The aspiration for world empire, for the greatest glory, for reverence along with the gods, therefore, suggests that the meaning of emancipation here is living without confines and constraints, without bounds. Boundless glory, a boundless empire, brings "freedom" and "liberation" in these senses. This is why, even though the language of liberation is in the texts here and there, it is the pursuit of glory through world empire – the "augmentation" of power, as Alcibiades terms it – that is most significant to the meaning of crossing over. The crossers cross ready to live and die for ultimate honor and glory usually reserved for the gods. Xerxes seeks it in "showing to all" an empire "that has the same limit as Zeus's sky." On "Persian power," Xerxes once reflected that "it was by risking dangers" that it was acquired. "Big things are won by big dangers," he said,[12] and in Pericles' exhortation on "the dignity of Athens" he echoed Xerxes: "With the greatest dangers, communities and individuals acquire the greatest glory."[13] "Facing danger" and dying with "vengeance upon their enemies" entails the "most glorious of hazards."[14] Qualitatively, the crossers always seek the greatest, the more, the most. Pericles may have been an exception in intentional terms – he advocated not expanding the empire – at least while the empire was being challenged, but not when it came to everlasting glory as its primary pursuit. Alexander seems to thrive in this Periclean way, constantly testing and demonstrating his "courage," "fearlessly facing perils of war,"[15] "inspiring" his soldiers "to win glory," and assessing himself "based on the extent not of my life but of my glory."[16] Near the end of his journey, when measuring his successes in having become so quickly and at such a young age "now conqueror of both continents," he asks: "Do you think I can relinquish this quest for glory, the one thing to which I have dedicated my entire life? No, I shall not fail in my duty and wherever I fight I shall believe myself to be playing to the theater of the world."[17] Livy, too, makes the pursuit of glory on all sides part of his account, often with reference to the glory of a particular figure (e.g. a Roman consul, Philip, Antiochus, Hannibal), but also describing, as we have seen, early in his account of the wars how the Pergamon and Rhodes could have "won the splendid title of 'Liberators of Greece' ... [but they] handed over to the Romans the glory of conducting it to a successful end."[18] By becoming the "liberator," therefore, by continually making the empire boundless, and by gaining the reverence reserved for the gods, one earns the greatest glory. This is, at the most macro level, the ultimate purpose of crossing over in the passage from Greece to Rome as depicted in the histories of those ages, and any *liberation* is connected with it, not political freedom.

Notes

1 *H*, 8:144, 611. It is worth noting as well that Alexander saw at least his battle against the Persians as self-defense, given their attacks and aggressive intentions on Europe. "I am not the aggressor in this war, but acting in self defense" (*HA*, 4.1.13, 51).
2 *H*, 8:143, 610–11; 5:78, 389; *HA*, 10.2.6, 241.
3 *PW*, 6.87.2, 409; 6.82.3–4, 407.
4 *RM*, XXXIII.30, 125; see also XXXIV.59, 191.

WHEN WORDS MAINTAIN THEIR MEANINGS ...

5   *RM*, XXXIV.32, 173.
6   *RM*, XXXIII.33, 127.
7   *RM*, XXX.III.21, 125.
8   *RM*, XXXV.32, 217.
9   *RM*, XXXV.33, 218, XXXI.44–46, 225–27.
10 *RM*, XXX.III.21, 125.
11 A similar question could be asked about Xerxes' pronouncement to his troops before crossing the Hellespont that their cause was "our common good" (*H*, 7:53, 489).
12 *H*, 7:50, 488.
13 *PW*, 1.144.3, 85.
14 *PW*, 2.42.4, 115.
15 According to Curtius Rufus, his words (*HA*, 2.6.24, 227).
16 *HA*, 9.6.18, 227.
17 *HA*, 9:6, 21, 227; cf. 9.2.31, 217; 9.9.22, 221.
18 *RM*, XXXI.16, 35; cf. XXXV.42, 223.

VII
Crossing as war, part II
Attacking, killing, burning, plundering, etc.

Glorious achievements ...
are more keenly remembered than inglorious.[1]

Along with these macro-level constitutive purposes, crossing over has additional micro-level layers of meaning in these works. No attempt to elaborate its meaning can ignore them. As the crossers make their way on the paths of war, they cross not only for glory at the grandest level, but more simply, as it were, "to fight, to face danger, to shed blood."[2] As expressed in "a shout that came from all sides" to the Roman consul before the decisive Battle of Magnesia between Rome and Antiochus, the crossers cross with "eagerness" "to do battle" and "to slaughter"[3] – to satisfy what Livy calls "a lust for battle"[4] and Curtius Rufus terms a desire "to expose" themselves "to many dangers."[5] They cross with "contempt"[6] and "enmity" for "their enemy." They cross in "blazing anger."[7] Called upon to "show zeal"[8] and "valor,"[9] they cross with the bravery of their forebears on their minds.[10] They "lay hold of war with eagerness."[11] And, of course, they cross to "win."[12]

Thucydides paints a fascinating picture of the subjective motivations for the Athenians who crossed to conquer Sicily. Among those who "fell in love with the enterprise," "the older men thought that they would either subdue the places against which they were to sail, or at all events with so large a force, meet with no disaster; those in the prime of life felt a longing for foreign sights and spectacles, and had no doubt that they should come safe home again; while the idea of the common people and the soldiery was to earn wages at the moment, and make conquests that would supply a never-ending fund of pay for the future."[13] Crossing here has the micro-level constitutive meanings of being "in love" with the practice itself, of *subduing other places with great force*. It includes the remarkably confident ("no doubt") expectation of "meeting no disaster," personal longings for sightseeing, and economic hopes for present and future wages. The imperial objectives of crossing thus do not only belong to the leadership. Thucydides characterizes the Sicilian expedition as an "enthusiastic" societal project involving many people – "the majority" – with different background characteristics and varying subjective motivations. Those who opposed the expedition "kept quiet" to avoid "appear[ing] unpatriotic."[14]

The multiple constitutive purposes of crossing over among those who participate in the practice suggest that it is a form of human activity that sees action and possible suffering in the face of danger as primary or fundamental to human existence. Xerxes may have articulated this underlying outlook best when he scolded his more cautious advisors not to take account of everything. "As each opportunity arises, if you were to take account of everything that is involved, you would never do anything. It is better to have a brave heart and endure one half of the terrors we dread than to make forecalculations of all the terror and suffer nothing at all."[15] "*So we cannot either of us retreat, but the struggle is on, for doing and suffering* ... "[16] The crossers are doers – of war, travel, wages, etc. – and they cross prepared both to suffer and to bring suffering to others.

In so doing, the micro-practices associated with crossing are in fact quite various. Crossers carry out all practices of war. A full accounting of these practices is beyond the scope of this work, but I wish to attempt to identify those among them that are nearly directly related to the very practice and explicit mentioning of crossing, where the practices of war could not have happened without the parties having first crossed, indeed without their having first *crossed the Hellespont*. I have in mind general war-related activities like carrying war imperia,[17] building and strengthening war alliances,[18] exhorting for war,[19] following the commands of the leadership,[20] bringing about revolts,[21] and relaying messages of war.[22] However, I also have in mind the multiple micro-level practices that take place as a direct result – and therefore in direct relation to – crossing. Such practices further elaborate the meanings of crossing over, both in the historical accounts and in the very outlooks constitutive of those engaging in them. These are many.[23] We have seen some of them in the example of Croesus above. Crossers cross to attack,[24] assail,[25] arrest,[26] avenge,[27] accept surrender,[28] batter, besiege,[29] blockade,[30] and burst in. They bring to heel[31] and steady pressure to bear. They pillage and burn,[32] and they butcher, capture,[33] charge,[34] cause famine, colonize, civilize, crucify,[35] and cut people down at random. They damage[36] and defeat, demolish and destroy, despoil and devastate, dismember and drag, dislodge and drive "the enemy like cattle."[37] They enslave, execute, exile, expel, and fall upon the enemy.[38] They hack and harass;[39] they harm, hunt, and hurl missiles and spears.[40] They chop. They intend to use open force, injure, insult,[41] inflict heavy casualties,[42] and instill panic. They kill. They loot, lay waste to everything,[43] and lust. They maraud,[44] massacre, molest, murder, occupy, overrun,[45] penetrate,[46] rip apart, pursue,[47] rape, ravage, raze,[48] reduce,[49] rob, rout,[50] sack, seize, satiate their wrath, and reign confusion and death. They show no mercy to resistance. They shanghai,[51] slaughter,[52] slay, shower with missiles,[53] smash, surround, and stick to their heels.[54] They spare neither youth nor age. They stab faces, backs, and beasts. They storm,[55] stir up trouble, and strike panic, fear, and terror. They take. They torture. They trample.[56] They violate. They whip.[57] They wipe out.[58] They plunder and pillage. Often they do many of these things simultaneously. They "fill lands and seas with armaments and fighting men,"[59] and then plunder more. In short, they make the world an abode of war.

All of the following selected examples occur in direct relation to a crossing of some kind. In each case, the crossing involves one of these destructive practices:

> After crossing the Bosphorus, Darius "*enslaved*" the Getae[60] and "the inhabitants" of Eretria. Mardonius "*added* the Macedonians to their already existing slaves."[61] Darius' troops "put to shore at Naxos; for they *made this their first point of attack* ... The Persians *made slaves* of all ... *burned* ... their temples and their city."[62] Then they "put their ships into ... the land of Eretria, and ... entered and *plundered and burned* the temples in retaliation for the temples that were burned in Sardis, and they *enslaved* the inhabitants, according to the orders of Darius."[63]
>
> Xerxes says that he "will not stop till I have *destroyed and burned* Athens."[64] Artabanes, Darius' brother, recalls to Xerxes how the latter "bridged" the river Ister, "*crossed over to attack* the Scythians."[65] Xerxes' troops "*set* [Phocis] *ablaze and ravaged* it, and they *put fire to* the cities and holy places. On they *marched* by the banks of the Cephisus and *ravaged all*, and they *burned down* the city of Drymus, and Charadra and Erochus and Tethronium and Amphicaea and Neon and Pediea, and Tritea and Elatea, and Hyampolis and Parapotamii, and Abae, where there was a rich shrine of Apollo, with store of many treasuries and dedications, and there was and still is an oracle there. This holy place they too *plundered and burned*. And they *pursued and caught* some of the Phocians near the mountains, and some women, too, they *murdered* with the multitude of those that raped them."[66]
>
> "The Delphians ... were *reduced to every sort of terror*."[67]
>
> "The Persians *established* themselves on the hill opposite the Acropolis that is called by the Athenians the Areopagus, and they *besieged* the Acropolis in this way: they *wrapped tow around their*

arrows and set them alight and shot them into the barrier."[68] They "*butchered* the suppliants" on the Acropolis, "*burned* Thespia and Plataea ... [and] *plundered* the shrine and *set* the whole acropolis [in Athens] *on fire*."[69] And Mardonius *burned* Athens again, and "where walls or houses or temples were still upright he *cast down and destroyed*."[70] At Plataea, "the Persians *killed without mercy, sparing neither animal nor human*. When they had had enough of the *slaughter*, they *surrounded* the remainder and *drove them* into Mardonius's camp."[71]

After gaining the upper hand in the Hellespont, "the Athenians and their general, Xanthippus, were for staying where they were and for *attacking* the Chersonese. So ... [they] *crossed over* from Abydos into the Chersonese and *besieged* Sestos."[72]

The Athenians under Pericles "crossed over" and subdued the Euboean revolt;[73] then, "while they settled the rest of the island by means of agreed terms, they *expelled* the people of Histiaea and *occupied* their territory themselves."[74] At the Corcyrean revolution "some five hundred ... exiles who had succeeded in escaping took some forts on the mainland and, *becoming masters* of the Corcyrean territory on the mainland, *made this their base to plunder* their countrymen in the island, and *did so much damage* as *to cause a severe famine* in the city. They also sent envoys to Sparta and Corinth to negotiate their restoration; but meeting with no success, afterwards got together boats and mercenaries and *crossed over* to the island, being about six hundred in all; and burning their boats so as to have no hope except in *becoming masters* of the country went up to Mount Istone and *fortifying* themselves there, *began to harm* those in the city and obtain command of the country."[75]

Lacking funds to support additional forces, the Athenians ordered the Thracians to return to Thrace. Diitrephes, the leader of the Thracians, "was instructed as they were to *pass through* Euripus ... [and] if possible on the voyage along the shore *to injure* the enemy." Diitrephes then "sailed across the Euripus ... from Chalcis in Euboea and disembarking in Boeotia led them *against* Mycalessus ... He passed the night unobserved near the temple of Hermes, not quite two miles from Mycalessus, and at daybreak *assaulted and took* the city ... *bursting* into Mycalessus *sacked* the houses and temples, and *butchered* the inhabitants, sparing neither youth nor age, but *killing* all they *fell in* with, one after the other, children and women, and even beasts of burden, and whatever living creatures they saw; ... Everywhere confusion reigned and death in all its shapes; and in particular, they *attacked* a boys' school, the largest that there was in the place, into which the children had just gone, and *massacred* them all. In short, *disaster falling upon* the whole city was unsurpassed in magnitude, and unapproached by any in suddenness and horror ... "[76]

When the war goes badly, " ... some persons [from Athens] *crossed over* from Samos and had an interview with Alcibiades, who immediately offered to make first Tissaphernes, and afterwards the King, their friend, if they would *give up the democracy* and make it possible for the king to trust them. The most powerful citizens who also suffered greatly from the war, now had hopes of *getting the government into their hands* and of *triumphing over the enemy* [Sparta and its allies]."[77] These were the powerful "oligarchic conspirators" who take power to defeat Sparta, but the Athens-Persian alliance fails to occur as Alcibiades had been deceiving them. The conspirators nonetheless "*deprive* the Athenian people *of its freedom*," according to Thucydides.[78] (*Crossing to triumph over one's enemy, to deprive of freedom.*)

Alexander "*stormed*" Miletus, "sparing the inhabitants but *selling the captured soldiers into slavery.*"[79] At Syria, during Alexander's invasion: "The Syrians, not sufficiently cowed by military disasters, refused to recognize the new authority, but they were swiftly *reduced and brought to heel*."[80] "Alexander changed horses – he had exhausted several – and began *to stab at the faces* of the Persians still resisting and *at the backs* of those who ran. It was no longer a battle but a *massacre* ... "[81] Afterwards, the Macedonians "first *pillaged* more than they could carry ... Now they came to the women, and the more these prized their jewels, the more *violently they* were *robbed* of them. *Not even their persons were spared the violence of lust.* They filled the camp with all manner of lamentation and screaming in reaction to their individual misfortunes, and *villainy of every shape and form* manifested itself as the *cruelty and license* of the victor *swept through* the prisoners irrespective of rank or age."[82]

As Alexander "make[s] haste" for the Persian treasury, "he *demolished* the villages in the vicinity."[83]

At Persepolis, Alexander "told [his troops] that no city was more hateful to the Greeks than Persepolis, the capital of the old kings of Persia, the city from which troops without number had poured forth, from which Darius and then Xerxes had waged an unholy war on Europe. To appease the spirits of their forefathers they should *wipe it out*, he said ... *cruelty as well as avarice ran amok* in the captured city; soldiers laden with gold and silver *butchered* their captives now of no worth, and *cut down* people they came across at random anywhere ... "[84] "And they got up, *drunk, to burn* a city which they had spared under arms. Alexander took the lead, *setting fire* to the palace, to be followed by drinking companions, his attendants and the courtesans ... Such was the end of the palace that had ruled the East."[85] "After *ravaging* Persian territory ... ," Alexander says to his troops: " ... our empire is new and, if we are prepared to admit the truth, insecure; the barbarians still hold their necks stiff beneath the yoke. We need time, men, for them to *develop more pliant dispositions* and for civilization *to moderate their wildness*."[86] Attacking the Mardians in a thick forest, "Now the local people, practiced in crawling through the undergrowth ... had on this occasion also entered the woods, and were *harassing* their enemies *with missiles* from their hiding places. *Like a hunter*, Alexander *explored their lairs* and *killed* several of them."[87]

At Branchidae, Alexander met former Milesians (from Miletus in Ionia) who had settled in Persia. They surrendered gladly but were seen by the Milesians among Alexander's troops as traitors. "[T]he signal was given to *sack* the city which provided refuge for traitors, *killing* the inhabitants *to a man*. The Branchidae, who were unarmed, were *butchered* throughout the city, and neither community of language nor the olive branches and entreaties of the suppliants could curb the *savagery*. Finally, the Macedonians *dug* down to the foundations of the walls in order to *demolish* them and *leave not a single trace* of the city. Woods, too, and sacred groves, they not only *cut down* but actually *uprooted*, so that *nothing would remain* after the removal of the roots but empty wasteland and barren soil."[88]

When some of his troops rebel, Alexander *besieges* several cities; one "was *demolished* so that its *destruction* could serve as an example *to keep others in line*."[89] At Nautaca, "he *crossed* the shattered fortifications and *moved his forces towards* the outcrop [facing the river] ... [and] issued *orders for trees to be felled and rocks piled* together. Unacquainted as they were with works of this kind, the barbarians were struck with sheer panic when they suddenly beheld the structure that was thrown up. Alexander thought they could be *frightened into submission*, so he sent Oxantes, a fellow tribesman of theirs but subject to himself, to urge their leader to surrender. In the meantime, *to increase their fear, siege-towers were moved forward and a barrage of missiles flashed* from the siege-engines."[90]

At Alexander's first engagement after crossing into India, "*to strike terror* right at the start into a people which had, as yet, had no experience of Macedonian arms, Alexander told [his commander] *to show no mercy* after the fortifications of the city under *siege* had been fired. Riding up to the walls [of the nearest city] ... Alexander was hit by an arrow, despite which he took the town, *butchered* its inhabitants to a man, and even *unleashed his fury* on its buildings."[91] Alexander gave the following instructions to disable

Porus' riders and elephants: "I am going to *attack* the enemy left wing ... [You] *attack* the enemy while they are in confusion ... *Dislodge* the riders and *stab* the beasts."[92] " ... Croenus made a vigorous *attack* on the left wing."[93] Against Porus' army, Alexander's army "*released a thick barrage of missiles* on both elephants and driver, and the phalanx also proceeded *to bring steady pressure to bear* on the frightened animals."[94] The elephants trampled on some Macedonians. "Then the Macedonians began to *use axes* – they had equipped themselves with such implements in advance – *to hack* off the elephant's feet and they also *chopped* at the trunks of the animals with gently curving, sickle-like swords called *copides*. In their fear of not just dying, but of suffering novel kinds of torment, *they left nothing untried*."[95] After victory, Alexander "ordered that *no mercy be shown* to any who resisted."[96] After Porus' capture, and believing him dead, Alexander "ordered his body to be *stripped*."[97] After crossing the river Hydaspes, "first *to attack* the Indians were the Scythians and the Dahae [among the Macedonian troops] ... "[98] After Alexander "crossed the river and marched into the interior of India,"[99] he came to the river Hiarotis and "*took* the nearby town with a military cordon and *imposed* a tribute on it after *taking hostages* ... Alexander now dispatched Perdiccas and a light-armed unit *to ravage* the area. He then transferred some of his troops to Eumenes so that he could help *force the barbarians into submission*."[100] In the country of Sibi, " ... after *crossing* the water Alexander *forced them* [the tribes defending the city on the river bank] *to flee* and *blockaded* them within their city walls, which he then *took by storm*. The adult males were *executed* and the rest of the population *sold into slavery*."[101]

Upon hearing that Alexander had been injured in battle, the Macedonians "*smashed* through the wall *with pick-axes* and, *bursting* into the city where they had *made the breach*, they *cut down* the Indians, more of whom took to flight than dared engage the enemy. Old men, women, children – *none was spared*. Anyone the Macedonians encountered they believed responsible for their king's wounds. *Mass slaughter* of the enemy finally appeased their just rage."[102] In the territory of King Sambus, "According to Clitarchus, 80,000 Indians were *slaughtered* in this area and many captives were *auctioned off* as slaves."[103]

"Let Macedonia instead of Italy," the Roman consul declares, "*be the scene of fighting*; let it be the cities and the countryside of the enemy that *suffer the devastation of fire and sword*."[104] The Romans *attack* Chalcis, held by Philip's forces. There, they *burn and slaughter*, *take booty* and *throw down and dismember* Philip's statues.[105] When Philip gets word, "in quest of *revenge* ... he *made for*

Chalcis ... [which was] still smoldering ... he therefore *recrossed* the strait [Hellespont] by the bridge and made his way through Boetia to Athens ... he *halted* and ordered his army to *pitch camp* and rest; *intending to use open force ... to glut his rage with a long desired massacre*, for there was no Greek city so hateful to him as Athens ... [H]e spurred his horse, *elated by his rage*, and *equally by the prospect of glory* ... he *pressed into the thick* of the enemy, *instilling* unbounded enthusiasm into his own men, and *corresponding panic into the enemy* ... [H]e *pursued* them and *drove* them inside the gate; and then when he had *caused even greater slaughter* among the Athenians as they huddled in terror in the narrow passage," he withdrew.[106] "He then *pitched camp* ... all the sacred sites and resorts of pleasure were *burned* down; the building, and even the tombs were *demolished. Nothing* whether under the ownership of Gods or men, was *preserved* from his ungovernable fury."[107] "On the previous occasion he had directed his *destructive activities* to the *demolition* of the tombs in the suburbs; now, to *avoid leaving anything unviolated*, he gave orders for the *demolition and burning* of the temples of the gods, the consecrated shrines of the Athenian demes ... It was not enough for Philip simply to *demolish* the temples and *overturn* the images; he went on to *order the stones be broken up* so that they should not be heaped up whole in piles of ruins. And when his *wrath had been sated* – or rather when material for the exercise of his wrath had been exhausted – he withdrew from enemy territory ... "[108]

Antiochus "left Ephesus with his fleet and sailed for the Hellespont, and ordered his land forces to *cross* from Abydos to the Chersonese ... in order *to remove any threat* from the Thracians, he set out in person *with half his land forces to lay waste* to the nearest parts of Thrace ... "[109] "He clearly understood – there was indeed no doubt about it – that on the fate of this city, which was the first *attacked*, depended the question of whether he should henceforth be despised by the whole Thessalian nation or be feared by them. He therefore *sought to strike terror into the besieged from all sides and by every means* ... After these successes ... the king marched to Crannon with his whole army and *captured* the place ... He then *took* Cierium and Metropolis ... thus *getting into his hands* all places in that district except Atrax and Gyrto. Next he decided *to attack* Larisa ... Ordering the elephants to be driven in front of the standards *to strike terror* into his opponents, he *marched* up to the town in battle order."[110] The Roman historian Valerius Antias records that Villius, the Roman commander, "*crossed over* [the Aous river] and *engaged the enemy in a pitched battle*. The king, according to this account, was *routed* and *put to flight*, and *driven away* from his camp; 12,000 of the enemy were *slain* in the battle; 2,200 were *taken prisoner*, with the *capturing* of 132 standards and 230 horses."[111] The Roman "consul *crossed* into the region of Epirus ... *advanced* ... *attacked* ... *captured* ... Phaloria was *sacked and set on fire*. The consul then *moved against* ... "[112] Livius "told his men to remember Roman valour, and *not to regard* the king's slaves *as men*."[113]

Antiochus' admiral "Polyxenidas assumed that the enemy would sail to Samos to join the Rhodian fleet, and setting out from Ephesus he first lay off Myonessus; from there he *crossed* to the island called Macris so that he could *attack* any ships of the passing fleet ... [the waves] began to roll higher ... and he saw that he could not reach the enemy. He therefore *crossed* to the island of Aethalia, so that on the next day he might from there *attack* the ships as they made for Samos from the open sea."[114] After crossing the Hellespont, Roman "marines *devastated* the country far and wide ... "[115] At Phocaea, the Roman praetor "first *moved up a ram*, and started *to batter the walls and towers*."[116] At Magnesia, the Roman "horsemen *pursued* the enemy all over the plain, the cavalry of Eumenes leading the way, followed by the rest of the cavalry, and they *cut down* the hindmost as they came upon them ... In the camp also *great slaughter* was done, greater, perhaps than the *slaughter* in the field of battle. It is said that up to 50,000 infantry were *slain* on that day, and 3,000 cavalry; 1,400 prisoners were *taken* and 15 elephants, with their drivers, were *captured* ... On that same day the victors *sacked* the enemy camp and returned to their own camp with a large quantity of plunder. On the next day they *despoiled* the bodies of the slain and *rounded up* the prisoners."[117]

When it comes to plundering, crossing takes on additional meanings in these classic stories: having access to everything, seizing, carrying off, making off, securing the booty, taking possession.[118] As early as the Ionian revolt, Aristagoras promised the Spartans and Athenians the "riches of Asia"[119] for their support, since in Asia, "men that live on that continent have an abundance of good things such not all other men have."[120] Similarly, Mardonius, Xerxes' cousin, says "Europe" is "a very fair land and bore every sort of cultivated tree, was high in fertility, and it was the Great King, alone of all mortals, who *deserved to own* it."[121] He advised "bridging the Hellespont" and "*making war* on Athens,"[122] and then he "*captured booty*" at Plataea.[123] After Athens defeated the Persians at the Hellespont, "having [executed Artayctes], they sailed away to Greece, *bringing with them the rest of the stuff* and, especially, the gear of the bridges, intended to dedicate it at their shrines."[124]

Alexander, too, promised his men before battle with the Persians that, "victory gave them *access to everything*. It would not be fruitless labor ... they were being *offered the spoils* of the East."[125] He tells the Illyrians and Thracians who "usually made their living by looting ... to *look at the enemy line agleam* with gold and purple – *equipped with booty* not arms! They were men, he said, so *they should advance and seize the gold* from this *cowardly bunch of women*."[126] After battle, "Alexander's men had *made off* with a huge quantity of gold and silver ... and, since they *pillaged* more than they could carry, the paths were littered everywhere with the meaner articles which they had greedily cast aside after comparing them with superior goods."[127] "[T]he wealth of [Persepolis] eclipsed everything in the past ... [The victors] *ripped apart* royal robes as each man *grabbed* a piece for himself, and they *hacked* to pieces with axes vases that were precious works of art. *Nothing was left intact*, nothing removed in one piece. Statues were *dismembered* and individuals *dragged* away the limbs they had broken off."[128] After the defeat of Porus, Alexander promised "*rich plunder*: the area for which they were bound was renowned for its wealth. In fact, he said, *the spoils* from the Persians were cheap and paltry in comparison, and the soldiers would now *fill Macedonia and Greece*, not just their own homes, with pearls and precious stones, gold and ivory. *The men were eager for both riches and glory* ... "[129] "*So it is not so much to glory that I lead you as to plunder*. You *deserve to take* home riches ... "[130] At the area where the Hydaspes joins the Acesine, in the country of the Sibis, "he *ravaged* the countryside and took its capital town ... "[131] And "he *occupied* [Patalia] and *ravaged* the countryside. *Large quantities of booty were taken from* here in the form of sheep and cows, and a great amount of grain was *found*."[132] At the Herita, "Three armies [Alexander's divisions] were thus simultaneously *looting* the Indians, and rich *spoils* were *carried off*."[133] Exhausted, however, the Macedonians, "proceeded to burn the spoils they had taken from the enemy, spoils for which they had *penetrated* the furthest reaches of the East."[134]

The Roman commander who promised his troops an empire "from Gades to the Red Sea" and reverence for the name of Rome next to the Gods if they defeated Antiochus, also said: " ... for *your reward* not only those things now in the royal camp will *come into your hands*, but also *all that equipment daily expected from Ephesus will be booty*; and afterwards you will open Roman rule to Asia and Syria and all the realms with all their *riches as far as the rising sun*. And after that, what will prevent *our having the Ocean* as the boundary of our empire ... "[135]As the Romans crossed to Asia, "they committed an act of war in *sacking* the temples and *carrying off* the statues" at Bacchium, the island overlooking Phocaea. "Then they *crossed* to the actual city ... and the *attack* was *launched*."[136]

One could go on.

These various meanings associated with crossing over are related. Moving an army is related to securing alliance is related to attacking is related to storming is related to slaughter is related to booty is related to honor is related to vengeance is related to reverence. Reverence is related to righteousness is related to domination is related to expansion is related to booty. All are connected, as in Xerxes' statement: "I find that there is *at once honor for me to win a land* that is not less in size and not less fertile but far more productive than what we now own; *and,* besides this, *vengeance and requital.*"[137] Follow the internal discursive relations between these values and practices long enough and one makes it to the shores of the Hellespont, for each of these values and practices is, in the final analysis, related to crossing from Europe to Asia or Asia to Europe by passing over the Hellespont.

> Livius was already on his way ... to the Hellespont with [his ships] ... his intention being to make the necessary preparations for *the crossing of the army.* He first *took the fleet* into the port called the "Harbour of the Achaeans" [the Greeks who fought the Trojan War], and from there went up to Ilium [Troy]; and *after sacrificing* to Minerva he gave friendly hearing to delegates from neighboring places, from Elaeus, Dardanus, and Rhoeteum, who came *to hand over* their cities to his protection. From there he *sailed to the entrance of the Hellespont,* where he *left ten ships on guard* off Abydos, and *crossed with the rest of the fleet to attack* Sestos.[138]

In the end, when we talk in terms of *crossing over,* or when the historian storytellers and the actors do, we and they are talking in one language, about one single practice with many and varied but interrelated characteristics. This evident consistency in usage in the seminal historical texts from Greece to Rome suggests a pattern, a form of conceptual stability in the conception of political space, from *polis* to empire with no significant shift in meaning.

Before bringing this discussion to a close, it seems fruitful to consider whether or not these texts offer any alternatives to these decisively dominant meanings of *crossing over.* The search for alternatives leads in at least two directions. First, one may examine explicit usages of crossing or crossing over that may be read as meaning something different from requiring arms or inspiring enmity, fear, and the desire for glory and booty. Second, one may comb these texts in search of alternative relationships to liminal spaces or borders more generally. Both directions reveal that these texts offer more complicated sensibilities about and around both crossing over borders and borders more generally. In one, crossing means *taking flight*, and in the other, crossing loses its meaning and relevance in the figure of the Medizer. These two alternatives deserve some attention, but it must be stated from the outset that in the former the difference does not amount to much of a difference, and in the latter the alternative does not get much attention. Thus neither possible alternative displaces the dominant significance of *crossing over* that I have outlined here.

Notes

1 Rosalind Thomas, "Introduction," in Strassler, *The Landmark Thucydides*, xxxiv.
2 Coenus of Alexander's army (*HA*, 9.3.5, 218).
3 "[T]he consul should lead the army out straightaway and make full use of the eagerness of the troops, who felt as if their task was not to do battle with so many thousands of the enemy, but to slaughter so many thousand of cattle ... they were ready to invade ... " (*RM*, XXXVII.39, 316).
4 Used twice to describe the Roman disposition at the Battle at Aous after crossing to engage the King (*RM*, XXXII.10–11, 77–78).
5 *HA*, 9.2.8, 215; Diodorus, in *HA*, 24.
6 e.g. the Roman feeling for Antiochus' forces at Magnesia, when the latter declined immediate battle. "No enemy was ever regarded by the Romans with such contempt" (*RM*, XXXVII.39, 316).
7 At the Battle of Corycus when the king's ships seize a Roman ship: "At this Livius, in blazing anger, went for the enemy with his flagship" (*RM*, XXXVI.41, 277).
8 Xerxes at the Hellespont, *H*, 7:50, 487.
9 Consul Livius in *RM*, XXVI.44, 278.
10 *PW*, 4.95, 275; *HA*, 3.10.7, 41; *RM*, XXXVI.44, 278.
11 Xerxes, *H*, 7:53, 489.
12 e.g. *H*, 7:50, 488; *HA*, 3.11.27, 44.
13 *PW*, 6.24.3–4, 375.
14 *PW*, 6.24.3–4, 375.
15 *H*, 7:50, 487.
16 *H*, 7:11. 473–74.
17 "The senate decided that the consul, Publius Aelius, should send a man of his own choosing, vested with the imperium, to take over the fleet brought back from Sicily by Gnaeus Octavius, and *to cross over* to Macedonia" (*RM*, XXXI.3, 25).
18 Brasidia, the Spartan commander, "*crossed over* by night to Scione" to call a meeting of the Scions who had just revolted from Athens (*PW*, 4.120.2–3, 288); and Attalus who "*crossed* the Piraeus *with a view towards strengthening his alliance* with Athens" (*RM*, XXXI.1, 34; cf. XXXII.40, 107; and XXXIII.31, 125).
19 Attalus presents "an *exhortation to embark* on the war" against Philip (*RM*, XXXI.15, 34).
20 On Alexander's Macedonian army, Curtius Rufus writes: "It was an army ready to stand its ground [against Persian attack] and *follow* its leader ... " (*HA*, 3.2.26–27, 31).
21 During a revolt from Athens, a Theban rebel "*crossed* the mountains and *brought about the revolt*" at Eresus" (*PW*, 8.100.3, 541). A Persian commander, Memnon, escaping Alexander's assault on Ionia, "had captured Chios and Lesbos and was

now preparing to *cross* to Europe," where he had "distributed money in Greece to *foster dissension* there" (*HA*, 25).

22 Darius sent a "horseman" from Sardis across the Hellespont to give his general Megabazus the message "*to move* the Paeonians *out* of their accustomed country and *bring them* to himself – and their children and womenfolk" (*H*, 5:14, 361). Megabazus read the message and "*marched upon* Paeonia"; he "*fell upon*" them and "*drove* [them] *out*" of their native land and *brought them* to Asia" (ibid.) by crossing the Hellespont.

23 As previously, I provide illustrative citations in the footnotes only for usages not illustrated in the forthcoming text.

24 e.g. *H*, 9:114, 661–62; *RM*, XXXVI.30, 266; XXXVII.21, 299; XXXVII.37, 315.

25 Alcibiades tells the Spartans that "to assail the empire and city of Carthage" was one of Athens' intentions of its expedition to Sicily (*PW*, 6.90.3, 413).

26 The Spartans "*cross over* to Aegina, intending to arrest those of the Aeginians who were most responsible betraying Greece" (*PW*, 6.48–49, 388).

27 *HA*, 7.5.35, 161.

28 e.g. *RM*, XXXVI.14, 250; XXXVII.44–45, 322.

29 e.g. Alexander "besieged" the Marmares (*HA*, 25); Gaza (*HA*, 4.6.7, 74); Mitylene ("siege," *HA*, 4.4.22, 63); the Uxians (Alexander "*crossed* the Tigris ... and proceeded to besiege the town," 5.3.7, 98); Nysa (8.10.10, 199); and Beira (8.10.22,200).

30 Uncited practices will be illustrated in the forthcoming text.

31 The Macedonians "swiftly reduced and brought [the Syrians, who refused] to heel" (*HA*, 4.1.5, 50).

32 e.g. " ... at Maracanda ... after leaving a garrison in the city, Alexander pillaged and burnt the neighboring villages" (*HA*, 7.6.10, 162).

33 e.g. *PW*, 6.101, 3–6, 421; *HA*, 8.10.22, 200.

34 e.g. after "crossing" the Granicus, Alexander "immediately *made his charge* with thirteen cavalry squadrons" (Plutarch in *HA*, 23); after crossing the Tigris, he "ordered Ariston, the commander of the Paeonian cavalry, to *charge* [the Persians] at full gallop" (*HA*, 4.9.24, 72).

35 As seen above, *H*, 9:120, 663–64; see also, e.g. after Alexander's victory at Tyre (*HA*, 4.4.17, 61).

36 e.g. "It was to damage Boeotia that they [Athenians] crossed the frontier and built a fort in our country ... " (*PW*, 4.92.1, 276).

37 In reference to the Macedonians: "So the Persians were *driven on like cattle* by a mere handful of men" (*HA*, 3.11.17, 43).

38 The Argives "*crossed* unperceived from Epidaurus ... and *fell upon* the Athenians" when Athens attacked Aegina (*H*, 5:86, 392).

39 At the Battle of Corcyrus, "The Romans and Eumenes pursued [the enemy] with commendable pertinacity so long as the rowers could keep going and while they still had hopes of *harassing* the enemy rear" (*RM*, XXXVI.45, 278).

40 At the Battle of Magnesia, the Romans "hurled missiles" and "hurled their spears into the disordered army" (*RM*, XXXVII.42, 320).

41 e.g. *H*, 4:159, 338.

42 Alexander "*crosses*" the Granicus; Parmenion "*attacks*" on the left, "while on the right Alexander *inflicted heavy casualties* on the enemy" (Diodorus in *HA*, 23).

43 "Laying waste to the whole area, [Alexander] entered Persia ... " (*HA*, 5.3.17, 99; cf. 3.5.6, 33).

44 Persians at Delphi (*H*, 8:35, 568).

45 The Persians "*overran* all Phocis" (*H*, 8:32, 568). Mardonius' "cavalry went in advance and *overran* the country about Megara" (*H*, 9:14, 617).

46 Amyntas, defector from Alexander, *"crossed* to Cyprus ... to make for Egypt ... *penetrated* as far as the harbor-mouth of Pelusium by pretending that he was the advance guard of Darius" (*HA*, 4.1.27–29, 52–53).

47 e.g. Alexander "proceeded to give chase to the fugitives" (*HA*, 1.11.16, 43) after victory over Persians. The Macedonians further *"crossed* the Caucusus" and *"crossed"* the river Oxus *"in pursuit of* Bessus" (*HA*, 7.5.18, 28, 159–60).

48 After Alexander crossed the Hellespont, some Persians fled to Halicarnassus, Alexander went there; the Persians crossed to Cos, with Alexander "ordering the city [Halicarnassus] *razed"* (Didorus in *HA*, 25).

49 e.g. the Scythian view of Darius' invasion: "the moment he *crossed* to this continent, he *reduced* every people that lay in his road" (*H*, 4:118, 323).

50 e.g. *H*, 5:113–16, 406; *RM*, XXXVII.16, 294.

51 e.g. Xerxes "forced all the peoples that lay in his route to serve with him" (*H*, 7:108). The Athenians in Sicily "marched against those who refused to join, and forced some of them to do so" (6.88.5, 410).

52 e.g. Alexander on "crossing the Tanais" and invading Scythia: "suppose we *cross* the Tanais and with a bloody slaughter of the Scythians demonstrate that we are universally invincible – who then will hesitate to submit to us when we are also the conquerors of Europe" (*HA*, 7.7.12, 165).

53 e.g. *HA*, 8.10.31, 206; 8.14.25, 209; 8.14.40, 210.

54 Darius heard Alexander was ill and "marched to the Euphrates so swiftly as his heavily burdened force would permit ... [and] managed, in his haste to seize Cilicia, to *get his army over* in five days ... now struck camp and *crossed* the river Pinarus, *intending to stick to the heels* of what he believed was an enemy in flight" (*HA*, 3.8.16, 38).

55 e.g. *HA*, 24–25; *RM*, XXXVI.44, 278.

56 e.g. Alexander to his troops, before battle with the Persians, "reminded them ... of all the cities they had *stormed* or which had capitulated, of the territory that now lay behind them, all of it *subdued* and *trampled* beneath their feet" (*HA*, 3.10.7, 41).

57 e.g. Alexander sought "to bring even nature to her knees" by capturing a mountain peak held by the Sogdians, where their leader Arimazes taunted Alexander by asking him sarcastically whether he could fly. "With you," Alexander tells his men, "I have *crossed* mountain chains snow-covered throughout the year, entered the defiles of Cilicia, and endured without exhaustion the fierce cold of India ... Nature has set nothing so high that it cannot be surmounted by courage." Following his capture of the peak, he captured Arimazes, his relatives, and the foremost nobleman of his people. "All of these Alexander ordered to be *whipped and crucified* at the foot of the rock" (*HA*, 7.11.8–11, 173). He also "crucified" the chieftain of the Musiconi tribe, who had led the tribe in rebellion (*HA*, 9.8.116, 231).

58 e.g. the Romans crossed the pass at Thermopylae and *"wiped out* a great part of the enemy column, soldiers who halted through weariness, or who had become scattered through losing their way ... " (*RM*, XXXVI.19, 257). Wiped out was also Antiochus' expression when he sought support against the Roman invasion, saying that "the *crossing* of the Romans into Asia" was "to *wipe out* all kingdoms ... " (*RM*, XXXVII.25, 302).

59 The words of the Aetolian commander in exchange with Spartan leader Nabis: "Antiochus, he assured him, had already *crossed* into Europe, and would soon be in Greece; he would fill lands and seas with armaments and fighting men" (*RM*, XXXV.35, 220).

60 *H*, 4:93, 315.

61 *H*, 6:4, 425.
62 *H*, 6:97, 447.
63 *H*, 6:101, 449.
64 *H*, 7:8, 469.
65 *H*, 7:10, 477.
66 *H*, 8:32–33, 567–68.
67 *H*, 8.36, 568.
68 *H*, 8:52, 574.
69 *H*, 8:53, 574.
70 *H*, 9:13, 617.
71 *H*, 9:39, 630.
72 *H*, 9:114, 662.
73 *PW*, 1.114.3.
74 *PW*, 1.114.3, 63.
75 *PW*, 3.85.2–3, 201.
76 *PW* 7.29–31, 443–44.
77 *PW*, 8.48, 509.
78 *PW*, 8.68, 520.
79 *HA*, 24.
80 *HA*, 4.1.5, 50.
81 *HA*, 4.15.31–32, 88.
82 *HA*, 3.11.20–22, 44.
83 *HA*, 5.5.4, 103.
84 *HA*, 5.6.1–6, 105.
85 *HA*, 5.7.5, 8, 107.
86 *HA*, 6:3.6, 122–23.
87 *HA*, 6.4.17, 127.
88 *HA*, 7.5.33, 161.
89 *HA*, 7.6.6, 163.
90 *HA*, 8.2.24–25, 181–82.
91 *HA*, 8.10.5, 198; cf. where Alexander "struck terror into the Indians in their disordered flight" (8.11.23, 203).
92 *HA*, 8.14.14, 208.
93 *HA*, 8.14.17, 208.
94 *HA*, 8.14.25, 209.
95 *HA*, 8.14.29, 209.
96 *HA*, 8.14.38, 210.
97 *HA*, 8.14.40, 210. Alexander later respects and bestows power on Porus (8.14.44–45, 210–11).
98 *HA*, 8.14.5, 207.
99 *HA*, 9.1.8, 212.
100 *HA*, 9.1.14, 19, 213.
101 *HA*, 9.4.3, 220.
102 *HA*, 9.5.19–20, 224.
103 *HA*, 9.8.15, 231.
104 *RM*, XXXI.7, 28–29.
105 *RM*, XXXVI.23, 41–42.
106 *RM*, XXXI.23–24, 42–44.
107 *RM*, XXXI.24, 43.
108 *RM*, XXXI.26, 46.
109 *RM*, XXXIII.38, 132.
110 *RM*, XXXVI.9–10, 244–45.

111 *RM*, XXXII.6, 73.
112 *RM*, XXXII.14–15, 81.
113 *RM*, XXXVI.45, 278.
114 *RM*, XXXVII.13, 290.
115 *RM*, XXXVII.13, 291.
116 *RM*, XXXVII.32, 310.
117 *RM*, XXXVII.43–44, 321–22.
118 e.g. *H*, 4:159, 338 (the Greek colonization of Libya); and *PW*, 6.2.4–5, 361 (the Sicilian colonization of Cycana).
119 *H*, 5:97, 400.
120 *H*, 5:49, 375.
121 *H*, 7:5, 467.
122 *H*, 7:5, 467.
123 *H*, 9:39, 630.
124 *H*, 9:121, 664.
125 *HA*, 3.10.5, 41.
126 *HA*, 3.10.9–10, 41–42.
127 *HA*, 3.11.20, 44. See also *"securing the booty* at Damascus" (4.1.4, 50).
128 *HA*, 5.5.4–5, 105.
129 *HA*, 9.1.2, 212.
130 *HA*, 9.2.27, 217.
131 *HA*, 9.4.4, 220.
132 *HA*, 9.8.29, 232.
133 *HA*, 9.9.6, 235.
134 *HA*, 9.9.12, 236.
135 *RM*, XXXVI.17, 254.
136 *RM*, XXXVII.21, 299.
137 *H*, 7:8, 469.
138 *RM*, XXXVII.10, 286.

VIII
Alternatives, part I
Crossing in flight

Some different meanings occur now and then in the explicit meaning of crossing or crossing over, but these generally occur in the context of the strategic actions of war – making them weak alternatives to the dominant meaning. As the crossers "pursue" "the" "enemy," for example, those pursued *take flight* and, in the process, *cross* as well. "Pursued" by the Persians, for example, the Scythians, "*crossed* the Tanais."[1] Ironically, when the Scythians arrive at the Agathrysi's neighboring territory, they are seen as invaders, and the Agathrysi stop them "to bar any invaders from *crossing*" – read invading.[2] Histiaus, the planner of the Ionian revolt, "crossed to Chios"[3] to escape. During the first Persian invasion of Europe, the Athenians take the advice of the Eretrians, who were facing destruction, and "*crossed over* to Oropus *[to] save themselves.*"[4] Thucydides writes that Athens left the battle scene at Corcyra and "*crossed over* to the island opposite." Once there, they "sent a herald, and took up under truce the bodies which they had left

61

behind."[5] During the Sicilian expedition, Alcibiades fled trial in Athens and, as "an outlaw, *crossed* in a boat ... to the Peloponnese."[6] He took flight, that is. In his flight from Alexander, Bessus "crossed the river Oxus ... "[7] Antiochus left Thermopylae and "*crossed to* Ephesus" in retreat.[8]

In each of these, crossing means taking flight or moving to a presumably safer place, and in each, taking flight occurs in the strategic context of war; that is, as part of war, as redeployment. This connection suggests an intimate conceptual relation with, not an alternative to, the dominant meaning of the concept. Most of the parties that were crossing-as-fleeing were still involved in war and, as such, prepared to cross for more war just as they had crossed to avoid being killed in it. At Corcyra, Athens took up the bodies and the next day they sailed to Corinth and "laid waste to the country."[9] Histaius and Alcibiades moved to safer places to continue to fight, to their death.[10] Similarly, after Bessus crossed the Oxus, he "burned the boats used for crossing to stop the enemy using them, and started levying fresh troops ..."[11] So, they crossed, gathered more fighting bodies, and then continue to lay waste. As such these usages are about "carrying on the war"[12] and do not constitute alternative meanings of crossing a border.

One dramatic exception to crossing and carrying on the war may be found in the calamity that befell the Athenians at Syracuse after they attempted to cross to safety.[13] They were all slain before they could take up arms again. Their general Nicias "*crossed over* [the river Ereneus], and posted his army upon some high ground upon the other side." The Athenians tried to get to the Assinarus river, "supposing that they should *breathe more freely* once across the river ... Once there, they rushed in, and all order was at an end, each man wanting *to cross* first, and *the attacks* of the enemy make it extremely *difficult to cross at all*."[14] Crossing here means taking flight, but this proved impossible and they were "forced to huddle together," where they "trampled one another" and were "showered" by missiles of the Syracusans and Peloponnesians.[15] This crossing for safety during war was a total failure. Indeed, there seems to be no safety when *crossing* is involved, for the dominant matrix of meaning remains in place. After Nicias crossed, he was himself "butchered" and the imperial cycle recharged itself once more: motivated by this victory, Sparta saw the "supremacy of all Hellas"[16] within reach, and the Persians again attempted to rule Ionia by allying with Sparta and "causing a revolt from Athens."[17]

Notes

1   *H*, 4:122, 324. Similarly, Paeonian captives of the Persians escape during the first Ionian revolt and, pursued by the Persians, "ran away to sea ... [and] *crossed over* to Chios" (*H*, 5:98, 40).
2   *H*, 4:125, 325.
3   *H*, 6:2, 410.
4   *H*, 6:101, 448.

5   *PW*, 4.44.5, 248. See also, the Sicilians had initially *"crossed over* to Sicily ... *fleeing from* the Opicans" (*PW*, 6:2.4, 361).
6   *PW*, 6.61.7, 395.
7   *HA*, 7.4.21, 156.
8   *RM*, XXXVI.21, 258.
9   *PW*, 4.45.1, 248.
10 *PW*, 6:28–30, 419–20.
11 *HA*, 7:4.21, 156.
12 *PW*, 7.47.4, 455. See also, e.g. *PW*, 3.22–23, 168–69.
13 There may be a second exception in this regard, but the political character of this crossing is not entirely clear in the text. Herodotus tells of when the Amazons, who settled in Scythia and took Scythian husbands, asked their husbands to "move out of this land and cross the river Tanais and live there" in order to maintain their "old way of life," which had been impossible among the Scythians. Their husbands agreed and "they *crossed* the Tanais and journeyed toward the rising sun a distance of three days" and settled there. Herodotus does not describe the events of this settlement, so the character and consequences of this settlement is unclear, other than crossing here means *journeying elsewhere to live* (*H*, 4.113–16, 322–23).
14 *PW*, 7.84.2–5, 476–77.
15 *PW*, 7.84–87.86.1, 477–78.
16 *PW*, 8.2.4, 482.
17 *PW*, 8.6.1, 485.

IX
Alternatives, part II
In praise of the Medizer

I had nothing, but lacked nothing.[1]

The search for more fundamental alternatives to approaching liminal or border spaces leads, in these classical texts, directly to the figure of the Medizer. The concept borrows on but should not to be confused with "the Medes," the name of a people and an empire.[2] "Mede" and "Persian" are used interchangeably at times in Greek discourse.[3] In the classical sources, the Medizer literally refers to the peoples in Greece who "gave earth and water"[4] to the Persian king, or, in other terms, who "came to an agreement with Xerxes" and went over "to the Persian persuasion," "bent their necks to the Mede," or "turned to the Persian interest."[5] It is often used with strong connotations of betrayal and disloyalty (double crossing, as it were), because it connotes "contempt of the laws [of one's country] and imitation of the barbarians" and being an "outlaw" or "traitor" as the Spartans and Athenians described their generals Pausanias and Themistocles, respectively – "the most famous men of their time."[6] Both committed "Medism"[7] by concluding alliances with the king. During his secret alliance, Pausanias "went out in Median dress ... [and] kept a Persian table,"[8] and Themistocles who, having been ostracized by Athens, joined the king's court, "studied the Persian tongue and customs" and "attained very high consideration there."[9] To be charged with "Medism"[10] was thus to be charged with going over to the other side in loyalty, thought, sentiment, and conduct.

Herodotus conceptualizes the Medizer as the unprincipled opposite of the highly principled Athenians: "[The Athenians] chose that Greece should survive free, and it was they who awakened all the parts of Greece that had not Medized, and it was they who, under Heaven, routed the king. Not even the dreadful oracles that came from Delphi, terrifying though they were, persuaded them to desert Greece; they stood their ground and withstood the invader when he came against their own country."[11] Similar meanings can be found in the expressions of the Athenians themselves. At Sicily, their representatives claim that during the war with "the Mede," the Ionians and Aegean Islanders were "kinfolk, [who] came against their mother country, that is to say against us, together with the Mede, and instead of having courage to revolt and sacrifice their property as we did when we abandoned our city, chose to be slaves themselves, and to make us slaves. We, therefore, deserve to rule because we placed the largest fleet and an unflinching patriotism at the service of the Hellenes, and because these, our subjects, did us harm by their ready subservience to the Persians ... "[12] Medizing thus carries shared meanings of being of questionable patriotism, choosing wrongly by going to the other side, being of value and giving sustenance to the king (acting under his influence, not freely, enslaved), surrendering, lacking courage, failing to stand one's ground, desertion, disloyalty, coming against and failing to make sacrifices for one's mother country, doing it injury and harm, etc. It describes with a short label one who shifts sides or takes on values, loyalties, and practices other than those of one's people and "own/mother country." The Medizer is seen as not properly resisting influence stemming from outside one's home society but rather submitting to it – becoming in the process a disagreeable danger, an enemy, a person without commitment and loyalty to the things that ought to be cherished and loved. Medizers are traitors. The Athenians, for example, accuse the Aeginetans who give earth and water to Darius of "betraying Greece"[13] and have the Spartans "cross over to Aegina" to arrest them.[14] In Thucydides' account of the Theban speech at Plataea, Medizers are contrasted with Atticizers, the latter used for those who "went over to the Athenians."[15] Medizers abandon what was understood to be the basis for all Greeks to "take common action" – their "common Greekness," as the Spartans called it, forged out of the diversity of their more local attachments.[16]

A poignant example of the Medizer-as-crosser – and one that involves an attempted crossing over the Hellespont – may be seen in Thucydides' description of what transpired when Aristeus of Corinth, Timagoras of Tegea, Pollis of Argos, and three Spartan envoys (Aneristus, Nicolaus, and Protodamus) sought to conclude a secret alliance between Sparta and the king. Sitacles, the son of the Thracian king, had allied with Athens to prevent such an alliance. The Athenians convince Sadocus, the son of Sitacles, "to prevent their *crossing over* to the king and doing their part *to injure* his city. He [Sadocus] accordingly had them seized as they were traveling through Thrace to the vessel in which they were to *cross the Hellespont*."[17] Herodotus expresses their aim in crossing the Hellespont in the dominant and very conventional sense – they were crossing to injure and to make a war alliance with the king. The meaning of crossing is consistent with the general pattern, though the injurious intention is placed on the bodies of the Medizer, not, in this case, on an entire army. Sadocus ordered the men to be given to Athens. There, they faced the swiftest treatment for their disloyalty, betrayal, and alliance with the other side: "the Athenians, afraid that Aristeus, who had been notably the prime mover in the previous affairs of Potidaea and their Thracian possessions, might live to do them still more mischief if he escaped, slew them all the same day, without giving them a trial or hearing the defense which they wished to offer, and cast their bodies into a pit ... "[18]

The Medizer is mischievous and eliminable. The very label casts an unfavorable prejudice towards the Medizer, expelling the Medizer from the world which he/she/they are seen as having abandoned. The term is one of forced exile. While seeming to give the said Medizer an alternative place in the narrative, the very term casts the Medizer into the veritable narrative pit wherein its subjective and intersubjective valuations are rendered through – domesticated to and erased by – the terms of the dominant narrative. In other words, the meanings of Medizing are all constituted through the conceptual worlds of non-Medizers. Whatever significance those said to be Medizing may offer is paradoxically represented and erased in the very concept that values *non-Medizing*. The dominant non-Medizing character of the discourse of crossing over thus signals but represses other ways of valuing what it might mean to cross over.

In identifying Medizing as "going over to the other side," for example, the dominant discourse of crossing over occludes the possibility that the Medizer may signify "sides" differently. "The Medizer," that is, may not be adequately (hermeneutically) characterized as either "going over to the other side" or "resisting the loyalties to one's mother country." Indeed, the figure of the Medizer appears to resist the very authority of the dominant discourse of crossing over. The Medizer essentially represents the possibility that what is rendered by historical actors and historians within the dominant metaphysic as border crossing may be considered otherwise. I am speaking about the figure of the Medizer – the conceptual possibility – not those who actually gave earth and water to the king. Medizing stands for resistance to the dominant conceptualization of political space. Its core feature is to have a different view of what are conventionally described as spaces that one *crosses*, or must be *crossed*, and what it means to move in and between such spaces. In suggesting that one need not *cross* or *cross over* (as understood in the dominant grammar of *crossing over*) at such spaces, the Medizer acts against the honor of the dominant worldview. The Medizer is *inglorious*.

As we have seen in the examples of Pausanias and Themistocles, Medizers are those in the classical histories whose choices, values, and conduct contrast with the dominant discourse of crossing over in precisely this way. At the "border" they see something other than the necessity of violence or the quest for spoils. They see possibilities for cooperation, friendship, company, cultural exchange, and learning. The reader encounters these examples very rarely, but when one does, it takes the imagination of the world of these texts in different directions than the dominant discourse of crossing. A critical review of some of these examples, large and small, suggests that important alternatives appear in these texts – in Alexander's Medism, Herodotus' form of comparative inquiry, and several short but significant passages – but that each remains fundamentally contained and thus constrained by the dominant discourse of *crossing over* and the bordered world within which that practice alone makes most sense. The existence of these alternatives, however, enables us to extend our thinking beyond this discourse into ways and forms of being that defy the tradition of crossing.

Alexander's example. In spite of his reputation as a peerless and consummate warrior, Alexander was charged essentially with Medism on several occasions by his own troops for displaying respect towards some of those he conquered, especially the Persian royal family, and for abandoning Macedonian social practices in favor of foreign customs and relations with the conquered. For example, he apologized when he inadvertently offended Queen Sisigambis by suggesting, out of "respect,"[19] that she make gifts made of wool with her granddaughter. Curtius Rufus writes that, "To Persian women nothing is more degrading than working with wool." So Alexander went to the queen, addressed her as "Mother," and said, "I was led into error by my own customs. Please do not take offence at my ignorance. I have, I hope, scrupulously observed what I have discovered of your conventions. I know that among you it is not right for a son to sit down in his mother's presence without her permission, so whenever I have come to you I have remained on my feet until you beckoned me to sit. Often you have wanted to show me respect by prostrating yourself before me but I have forbidden it. And the title due to my dear mother Olympias I give to you."[20] His acknowledgement of the limitations of his "own customs," his apology and recognition of his own ignorance, his hope to observe scrupulously the queen's customs – these suggest a profound regard for the ways of his royal "captives" and a willingness to understand and to act in those ways. Curtius Rufus describes a transformation that set in: "He began to ape the Persian royalty with its quasi-divine status ... His claim was that he was wearing Persian spoils, but the fact was that with the clothes he had also adopted Persian habits ... Furthermore, he sealed letters sent to Europe with the stone of his old ring, but on those written to Asia was set the seal of Darius' ring ... he had also forced Persian clothing on his friends and on the cavalry, the élite of the troops."[21] He also built royal quarters, equipped with concubines and eunuchs for sex, and he married Roxanne, the daughter of Oxyartes.[22]

Both Curtius Rufus and some of the major figures in his history question the depth of Alexander's respect. Curtius Rufus represents his apology to Sisigambis and his marriage to Roxanne as strategic imperial consolidation,[23] and he criticizes Alexander's immoderate forms of social activity as a descent "into the depraved customs of foreigners and conquered nations."[24] Some of Alexander's own troops rejected Alexander's transformation. According to Curtis Rufus, "They found [wearing Persian clothes] distasteful ... "[25] The veterans from the time of Alexander's father Philip, "displayed open revulsion," both to the new ways and to Alexander's sexual licentiousness. "Throughout the camp one sentiment and one view found expression, that they *had lost more by victory* than they had gained by war, and that at that very moment they were experiencing defeat, surrendering to the ways of aliens and foreigners. How could they face people, they asked, returning home dressed like captives? They felt ashamed of themselves now, they said, and their king resembled one of the conquered rather than a conqueror ..."[26] "His friends" were also "ashamed that he had chosen his father-in-law at a dinner party and from subject peoples ... "[27] They viewed Alexander's change as a loss, as shame, surrender, as a descent into the decadent ways of the alien and foreign, inferior enemy, as offense.[28] When plotters admit to wanting to assassinate Alexander, one of them, Hermolaus, says, "we could have tolerated [executions of some of their leaders and shortage of booty], until you delivered us to the barbarians and (a novel twist!) sent the victors under the yoke! But you revel in Persian clothes and Persian etiquette; you abhor the customs of your own country. Thus it was a king of the Persians, not of the Macedonians, we wanted to kill, and in accordance with the conventions of war, we pursue you as a deserter."[29] The essence of the charge was Medism: Alexander had placed his loyalties with the other side and now sought to subdue his own. "You wanted Macedonians to kneel before you and worship you as a god. You repudiate your father Philip ... We are free men – are you surprised that we cannot bear your vanity? What can we hope for from you if even innocent men must either face death or – a fate worse than death – a life of slavery?"[30]

For his part, Alexander characterizes his adoption of some foreign practices as partly strategic and partly a matter of respect about which there is nothing to be ashamed. In language that mixes terms of imperial strategy with supremacist conceptions shared with his troops, he says that his strategy is required to "tame" "a pack of wild animals" "by the passage of time."[31] "The barbarians still hold their necks stiff beneath the yoke" of enslavement. "We still need time, men, for them to develop more pliant dispositions and for civilization to moderate their wildness."[32] The "high regard" he shows to the Persians "was to make the people I conquered in warfare feel no regret at my victory ... Possession achieved by the sword is not of long duration, but gratitude for kindness shown is everlasting. If we wish to hold Asia and not merely *pass through* it we must impart our clemency to these people – it is their loyalty which will make our empire stable and enduring."[33] Alexander also defended his actions as principled, claiming in response to charges of desertion made by Hermolaus that there was nothing to be ashamed about in adopting the practices of the conquered peoples: "[Hermolaus] claims, I am foisting Persian habits on the Macedonians. True, for I see in many races things we should not blush to imitate, and the only way this great empire can be satisfactorily governed is by transmitting some things to the native and learning others from them ourselves."[34] Alexander responds to the charge therefore by turning it back on his accusers. Hermolaus is "the "traitor" ... for wishing "to abort this glorious enterprise" – the "subjugation" of "the whole world" – and seeking "to deliver up the Macedonians to the races they had conquered by eliminating their king."[35] Alexander is not the traitor; those who threaten his imperial work with accusations of betrayal are. Hermolaus was executed by torture.

Insofar as the principled defense of learning from the Other appears in the context of the rationale for imperial stability, at least in his reported declarations, Alexander's example does not convincingly classify as Medism except in the eyes of his accusers. In essence, he adopts and adapts to the customs of others in order to conquer even better and to have more power over them. In relation to the dominant terms of the discourse of crossing and crossing over, Alexander's example is therefore not betrayal but conformity with the main terms and meanings of the discourse of *crossing* to *conquer*. "Learning" here means learning for empire and favors the imperial strategy. It includes a portion of respect and openness to the limits of one's own understanding, but it is undertaken within his initial, primary, and undiminished conception of his purposes – to rule, not to relate to liminal spaces between peoples in ways that differ from the general outlook of imperial rule and domination. Learning, respect, and openness become instrumental to holding, possessing, and conquering. These aims comprised Alexander's greatest "hope" in "crossing."[36]

Herodotus' inquiry. Herodotus never said, "I crossed," but, as a storyteller, he traveled and conversed, and in doing so, his example suggests a second possible alternative to the dominant discourse of crossing over. *The History*, like that of the other texts under consideration here, however, frequently evinces Orientalist characteristics typical of the general Hellenocentric outlooks of the time. For example, Herodotus frequently describes other peoples in terms of what they lack,[37] and when he appears to favor something, it is usually stated in a way that reaffirms broader Hellenic values.[38] Nonetheless, on occasion, Herodotus strives to learn things outside conventional expectations. When he learns, for example, that in Scythia the cattle do not grow horns "because of the cold," he says. "But I wonder all the same – for this *History* of mine has *from the beginning sought out the supplementary to the main argument –* … "[39] In this way, Herodotus wonders and seeks to understand beyond conventional understandings. Thus at times, non-Hellenics occupy a place in the discourse other than lacking what Greeks possess. He asserts, for example, that the Greeks have received some of their fundamental beliefs from others, the Egyptians especially, rather than invented them,[40] and he espies shared values at the political level. The Egyptians and Greeks shared laws, like the declaration of a "means of livelihood" law that Solon the Athenian "took" from King Amasis, "a great lover of the Greeks."[41] Similarly, Herodotus records that Persian governance in Ionia following the first, failed Ionian revolt in 493 included "some very useful things": The viceroy of Sardis, Artaphernes, "forced on the Ionians certain compacts: that they should submit their quarrels with one another to law instead of plundering and harrying one another," and "the most wonderful thing that happened … For here in Ionia Mardonius put down all the princes and set up democracies in the cities."[42]

To be sure, Herodotus considers the Persian establishment of "democracy" wonderful through the Athenocentric outlook, because it reaffirms his value. Similarly, when he states that the Ionians "have founded cities in the most beautiful setting of climate and season of all mankind that I know,"[43] he is of course expressing a judgment in and through his own conception of the beautiful. What may be significant, though, is that his account also allows us to challenge dominant assumptions within the discourse of crossing over that those on the other side of a border somehow must be approached with violence, or at least with readiness to be violent. He allows the reader to make sense of concepts commonly understood as particular to the Greeks as having some value on the other side. These include the common good, unity amidst difference, justice, and liberty. Herodotus quotes Xerxes appealing to "the common good" of his troops at the Hellespont,[44] and *The History, The History of Alexander*, and *Rome and the Mediterranean* all mention the tremendous heterogeneity of the Persian forces, enabling us to see some form of commonality forged out of diversity on both sides.[45] While these forged commonalities are no doubt outcomes of various forms of power, we can nonetheless say that there was unity among diversity on both sides of battle.

The idea that concepts of justice and liberty existed on both sides of battle runs fairly strongly against the Hellenocentric grain of the historical narratives, with its basic assumption that these political values, especially liberty, are particular to the Greeks, especially to Athens.[46] Curtius Rufus' discourse, for example, is often colonial in the sense that he repeatedly records differences as evidence of the "backward" and "extremely uncivilized" character of "barbarians."[47] Yet, he also notes alternative concepts of justice. "The Abii," for example, "were generally regarded as the barbarians with the best sense of justice." This could mean "as good as it can be," or it could mean "the best." He continues, "they refrained from warfare except under provocation and they exercised their liberty with restraint and impartiality, setting those of humble birth on equal footing with their leading citizens."[48] By suggesting liberty may be found on the other side of the border, is Curtius Rufus crossing over a border in other ways? He also acknowledges the "hospitality"[49] shown by those defeated by Alexander and, though incredulous to find it "amid such degeneracy" in India, he finds "an interest in philosophy," too.[50] "There is an unkempt, squalid class of men called 'wise men'."[51] The "barbarians" have wisdom, too.

Concerning liberty, each of the texts analyzed here is rich with examples of parties on one side or the other resisting or refusing to submit to conquest in such a way that it would be hard to deny, within the terms of the stories told, those parties some conception of liberty. While the Athenians are the main symbol of resistance and freedom in *The History*, we also learn that Xanthans collectively immolated themselves in the citadel rather than submit to Harpagus, Cyrus' general.[52] Many parties subject to Athenian imperial power sought what they describe as their liberty from enslavement.[53] Similarly, those facing conquest by Alexander resisted and refused to submit, like the Marmares, the Syrians, and the townspeople of the unnamed second city Alexander took after crossing into the country of the Sibi.[54] In Livy, too, we see resistance founded on the idea of living independent or free from imperial subjugation – among the people of Abydos on the Hellespont and Phocaea in Anatolia, for example.[55]

These and many other examples of resistance in the face of imperial conquest suggest that living freely in the sense of not being subjugated by an outside power was widespread. The Athenians, Spartans, Ionians, Syrians, Macedonians, Tyreans, the people of the country of the Sibi, the Marmares, the Phocaeans all wanted to live freely in this sense. Moreover, a case might be made that a concept of liberty also existed among the Persians. They established some democracies, and they fought, in Xerxes' words, because they assumed that if they did not fight, they would be attacked by Athens. Furthermore, in the final page of *The History*, Herodotus tells us that they "went away" from Ionia, taking to heart the idea that "from soft countries come soft men." That is, they came to disagree with those who said that they should "take other lands," and to agree with Cyrus' judgment. Recall it was Cyrus who asked Croesus, "Who of all mankind persuaded you to make war upon my land and to be my enemy rather than my friend?"[56] They now followed those who "chose to rule, living in a wretched land, rather than to sow the level plains [under Athenian power] and be slaves to others."[57] The Persians chose, that is, to leave Ionia, now under Athenian power, rather than be slaves. A Medized reading of the histories examined here might read these and all refusals to submit to all crossers not as evidence of their "recalcitrance,"[58] but as a desire for liberty.

In short, Herodotus and the others thus bring out and permit us to see commonalities beyond singularly conceived and essentialized Greek, Hellenic, Roman, or "Western" values. Reading the classical historians against their Orientalist tendencies, one may see a different orientation to borders than emphasized in the dominant discourse of *crossing over*. When the historians write across the border, they do not do so as strategic action or in pursuit of power, as we saw in Alexander's example.

Identifying commonalities across known borders may not replicate the fundamentally violent spatial outlook of crossing over, but it also does not challenge it. Herodotus wandered his world and came to understand much about life practices in various societies – "the Egyptians," "the Massagatae," "the Scythians," etc. – but he did so within the basic framework of political space wherein "crossing" a border entails going well armed, etc. Moreover, we do not see Herodotus consciously transforming himself through his learning, as we saw in Alexander's practices of rulership. Herodotus remains the historical inquirer, and thus the borders between him and his interlocutors remain after the conversation what they had been before. This is not to ignore his contribution to thinking about moving across borders in different ways. He opens *The History* by considering the multiple, contrasting stories of the causes of the rift, enmity, and wars between various parties, especially between the Greeks and the Persians. *The History* thus encourages deep interpretive curiosity and leaves us pondering possibilities otherwise. However, is this a sufficient challenge to the dominant narrative of crossing over, especially when his narrative so prominently reiterates crossing-as-violence? Herodotus may have had his conversations and noted Cyrus' reservations about taking the lands of others, but, ultimately, these aspects of his storytelling do not fundamentally challenge the basic framework of political space. Perhaps what Herodotus offers is an alternative way to view those on the other side of borders that most often get crossed militarily. In this regard, his alternative is history, or, as the title of his work may also be translated, inquiry. He extends conversations and inquiry in directions other than war, in the context of war, between parties that have been, are, or will later be at war. And that is the rub. He makes it possible to cross without weapons but still posits, and reiterates, the existence of those borders as sites for war, war that people may undertake given their interpretations of the events that brought them to such a point.

The other works similarly reinforce the dominant political-spatial outlook, in my judgment, even more than Herodotus. Thucydides' favorite personalities appear to be those leaders, like the Pericles, Brasidas, or Phrynichus,[59] who urge action within one's knowable limits. In Thucydides' famous critical phrase they do not "grasp for more" – act beyond the limits of prudence within the circumstances they face. The strong implication is that such grasping by leaders like Alcibiades brought about Athens' self-destruction. Thucydides' critique of those who grasp for more, then, challenges the dominant imperialist framework of crossing. Cross less, he might have said. Again, therein lies the rub, for, like Herodotus, Thucydides does not so much criticize the overarching framework of crossing as suggest that crossing be minimized within the existing power structure – indeed, within the existing Athenian imperial power structure, from whose vantage point Thucydides on occasion writes – however essentially violent the border structure might be. This explains the underlying appeal of *The Peloponnesian War* to the contemporary realist imagination. The work is consciously set within the tradition of imperial power, its growth and consequences. "The growth of the power of Athens, and the alarm which this inspired in Sparta, made war *inevitable*."[60] Both classical historians trace and examine the causes and consequences of imperial power. More than *The History*, *The Peloponnesian War* is suggestive as well about the powers of exhortation and about the social and political consequences of war. This is especially apparent in the passages on the Corcyraean revolution, where war is described as "a rough master."[61] Revolution brings degeneration. Grasp at less, Thucydides urges; otherwise you will lose the power and order you have within the existing system of power. Grasp at more and you will upend the order of things upon which precious life and able leadership rest. Avoid getting "carried away" as the Athenians did "by Alcibiades."[62] Curtius Rufus does not favor disturbing the existing disciplinary forms much either. He is most critical when Alexander is "reveling" among the "barbarians." As in Thucydides, radical changes entail moral corruption. Indeed, for both Thucydides and Curtius Rufus, grasping at more is a kind of overstepping, a kind of *crossing over limits* in an undisciplined fashion that brings self-destruction and degeneracy in the coherence of a unified identity and entity.

In short, where the authors transgress the borders of war through inquiry, they remain within the borders made by war. To find a figure of the Medizer who challenges the discourse, therefore, we must look further. A close reading suggests that a few examples are buried within the narratives of these texts. I shall mention four. Each offers a potentially more serious alternative to the dominant meaning of crossing over.

Going back, or signs that say "return." Three times in the fifth chapter of *The Peloponnesian War*, Thucydides describes how the Spartans did not cross/invade Argive territory because "the frontier sacrifices" were not favorable.[63] So, three times, he says, the Spartans "went back" to Sparta. They "returned home,"[64] "went back again,"[65] and "went back again."[66] Although these practices preserve bordered life, and life within borders, they appear to be genuine alternatives to crossing over in either war or inquiry. Go back. While the gods (or their invocation), oracles, or religious and spiritual practices of one sort or another may contribute to war, they seem also to prevent it from happening.

To let be in the limits existing between: The words of Nicias and the Scythian elder. Nicias both cautioned against the Sicilian crossing and led it, so his example is complicated. Yet we find in his exhortation against the expedition language that is at odds with the dominant discourse: he called on the Athenians to "vote that the Sicilians be let in the limits now existing between us – to enjoy their own possessions and to settle their own quarrels."[67] Alcibiades called this "inaction."[68] I see it as an alternative to crossing over. A similar example comes in the form of a communication delivered to Alexander by the eldest of the Scythians, who scolds him for his "greedy" adventure, for "coveting things beyond your reach."[69] The Scythian suggests that, though weaker, the Scythians can harm Alexander, but more importantly states: "We have never set foot in your country. *May we not live in our endless forests ignorant of who you are and where you come from? We cannot be slaves to anyone and do not wish to be anyone's masters.*"[70] Here we get the glimpse of a view similar to Nicias' – that those eying the lands of others should consider remaining within existing "limits" and let those beyond those limits enjoy their own possessions and govern themselves. Of course, like the frontier sacrifices, "letting" others "be in the limits now existing between us" still does not challenge the very positing of spaces among and between societies as borders that must either contain violence or be *crossed*. It also seems to ignore routinized forms of not living within limits in the context of activities unrelated to war (e.g. economic and cultural exchanges).

However, the elder in effect recognizes these tensions. He accounts for social intercourse of other kinds,[71] reprimands Alexander for being a violent bandit, and advises him both to place "constraints on your prosperity" and not to forget "your condition":

> You proudly claim you come in pursuit of bandits, but to all the people you have visited *you* are the bandit. You took Lydia, overran Syria; you are in control of Persia; ... Now you are stretching out your greedy, insatiable hands towards our flocks. Why do *you* need riches? They merely stimulate your craving for more. You are the first man ever to have created hunger by having too much – so that the more you have the keener your desire for what you do not have ... In your case victory spawns further war. No matter how far you surpass others in power and strength, the fact remains that nobody wants a foreign master ... Put some constraints on your prosperity – you will more easily control it ... Finally, if you are a god, it is your duty to confer benefits on mortal men, not filch their possessions from them. But if you are a man, always remember that is what you are. It is folly to have your mind on things that make you forget your condition.[72]

Un-common ties. The histories of Curtius Rufus and Livy report that some of the troops involved in battle acted against the expectations of the discourse of crossing on account of having ties with the conquered. During the long

Macedonian siege of Tyre, for example, the Sidonians among the conquering force entered the fallen city but "remained aware that they were related to the Tyrians (they believe that Agenor had founded both cities) and so they secretly gave many of them protection and took them to their boats, on which they were hidden and transported to Sidon. Fifteen thousand were rescued from a violent death by such sabotage."[73] Similarly, the allies of Rome, King Eumenes and the Rhodians, persuaded the Romans not to destroy Iasos, an Ionian city held by Antiochus and under siege by the Rhodians, since "there were exiles from Iasos among the Romans" who "begged the Rhodians with repeated and urgent appeals, not to allow an innocent city, *a relation as well as a neighbor*, to perish. The only cause for their exile, they said, was their loyalty to the Romans: and those who remained in the city were kept under by the same oppression of the king's garrison as had driven the speakers into exile; in the minds of the people of Iasos there was but one resolve: to escape enslavement to the king." Livy tells us that, "the Rhodians, moved by their entreaties, which had the support of King Eumenes also, prevailed on the commander to raise the siege, by reminding him of their own ties with the place, and by expressing sympathy for the plight of a city beset by a royal garrison."[74]

These alternatives open up possibilities other than the use of sheer force between parties that are either prepared to go to war or are already at war. They suggest that retreat from the edge of war or negotiations might be preferable to conflict. Each example alerts us as well to the fact that these forms of action were not simply individual. The Sidonians, in plural, acted, and we know that Nicias' opinion carried among the minority of Athenians – those who kept quiet to avoid being labeled "traitors." As I have already suggested, however, it is not clear if their practices go far enough in rejecting crossing for war. The overarching logic of the border remains in place, between "friends" and "enemies." Although peaceful relations exist, we still see a conception of political space that posits – against the reality of other forms of intercourse of the time – separate groups or states, living side by side as "enemies" or, now, "friends." For example, Nicias talks about staying within limits. Whereas, in the figure of the Medizer, other things may be possible.

The Medizer appears to constitute spaces in between with other meanings, including meanings where the very concept of border (signified as something to be *crossed*) becomes unnecessary. That is to say, the Medizer is not constrained by commonalities of the communal self – for safety or for interest – or by borders, because the Medizer makes possible something other than *crossing*. The limits Nicias describes have been determined by war, colonization, etc. As Alexander wrote to Darius, "It is war that will determine the boundaries of our respective empires and each shall have what the fortunes of tomorrow assign to us."[75] By contrast, the figure of the Medizer offers the possibility of a different tomorrow where the emphases are altered, where perhaps some conceptual change and political innovation is genuinely possible. In short, the Medizer points the way towards a more radical set of possibilities.

Given how this meaningfulness is largely silenced or dismissed in the wars and the narratives of war, these possibilities are not salient within the historical narratives. I can only be suggestive at points where they make brief appearances in our understanding. Something else seems available. This something else is only faintly recognizable in the dominant languages of political space, since it is always rendered as betrayal. It is inscrutable and troublesome because its meaningfulness has been domesticated to and written out of the classical histories. However, the presence of the figure of the Medizer shows it to have existed and, more significantly, it shows the possibility of dispensing with the dominant outlook of *crossing over* as a meaningful category of human existence. The spaces between collectivities – that appear that they must be *crossed* – can be understood, and related to, otherwise. They can be given other valuations and significances. Only in the slightest ways do suggestive modes of something-other-than-crossing emerge in these classical texts. The Medizer is largely cast into the pit of irrelevance, but the idea for alternative possible relations across what are most commonly understood as borders that must be crossed is not.

The idea appears to have existed among those thrown into the pit for their "betrayal," but we never get a sense of their purpose, other than through the dominant discourse of betrayal. It appears perhaps as well among the Athenians, whose opinion on the Sicilian expedition has been recorded as "the few that did not like [the idea] feared to appear unpatriotic by holding up their hands against it, so kept quiet."[76] These voters may or may not have been of the exact same opinion of Nicias. The idea also appears in key figures whose multilingualism and/or adoption of foreign customs we learn about: Pausanias, Themistocles, Anacharsis of Scythia (who adopted Greek customs while traveling in Greece and was killed for it[77]); Darius – the one Alexander subdued – who "had some knowledge of Greek,"[78] and Philotas, who encouraged multilingualism and was tortured and stoned to death for conspiring against Alexander. Far from displaying sympathy, Alexander accused Philotas of being "contemptuous of our way of life."[79] Philotas responded to the charge "that I disdain to communicate in my native language, that I have no respect for Macedonian customs (which means I have designs on an empire I despise!)" with a principled defense of what might be called new forms of globality of the time: "That native language of ours has long been rendered obsolete through our dealings with other nations," he averred, "conqueror and conquered alike must learn a foreign tongue."[80] For Philotas, the categories of conqueror/conquered remain, but his claim that unitary linguistic identities have been "rendered obsolete" presses against their rigid boundaries somewhat. Similarly, the idea of the Medizer may also be found in a captured Lycian prisoner who "was one who spoke Greek and

Persian,"[81] or among those Curtius Rufus calls the "troublesome" Scythians who live in both Europe and Asia: "The Scythians, who remain today troublesome neighbors, with settlements in both Europe and Asia."[82] Curtius Rufus does not elaborate on their troublesomeness, but perhaps it has something to do with their not fitting easily into one of his categories, for he continues: "Those living across the Bosphorus are considered Asiatic, the Europeans being those whose territory extends from the west of Thrace to the river Borysthenes and from there in a straight line to the Tanais, the river which separates Europe and Asia."[83] Perhaps the sentiment of the Medizer appears as well in the unlikely voice of Antiochus who, while suing for peace after the Romans crossed the Hellespont, before the Battle of Magnesia, sent a message to the Romans asking them to "bear in mind the human condition – that they should show moderation in exploiting their own situation and refrain from harshness in dealing with the situation of others."[84] Antiochus goes on immediately to say, "Let them confine their empire in Europe."[85] These are the words of a rival imperial power, but his request that the Romans consider refraining from harshness opens other possibilities for relations "between" human beings, ones other than crossing for war and violence (e.g. doing much less harm). Unlike the solidaristic alliances above, Antiochus does not base his appeal on common ties. It is a direct appeal to the most powerful empire on earth to refrain from and stop treating others harshly.

Medization therefore entails something more than subscription to the imperial ideals of power and stability of rule, and even more than the Hellenic ideal of liberty. Medizing is the radical opposite of crossing, where spaces that, in the dominant narrative, are "crossed" may be filled with other possibilities because they are given different meanings. For those who *cross over*, war and violence are always necessary and inevitable. The Romans reject Antiochus' pleas, saying, "you should have resisted us at the Hellespont."[86] That is, they reiterate the primary meanings in the languages of the crossing over. Battle is the language they know. Only resistance – or surrender – is acceptable. For the Medizer, there are other alternatives. Stop what you're doing. Go back. The Medizer appears not to subscribe fully to the grammar of *crossing over*. In this sense, the Medizer questions the primary conception of whatever is being posited as a border between human collectivities. If the dominant narrative conceptualizes political space as potentially and actually occupied by and filled with hostility and antagonism, pursuit of supremacy among supreme equals and surrender for unequals, greatness for those who achieve and suffering for those who succumb, then the Medizer, rather than being a military threat, is a true threat to the dominant discourse of crossing over. In fact, the Medizer suggests that the border to be crossed may not be there. A different kind of relationship with both political space and those with whom one comes into contact is possible. If spaces exist between human beings – and they seem to – they are not bordered or bounded as the crosser imagines them and thus do not need to be *crossed*. Other possibilities are available – leaving each within limits, learning languages, etc. However, after careful review, these possibilities are only suggested – they are not emphasized and explored – within the narratives of the seminal histories of Greece and Rome.

Notes

1 Abdalonymous, *HA*, 4:1:25, 52.
2 The Median Empire was conquered by the Achaemenid Persian Empire of Cyrus, himself born to Medean royalty but banished as a threat by his grandfather, whom he later defeated.
3 e.g. *PW*, 1.74.4, 43; *PW*, 6.82.4, 407. At Thermopylae, Herodotus writes, "the Medes charged the Greeks full tilt ... " (*H*, 7:210, 545).
4 e.g. *H*, 7:32, 481.
5 *H*, 6.99, 447, 6:109, 457, 8.31, 567; *H*, 7:139, 514; 7:172, 530–31. "That was the expedition to Thessaly when the King was about to *cross into* Europe and was still in Asia – indeed at Abydos. So, the Thessaleans, being abandoned by their allies, *Medized* ... " (*H*, 7:174, 531).
6 *PW*, 1.38.6, 79.
7 *PW*, 1.135.2, 76.
8 *PW*, 1.133.1, 1.132.1, 72.
9 *PW*, 1.38.1–2, 79.
10 *H*, 7:205, 542.
11 *H*, 7:139, 515.
12 *PW*, 6.82.4–6.83.1, 407.
13 *PW*, 6:49.1, 427.
14 *PW*, 6:50, 427.
15 *PW*, 3.62.2, 190.
16 *H*, 7:145, 518; 8:144, 611; cf. Herodotus' affirmation of this judgment (7:139, 514) and Themistocles' statement on "our stock" (8:22, 564).
17 *PW*, 2.67, 2, 129.
18 *PW*, 2.67, 4, 129. Thucydides writes that the Athenians considered this punishment justified in response to the Spartan practice of slaying and casting the bodies of Athenian and Athenian-allied sea merchantmen into pits.
19 *HA*, 5.2.18, 97.
20 *HA*, 5.2.19–22, 97; see also, *HA*, 3.12.21, 46; 3.12.22–23, 46; and 3.12.25, 46.
21 *HA*, 6.6.5–6, 128.
22 *HA*, 6.6.8, 129.
23 *HA*, 5.3.1–3, 98; 8.4.23–25,186.
24 *HA*, 6.2.3, 120; cf. 9.7.15, 229 and 6.3.5–8, 120.
25 *HA*, 6.6.7, 128.
26 *HA*, 6.6.9–10, 129; see also 9.3.10, 218.
27 *HA*, 8.4.30, 187.
28 They were "offended by the substitution of foreign customs for their established traditions" (*HA*, 8.5.20, 189).
29 *HA*, 8.7.11–13, 193.
30 *HA*, 8.7.13–14, 193.
31 *HA*, 6.3.8, 122.

32 *HA*, 6.3.6, 122. "They are all of the same stock, while we are foreigners and racially different. Everybody finds it easier to be governed by his own people, even if the man in charge is more to be feared" (6.3.10. 122).

33 *HA*, 8:7:12–13, 194.

34 *HA*, 8.9.10–13, 194–95.

35 *HA*, 8.8.17, 195.

36 As in his speech to his "Asiatic" soldiers: "When I was *crossing* from Europe to Asia, I hoped to *annex to my empire* many famous peoples and large numbers of men ... I had believed everything here to be swamped in luxury and, through excessive prosperity, submerged in self-indulgence. But, in fact, your moral and physical strength makes you just as energetic as anyone in the performance of your military duties." Thus Alexander accords "respect" for their elevation in his estimation. He reaffirms his values that he now sees manifest in them, including "loyalty," "courage" and "obedience": "your dedication to loyalty is no less than your dedication to courage. I make this statement for the first time, but I have long known it to be true. For that reason I have selected younger soldiers from among you and integrated them in the main body of my troops. You have the same uniform and the same weapons. Your obedience, however, and your readiness to follow orders far surpass everybody else's. That's why I married the daughter of the Persian Oxyartes, feeling no hesitation about producing children from a captive. Later on, when I wished to extend my bloodline further, I took Darius's daughter as a wife and saw to it that my closest friends had children by our captives, my intention being that by this sacred union I might erase all distinction between conquered and conqueror. So you can believe that you are my soldiers by family, not conscriptions. Asia and Europe are now one and the same kingdom. I give you Macedonian arms. Foreign newcomers though you are, I have made you established members of my force: you are both my fellow citizens and my soldiers. Everything is taking on the same hue. It is no disgrace for the Persians to copy Macedonian customs nor for the Macedonians to imitate the Persians. Those who are to live under the same king should enjoy the same rights" (*HA*, 10.3.7–14, 244–45). Thus, Alexander was charged with betrayal because he refused simply to see those he conquered as subordinate beings, yet his discourse is riddled with strategic imperatives of empire. His death seemed to confirm a successful ruling strategy: Curtius Rufus notes that, when he died "barbarians and Macedonians alike, and in the general grief, conqueror and conquered were indistinguishable. The Persians recalled a master of great justice and clemency, the Macedonians a peerless king of outstanding valour; together they indulged in a kind of contest in mourning" (10.5.18, 247). It is said as well that, with news of his death, Darius' mother Sisigambis "ripped off the clothes she wore and assumed the dress of mourning; she tore her hair and flung herself to the ground" (10.5.19, 247).

37 e.g. "The Persians themselves do not have [marketplaces], nor is there any such marketing among them" (*H*, 1:153, 103). "They do not use doctors at all" (1:197, 123); "they auction their children" (1:196, 123).

38 e.g. "The Persians welcome foreign customs more than any other people. For instance, they decided that Median dress was more beautiful than their own, and so they wear it. They wear Egyptian breastplates for their wars. Wherever they learn of enjoyments of all sorts, they adopt them for their own practice. From the Greeks they have learned to lie with boys." Herodotus here appears to praise their cultural flexibility, but we may wonder if this respect arises out of a sense that it is a good thing that they imitate others. Would he congratulate the Athenians if they displayed the same disposition? Cf. "In their reverence for the gods, [the Egyptians] are excessive, more than any others in the world" (*H*, 2:37, 146).

39 *H*, 4:30, 290. Cf. "They kiss one another on the mouth," "drink a lot," "eat roots of all kinds" (1:202, 125). "The women piss standing upright, but the men do so squatting" (1:35, 145). In India, he sees different "style(s) of life" (3:100, 255), some he describes, and then he talks about "other Indians: These will not kill any living thing ... When one falls sick, he wanders into the desert and lies down, and no one troubles about him, whether he is sick or dead." "Among the Indians I have spoken of, sexual intercourse is quite public, as it is among the animals." The Agathyrsi "wear jewelry a lot; they enjoy all their women in common ... have neither envy nor hatred against one another" (4:104, 319). On camels in India, he says, "The Greeks know camels, so I will not write to describe their shape; *but I will tell something that is not known.* The camel in the hind legs has four thighs and four knees, and its genitals are turned toward the tail behind its hind legs" (emphasis added, 3:103, 256).

40 "Certainly the Egyptians did not get the name of Heracles from the Greeks, but rather the Greeks got it from the Egyptians" (*H*, 2:43, 149). "That these gods came from the barbarians I found on inquiry to be true" (2.50, 153). "The Egyptians were the first people to organize holy assemblies, processions and services of the gods, and it was from them that the Greeks learned these things" (2:58, 156–57).

41 *H*, 2.177–78, 208. King Amasis also helped Greeks settle and establish "the Hellenium" in Egypt and "he dedicated offerings in Greece" (*H*, 2.178 and 2.82, 208, 210).

42 *H*, 6:42–43, 424–25. In the next line, Herodotus notes that, "having done so, [Mardonius] hastened off to the Hellespont." The next several sentences rekindle the dominant narrative: "Having collected this huge force of army and fleet there, the Persians *crossed* the Hellespont *with the ships* and *marched* by land through Europe ... to *subdue* as many Greek cities as possible ... " (*H*, 6:44, 425).

43 *H*, 1.142, 99.

44 *H*, 7.53, 489. "Show zeal, for it is our common good that is the cause of our endeavor."

45 "What nations did Xerxes not bring out of Asia?" Herodotus asks. See also, especially *H*, 3.2.9–12, 28; and *RM*, XXXVII.40, 317–19.

46 The Athenians say it is "not their custom ... to do obeisance to a human creature" (*H*, 7:136, 513) and are credited by Herodotus as being the "saviors" of freedom. Many contemporary historians are of the mind that had the Athenians not defeated the Persians, "Greek freedom would have been curbed and with it, the political artistic, dramatic, and philosophical progress which has been a beacon to Western civilization" (Robin Lane Fox, *The Classical World: An Epic History from Homer to Hadrian*, New York: Basic Books, 2006, 104, 100). Compare, *H*, 7:135, 513.

47 *HA*, 7.3.6, 153; also, e.g. 7.2.19, 181.

48 *HA*, 7.6.11, 162.

49 See e.g. *HA*, 8.12.15–17, 204.

50 *HA*, 8.9.31, 197–98.

51 *HA*, 8.9.31, 198.

52 *H*, I.176, 113.

53 The Boeotian Pagondas called on his army "to resist the foreign invader" (who had "*crossed the frontier*"), namely Athens, who is "trying to enslave near and far alike" – "always ready to give battle for the liberty of their own country" (*PW*, 4.92, 273–74). Hermocrates, the Syracuse leader, similarly rallies his people "to resist the invader" and thereby "escape disgraceful submission to an Athenian master" (6.78.4, 405).

54 Marmares and Syrians discussed above. After destroying the Sibi, Alexander "attempted to take a second city by assault, but he met fierce resistance and was driven back ... when he persisted with the siege, the townspeople lost all hope of saving themselves, and set fire to the buildings, burning themselves in the blaze along with their wives and children" (*HA*, 9.4.6, 220).

55 The "Abydosians bound themselves to take their own lives and destroy the property" as Philip took "the gold and silver," Livy writes. "But he lost the human booty," since the Abydosians "sought every means of suicide" (*RM*, XXXI.19, 38). It was this "slaughter of the people of Abydos," Livy adds, that "aroused [Rome] against Philip" (ibid.). The Romans also faced resistance from the Phocaeans: "The townsfolk resisted so stubbornly ... even when the fighting stopped, [they] did not break off for rest." Eventually they surrendered, but only after "stipulating that they should not be treated as enemies" (XXXVII.32, 31). When Antiochus "tried to bring all the cities of Asia under his dominion, as they had been in times gone by," he, too, found the inhabitants of the Hellespont prepared to resist. He "ordered his troops ... to frighten by a display of terror" and then tried to persuade them to gain liberty as his gift. "To these approaches the people replied that Antiochus ought not to be surprised or enraged if they refused to submit with equanimity to the deferment of their hope of freedom" (XXXIII.38, 131).

56 *H*, 1:87, 74.

57 *H*, 9:122, 664.

58 *RM*, XXXVII.32, 310.

59 An oligarch who Thucydides describes as "a man of sense": "As he spoke, so he acted" (*PW*, 8.27.5, 497).

60 *PW*, 1.23.6, 16. Compare Herodotus, who analyzed Croesus' concern about "growth [and consequences] of the power of the Persians" (*H*, 1:46,52).

61 *PW*, 3.82.2–4, 199.

62 *PW*, 5.45.4, 328.

63 *PW*, 5.55.3, 336.

64 *PW*, 5.54.2, 335.

65 *PW*, 5.55.3, 336.

66 *PW*, 5.116.1, 357.

67 *PW*, 6.13.1, 357.

68 *PW*, 6.18.6–7, 373.

69 *HA*, 7.8.14, 168.

70 *HA*, 7.8.16, 168. Herodotus records that the Scythians killed their own who "went traveling to Greece and adopted foreign customs" (*H*, 4.76, 308).

71 "To give you some idea of the Scythian race, we have been provided with the gifts of a yoke of oxen, a plough, an arrow, a spear, and a cup. These we use with our friends and against our enemies. We give to our friends crops produced by the toil of our oxen, and with them we use the cup to make libations to the gods. Our enemies we attack at long range with the arrow, and at short range with the spear" (*HA*, 7.8.18, 168).

72 *HA*, 7.8.16–30, 168–69; cf. *H*, 3.21, 220, 3.25, 221.

73 *HA*, 4.4.15–16, 61.

74 *RM*, XXXVII.17, 294–95.

75 *HA*, 4.11.21, 77.

76 *PW*, 6.24.4, 375.

77 *H*, 4.76, 308.

78 *HA*, 5.11.4, 112.

79 *HA*, 6.9.36, 138.

80 *HA*, 3.10.23, 140.
81 *HA*, 5.4.11, 101.
82 *HA*, 6.2.13, 121. This description resonates with the voice of Thucydides who said of the Scythians that "they are not on a level with other peoples in general intelligence and the arts of civilized life" (*PW*, 2.97.6, 151). The identity of the Scythians seemed to have perplexed the classical historians.
83 *HA*, 6.2.13, 121.
84 *RM*, XXXVII.35, 313.
85 *RM*, XXXVII.35, 313.
86 *RM*, XXXVII.35, 314.

X
Crossing the Hellespont

Let us try to summarize and take account of the larger picture I have sket-ched concerning the intersubjective meanings constitutive of political space in the passage from *polis* to empire. Some cross to fight and die a glorious death; they bear enmity and trust in force. They entrust themselves to force,[1] always grasp for the more and the most, and hold vengeance upon what they call their enemies – all in the pursuit, *inter alia*, of booty, trophies and prizes.[2] Fear fills the spaces between what they see as sides. For them, "the struggle is on" and they are prepared to do, die, suffer and visit suffering upon others, such "that either everything here shall fall to the domination of the Greeks or everything there to the Persians. There is no middle ground for this enmity."[3] In this view, borders are crossed and are seen as necessary to check the violence that they in fact fail to contain. Others – I have called them the Medizers of varying degrees – are subordinated discursively, har-assed, charged, and dismissed by the former, and appear to live without/ outside of the enmity of the crosser. They distrust in force. Fear does not guard the space between them. The struggle is not on. They suffer mis-characterization and erasure in the narratives of crossing. There may be no middle ground (for fear or anything in particular), because there may be no ends between which a presumed middle is conceived.

Crossing the Hellespont has a special character in this matrix of meaning.

In one sense, the dominant one, it is the edge, the boundary, the border between Europe and Asia, "West" and "East", across which great differences are said to reside. It is where armies have set themselves on edge and been launched to pursue dreams of reciprocal colonization and conquest, in search of honor and greater possessions. Even the classical, mythopoetic crossings are not free from violence. The consummation of love between Hero and Leander in Marlowe's *Hero and Leander* has been read as a metaphor for violence – Leander's "assault" on "the vulnerable body of his beloved, robbing it of its most cherished value."[4] When Byron swam across the Hellespont, he did so with Lieutenant Ekenhead of the British navy – from the royal brig, the *Salsette*, on which he traveled.[5]

In another sense, the Hellespont is a metaphor for the precarious and tumultuous character of all liminal spaces, where differences as significant as those imagined historically between "West" and "East" exist. In any era, it seems, the Hellespont can be everywhere. It exists at every putatively bordered site, every borderline, where unfamiliarity and seemingly opposite entities face each other.

Approaching the actual Hellespont, the crossers seem spellbound by its overwhelming natural power – they pray, consecrate, sacrifice and imagine their predecessors. This was not unique to Greek and Roman eras. Dreams of conquest and glory seem to occur at the shores of the Hellespont to every aspiring world emperor. The historian of the Ottoman Empire, Edmund Creasy, writes that the Ottoman historians tell of a vision that Süleyman Pasha saw "as he mused on the sea-shore near the ruins of Cyzicus. They tell how the crescent of the moon rose before him as the emblem of his race, and united the continents of Europe and Asia with a chain of silver light, while temples and palaces floated up out of the great deep, and mysterious voices blended with the resounding sea, exciting in his heart a yearning for pre-destined enterprise, and a sense of supernatural summons. The dream may have been both the effect of the previous schemings and the immediate stimulant that made Solyman put his scheming into act." Like those before and after him, his imagination set itself on the other side of the Hellespont as potentially within his grasp and dominion. "With but thirty-nine of his chosen warriors" – he is about to cross – "he embarked at night in a Genoese bark on the Asiatic side of the Hellespont, and surprised the Castle of Tzympe, on the opposite coast ... [A]nd the victors never left the continent on which they had conquered."[6] Nor, it seems, is the desire for vengeance exhausted. Like Antiochus and the Romans, the Ottoman Sultan Mehmet, the Conqueror of Istanbul/Constantinople, visited Troy, praised the memory and deeds of the Trojans, and "reported[ly] said, shaking his head a little, 'God has reserved for me, through so long a period of years, the right to avenge this city and its inhabitants ... It was the Greek and the Macedonians and Thessalians and Peloponnesians who ravaged this place in the past, and whose descendants have now through my efforts paid the just penalty, after a long period of years, for their injustice to us Asiatics at that time and so often in subsequent times'."[7] The imagination that comes to empire builders on the shores of the Hellespont is strong and consistent,[8] and the historians who record those imaginings are similarly consistent: "*Crossing the Hellespont* in 334," writes Robert Strassler in 1996 in his "Epilogue" to *The Peloponnesian War*, "Alexander *completely destroyed* Persian military power in a series of brilliant victories in just three years ... Ten years later, when he died in Babylon, the independent polis was well on its way to oblivion, and the Hellenistic world was born."[9] From *polis* to empire, crossing and destroying.

What is the power of the Hellespont that it so compels the political and historical imagination? Perhaps it is its rushing waters – flowing in one direction on the surface, another in its depths. What lies in the middle, or on the other side, can be viewed but not known from its distant shores, but the distance is collapsed as one extends one's imaginative grasp across this natural wonder as "the border" between "East" and "West," Europe and Asia. A rift, an obstacle, a bridgeable seam. Perhaps the dangerous glamour of crossing it lies in the ceaselessly undulating power of its "wine-dark"[10] currents. Swishing back and forth, across the straits, connecting yet separating the two mythologically separated worlds. The water's tides carry one off, not the other way around. Kinetically pulsating, they direct your desires, not you theirs. One can float and reach the other side or sink into its depths. It is nearly impossible not to plunge. Moreover, remaining in place on its banks runs counterintuitive to memory, a betrayal of the tradition. The other side, reachable, unreachable, ending in life, life not ending, calls. What lies on the other side? Unfamiliarity, and certain heroic victory or death, gain or loss, glory or subordination: Penetration for the sake of displaying one's power to the world. Death calls – either in fame or disaster – and it is *death, everlasting life*, to which the imagination of the crosser cannot yield.

Approaching the Hellespont metaphorically, and with the Medizer in mind, enables us to see that one's options for conceptualizing space and moving within it are much more open than the classical crossers have permitted. *Whether their imaginations control us or we revive ours is the key criterion to any less mutually destructive, more meaningful future.* The Medizer offers another way of reaching, or not reaching, the other side: something other than glory, expansion, and imperialized liberty through eternal renown is possible. A world that is not an abode of war, worlds that are not abodes of war. But one must endure the accusations of betrayal. The Medizer sees and lives within political space differently. One cannot be sure from the stories we have studied thus far, but perhaps the Medizer might see beauty where crossers see bounty, life where crossers see terror and hopes for death, sympathy and reciprocal ties where crossers see strategic advantage and are always prepared to engage in either imperial subterfuge, ravaging, or research to maintain an upper hand.

Notes

1 e.g. *HA*, 8.12, 203.
2 *HA*, 7.7.14, 165.
3 *H*, 7:11, 473.
4 Patrick Cheney writes: "When Marlowe finally fulfills the reader's desire, he breaks down the hymeneal walls of myth and metaphor itself: *Leander now, like Theban Hercules; Entered the orchard of th' Hesperides; Whose fruit none rightly can describe but he; That pull or shakes it from the golden tree* ... By likening Leander to the mighty athlete Hercules stealing the immortalizing apples from

the garden of the Hesperides, Marlowe constructs a rather dubious icon: the male's sexualized quest for transcendence" (Patrick Cheney, "Introduction: Authorship in Marlowe's Poems," in Patrick Cheney and Brian J. Striar, *The Collected Poems of Christopher Marlowe*, New York: Oxford University Press, 2006, 19).

5 Byron mentions Ekenhead in his poem, *Don Juan*: "A better swimmer you could scarce see ever; He could, perhaps, have pass'd the Hellespont; As once (a feat on which ourselves we prided); Leander, Mr. Ekenhead, and I did" (Allan Massie, *Byron's Travels*, London: Sidgwick & Jackson, 1988, 56–57).

6 Sir Edward Creasy, *History of the Ottoman Turks*, New York: H. Holt and Company, 1877, 18–21.

7 Kritobulos, *History of Mehmed the Conqueror*, Princeton: Princeton University Press, 1954, 181–82. This work is full of crossings of the kind analyzed here.

8 For the nineteenth and twentieth century, pan-Hellenic *enosis* version of this imaginary, see Michael Llewellyn Smith, *Ionian Vision: Greece in Asia Minor 1919–1920*, London: Hurst, 1998. Llewellyn Smith notes in a few usages of the *crossing* idiom that when Turkey gained the upper hand in battle against the invading Greeks, the British allies of the latter "agreed on firm action including the use of force to prevent the Turks from crossing into Europe" (ibid., 316). Here, the site in question is the Bosphorus, but it is interesting and, again, important to see continuity in meaningful usage of *crossing over*.

9 Robert Strassler, "Epilogue," in R. Strassler (ed.) *The Landmark Thucydides: A Comprehensive Guide to the Peloponnesian War*, New York: Simon and Schuster, 1996, 554.

10 Homer, *The Iliad*, New York: Penguin, 1990, 217 (7:102).

XI
A tradition of meanings

The classical texts construct a world of meanings within which crossing over a border is embedded in shared understandings of borders and life on and around them. Crossing occurs for similar purposes, in similar ways, and with similar forms of significance – as an aggressive armed practice that views those on the other side of what is crossed as objects of war and their bodies and properties, personal and collective, as objects of conquest, seizure, and possession. Crossing over is, moreover, a central term of willful and resolute action throughout these seminal texts. It is almost the one concept without which the seminal events characterized in them – the Persian/Greek, Peloponnesian, and Roman wars over Europe and Asia and the conquests of Alexander – cannot be told. It supports permanent distinctions between self and enemy, distinctions by which the world is continually made and remade, making a particular world. It is noteworthy that these texts reference and methodologically imitate each other in important ways. Thus meanings within them resonate through and between each, bringing seemingly separate seminal events into a similar history – indeed, the (glorious) history of "the West," now shown to be one in which its major actors, on all sides, consistently mean to engage in a particular kind of practice – linking each separate moment to a kind of collective identity, one shared on all sides of the borders, as constructed in the seminal texts of "the West."

That the authors sometimes offer (or appear to offer) conservative critiques of some of these crossings does not weaken the power of the construction they offer – a construction that is reinforced in their equally patterned condemnation or discursive dismissal of alternative forms of crossing – in the figure, for example, of the Medizer (the violator of standard crossings and permanent target of suspicion, anger, and accusations of treason). Such forms of crossing otherwise or not crossing at all – some exceptions to the rule – exist within these works, but they are submerged and thus rendered nearly irrelevant within the dominant paradigm.

This account seems necessary at this point in history not only because this world of meanings is still significantly with us. It is important as well insofar as some of these texts have acquired the status among contemporary historians or observers of international politics of classical guides or sacred sources of wisdom for contemporary imperial politics.[1] Against this impression, I suggest that these texts posit destructive mythological constructions as the bases for Western (or any) experience, establishing a way of thinking about crossing borders that entails visiting "horror," disaster, and death upon peoples on the other side, because all space outside the home space is seen as an abode of war. While these works have many valuable uses, they are no longer, if they ever were, valuable sources of wisdom concerning global political relations as such. They frame the border as necessarily a space of enmity and hostility. In them, establishing and maintaining borders becomes necessary to political life, for the borders are constraints to the violence human beings "know" they can and will enact on each other when crossing them. These works thus produce an indelible and questionable picture of the species as universally aggressive, borders as necessary and natural requirements of political practice (permanent states of siege within a bordered humanity), and a/the world as a place for perpetual, sectarian, vengeful, expansionist wars to decimate forms of life on the other side of the border. I must emphasize they promote these fantasies whether the crosser is coming from the direction of the west or east. The sides change but the concept that is constructed and conveyed within these classics of "the West" does not: it's about "doing injury." That contemporary political realists wish to see their "enemies" as mirror oppositions of themselves is not surprising given the deep, reciprocally distrustful construction of each in the wisdom of the foundational stories of Western civilization.

In the transition from *polis* to empire, the language of crossing over borders, of this dimension of space and the human political relationship to it, is consistently and predominantly that of violence. As such, these texts, if they are practical sourcebooks, are guides for war, or for a limited form of calculating, strategic politics that occurs during war. They do not enable us to cross over – *so to speak* – war itself. They exude suffering, bitterness, and an imperialistic view of human achievement, where conquest and achievement are essentially synonymous. Their ongoing popularity may be based in their reinforcement of the violence of a so-called realist view of global possibilities, along with imperial fantasies of crossing as possessing, saving, and/or assaulting and slaughtering.

If my account is compelling, we might both amend our view of the roots of the Western tradition and espy a vision of political space that not only remains quite stable from Greece to Rome, but, perhaps, also thereafter for quite a while, down to this day. Scholars of "the Middle East," for example, are profoundly familiar with the enduring quality of the violent and imperial imagination within "the West" of its borders. In his important study of European views of "the Orient," Thierry Hentsch shows how, since the nineteenth century but with roots that sprouted much earlier, "the West ... denigrated [the Orient] in order to reassure (or frighten) itself."[2] The very term, "The Middle East," was a product of Western military strategy: it was coined in 1905 by the American naval captain Alfred T. Mahan, while he plotted British naval strategy in the Persian/Arabian Gulf.[3] Military considerations, that is, are embedded in the concept, "The Middle East," as the posited border and liminal space between "the West" and "the East," and its usage in contemporary scholarly and political discourse, educational curricula, media, etc. most often reiterates this meaning. This embedded strategic and military view of "the Middle East" is not all that exists in today's "the West," but it is unmistakably omnipresent.

A more detailed account of this more recent part of the story awaits elaboration at another time, but I want to suggest that the classical understanding of crossing over endures in a relatively stable fashion in the history of "the West," from *polis* to empire, empire to nation-state, and nation-state to globalized world. In the latter context, the discourse of crossing over continues to be reflected in dominant, contemporary prejudices about "traveling" to and from places across the Hellespont. Thanks to *National Geographic*, the *Discovery* channel, itinerant journalists, and modern travel writers, the people and places "on the other side" are perhaps now seen as curious and beautiful in cultural and historical terms – almost as Herodotus portrayed some of the peoples and places he visited in his journeys. However, as in Herodotus, these societies are still profoundly represented through what they lack, and the attributes that they are said to lack – like freedom, adequate education, health, wealth, stable and honest/noncorrupt government – are precisely those things that, within the dominant understandings of "Western" societies, would provide for "safety." From one metaphorical edge of the Hellespont to another, the Western traveler may be eager to travel across the border, but s/he always goes on guard. This is due to a widely shared belief once stated very well by a popular writer on Turkey who spoke – as if it were an objective fact – of "this country's political and psychological underdevelopment."[4] Depictions of societies outside "the West" as inadequate in terms of "developmental" measures inevitably reduce these societies in the eyes of the Westerner, and thus – among many other untoward effects – increase fears and suspicions about the people living in them. The visiting European Union parliamentarian, attempting rightly to criticize Turkey's objectionable record on press freedom, carelessly generalizes: "The Internet Law is just one symptom of the challenge the society has in the scope of freedom of expression in general."[5] "The society?" "In general?" Such pronouncements are pervasive. Not that this destroys an interest in travel, but travelers routinely make "safety preparations" a priority. I can't tell you how many tens of inquiries I've had from students and their parents about the safety of traveling to "Turkey" or "the Middle East" more generally. The essential view of a world divided by two abodes, safety on one side and danger/terror on the other, is a lived reality in the Western experience. The shores of the Hellespont shift from the various edges of Western engagement with other worlds (other "Easts," "the South") and over time, but the view of political space remains, sometimes in a partially updated form, the same.

As I say, establishing the enduring, contemporary life of the discourse of crossing over awaits another time. For now, I hope to have shown that there is a patterned way of thinking in the formative experience of "the West" about what it means to cross over a border, indeed and especially, the border between "Europe" and "Asia." A participatory reading of Herodotus, Thucydides, Curtius Rufus and Livy suggests the presence of a deeply enduring sensibility constitutive of "the West" and articulated in "the West's" own seminal accounts of its primary political experiential foundations, a constitutive way of thinking, talking, imagining, feeling, and valuing the significance of the border between "the West" and what "the West" describes as "the East" as a site of danger. An analysis of this enduring conceptualization of the world shows the roots of broader concepts of "civilizational borders," and, importantly, shows a hostile and destructive orientation towards the peoples and places over the border, generally and especially the border between Europe and Asia. It shows as well that this pattern precedes the Crusades as well as the more recent, imperial and colonial codings of the territorial and "civilizational" boundaries between Europe and "the Orient," or "the West" and "the East" (or "Islam").

Indeed, bringing to life the meaning of crossing a border in the seminal texts of the classical era illustrates conceptual stability in "the nature and quality of the life that men could attain in political association" within the Western tradition.[6] Alongside the pattern of conceptual innovation in the transition from *polis* to empire lies an equally tenacious human conceptual phenomenon – a phenomenon of permanent and persistent conceptual reaffirmation of longstanding meaning in the history of "the West," a capacity for profound metaphysical and conceptual stability and non-transformation, for deep and enduring continuity.[7] I thus suggest a slight shift in emphasis in "the West's" self-understanding as a tradition of conceptual innovation, one drawn from the era in which this dimension is understood to have taken shape. In the meanings constitutive of "crossing a border" in seminal Greek and Roman texts, nothing was significantly thrown out of balance, no past valuations substantially modified, no new dimension or attitude convincingly acquired, no change in the criteria of application or range of reference apparently achieved;[8] in a word, no conceptual change occurred. Whatever innovation exists in "the West's" political conceptual capacities should be seen against this background of conceptual fixity. In specific ways, things remained – and still remain to an important extent – quite stable. Finally, because these texts exhort us not only to understand their worlds, but to be beings in the world in particular ways, my hope is that this exercise of disclosing, revealing, remembering, and highlighting the destructive and life-negating associations of border crossing, of embracing them for reflection and scrutiny with the "extra edge of consciousness" that conceptual awareness affords,[9] will allow us to dethrone them as terms of ongoing significance and resist their lasting grip on us.

One should have no illusions, however, about the possibility for transformation. The dominant tradition is centuries old, and, as we have seen in our analysis of alternatives, it frequently underlies even ostensible acts against it. It is part of the truly intersubjective conceptual inheritance of what is called Western civilization, within and across generations, with ongoing discursive power to constitute the meaning and significance of political space. In this tradition, the Hellespont today is, as Anthony Pagden avers, "the selfsame corner of the world" where "the battle lines" between "West" and "East" were drawn "more than twenty three centuries ago." For Pagden, these lines are now "very much where they were then."[10] However, resolute declarations of the inherited significance and border-like character of the Hellespont – the continually solved and resolved character of the border in contemporary writing and what it must mean – need not constrain defiance of this imaginatively violent, antagonistic and destructive cultural legacy. Alternative understandings – traitorous ones like Medizing, staying back, letting Others be, and forging uncommon ties – are available. The highly stable, classical conceptualization of political space in the passage from Greece to Rome to Turkey has its voice, but it is only one voice among others.

In the next part of this work, I want to take up the question of what it might mean to approach the life worlds across the Hellespont(s) in a fundamentally different way than they are understood in the violent discourse of crossing over. Let us leave the figure of the Medizer aside for the time being. That figure is, after all, part of the discourse of crossing over; it is the crosser's dialectical other, represented and signified in and through the language of the crosser; the Medizer is internal to the discourse of crossing over without which that discourse might not exist. One can champion the Medizer's causes, but what we may say may emerge from other discourses and languages of life. There may be other ways, other possibilities, for living and being in relation to borders and the worlds on their different sides of them. I want to try to write about something different, something other than crossing over, about approaching political space differently, hermeneutically, open to having one's prior understandings fundamentally altered in relation to the experience to which one opens oneself up and adjusts.

Much of what I say is based on my nearly twenty years of work, as a teacher and person with life, study, and teaching experience in Turkey. I want to try to convey how the "closer" I have felt in relation to lessons I have learned from stories told and forms of life on the other side of the Hellespont, the less I feel I understand (in) my old sense of understanding, the less I remain able to possess (in) my old sense of possessing, the less I am able to be (in) my old sense of being, the less I am able to participate in a world where a confident fear guards the space between the shores of the Hellespont. What I have to say here stems from a realization of the limits of my inherited understanding in relation to the meanings and understandings of peoples living on the other shores of the Hellespont, and an awareness emerging from this realization, that the ways of life and being on the other side of the Hellespont provide the basis not for hostility and fear but for hospitality, regard, esteem, solidarity, and – the most difficult adjustment – justice, and thus a way of being and relating to global spatial relations that undermines the eternal validity of the classical discourse of crossing over. In what follows, then, I seek to approach the limit and liminal space of the Hellespont differently.

Is it possible to *be* otherwise in relation to all borders characterized and inherited through memory within the classical Western tradition, in one form or another, as fatal?

Notes

1 See previous chapters and, e.g., work by Victor Davis Hanson, including an explicit statement of the relevance of the classical texts to "conflicts of our times" in his, "Introduction: Makers of Ancient Strategy, from the Persian Wars to the Fall of Rome," in V. Davis Hanson (ed.) *Makers of Ancient Strategy, from the Persian Wars to the Fall of Rome*, Princeton University Press, 2010, 1–10. Also, Curtius Rufus' account of Alexander's conquests has appeared in the analysis of the American war in Afghanistan (S. Jones, *In the Graveyard of Empires: America's War in Afghanistan*, New York: W.W. Norton & Co., 2009, 3–5).
2 T. Hentsch, *Imagining the Middle East*, Montreal: Black Rose Books, 1992, 205.
3 R. Davison, "Where is the Middle East?" *Foreign Affairs*, 38, 1960, 667.
4 S. Kinzer, *Crescent & Star: Turkey in Between Two Worlds*, New York: Farrar, Straus and Girouz, 2001, 24.
5 Comment by Marietje Schaake in Ö. Öğret, "Gap Remains Between Turkey and EU, EP Politician Says," *The Turkish Daily News*, 6 November 2010, www.hurriyetdailynews.com/default.aspx?pageid=438&n=ep-member-disagrees-with-protecting-ataturk-with-bans-2010-11-05 (accessed 9 November 2010).

6 S. Wolin, *Politics and Vision: Continuity and Innovation in Western Political Thought*, Princeton: Princeton University Press, 2004, 67.

7 Perhaps "truly novel ideas in the domains of morals and politics are extremely rare and the history of political thought can demonstrate how rare they are" (M. Sibley, *Political Ideas and Ideologies*, New York: Harper Collins, 1970, 6–7).

8 I draw these criteria from James Farr's criteria for conceptual change; see J. Farr, "Understanding Conceptual Change Politically," in T. Ball, J. Farr, and R. Hanson (eds) *Political Innovation and Conceptual Change*, Cambridge: Cambridge University Press, 1989, 31.

9 R. Williams, *Keywords: A Vocabulary of Culture and Society*, Oxford: Oxford University Press, 1983, 24.

10 A. Pagden, *Worlds at War: The 2,500-Year Struggle between East & West*, New York: Oxford University Press, 2008, 538.

Part Two

ON THE FATAL BOUNDARIES

I shall give distinction to places that have none.

Alexander[1]

Manlius, they said, had been eager to cross the Taurus range and he had with difficulty been restrained by the entreaties of his subordinates from his intention of testing the prophecy of the Sibylline verses foretelling disaster for those who crossed the fatal boundaries; nevertheless, he had brought up his army and encamped almost on the crest of the range at the watershed.

Livy, Rome and the Mediterranean[2]

The Taurus mountains are now the boundary of your empire; of all that lies within this limit, nothing should seem remote from you.

Rome's allies from Rhodes[3]

The state has issued an edict against us
The edict is the sultan's but the mountains are ours.

Dadaloğlu[4]

Come, soul brothers, let's band together,
Brandish our swords against the godless,
And restore the poor people's rights.

Pir Sultan Abdal[5]

I
Introduction

When the Romans defeated Antiochus, they proudly banished him to what they described as "the furthest boundaries of the world,"[6] or "the furthest corner of the earth."[7] What they meant was "beyond the Taurus mountains"[8] of Eastern Anatolia/Asia Minor, the area that now marked the sovereign political boundary of their empire in the east. The Romans attached political and mythological significance to this boundary. Both Livy and speakers in his *Ab Urbe Condita* consistently describe the mountains along the Taurus range as the limit of Roman dominion and the boundary between safety on one side and danger on the other. This was "on account of some verses in the Sybilline oracles threatening slaughter and destruction to those Roman armies which should pass that limit."[9] The Taurus Mountains were thus *the* fatal boundaries: On one side, the Romans secured peace and life; on the other they prophesized disaster and death.

Livy relates, for example, that when the Roman General Manlius had the "intention of testing the prophecy of the Sibylline verses" by crossing the Taurus range, "he had with difficulty been restrained by the entreaties of his subordinates" because "the king's [Antiochus'] forces made no move." That is, Manlius "found no excuse for war" and, rather than crossing and testing the prophesies, he "brought his army up" to the crest of the range at the watershed, "encamped" there, and then led his army back around "to attack the Gallogrecians" on the nearer side instead.[10] Thus, *pax/bellum Romana* reigned on the nearer side of the Taurus range, and death and disaster on the other. The political and mythological limit of Western imperial antagonism at this moment, its frontline of achievement and defense, had moved from the sea of Helle that split "Europe" and "Asia" to a new point of threat – the Taurus Mountains. What had once been true on the eastern shores of the Hellespont was now transferred through political experience and oracular myth to the mountains of the Taurus range: If one is to cross them, one must be prepared to assume the greatest of all risks and ready to confront danger guaranteed by higher forces. On one side of the border is the homeland, on the other lies land *fatalis*, the land of prophesized doom.

The story repeats itself as the border moves further over time in the eastern direction ... Eventually, it is right next door ...

Recognizing the enduring power of this disposition and turning to the here and now, we must, today, ask: Is a differently constituted disposition in relation to this constantly repeated *limit* – the Hellespont, the Taurus range, the – possible? Is a different kind of risk available? Is it possible to approach this limit otherwise, that is, outside the experience of the limit *as it is pre-constituted and essentially given as fatal* in the Western imagination? Is it possible not *to cross*, but to be taken elsewhere when at the limit, away from the certain vile fantasies and deadly prophesies of *crossing the Hellespont* – to another place where, perhaps, the closer one gets to the limit the less one knows about it and the less one is prepared to be there; the more one moves beyond the limit the less one understands how one previously understood and the less one is what one was: where old translations become untranslations and new translations become untranslatable, the more one understands the less there is to gather and grasp, and one stops grasping and begins living otherwise, not *to* ... What might yet come through at and beyond the limit that would be otherwise? Not through direct translation but through some mediated form of simultaneous solidarity and estrangement. *Today, right now, and for tomorrow* – from the places in the world called home, where people live, labor, and make beautiful things of life, even as life is never as sweet, easy, and free from the violent designs of others as it ought to be.

Notes

1 *HA*, 9.6.22, 227.
2 *RM*, XXXVIII.45, 378.
3 Representatives of Rhodes, to Rome, in a post-war effort to "deny the ambitions" of other rulers (*RM*, XXXVII.54, 333).
4 Dadaloğlu, quoted in T.S. Halman, *A Millennium of Turkish Literature: A Concise History*, Syracuse: Syracuse University Press, 2011, 27.
5 Pir Sultan Abdal, quoted in Halman, *A Millennium*, 27.
6 *RM*, XXXVIII.60, 396; also, XXXVIII.8, 340.
7 In defense of Lucius Scipio at his corruption trial, *RM*, XXXVIII.59, 395.
8 *RM*, XXXVIII.12, 344; also XXXVII.7, 340; XXXVII.8, 341; XXXVIII.39, 372; XXXVIII.53, 388; XXXVIII.38, 369.
9 Nathaniel Hooke, *The Roman History, from the Building of Rome to the Ruin of the Commonwealth*, Volume 5, London: T. Davison, 1818, 297, books.google.com/books?id=puzQAAAAMAAJ&pg=PA297&dq=livy+the+fatal +boundaries#v=onepage&q=fatal%20boundary&f=false (accessed 24 September 2009).
10 *RM*, XXXVIII.45, 378.

II
The Village of Değirmenoluk[*]

High above the shores of the eastern Mediterranean, amidst the palpitating beauty of the Taurus highlands where the jagged rock cliffs make one shiver, a boy takes flight from a punishing life of toil and abuse under the aegis of a cruel feudal lord.[1]

Only the thorny eryngo thistles grow in the fields of his village, and the thistles are so thick that not even a snake can slither through them. In the summertime, the thistles turn from light springtime green to blue, first bright blue and then the most stunning, deep blue. If a breeze blows at the end of the day, the blue thistles swish and ripple across the plain like a sea. At sunset, the field of thistles turns red. In autumn, they dry and change from blue to snow-white as thousands of snails cover their stems.[2]

---

[*] The following selected stories are conveyed from Y. Kemal, *İM1*. The italicized portions of the text relate to selected aspects of the story's narrative in a condensed and paraphrased fashion. The non-italicized portions are significantly more faithful to the language of the storyteller. As discussed in the Introduction, I do not view what is manifested here as translation in a conventional sense: I am *conveying* the stories, and, at times, the language of the stories, in the company of the storyteller and readers of this work, with all the liminal *différance* such an effort entails.

When İnce Memed, Slim Memed, works the land, the thistles rip his legs like the bite of a dog. And when not working, the lord, Abdi Ağa, beats him ruthlessly all over his body. Just yesterday, İnce Memed took such a beating.[3]

And so İnce Memed runs. He runs and runs, through the tall, thick thistles, panting and dripping blood where the prickly thorns scratch, slash, and slice the skin of his legs. Tiring, unsure of what lies ahead, he's determined to find the village that he once heard about, if he doesn't die from hunger now, that is. He considers resting, but remembering Abdi Ağa's men may be on his heels, he keeps running, hopelessly now and hopefully then. He runs and runs, his heart beating fast, out of the thistles, over the mountain rocks, and through the trees, startling the lizards and partridges he runs past.

Sweating, stinking, and exhausted, he tires as the sun sets. His knees give way, and he sits down on a small slope. A sweet flower aroma comes to him. He looks further down the hill and catches faint sight of an earthen hut below. His heart beats with happiness. Could this be the village? A light purple smoke wafts from the chimney. Then he hears what he thinks are sounds of footsteps behind him, rises, and takes off again. "I'll make it and say to them I've come to shepherd for you. I'll plough and plant the fields ... I'll tell them my name is Kara Mıstık, that I have no parents ... I have no Ağa either. I'll shepherd your flock. I'll plough your fields. I'll be your child. I will. My name is not İnce Memed. No, I'm Kara Mıstık ... " He breaks down and sobs. It's getting darker ...

Pausing, he approaches the first house. A man with a long beard is immersed in his work with a saddle. The man glances up, sees a shadow in the yard coming a few steps towards him and continues to work. When it gets too dark to see anymore, the man puts his work aside, rises and sees the figure still standing there. "Hişt! Hişt! Hiştişt!" the man says, "What are you doing there?"[4]

"I'll," the boy said,[5] "be your shepherd, uncle. I'll plough the fields. I'll do all sorts of work for you, uncle."

The man reached out to the figure and led him in.

"Just come inside, we'll talk about everything later."

A piercing northeast wind blew. Memed shook and shivered. He shivered so, as if he was going to fly.

The man hollered to the woman inside, "Throw some wood on the fire. The boy is shivering."

"Who's there?" she asked with surprise.

"Bir Tanrı Misafiri" – a Guest of God.

"Misafirin hiç de böylesini görmedimdi" – I've never seen a guest like this – she said, laughing quietly to herself.

"Gör işte!" – Have a look!

Once inside, Memed continued to shiver. "Yavru" – dear boy – the woman said, "You're hungry. I'll heat some çorba for you."

"I'll have some."

"It'll warm you up."

"It will stop my shivers."

Memed's eyes were glued on the steaming soup in the large copper kettle as the woman filled a tin bowl with döğme çorbası.

"Eat it quickly!"

"I will."

"Don't drink it so fast that your mouth will burn," the man said.

"Yanmaz" – It won't burn – Memed said. He smiled, his shivering stopped, and the old man and woman smiled, too.[8]

...

"Why would he run away?" the woman wondered ...

"Çok çok sıkıştırmışlar" – they treated him very, very harshly – the man replied.

"Yazık." What a shame. "Such a nice boy," she said. "Infidels – what do they want from a boy as small as a finger?"

"He can stay as long as his heart desires."[7]

****

The man comes to love Memed as a son, but Abdi Ağa finds Memed and marches him back to the village, where he punishes Memed and his mother, Döne. After the crops are harvested, he takes three quarters share instead of the customary two thirds, and when, as every year, the villagers line up in winter in front of his door half starving to plead for extra grains and supplies, Abdi Ağa scolds Döne for even bothering to come. He shoos her away and warns everyone else. "Up till now, no one in the village of Değirmenoluk has died of hunger. But she will die. Or if she has something to sell, let her sell it. But if you give her anything, or I hear that you did, I'll come to everyone's house and take back what I've given. Don't say I didn't warn you." Some in the crowd vocally agreed. They carried sacks of grains home, and the next day a warm scent of bread came from every house – except Döne's.[8]

****

Sixty years old and fit as an old plane tree, Durmuş Ali was the biggest man in the village. He ate a few pieces of the freshly baked bread to satisfy his hunger. Then his eyes began to tear up.

He turned to his wife, "To be honest, this isn't going down well at all."

"Why's that, Ali?" Hürü Ana asked, surprised.

"It's our İbrahim's family ... I can't get out of my mind what that heartless infidel Abdi has done. He sent Döne away yesterday without giving her a thing."

"Yazık," dedi. "If it was İbrahim ... "

95

"Abdi warned us that … "

"I heard."

"Are we going to allow two people in the middle of this huge village to starve?"

He fumed and boiled with rage. He shouted so loud that it was heard all the way on the other side of the village.

"Here's what I want you to do, my wife. Wrap up some of this bread and put some flour in a bag! I'm going to take them to İbrahim's family."

She prepared the things, and, with the bag and bundle in his hand, Ali stormed out of the house.

He calmed down by the time he arrived at Döne's front door.

"Döne, Döne! Open the door."

Inside, Döne and her son crouched motionless, like stones, in front of the stove where the flames had died out.

"Döne! Döne!"

After a while, Döne recognized the voice, pulled herself together, and rose. She made it to the door and, without the slightest sign of emotion, opened it.

"Come in Ali my brother."

"Why are you keeping me waiting outside all day, woman?"

"Come on inside, Ağam."

Ali leaned down and went inside.

"Why is your fire out?"

A ray of light, as tiny as the head of a needle, was flashing in Memed's eyes. It went out when he looked at Ali's kind and cheerful, fatherly face.

"Allah Kerim," Ali said as he handed the bundle to Döne. God is generous and kind.

"Öyledir zaar", Döne replied. That is how it is, I suppose …

…

After Ali, several other villagers brought food to Döne as well.

Abdi never knew a thing about it.[9]

****

One spring day, eager to see more of the world, Memed and his friend Mustafa set out to a nearby town in Çukurova, the Cilician plains. There, they are shocked to learn from an old man, Corporal Hasan, that the town has no ağas – that anyone who is wealthy is called "ağa," that just about everyone has their own fields, and that the shopkeepers in the market own their own shops. Memed listened in near disbelief as Hasan explained these things and the wider world: the rice fields and vineyards of Maraş, the Caucasus, Istanbul, Damascus, Beirut, Adana, Mersin, and Konya, where the great Mevlana is buried.

Memed lay awake that night and pondered the size of the world. He began viewing Değirmenoluk as nothing more than a small dot and the great Abdi Ağa as nothing more than an ant. Maybe this was the first time in his life that he genuinely thought about things. He thought about love and passion. And he felt enmity. In his own eyes, he started to grow up and see himself as a person. He tossed back and forth. "Abdi Ağa da insan, biz de ... " Abdi Ağa is also a human being, and we are too ... [10]

****

Memed and Hatçe loved each other and everyone in the village knew. But it had been arranged that Hatçe would marry Veli, the nephew of Abdi Ağa.

Abdi summoned Memed and demanded that he stop seeing Hatçe. "I hear you have your eyes on my nephew's fiancée. You ungrateful rascal, you enemy of honor. Boy, you have no idea of who you're dealing with. I'll destroy everything you have. I'll rip you into pieces and throw you to the dogs."

Memed stood there, still and quiet. This angered Abdi even more, and he gave Memed another beating. Memed clenched his teeth and chewed the cheeks of his mouth until they bled to keep himself from killing Abdi. He didn't say a word or lift a hand, except that tiny, needle-like flash of light came again and glistened in his eyes. [11]

****

Memed tells Hatçe that they should run away to where a better life is possible. Hatçe is afraid of what Abdi Ağa will do, but she and Memed run away that night.

Caught in a powerful thunderstorm, soaking wet and shivering, they take shelter in a rock cave where they manage to build a fire to dry their clothes and warm up. That night, they embrace each other in love. [12]

The next day, however, Abdi, Veli, and Abdi's men track the couple down and demand they give themselves up. Surrounded, Memed sends Hatçe home, promising to come for her when the trouble clears. In a gunfight, Veli is killed and Abdi is wounded, though Memed believes he has killed Abdi as well. Memed escapes and finds his way again to Süleyman's house. [13]

Süleyman decides to take Memed to the mountains to Deli Durdu and his gang of mountain brigands. Süleyman warns Memed not to stay too long with them. They are robbers and thieves, he says, not real eşkıyas. On their way up the mountain, he gives Memed some advice. [14]

"Memedim" – my dear Memed – "if you had done something wrong, if you had killed any other man, I would have turned you in to the authorities with my own hands."

"Actually, I wouldn't have killed any other man."

Süleyman stopped in his tracks. He took Memed by the collar, stared him straight in the eyes, and said:

"Look here my son İnce Memed! If you ever kill an innocent man, or someone who is only partly guilty, or if you kill someone for money, I'll kill you myself!"

"Bundan sonra insan öldürmeyeceğim." From now on, I won't kill anyone.

"But if you come across another Abdi Ağa and you don't kill him," Süleyman continued, "again you'll find my hands around your neck. If you come across a hundred Abdi Aga's, then kill every last one of them … "

"Söz," Memed said, smiling. I promise. "If I find a hundred, every one of them … "[15]

****

Abdi and his men frame Hatçe for Veli's murder. In the courthouse, the elderly judge knows Hatçe is innocent, but the cooked-up evidence is so strong that he has her sent to jail. An overwhelming sense of fear, hopelessness, and grief falls upon her. She's taken to the women's jail – a damp, crumbling cell, smelling of urine and with walls covered with the blood of dead mosquitoes.

In the village, Abdi's men beat Döne nearly to death.[16]

****

Süleyman introduces Memed to Durdu and his gang and, before he departs, admonishes Durdu not to underestimate his enemies or be cruel to the poor. "You can do whatever you want though with the haksız ve kötüler" – the unjust and corrupt.

Memed's eyes tear up as Süleyman departs. He wonders if he'll ever see Süleyman again. Maybe never, he thought to himself. The tears in his eyes grew larger. "Şu dünyada ne iyi insanlar var," he thought. What good people there are in this world.[17]

In clashes with the jandarma, Memed shows himself to be a brave eşkıya, but he never warms to Deli Durdu. Durdu takes pride in his reputation as the only eşkıya who strips his victims of everything they have, down to the very clothing on their bodies. Memed is appalled. "For a man to enter his village and house stark naked is worse than death," he says to Cabbar, one of the gang with whom he has grown close. "You shouldn't play with people. Bir yerleri var, bir ince yerleri, işte oraya degmemeli." Every person has a spot, a very soft spot, that shouldn't be touched. "Scare people yes, but you shouldn't humiliate them."[18]

****

The gang narrowly survives a skirmish with the jandarma, and Cabbar and Memed approach the tent of Kerimoğlu Ağa, a well-known nomadic elder, for supplies. Kerimoğlu welcomes them, but Memed hardly notices the greeting. He is completely taken aback by the beautiful carousel of colors inside the tent. "It's like paradise."[19]

"These young men are probably starving," Kerimoğlu Ağa said to his wife. "Quickly prepare some food."

Memed and Cabbar began to eat.

Kerimoğlu offered cigarettes as well.

"Neither of us smoke," said Cabbar, declining the offer.

"I'd like to say something to you," Kerimoğlu said, "but don't want it to offend you."

"Go ahead Ağam," said Memed. "Say what's on your mind."

"I'd like to say to you that, here in the mountains, you have no family or home. You've just come from a skirmish. You're covered with blood. Maybe you're hurt. Take off your clothes. The children will wash them right away. In the meantime, you can wear some of my clean ones. Don't think that Kerimoğlu is going to strip you down and turn you in. No wrong comes to anyone in Kerimoğlu's house. Kerimoğlu would die before anyone lays a hand on a guest. So you know, this is how it is."

"We've heard of Kerimoğlu, bre Ağa," Cabbar said. Turning, to Memed, "Look at what he wanted to say to us!"

"That's something … " Memed said.

"You shouldn't say that, young men," Kerimoğlu cautioned. "İnsanoğlu çiğ süt emmiştir." Human beings don't always behave with decency. "Her kötülüğü yapar, her iyiliği de yaptığı gibi." They commit every evil, just as they do every good.

One of Kerimoğlu's daughters entered the tent with soap and clean clothes, and Kerimoğlu left so that Memed and Cabbar could change.

"Bre Cabbar," Memed said, "ne iyi insanlar var şu yeryüzünde." What good people there are on this earth.

"Memed," Cabbar responded, "some people on the earth are neither zalim nor melun" – neither cruel nor cursed.

"Just look at this Kerimoğlu," said Memed. "Bak şundaki misafirperverliğe … " Just look at this hospitality …

After they changed their clothes, Kerimoğlu returned with an ointment and spread it over a small wound on Memed's head.

"This will heal in a couple of days," he told Memed. "When I was young, yavru, we were injured all the time. Everything comes and goes."

They talked some more and Kerimoğlu saw Memed and Cabbar off. "Come visit us again from time to time."[20]

99

Returning to the rest of the gang, Memed tells them about Kerimoğlu. "Şu dünyada ne kadar iyi insanlar var," he began. "Kerimoğlu thought of everything for us. He took care of my wound. He filled our stomachs. He washed our clothes. And on top of that gave us gifts of fresh clothes."[21]

Durdu hears of Kerimoğlu's riches and determines to take the entire gang to the tent.

Kerimoğlu greets each of them as they enter, "Hoş geldiniz misafirlerim."
Welcome my guests.

Memed smiled. "Thank you," he said.

Soon, though, his smile froze on his face. Some doubt gnawed at him inside. He wondered what Deli Durdu was going to do. Then he pointed Durdu out to Kerimoğlu. "This is our leader," he said.

Kerimoğlu was an experienced man. He glanced at Deli Durdu and motioned to Memed that there was something he didn't understand. Durdu was walking about, with a frown on his face and his head held high, without looking around.

"What's his name?" Kerimoğlu asked Memed.

"Deli Durdu."

"That's who this is?"

"That's him, right there."

The smile on Kerimoğlu's red face froze. His eyes became misty.

"The thief who robs people down to their underwear?"

"That's him."

When they entered the tent, Durdu was amazed almost as much as Memed had been earlier. An ornamented rifle hung on the wall. After throwing a hostile glance towards Kerimoğlu, Durdu spoke:

"Hand me that rifle and let's have a look, Ağa. Let's see what an Ağa's rifle looks like."

Kerimoğlu felt enmity in these words. Pangs ran through his heart. Inside, he told himself that a disaster was coming. This man's face was not a face, his eyes were not eyes.

As he handed Durdu the rifle, he asked, "Will you have something to eat right now or in the evening?"

Durdu's eyes flashed. "I didn't come to break bread or drink coffee," he said. "I came to plunder. If I eat or drink, I won't steal."

"Eat some food and then plunder," Kerimoğlu responded. "No one leaves the Kerimoğlu tent without eating first." His voice was shaking. The redness on his cheeks spread right to his nose and forehead. Then small beads of sweat appeared on his brow.

"Look, Durdu Ağa," he said. "These mountains are full of eşkıyalar. Until now, not one has ever sacked the Kerimoğlu home. If you're going to steal, then steal! *İşte ev önünde.* Here's the house, right in front of you."

From across the tent, Memed and Cabbar were devastated. They looked as if someone had just poured boiling water all over them.[22]

Durdu's men collect Kerimoğlu's money and gold.

With his eyes, Kerimoğlu tried to figure out Cabbar and Memed. They were standing behind him. Turning around, he and Memed caught each other's eyes. Memed lowered his. Kerimoğlu then looked at Cabbar. With disappointment in his eyes, he seemed to say, "Is this what you were going to do to me?"

...

Kerimoğlu remained where he was, motionless. He let Durdu's men take everything. His face was yellow. His lips shook.

With a firm, stubborn, and bossy growl, Durdu continued:

"Deli Durdu has a custom. Do you know what it is, Kerimoğlu? It's something that no other eşkıya does. In fact, no other eşkıya has sacked Kerimoğlu. Do you know my custom?"

Kerimoğlu gave no response.

"Deli Durdu's custom is this: he robs a man down to his underwear. So, take off your clothes Kerimoğlu!" he commanded.

Kerimoğlu gave no response.

"I'm talking to you. Take them off."

When, again Kerimoğlu didn't move, Durdu lost himself in a rage, grabbed Kerimoğlu and struck him hard just below his ear. Then he rammed him in the chest a few times with the butt of his rifle ...

Kerimoğlu staggered and was about to fall when Durdu grabbed his arm and hit him a few more times. "Take off your clothes!"

Groaning in pain, Kerimoğlu said, "Don't do this Durdu. No one till now has sacked the Kerimoğlu house. You won't get away with this!"

Durdu flew further into a rage. He dropped Kerimoğlu's arm and started kicking him.

"Etme. Etme." Don't. Don't, Kerimoğlu said from the ground. "You won't get away with this."

Durdu didn't stop. He stomped on Kerimoğlu some more.

"I know that I won't get away with this. That's why I'm stripping you down to your underwear. At least they'll say that I took the underwear of the great Kerimoğlu. Now do you understand?"

The women in the tent were sobbing. One of them flew herself onto Kerimoğlu. One of Durdu's men grabbed her and tossed her aside.

"If you don't strip down, if you don't take your clothes off with your own hands, I'll kill you."

The screams continued.

"Don't do this to me. Not in front of my entire family," he moaned.

Right then, Kerimoğlu's eyes looked to Memed, who was standing still, but trembling and biting his lip. Kerimoğlu implored him with his eyes and Memed felt something sizzle inside, bir şey "cızz" etti. His anger stirred inside. He turned to Cabbar. They looked at each other. Cabbar was biting his cheeks in anger, too. When he got angry, he bit his cheeks till they bled.

"Don't do this to me, Durdu Ağa," Kerimoğlu repeated. "Etme."

"Strip or I'll ... "

He placed the tip of gun barrel at Kerimoğlu's mouth. "Take off your clothes!"

Just then, in the blink of an eye, Memed flew out of the tent. "Don't move Deli Durdu, or I'll shoot," he shouted back inside. "Forgive me for this, but I'll shoot. What you are doing ... "

Then, from behind Memed, another reproachful voice came. "Durdu Ağa don't move! Let the man go and get on your way. I'll shoot. Our friendship goes way back. Don't let your death come from our hands." Ölümün bizim elimizden olmasın.

"Ölümün bizim elimizden olmasın," Memed repeated.

Durdu was totally taken by surprise. He never expected this.

"Demek böyle ha?" So that's how it is? he shouted back.

Then he turned his gun and fired two shots outside in Memed and Cabbar's direction.

"Look Durdu Ağa, that's not how it's done," responded Memed. Then he returned two shots that grazed past Durdu's ear. "Let the man be and get on your way. You've done enough. This is nothing but zulum, cruelty. Leave him be and get on your way!"

"Demek böyle İnce Memed? Demek? – Is that how it is İnce Memed? Is it?

"If you don't want to die, let the man go and come out of the tent."

Durdu kicked Kerimoğlu once more.

"Let's go friends," he said. "You'll get yours, İnce Memed. And you, too, Cabbar."

One of the men with Durdu, Recep Çavuş called out to Memed and Cabbar, "I really liked what you guys just did. Can I stay with you?"

"Stay Çavuş, stay," they said.

"You, too, Çavuş?" said Durdu.

"Me, too."

"Then you'll get yours, too."

Durdu went about fifty meters and then turned back and fired on them. "Today it's life or death!" he shouted.

They knew he would do this, so they had taken cover on the ground.

"Var git yoluna." Get on your way, "Durdu Ağa," Memed hollered. "Don't be childish!"

"It's either you or me, " Durdu said.

"Get going," said Cabbar, "Ölümün bizim elimizden olmasın."

Durdu stopped firing and took off with the remaining members of his gang.

After they left, Memed wondered what they could say to Kerimoğlu. "Ne diyelim?" What should we say to him? "Adamın yüzüne nasıl bakarız?" How will we look the man in the face?

Cabbar thought there was little they could say. "The man was good to us and we did him wrong. What should we say? Did you like what we did? This is what manhood is all about. Should we say, this is how we rob a man? Vazgeç!" – Let it go! – "Let's get on our way without being seen again."

But Memed was still wondering, "Ben ne deyim?" What should I say? "Ben ne deyim to Kerimoğlu?"

They approached the tent. They could hear cries and commotion inside. They opened the door. Two women kneeled over Kerimoğlu. They prayed and tended to his wounds.

"Kerimoğlu Ağa," Memed began. Everyone turned to look at him. At that moment, he felt that he wanted to leave without saying anything. But he couldn't.

"Ağa," he stuttered. "Kusura kalma." Forgive us. "We didn't know this would happen." Then he turned and started to run.

From behind him, Kerimoğlu yelled out, "Don't go without eating dinner my son. Gitmeyin ... " Don't go ...

Memed reached Cabbar and said, "Get up and let's go. I can't stay here any longer. My heart is burning so much for that man ... He's in pieces ... "

"Nothing can be done. What's done is done," said Cabbar.

"We should have killed that Crazy Durdu," Memed said.

"Killing him isn't so easy, Memed," said Cabbar. "He's a real clever scoundrel. If it were easy to kill him ... do you think I would have let him go like that!"[23]

****

Ali and Hasan are returning to their villages after working for three years in the Çukurova. With his earnings, Ali is planning to pay a dowry on a bride and to purchase a pair of oxen, a sweater for his mother, and a new roof for the family's house. Hasan is thinking of his son who was two when he left. He's not planning on telling anyone about the money he made. He's thinking of plowing the fields.[24]

Suddenly they hear a sound from the edge of the road. The sound of a trigger.

"Don't move."

"We're dead," Hasan said.

"We're done for," said Ali.

"Let's run. If they're gonna shoot, let them shoot. It's better to be shot than robbed. And if we aren't hit, we'll make it home."

Ali agreed. "Let's go … "

Shots rang out from behind them. Screaming, they hit the ground.

"Don't move from where you are. We're coming," a voice called out.

Ali and Hasan remained where they were.

Memed, Cabbar, and Recep Çavuş ran toward them.

Memed spoke, "Get up."

As if they were already dead, Ali and Hasan rose slowly to their feet.

"Where are you coming from?" asked Memed.

"From Çukurova, kardaş." From Çukurova, brother.

Cabbar smiled. "If that's the case, you must have made a lot of money. If not for you, we'd die of hunger. Give us the money."

"Just kill me," Hasan responded quickly. "For four full years … "

"Take out your money," Cabbar said.

"Shoot me now, Ağam."

"My fiancée has been waiting exactly six years," Ali said. "Just shoot."

"Exactly six years," Hasan said again.

Cabbar grabbed the bundle, soaking with sweat, under Hasan's arm and removed the money hidden inside a cloth.

"Please – shove your gun into my mouth and shoot me. I can't go home to my family with empty hands," said Hasan.

"Exactly six years. There's just no way. You have to shoot me. I can't go either."

"For four full years I drank Çukurova's poisonous water. I had malaria in my stomach."

"I'll kiss your hands and feet," said Ali to Cabbar, "just kill me."

"Kill me," Hasan repeated.

Memed's eyes began to water.

"Look here," he said, now speaking more compassionately. "No one is going to touch your money. Cabbar give him back his money. Take your money."

Hasan was stunned. Still frightened, he stuck out his trembling hand to Cabbar and took the money back. He didn't know what to say. "Allah uzun ömür versin size," fell from his lips. May God give you long lives. Then he started to weep.

"Uzun ömür," Ali said as well.

"Listen here," Memed said. "Don't travel through the Çanaklı flats. Deli Durdu's controlling them. He'll rob you down to your underwear. Good luck to you. İnşallah you'll embrace your fiancée, kardaş."

Hasan wept and wept, like a child. "Thank you. Thank you, kardaşlar. Berhudar olsun." May you prosper. "Let God save you from these mountains and reunite you with your loved ones."

They started to go, turned around to say a prayer, and then continued on their way.

As they took off, Ali echoed Hasan, "may you be reunited."

Hasan couldn't stop sobbing.

"Enough Bre Hasan," said Ali. "What's with the funeral dirge?"

"Şu dünyada ne kadar da iyi insanlar var," Hasan responded. "Did you see that lokma" – that tiny bite of a – "young eşkıya. If it hadn't been for him, the big one would have taken our money."

"No," said Ali. "They wouldn't have." And they decided to walk for two extra months if necessary to avoid the Çanaklı flats.

From behind, Memed said, "They'd have been happy if we killed them after taking their money."

"The tall one really begged to be shot!" said Cabbar.

"Who knows how hard and with what hope they must have worked," said Memed.[25]

****

Iraz, Hatçe's new cellmate, had burned her brother-in-law's house to the ground in revenge and grief for the murder of her son Rıza. Iraz had refused to marry her brother-in-law after her husband had died. This led to Rıza's death.

Hatçe thought it would be nice to have a can yoldaşı – a companion – in this lonely prison … but this poor woman was in so much pain. Who knew what had befallen her? No, she thought, she didn't want a can yoldaşı. This is an abominable place. No one should be pleased about anyone's coming here.

She wanted to speak with the woman and ask her, but couldn't quite bring herself to do so. Asking something of someone this depressed, someone struggling inside, caught between death and life, doesn't come easily. It's difficult to know what to say, what to ask. Hatçe was at a loss. All she could do was care for her.

It was evening, so she whipped up some bulgur soup on the stove. She took an onion and the soup that smelled of bitter oil inside.

The soup was still boiling a little. After it cooled down, Hatçe timidly approached Iraz.

"Teyze," Auntie, she said. "You're probably hungry. I made a little soup. Have some."

Iraz's eyes were completely empty. She stared straight into space, as if she were blind, and she looked like she couldn't hear a thing either.

"Teyze," she hesitantly repeated. "Teyze, have a little soup. Not a lot, just a little. You're probably hungry now."

Iraz wasn't even paying attention. Her eyes were completely empty. Turned to stone. Didn't even blink.

That night Hatçe couldn't sleep. The next day was the same. Iraz was the same. The following day, Hatçe awoke determined.

"Teyze!" she said. "I'll do anything, teyze! Etme!" Don't do this!

She took Iraz's hands in hers.

"Etme n'olur!" Please, don't!

The woman turned her wide open eyes to Hatçe. Her totally weary and dark eyes, with no light or glimmer left in them.

Hatçe insisted. "Tell me your troubles, teyze. I'll do whatever you need, teyze. Is there anyone who comes here without troubles? What would a person without troubles be doing here? Isn't it like that, teyze?"

Iraz whimpered a few words, "What are you saying kızım," my girl?

Hatçe was happy that Iraz had opened her mouth and spoken. She felt as if a huge weight had been lifted.

"Why are you like this, teyze? You haven't spoken ever since you arrived. And you haven't taken even a bite of bread."

"My son was valuable to his country. My son was the handsome one of the village. Is that a lot?" she said, and then fell quiet.

"When I saw you," Hatçe said, "I forgot my own troubles. Open up and tell me yours, teyze."

"If I burn down the house of the one who killed my son, if I break down its doors, is it a lot? If I kill each of them one at a time, is it a lot? If I cut them to pieces … "

"Ooohh my teyze, ooohhh! Damn!"

"The handsome one of the village," Iraz whimpered again. "If I kill them all, is it a lot?"

"Ooohh my, ooohh," Hatçe repeated.

"And then they brought me and threw me in here. And the one who killed my son walks around freely in the village. Let some others die, not me!"

"Hatun teyzem," Hatçe said. "You've already died from pain. You haven't had a bite to eat since you arrived. I'm going to make some soup."

This time, Hatçe decided to put lots of fresh butter in the soup. About a month after she had arrived, Hatçe had started to wash the clothes of some of the wealthy prisoners. She had saved a bit of money as a result. She sent the girl who brought things to the prisoners from the market to go and get some fresh butter. She was happier now. At least the woman now spoke. Konuşan insan, öyle kolay kolay dertten ölmez. A person who talks about their troubles doesn't easily die from them. It doesn't bode well for the person who doesn't talk, who buries things inside. This is why Hatçe was happy.[26]

As the days passed, Iraz and Hatçe became like mother and daughter, maybe even closer. The water they drank went down the same pipe. Their separate troubles became one. Hatçe learned all there was to know about Rıza and Iraz learned all there was to know about Memed. While Hatçe wished for news of Memed, Iraz tried to think of ways to prove who killed Rıza. And they spent their entire days and nights knitting socks, socks embroidered with the most sorrowful designs. The socks made by the girl who killed her fiancé and the woman whose son was murdered became famous. Knitted webs of sad colors and emotionally piercing designs. As long as the town had existed it had never seen embroidery this powerful, this painful, this beautiful.[27]

****

Memed, Cabbar, and Recep Çavuş enter the village to take Memed's revenge on Abdi Ağa. When they arrive at his house, however, they learn that he has gone to another village to hide. Everyone expects Memed to punish the ağa's family but, after the women implore him to find Abdi and kill him – o gavur, that infidel – not their small children, Memed again shows mercy. Recep Çavuş is annoyed. "With this heart of yours," he says to Memed, "you can't be an eşkıya or get your revenge."[28] *But Memed's mercy – "as wide as the sea" – becomes well known. Durmuş Ali tells Memed, "It was clear when you were born that you were going to be a good man. You did good by not killing the children."*[29]

Memed and his friends approach the relative's house where Abdi is hiding. The family denies that Abdi is there, but a gun battle with Abdi inside breaks out. A spark triggers a fire and winds carry the flames so quickly through the house and village that soon the entire village burns to the ground. Everyone thinks that Abdi is killed in the fire, but he survives by hiding in the family's belongings as they are carried out of the burning house. Memed and his friends retreat to the mountains. Along the way, Recep Çavuş dies from wounds he had suffered in the skirmish with the jandarma before the incident at Kerimoğlu's.[30]

****

During Memed's time there lived an old eşkıya, Koca İsmail, who was over ninety years old. He told stories of the old days in the plains of Çukurova.

"Fifty or sixty years ago, Çukurova was deserted in those days. It was just swamp and thicket. There were only tiny fields at the foot of the hills ... Then the migration began with a boom, the Turkmen migration ... Çukurova's finest days. Spruced up the bare trees, the soil, and the world ... In red and green colors, the migration began with a boom.

"We set off, passed over the mountains and settled in the Binboğa highlands. When the winters came, we went down to the Çukurova flats. The thickets and reeds were no use at all. It was all marshland. In the plains, the weeds grew to your knees twelve months of the year. Gazelles roamed the plains. Skittish ones with black-bordered eyes. We hunted them with the finest horses. The courage of a horse can be seen when it hunts gazelles. Çukurova's reeds stretched as high as the poplar trees. On the edges of the lakes, the tiny pedals on the reeds, radiating light like the light of day, spilled into the water. Daffodils spread over the whole of Çukurova from top to bottom. The winds of Çukurova carried their aroma day and night. Bir belalı işti, it was tough work, Çukurova. The white, frothy waves of the white-capped sea hammered it hard.

"The Turkmen tribes set up their many tents. Curly plumes of smoke rose everywhere. The Tecirli tribe settled on the Osmaniye Toprakkale plain, that is, in the upper areas on the sea side of the Ceyhan River that leads straight to the mountains. Below it, the Cerit tribe settled in the Ceyhanbekirli, Mustafabeyli, and Ceyhan district, the Bozdoğan tribe between Anavarza and the Hemite castles, the Lek Kürtleri between Anavarza and Kozan, the Sumbaslı tribe between the Sumbas river and the Toroslar, and the Tatarlı tribe between what is now the Ekşiler village and Kadirli. And sometimes they changed their locations. The Bozdoğan and Cerit tribes exchanged places. The most powerful tribe was the Avşar tribe. They settled wherever they liked. There was no getting in their way.

"This is more or less how I remember it. A huge conflict started with the Ottomans. There was a Bey named Kozanoğlu. He lived in what is now Kozan. In the beginning, all the tribes clashed with the Ottomans. Then came the Ottoman iron fist. They captured Kozanoğlu and took him away. And they exiled the Avşar to Bozok. They were scattered. The türküs of Dadaloğlu tell about the defeat of the tribes. And there was an elegy written for Kozanoğlu."

Koca İsmail paused here. Tears gathered in the hollows of his eyes. Lips trembling and in a deep, rich voice, he recited the Kozanoğlu elegy.

> Çıktım Kozan'ın dagına – I climbed Mount Kozan
> Karı dizleyi dizleyi – My knees pushing and pushing the snow
> Yarelerim göz göz oldu – My wounds punctured like eye-shaped
> holes
> Cerrah gözleyi gözleyi – Searching for a healer
>
> Olur mu böyle olur mu – Can it be like this, can it be
> Evlat babayı vurur mu – Does a son shoot his father
> Padisahın askerleri – Soldiers of the sultan
> Bu dünya böyle kalır mı – Will the world remain like this?
>
> Kara Çadır eğmeyinen – May the Dark Tent not bend
> Ucu yere değmeyinen – May its tips not touch the ground
> Ne kaçarsın koç Kozanoğlum – Why are you fleeing my ram
> Kozanoğlu

Beş bin atlı gelmeyinen. – May the five thousand armed riders not come.

"So it was that after all that, the Ottomans broke the tribes and moved into Çukurova. They distributed land and handed out deeds. They posted soldiers on the roads to the mountains so that we couldn't go to the highlands. No one could go there. The tribes continued to fall into ruin. Some from malaria, some from the heat ... epidemic spread ...

"The tribes never intended to settle and stay in Çukurova. But the Ottomans would give them vines and trees to plant. The tribes would first burn the roots and then plant them. That's why there are no trees in any of the villages now.

"Later, when the Ottomans noticed that all the tribes were disintegrating, they granted permission to go up to the highlands in the summer.

"And much later, the tribes began to turn their settlements into villages, and then to plant crops. That was the end of them. All that was solid melted into air. The world turned upside down. Humans got lazy. What the Ottomans wanted was accomplished."

Whenever Koca İsmail talked about the tribes he talked for days on end, never tiring. It would make him long desperately for an özgür bir dünya, a free world.

He would preface everything he said with, "I'm someone who saw Dadaloğlu." He was very proud of this.

"In 1917, 1918, 1919, 1920 ... the first world war and the defeat of the Ottomans, Çukurova was filled with deserters and eşkıyalar. And the Toroslar couldn't be passed because of the eşkıyas there.

"When the French occupation forces arrived in Çukurova, the eşkıyas and the deserters and the people of Çukurova, young and old, best and worst, wayward, good, bad, and the poorly raised, came together and fought to drive the enemy out. And they did. The enemy was driven from the entire country. A new regime arrived, a new era was opened.

"Some years after settling, towards the end of the nineteenth century, the conditions gradually made it necessary for the people to be tied to the land. The land slowly grew in value. The Turkmen who in no way wanted to settle and fought in every way not to do so, left the highlands and embraced the land. The fertile lands of Çukurova yielded forty to fiftyfold. No one had ever seen anything like it before. If you look at Çukurova in the years after 1900, we can see that almost all the marshes retreated at least a bit, the thickets were cleared and made into fields, and at least half or close to half of the completely unplanted Çukurova earth was planted.

"The new regime tried to end the small feudal lords (derebeyiler), the growth of the lords, and their absolute rule. In fact, the feudal system had been collapsing in those years all by itself. Many of the lords had fought to possess the land, to take as much of the empty land as possible. And they succeeded.

"They used every means to snatch the land from the hands of the poor people. Some used law, some bribery, and some force. The lands of the rich increasingly grew. A struggle began between the new rich and the people, who were seeking their rights and making desperate efforts for the land.

"The rich started to use the eşkıyas from the mountains as a weapon of force against the people. These eşkıyas grew in the mountains and gave the ağas protection against the regime. Without them, almost none of the ağas would have remained. And those ağas who couldn't find eşkıyas behind them in the mountains sent new eşkıyas to the mountains. As a result, the Toroslar were teeming with eşkıyas.

"Then, the interests of the ağas on the plains started to conflict, and they clashed in the mountains. The gangs in the hills continually fell upon each other, killing both each other and the poor people. And so the lands of the ağas grew.

"Ali Safa Bey was the son of one of the ağas who had fallen into poverty. In spite of being poor, the father schooled his son first at the Adana Sultan School and then sent him to Istanbul Law School. For some reason, Ali Safa Bey left half way through and returned to town to start practicing law. After going in and out of a lot of business, he came to his senses and got to work acquiring land.

"Because of the poverty, he first tried every cunning way to take back from the villagers all the land that had been taken from the hands of his father. That's how he discovered the tricks of grabbing land. He was not to be satisfied.

"The villagers by then were different from the villagers who had first settled, even from those who came right after them. The villagers now understood that land is gold, and they clung to it. A battle began between them and Ali Safa Bey that lasted for years. In this war, that son of a bitch Ali Safa Bey showed who he was. He devised various schemes and means to take the land from the hands of the villagers. In the beginning, using a tried and true method, he would take the side of two or three villages that had become enemies and fallen into conflict, and with the help of that side grab the lands of the other. This was the easiest way, and it was very effective. But it doesn't work for very long. The villages in conflict understand the situation and figure out who the real enemy is. They figure it out, though only after at least half of their land is gone. Ali Safa Bey's estate multiplied by the size of the lands of two or three villages.

"Over the years, Ali Safa Bey found all sorts of means and methods. Every one of them was exposed within a year or two. But, despite everything, he came out profiting. Little by little, at the end of every year, his estate grew.

"The situation came to a point where all of Ali Safa Bey's tricks were well known. No villager would fall into his traps. All possibilities, all options were cut. But still Ali Safa Bey found hope.

"In these days, there were eşkıyas in the mountains – deserters, thieves, murderers, rebels ... This time, Ali Safa Bey looked to them to secure his interests. He forged an agreement with the heads of one or two of them. And one or two of his own men went to the mountains. His eşkıyas rained hell upon the villagers. Now, whatever Ali Safa Bey said was done. After this, if any villager had a heart, it stirred with fear!!! In one night his house would be destroyed, his wife kidnapped, and he was tortured and murdered. Everyone knew that Ali Safa Bey was behind all this. No one could touch even a hair on his head. The jandarma went after the eşkıyas and shot at them.

"Ali Safa Bey's method became so familiar that the other ağas used it as well. As a result, the land of Çukurova began to be painted red with blood. Everyone started shooting everybody else. The eşkıyas in the mountains split into two or three or five or ten and attacked one another. In a single night, one gang would suddenly break up and another suddenly form.

"Only eşkıyas like Gizik Duran, Kürt Reşit, and Çötdelek, who were independent and didn't pay attention to the provocations of the ağas, strove as much as possible to protect the poor people against the ağas and eşkıyas. Although in the Toroslar the name and fame of many killers is forgotten, türküs for these eşkıyalar still travel around by word of mouth.

"İnce Memed's going to the mountains coincided with the battles between the eşkıyas who were securing the interests of the ağas and, in Çukurova, the groaning and suffering of the villagers whose lands had been taken by force."[31]

****

Memed and Cabbar walk all night, without saying a word. They reach the Akçaçam cliffs at dawn and look back over the plains where clouds of smoke rise in the village. Thinking Abdi is dead, Memed becomes determined to return to Değirmenoluk, gather the villagers and say, "Abdi Ağa is gone. The oxen that you have are now yours. There's no such thing anymore as part-nership. The fields are now yours, too. Cultivate them as much as you like." Cabbar is excited by the idea, and they walk to the village where Memed shares his plan with Durmuş Ali.[32]

"In the old days these lands belonged to everyone," he explained. "Before that infidel's father arrived. He did everything he could to take the lands from us. Before him everybody worked the lands they wanted, however they wanted."

"That's it," Memed said with some excitement. "That's how it will be again. Exactly like that."

Durmuş Ali bowed his head forward in thought as Memed continued:

"It will be like that again. Just like that. What do you say?"

"Keşki öyle olsa," Durmuş murmured, his eyes starting to fill with tears. If only it were so.

"Olacak," Memed repeated. It will be. He asked Durmuş Ali to call the villagers together so he could tell them what will be done.

"They will be liberated from slavery and servitude. What everyone grows will be theirs. The oxen in their hands will be theirs ... "

"Keşkiii!!!" exclaimed Durmuş Ali.

"The days of servitude are over," Memed affirmed. "With my gun in my hands, I'll guard these lands until death. And even thereafter ... "[33]

The rest of the villagers were hesitant at first. But as news of Abdi's death sank in, they became enthusiastic. The village filled with an unbelievable amount of commotion. Everyone let loose. Dogs howled, roosters crowed, and chickens ran from place to place. Children wept. In the barns, the donkeys brayed and the horses neighed. Ever since Değirmenoluk was Değirmenoluk, no such roar had ever been heard ... shrieks of joy, drums, türküler, and chants. "Bizim İnce Memedimiz. Our İnce Memed, Our İnce Memed ... "[34]

"Everyone will plant the fields as much as they like. No more giving two thirds."

"No more starving in the middle of the winter."

"No more begging like a dog."

"Our İnce Memed."

"No more selling the cows."

"No more oppression."

"Everyone can go where they like."

"Everyone can even take in a misafir" – a guest.

...

"Hatçe will be free."

"The five villages will put on a wedding."

"Bizim İnce Memedimiz."

...

The celebration went on for two days and nights. Then Memed asked everyone why, when it came to ploughing the fields, they hadn't thought of burning the thistles that made their work more difficult. "Wouldn't it be easier to plough then?" he asked.

"It would be," they agreed.

"Then we're going to burn the thistles – çakırdikenliğe ateş vereceğiz – he announced. "Ondan sonradır ki çift koşulacak." From now on, the fields will be ploughed.

"No longer will the thorns cut the legs of the oxen or the farmer," declared Durmuş Ali.[35]

They gathered the dried thistles and built a huge pile. Durmuş Ali took a piece of tinder and shoved it into the pile. Swirling flames consumed the heap. The villagers drew back and watched the thistles burn. Türküler, cries, dancing, and an overflowing sense of joy spread as the fire leapt across the plain. Cabbar fired shots into the sky.

Topal Ali came, however, and brought the news that Abdi did not die.

The villagers were immediately beside themselves in fear. Cabbar tried to reassure them. "If not today, then tomorrow." But Hürü Ana, Durmuş Ali's wife, cried out, "Oh the troubles that afflict us ... Now this ... Vay vay! Vay vay vay! Oh oh! Oh oh oh!"

The roar of celebration stopped. People returned to their homes, dogs stopped barking, and the roosters ceased crowing. It was as if there was not a single living creature left in the village. Some of the villagers turned against Memed. Sümsük, savsak – stupid and careless, "he became an eşkıya and he burned a village down ... look at him ... he boasted of killing Abdi, our Ağa ... Our Ağa can kill a hundred dogs like him with one shot. Our Ağa." They went to Abdi's house and congratulated his wives and children.

Memed supporters were distraught. They didn't go outside. For Durmuş Ali, it was like death. Hürü Ana fell ill and became bedridden. She didn't utter a word. Nor did Memed.[36]

****

Abdi and Ali Safa Bey hire Kalaycı, a famous eşkıya, to go after Memed, but Memed and Cabbar defeat Kalaycı and his men, and word spreads throughout Çukurova that Memed escaped the battle without a scratch. The villagers begin to take risks to protect İnce Memed.[37]

Yearning to see Hatçe, Memed slips into Çiçeklidere village in disguise to visit her in prison. They are speechless in each other's presence, but Memed learns that Hatçe and Iraz are to be transferred to another prison. The day of the transfer, Memed hides by the side of the road and takes the jandarma by surprise, stopping its convoy by shooting one of the soldiers in the leg. After a long standoff and gunfight, the soldiers release Hatçe and Iraz to Memed. The three receive shelter from some villagers who are more than happy to feed and care for "our İnce Memed."[38]

****

"It may be me today, but it's you tomorrow," Abdi told Ali Safa Bey. "This is what frightens me most ... So what if there are eşkıyas in the mountains. What is an eşkıya, anyway ... But this! This worries me. The issue is the land … Bir aklına düşerse köylünün, önüne geçilmez. If the idea gets into the mind of the peasant, there'll be no preventing it. It's not my being killed that worries me, it's this. You know this, Ali Safa Bey. If you ask me, the boy needs to be killed immediately, without another day passing. Bu oğlan eşeğin aklına karpuz kabuğu düşürdü. The boy's planting dangerous seeds in the minds of others. Don't let the opportunity pass another day … "

"I understand Ağam," said Ali Safa Bey. "I understand, but don't worry. If they don't bring his head and toss it on your front doorstep today, they'll do it tomorrow. Don't worry!"

Ali Safa Bey had ordered the jandarma sergeant Asım Cavuş, and an old ruthless eşkıya named Kara İbrahim to bring in Memed.

"I told them to cut off İnce Memed's head, put it on top of a stake, and bring it and plant it in front of Abdi Ağa's house. And that's what they'll do."

"He shouldn't live one more day," said Abdi. "Not one more day. İnşallah this is how it will be. What you have said will come true."

"İnşallah da var mı?" Ali responded. Can there be an inşallah here? "Mutlak öyle olacak." This is how it will definitely be. "Have you heard of Kara İbrahim?"

"I've heard of him."

"There, then!"[39]

With ruthless beatings, the jandarma turned whatever mountain village they entered into a scene of calamity. Screams of pain came from the families of the Taurus mountain villages. No one knew Memed's whereabouts. Those who pointed in some direction pointed in the wrong direction. Türküs were written and tales grew about how Memed had sprung the innocent girl Hatçe out of prison. Everyone left their work behind, and everywhere there was talk of İnce Memed.

In Değirmenoluk, the jandarma went straight to Durmuş Ali's house. They seized the old man and worked him over, but he didn't say a word. They threatened and grilled him. Nothing. They hit him with their rifles. Hürü Ana, holding tight to the old man like a scared bird, shouted at the jandarma. One soldier's baton quickly shut her up. The soldiers left the two old folks, dripping in blood, in the yard and went to the next house where they beat others.[40]

****

The high cliffs of Alidağı are barren rock and sharp as a knife. They'll cut through whatever roams upon them. They're covered with snow all four seasons. Because of the extreme cold, there's no sleeping at night atop the snowy heights of Alidağı.

Memed knew every rock, boulder, and cave there from when he used to hunt deer. This is the habitat of the long-antlered deer. At the peak there is a cave

114

with no direct path to it. Memed saw no other option. He knew the place well, and he knew that nobody else did.

"We'll make our home and live there," he tells Hatçe and Iraz.

"Till the amnesty comes," Hatçe responds."⁴¹

They spent the entire winter in the cave. They decorated it like a house more pleasant than that of a rich village ağa. They spread sweet smelling veronica grass on the floor and covered it with embroidered nomad kilims that gave off scents of spring. The kilims were given by Kerimoğlu as a dowry. Deer-skins covered the walls of the caves. Skins from deer with huge antlers. The antlers looked as though they had been polished. The fur of the skins glittered like gilt.

The winter was hard. To avoid freezing to death during the blistering storms on the top of the mountain they would huddle beside a fire they lit in the cave. For a month and a half, Memed had carved into the ceiling of the cave, opening a vent hole for the smoke to escape, but it wasn't enough. Smoke filled the cave, and during the storms they had to open the cave's entrance and step outside to breathe. They would freeze. When they felt like their hands and feet were about to fall off, they would throw themselves back inside the cave again, into the smoke.

They wrapped themselves in the deerskins, blankets, and kilims and clung to each other good and tight. When day broke, they peeled themselves apart, Memed went off hunting deer, and the women baked bread and knitted socks. The skins on the walls were the skins of the deer Memed shot. They would eat the meat and dry the skins. The entire winter there wasn't even one day when they didn't have meat.

Flour, butter, and salt were brought from the village by Topal Ali. He would leave them in a cave below for Memed to retrieve. Even he didn't know their whereabouts. So that there would be no trace in the snow, every time Memed left the cave he would drag a big ball of black shrub over his tracks. No matter how deep the tracks, the shrub would cover them, and its own trace would fade away within a half hour. They were safe no matter where the jandarma looked around Alidağı.⁴²

Iraz dreamed of taking revenge on the killers of Rıza and settling in Çukurova, in Adaca where the family had land, and where, as Hatçe recollected, "mounds of daffodils grow between the cliffs."

In one of his trips to the village, Memed is badly wounded in a clash with the jandarma. It takes two weeks for him to heal.⁴³

****

Abdi Ağa sends a scathing complaint to Ankara about not receiving his rightful share from the villagers, and, in town, he explains to the provincial governor and commander of the jandarma all that has happened. They are also angered and send the jandarma back to Değirmenoluk. The jandarma lock Hürü Ana in a shed and start the beatings again.[44]

****

Alidağı is blanketed again with snow, and the situation in the cave grows dire. There is nothing left to eat, and they are out of wood. Hatçe is pale and thin, but her belly is up to her nose: she is pregnant and, Iraz is sure, going to give birth at any moment.

One day the snow stops. "Either we should go into a village," Iraz tells Memed, "or we should get supplies up here, let's do whatever we're going to do … The child is about to come."

Memed leaves to get supplies, but Iraz later notices that he forgets to take the ball of shrub he uses to cover his tracks. She grows anxious.

Two days later, pale to the bone, Memed returns but knows he forgot the shrub and is afraid, too. "I was worried about you so I hurried back right away … "

Their fears are realized. A soldier has reported to Asım Çavuş that Memed was seen covering his tracks. The jandarma goes to the foot of Alidağı, with the entire village, shaken by the news, following close behind.

The first assault occurs towards evening. The jandarma ascends the mountain and, from above, hurls bombs into the mouth of the cave. Memed returns fire.

Hatçe starts to cry when she hears the sounds of gunfire. She is in labor.[45]

"Memed my boy," Asım Çavuş said, "Give up! You're totally surrounded. Closed in on all four sides. You can't escape. Soon an amnesty will come. Come and surrender! I don't want your death."

Memed gave no response. A shot shattered a stone right in front of Asım Çavuş.

Then the clash intensified. Shots rang out from both sides.

"I'll wait here a week, or a month," said Asım Çavuş. "Sooner or later you'll run out of ammunition."

Clenching his teeth, Memed finally spoke back.

"I know Çavuş, I know," he yelled. "That's how it will be in the end. Until then I won't leave even one of you alone. I'll shoot you all. I know Çavuş. I won't surrender. In the end, you'll carry my dead body from this cave. Do you understand Çavuş?"

"It's a pity for you. It's a pity for a man like you. If you shoot all of us, more jandarma will come. What will you gain? An amnesty will come this year. Come and surrender, İnce Memed!"[46]

Memed doesn't surrender, but he is injured. Hatçe gives birth to a boy, but her condition worsens. With ammunition running out, Memed decides to

116

surrender. *"Name my son Memed," he tells Iraz, and he calls out, "I surrender." Asım Çavuş is suspicious. He has the jandarma halt their fire and goes up to the opening of the cave.*

"Geçmiş olsun, İnce Memed!" he said. May the worst be over, İnce Memed!
    "Thanks."
Iraz crouched in the corner.
"I still don't believe you're surrendering, İnce Memed," Asım Çavuş said.
Memed was silent. He extended his arms for handcuffs.
Iraz suddenly jumped like an arrow from where she was sitting.
"Çavuş, Çavuş, do you think that you made İnce Memed surrender?"
She went to the corner, drew the kilim back from over the baby, and held him up.
"This is what made İnce Memed surrender! And you're proud to be a man."
Asım Çavuş hardly expected this. He looked at Hatçe, then at Iraz, and then at Memed. His mouth froze with a smile. He extended his hand to Memed and removed the handcuffs.
"İnce Memed!" he said, falling silent.
They stood there, face to face without saying a word.
"İnce Memed, under these conditions, I'm not a man who can accept your surrender."
He took five rounds from his waist and threw them on the ground. "I'm going. Shoot at me from behind," he said.
He threw himself outside, screaming as he did.
Memed fired at him from behind.[47]

Asım Çavuş told his troops that Memed had tricked him, and with a storm on the horizon, they should return before they all died from the cold. The huge storm came towards evening and Alidağı was again crowned in white.[48]

****

With İnce Memed alive, the villagers in Çukurova feel secure again. Everyone had received their land because of him, and his legendary evasion from capture protected them from the wrath of the cruel ağas. Koca Osman, the elder of Vayvay village near Alidağı, calls Memed "Şahinim" – My hawk. The villagers are excited that the coming amnesty will allow İnce Memed to settle in the village. Koca Osman has a home built for him in Vayvay.

Memed, Hatçe, and Iraz remain on the run, however, and near Alayar they are surrounded by the jandarma under Yüzbaşı Faruk.

Memed hears Hatçe's scream – "Yandım," I've been shot – but doesn't turn around. He fires round after round in the Yüzbaşı's direction. This is too much to bear. He fires off more rounds and then goes to Hatçe's side. She is laying flat out, lifeless, the child by her side.

117

Memed loses it, sprays more fire, and throws grenades at the jandarma. Iraz does as well. The Yüzbaşı is injured and the jandarma retreat. Memed weeps, and Iraz collapses in tears by Hatçe's body. She has the same look on her face she had the day she was jailed.

They take Hatçe's body to the village for a proper burial, and Memed, Iraz, and little Memed return to the mountains.[49]

****

They found a cave at the peak and sat down at its entrance. The leaves on the trees were falling. A bird chirped. A white rock dove rose from the cliffs across the way. A lizard hopped onto a log. Just then, the child in Memed's arms awoke and let out a cry ...

Iraz came over. She took hold of his hand and looked him in the eye.

"Kardaş!" Iraz said. "Kardaş!" "I'm going to tell you something, İnce Memedim."

Memed waited without moving.

"Kardaş. Give this child to me and I'll go to the villages of Antep. He'll die in these mountains. He'll die from hunger ... I've given up revenging my Rıza. In place of him, we have this one! Give him to me and I'll go. I'll raise this dear child."

Memed slowly lifted the child into her arms. Iraz took him and pressed him against her bosom.

"Rızam!" she said. "My Rızam."

She took off the guns slung around her body and placed them in a pile.

"Sağlıcakla kal İnce Memed," she said. Take care of yourself.

Memed held Iraz's arm. The child stopped crying. Memed looked into his face and eyes for a long time.

"Uğurola," he said.[50]

****

Cabbar brings news of the amnesty. "I'm going to surrender." Memed doesn't utter a word and enters the village in broad daylight with a darkened face, hollowed eyes, and a wrinkled brow. That small flash of resoluteness, though, shines in his eyes. He walks as though he's drunk and about to faint. Worried women watch with fear in their eyes. Children walk speechlessly behind.

Hürü Ana runs after him and grabs him by the collar. "You fed them Hatçe and now you're going to surrender? Abdi Ağa will come again and settle in the village like a pasha. Avrat yürekli, Memed. For the first time, Dikenlidüzü didn't go hungry. For the first time, it prospered. Are you going to stick us with Abdi Ağa again? Where is your courage İnce Memed? Are you really going to surrender? ... Look at all these villagers, look at these people looking

118

into your eyes. You're going to surrender? You're going to bring Abdi back upon us? Beautiful Döne's rolling over in her grave. Beautiful Hatçe's rolling over ... "

Koca Osman is there, too. "İnce Memed, Şahinim. Your home is ready. So are your fields. The villagers bought this horse for you, too. Not like the other eşkıyas. When you arrive in Vayvay, drums will sound to greet you, Şahinim. Ali Safa Bey and Abdi Ağa be damned ... Hop on the horse and be on your way."

Memed does just that and motions to Topal Ali to follow him. They meet outside the village, and Topal Ali tells Memed where he'll find Abdi. "At night he's scared to take a step out of his house." Memed rides off into the darkness.[51]

He dismounted in the courtyard in front of the house and tied the horse to the branch of a big dark mulberry tree. He used his dagger to lift the latch of the front door. There was a light on upstairs. He climbed the stairs by threes. When the women and children saw Memed, all hell broke loose and they scurried straight for the room in the back.

Abdi Ağa had been stretched out sleeping with his arms at his side. "What is it? What's going on?" he asked as he awoke.

Memed arrived, grabbed Abdi's arm, and shook him:

"Ağa Ağa! I'm here Ağa!"

Abdi Ağa opened his eyes. At first he couldn't believe it. Then he opened his eyes wide. Even the dark of his eyes turned white.

Outside a huge commotion stirred.

Memed drew his gun, aimed and fired into Abdi Ağa's chest three times. The wind from the shots put out the light of the lamp in the room.

Memed bolted like lightning down the stairs and jumped on his horse. Just then, the jandarma got word of what was happening and fired at the house. Memed rode the horse straight to the Toroslar.

****

At dawn he entered the village. Both he and the horse were drowning in sweat. The horse gleamed in the light from head to toe, beaming all over. It stood tall and upright. The villagers gathered around. Memed rode the horse right up to Hürü Ana.

"Hürü Ana! Hürü Ana!" he said. "It's done. Hakkınızı helal edin."

He rode off in the direction of Alidağı in a cloud of dust and was soon out of sight.

It was time to harness the animals and plough the fields. The five villages of Dikenlidüzü gathered together to celebrate. The young girls wore their prettiest outfits. The older women wore their finest sakiz-white scarves. The drums beat ... Even Durmuş Ali forgot his poor health and came out and danced. Later, early one morning, they all went out together and set the field of thistles on fire.

Not a word was heard from İnce Memed again. He dropped out of sight.

O gün bu gündür – Since then – Dikenlidüzü köylüler her yıl çift koşmadan önce, every year in Dikenlidüzü before they harness the animals and plough the fields, büyük bir toy düğünle ateş verirler. They burn the thistles with a huge wedding feast.

Ateş, üç gün üç gece düzde, doludizgin yuvarlanır. The blaze swirls fullblown on the plains for three days and three nights.

Çakırdikenliği delicesine yanar. Yanan dikenlikten çığlıklar gelir. The thistles burn like mad. Screams come from inside the burning thorny patches.

Bu ateşle birlikte de – and together with this blaze – Alidağın doruğunda bir top ışık patlar, a ball of light bursts atop Alidağı. Dağın başı üç gece ağarır, gündüz gibi olur. The mountain's peak turns white for three nights, just like in the daytime.[52]

Notes

1 *İM1*, 9, 10, 19, 32, 52–53.
2 Ibid., 12.
3 Ibid., 20.
4 Ibid., 15.
5 The narrative of the story in Turkish is told in the past tense.
6 Ibid., 15–17.
7 Ibid., 22.
8 Ibid., 52–59.
9 Ibid., 59–61.
10 Ibid., 79–80.
11 Ibid., 94.
12 Ibid., 101.
13 Ibid., 116–17.
14 Ibid., 122.
15 Ibid., 123–24.
16 Ibid., 148–55.
17 Ibid., 132.
18 Ibid., 159.
19 Ibid., 175.
20 Ibid., 177–79.
21 Ibid., 184.
22 Ibid., 188–89.
23 Ibid., 190–95.
24 Ibid., 196–201.
25 Ibid., 201–4.
26 Ibid., 214–16.
27 Ibid., 218.
28 Ibid., 243.
29 Ibid., 247.
30 Ibid., 284–85.
31 Ibid., 289–94.

32 Ibid., 304.
33 Ibid., 323.
34 Ibid., 324–25.
35 Ibid., 327.
36 Ibid., 328–32.
37 Ibid., 344.
38 Ibid., 373–85.
39 Ibid., 388.
40 Ibid., 390–91.
41 Ibid., 391.
42 Ibid., 402–3.
43 Ibid., 404–7.
44 Ibid., 409–10.
45 Ibid., 412–17.
46 Ibid., 418.
47 Ibid., 420–21.
48 Ibid., 421.
49 Ibid., 426–30.
50 Ibid., 430–31.
51 Ibid., 433.
52 Ibid., 436.

III
Vayvay[1]

The ancient, fractured ruins and remains of a Roman castle sit above the fertile plain of Anavarza. The cliffs on which the castle sits resemble a huge ship extending from north to south. The Anavarza ship forever forges slowly ahead on a still sea without wavering …

In the middle of the Anavarza plain is the Akçasaz marsh, a long, dark, buzzing, broad, impenetrable waterside thicket with tall reeds. The marsh thicket is so dense that neither can a bird fly nor a snake slither through it. On the edges of the marsh are the houses of the Türkmen villages built of dried reeds and straw … The Akçasaz begins in the south where the Savrun and Ceyhan rivers meet. In the north it ends just under the village of Vayvay.

The land of Anavarza is so fertile that it yields crops three times in a year. A new plant sprouts forth every day from this fresh and crisp, dark, oily, soft and fecund soil. Each plant is huge. The same flora that grow in other areas grow two, three, four times their size here. And the colors of the flowers, the fresh green herbs, and the trees are something to behold. The green is the green of crystal green, the yellow the yellow of pure, amber yellow. The red is ablaze, sparkling and shining, and the blue a thousand times blue. The wings and shells and backs of the birds, butterflies, beetles, and ants scintillate in a thousand extraordinary, magical colors. The beetles, butterflies, birds, and grasshoppers flurry about like a storm on the plain. You look one day and a burst of butterflies, flashing and scattering in a thousand colors, whirls and swirls on the Anavarza plains … Yellow, red, green, blue, white butterflies, each as large as a bird, intermingling in the thousands, in the millions, swirling in a huge butterfly twister, rising to the sky, floating down and spreading across the plain, and then suddenly rising again, taking to the air and clouds, making the world, an unattainable, awe inspiring, utterly magical world ...

The fireflies of the plains are huge, too. At night the fields are lit up like they have been decorated with the light of a million stars. The plants and herbs, trees and flowers, leaves and branches kindle and fade until morning. So many fireflies, flying hither and thither one on top of another. A twisting blaze of stars swirls about, with the flames on the ground and those in the sky surging, converging, and intertwining with one another ...

On the Anavarza plain, everything – the plants, trees, bugs, birds and animals – exist in an endless state of coming together and sowing more life. The beings on the Anavarza plain are unique creatures of an abundant, lush, scintillating, and magical world.

And, with fields of bright yellow daffodils surrounding it on all sides, no stench comes from the Akçasaz marsh. The daffodils blossom as large as roses, as their aromas blow gently from the soft soil and permeate every-thing – the heat, the rocks, plants, trees, people, flies, wolves, and birds. Everything in Anavarza smells of narcissus. The scent is strong under the sun in the heat of the day, so strong, that it makes the people of Akçasaz and all the other creatures, including the birds and wolves, groggy and dizzy ...

Coming down from the Toroslar onto the plain, the plain is as quiet as can be. Not a sound can be heard, not a bird, not a stream, not a soul. The flat plain absorbs them all. Especially when there's sun and heat, not a çıt can be heard. It stays like this all the way to the edges of Akçasaz. Then, all of a sudden, a boom erupts, astounds you and curdles your blood. All kinds of unfamiliar sounds blending together spring from the marsh. The crows and calls of shouting and screaming birds, the croaks of the frogs, the stirring of the marsh's waters, the strange sounds of insects, the humming buzz of the thicket, the rustling of the reeds, the crows of the roosters, the barks of dogs, and the howls of the coyotes all coalesce in the reeds and burst on the bor-ders of the marsh like a canon. Akçasaz frightens a person. And that's why people don't enter there easily ...

The land of Anavarza is not just land, it's gold, and one person who knows this is Ali Safa Bey. Ali Safa Bey feels the value of the land deep down inside. Everyone has some kind of ambition, some kind of thirst. Ali Safa Bey's incurable, blind love and desire, the worst kind of it, is for the fertile land of Anavarza. Every morning at sunrise, as the world awakens, he plants his feet solidly on the dark soil, his eyes flickering from the zest of the Anavarza plain. The awakening dazzles and overwhelms him. He's beside himself with the sight of the insects intertwined with one another, sleek and robust slithering snakes, huge green frogs sparkling with the freshest green and riding one on top of the other, speedy turtles, bugs with hard shells of a thousand dazzling colors, bees, birds, gazelles, huge flowers, overflowing crops, saturated rice paddies bursting in green, butterflies, streams, swamps, springs, paths, dust piles, the circling and falling silver clouds – this ebullient, enchanted, vibrant *dünya* – world – that resembles the awe of the apocalypse, endlessly mating and creating more life, and he seeks the rebirth of the world, his head spins and he's totally overwhelmed with joy. He wants to take the Anavarza plain into his arms and hold it tight.

When there was not an inch of land in the Anavarza plain, he took possession of many farms, but he remained unsatisfied. Why shouldn't he possess the entire Anavarza plain? Or at least why shouldn't he greatly expand his lands? Ali Safa Bey always says that life is a struggle. Even more so, much more, the land is a struggle. If life is not a struggle, nothing is. If the land is a struggle, it is the most sacred of all struggles. And what good is humanity in this world if it doesn't struggle? Ottan çöpten ne farkı olur? – What would make it different from grass or garbage?

But the struggle for land has gradually become more difficult. The enemy of this land, of Çukurova, of Anavarza, of the heat, the flies, the reed huts, of settlement – the Türkmen who were forcibly and with difficulty settled in the land have gradually understood that there's no remedy for their troubles other than the land. The days of buying fifty dönüms of land for five kilos of salt, a goat, ten lira, a sack of herbs, and a cow are long gone. Fifteen or twenty years ago, an entire village, land and yurts in all, could be bought for three thousand lira, and the villagers could settle in a different place. As for now, the situation had changed dramatically. Those living in reed huts are even prepared to shed blood for the land. When Ali Safa Bey was deeply bothered by something, he was able to see a more conniving way. He needed to be able not to show his ambition at all. It was his greed and the value that he gave the land that opened the eyes of the villagers. Contending with them was harder, but it was also more satisfying. It was a way of being that suited a person. And, something as valuable as the land shouldn't be so easy to take into one's possession.

Vayvay village is one of the villages of the Anavarza plain. It is slightly bigger than the others. The villagers there have become an obstacle standing in Ali Safa Bey's way. Nothing budges them, neither the eşkıyas nor fear of the government, neither promises nor threats, nothing. Like the white and yellow everlast flowers, the people of Vayvay have stuck to the land, stood their ground and struggled against all the troubles that came to them. If Ali Safa Bey could prevail against Vayvay village, the rest would be easy.[2]

****

A slight drizzle fell, faintly, like a misty fog. There was no breeze. Fog covered the Anavarza plain. The sun was rising. In the east, beyond the fog, a hazy skylight came and went. A man, covered in an embroidered wool cloak, his knees tucked tightly to his stomach, crouched asleep. His head rested atop his rifle that was laid out over the root of a thorny dark evergreen bush – the karaçalı. Overhead, just above the top of the karaçalı a flock of birds passed, squawking and squeaking and letting all hell break loose. The man opened his eyes, and then closed them. A short while later, he straightened up, rubbed his eyes, and glanced around vaguely. His body was numb, his knees ached. Stretching, he rose to his feet, felt a bitter taste in his mouth, and spat. His spit pierced a spider's web and fell on a branch of the bush. He leaned down, picked up his rifle, and slung it over his shoulder. His silver ornamented Circassian dagger hung downward from his left hip to his knees. Alongside that, above his waist he fastened his nagant pistol. Over his thick, hand-knitted, multicolored silk shirt hung three rounds of cartridges. The large black binoculars that hung from his neck looked brand new, as though they hadn't been touched. His embroidered sandals made from thick wool were also new. His hand-woven wool socks came up to his knees. He pulled up his light-brown wool trousers, dyed with the shell of walnuts, that are woven and worn by the villagers of the Toros mountains ...

He walked eastward. Exhausted, his knees buckled. He had been on the move for four days. He finished the food he had had in the afternoon the day before, but he wasn't hungry now. Hunger didn't enter his mind at all. Four days ago he was ambushed by soldiers at Savrungözü. There were a lot of soldiers, and they fired a hail of bullets at him. Thankfully the ambush occurred in the evening. And, when darkness fell, it had started to rain. Towards midnight, he snuck like a cat through the wall of soldiers without making a sound. There was no one living in the mountains any more. Soldiers were everywhere and throngs of well-armed villagers had joined them in hunting down the eşkıyas, bush by bush, cove by cove. Just a week ago, the famous Koca Ali, who had taken refuge on a steep mountain peak, was captured by thousands of villagers who scaled the mountain.

There was only one place he could find refuge, only one glimmer of hope, one path of salvation, and that was the village of Vayvay, with Koca Osman in Vayvay village.[3]

****

Veli, Koca Osman's neighbor, at whose door Memed first knocks, takes Memed to Koca Osman's.

"Osman Ağa, Osman Ağa, misafirin – your guest – has come, and I've brought him."

The door opened right away.

"Welcome, safalar getirdi konuk," a woman said. "Tanrı misafiri. Veli, come in as well. It's still early. Koca Osman is repairing a saddle, come in."

"I'm sleepy," the man said as he left.

"Thanks, Veli," said the woman, and she called the visitor inside. "Come in kardaş."

"Who's that who's come?" Koca Osman's deep voice came from over near the furnace.

"No one I recognize as far as I know. A Tanrı misafiri. Wearing an aba. Dağlı olacak – will be someone from the mountains."

"A dağlı?" Koca Osman asked. "Dağlı demek, dağlı, ha? Eh, welcome safalar getirdi. Come, come sit at the head of the fire, come sit over there. Is it raining?

"It's drizzling."

Koca Osman put his saddle down and gave the traveler, who remained standing, a good look from head to toe.

"Why are you standing there, sit down kardaş," he said. "My God, have a seat my boy. What happened to you?"

Koca Osman rose, placed his hand on his guest's shoulder, and bent down.

"Have a seat yavrum."

He didn't sit.

"Kamer, bring a döşek and spread it out on the floor for our valued visitor."

"I'm bringing it," she replied from the other room.

"My son," Koca Osman said, "visitor, your aba is very wet. Where are you coming from, where are you going?

"I'm coming from the mountains and I'm going to Koca Osman's," Memed responded in a happy voice.

"You're coming to Koca Osman's? That's strange."

"Strange," said the visitor.

Kamer Hatun brought the döşek, and spread it in the left corner of the hearth.

"Here you are, kardaş."

"Have a seat my boy," Koca Osman exclaimed. "Take off your aba and sit down. It's the first time in my life that I've seen a visitor who doesn't take a seat."

He was hesitant and couldn't quite reach his aba.

Kamer Hatun leaned over and spoke into Koca Osman's ear.

"There's something seriously wrong with this child."

"What could it be?" he asked with pity and worry. "Is something wrong with you visitor?"

The visitor smiled.

"You didn't recognize me Osman Emmi?" Memed said with a voice full of love.

Koca Osman got real close to the visitor, squeezed his shoulders, and looked into his face.

"İnce Memed, şahinim – my hawk – yavrum! You, misafir, you look like my yavrum, şahinim," he said with joy. He wrapped his arms around Memed and shook and shivered with chills from head to toe. "Is it you, is it you şahinim, my guest? Are you the Tanrı misafiri? Are you him?"

Memed was in no condition to utter even a single word. He stood frozen in place and drifted away in a sweet dream.[4]

****

Ali Safa Bey's men raid Vayvay köy and set Hasan Yobazoğlu's home on fire. Ali Safa Bey had previously traded his rare, purebred Arabian horse for the deed to Hasan's land. The horse was legendary in Çukurova. Ali Safa Bey had said that the horse was as smart as a person, that he understood absolutely everything. But the land of Vayvay was more valuable to him than the horse. After the deal, Hasan boasted that Ali Safa Bey wanted the land so badly that he would have traded his wife for the deed. That's why Ali Safa Bey sent his men to burn Hasan's house to the ground, leaving Hasan and his family homeless. During the fire, Hasan managed at the last minute to save the horse from the burning stable, but the horse escaped. This was bad news for Ali Safa Bey. He wanted the horse killed. It was like an open wound for him.

The blaze at Hasan's left the village in shock. Only Koca Osman wasn't particularly awed by it. Ali Safa Bey's men noticed that he spoke strangely and confidently that there was nothing to worry about – that a pure-hearted young man had arrived who was stronger than the huge government and who even the mightiest men should fear. When Ali Safa Bey's men reported back to the Bey, they told him that the villagers were good and scared, except for Koca Osman who looked like he was up to something. But Ali Safa Bey was confident as well. "We'll overcome whatever game or trap he has in mind. I'm strong. Strong and right."[5]

The elders of the village debated what to do. Ali Safa's man in the village, Zeynel, suggested the villagers move to another village in Çukurova. He said that Ali Safa Bey has the deeds of the land and the support of the government and eşkıyas. "He'll force us out. Sooner or later, he'll remove us," said Zeynel. Koca Osman thought this nonsense. "Half of those who already went, left out of fear, the other half from being worn down and losing hope. Only a few went with five or ten lira from Ali Safa in their hands. A few of them thought that they would find very good land. Things have changed now. The very good has changed. You haven't heard, but things have changed. There's nowhere in Çukurova to go and settle."[6]

****

Another raid.

"What is this Osman, what is happening to us?"

126

"Ali is trying to scare us, what could it be! This is a really old method."[7]

Koca Osman grabbed his rifle, went outside, and shot one of the men in the kneecap.

"I'm old, in the dark only the shadows move, and still I hit him," he told Memed later. "If another comes again tomorrow, I'll shoot him. The next day, another … each day I'll take one out, until there are none left … This time it was the kneecap. Next time I'll aim right for the heart."

Koca Osman was not alone in wanting to fight back. At the Muhtar's the next day, the village imam, Ferhat Hoca, said that human beings are subjects to God only. It is their duty to resist their enslavement to other human beings. Those who left the village, he said, are cowards. Since there's an Ali Safa Bey under every stone, they'll find only more misery where they go. They should stay and resist. "Allah kulu kul yaratmış, kulu kimseye kul yaratmamış. Diretmeyen insan Allaha karşı insandır."[8]

****

Koca Osman told Memed that while he was in the mountains, they had settled Seyran Kız, a young woman whose beauty and suffering at the hands of Ali Safa Bey's relatives was renowned, in the house prepared for Memed. Seyran talks only with Kamer Ana, but every night the villagers listen as she sings the most sorrowful laments with a voice that pierces the mountains and rocks. "Her rage burns like a flame inside," said Koca Osman. "It makes her even more beautiful."

Memed knew about Seyran. She was from Harmanca, in the mountains. She had come to Vayvay to be near her closest childhood friend, Aziz, after her father had Aziz sent to a relative in Vayvay, Seyfali, in order to keep them apart. In Vayvay, several good-for-nothing nephews of Ali Safa Bey started stalking Seyran. They lived on farms, but they had been to school and, along with Sergeant Zülfo of the jandarma, spent their time gambling, drinking, abusing women, stealing, and killing – many things that had never been seen among the Türkmen. They surprised people that human beings could be like this.

Seyran did her utmost to avoid them. One day, though, they ambushed Seyfali's house and abducted her. Rumors floated about one of them being in love with her as well as about how they had raped her. No one knew for sure what had happened, and no one would.

Aziz got a gun and so much ammunition that it weighed him down when he hung it on his body. He found the brothers and Zülfo in a hut in Bozkuyu, a village in the hills. He opened the door, kneeled at the threshold, and shot them one by one. Other than Seyran, no one inside was left alive. When he finished, he calmly took Seyran's hand, helped her up, and looked for a long time into her eyes. Then he kissed her forehead and ran down to Vayvay.

It was afternoon when he arrived at the jandarma station. He shot the first jandarma that came toward him. The others then barricaded themselves in the station and shot back. Aziz fired at them for three hours. Then he went and got some gasoline, rags, and matches, returned to the station, and set it on fire. As he did, he held the door closed so no one could escape. When the jandarma hurled themselves outside, he shot and killed them. More soldiers arrived and a long shootout followed in which many jandarma were shot. When he ran out of bullets, Aziz rose from where he had been firing, walked towards the jandarma as they shot him who knows how many times.

The jandarma displayed Aziz's corpse in front of the Jandarma Command for two days. The people looked upon his small body as they looked upon a saint – an aziz – with reverence and love. After two days, the jandarma threw the body into a pit. The people retrieved it and gave Aziz a proper burial.

Seyran was jailed. When her father heard the terrible news a few days later, he fell ill and died. Seyran's mother, brothers, and relatives came to Çukurova to see her, but she wouldn't speak a single word to them. When she got out of jail, she went right away, as she would every Friday from then on, to Aziz's grave among the myrtle bushes on the highest hill in town. There, she would sing the warmest, most soulful and stirring dirges with her beautiful voice. She moved into the house built for Memed after Memed dropped out of sight following the battle with Kalaycı, the eskıya hired by Ali Safa and Abdi to kill Memed. All night long, she sang such beautiful dirges for Aziz. The young girls of the village stayed up till morning memorizing them. They were now sung throughout Çukurova.

Seyran worked by herself. She accepted nothing from anybody. She was still beautiful, so beautiful that the villagers of Çukurova looked upon her not as a woman but as a sacred creation.

Seyran smiled only one time after Aziz was shot – when she heard that İnce Memed had killed Kalaycı. She hadn't been interested in anything since the day she arrived in Vayvay, but that day she burned with curiosity about İnce Memed. Memed would leave Vayvay before she could see him, but Koca Osman told her that, "he has such eyes, huge, grand eyes. When you look at his face, you can't see anything other than his huge, radiant, gleaming eyes. His eyes are so potent that, if you look at them for a long time, your heart beats quickly. No one can shoot him, if he's ever shot I'll be ruined. I won't be able to live, I'll die. Moreover, his trigger finger works so fine, so fine, his finger is so quick that you can't see it, he can't be shot. He'll come again."[9]

****

Koca Osman's behavior in the village had changed so much that people began to suspect he was hiding something. Before they could find out, Memed leaves Vayvay and heads for the Toroslar. He spends days in the mountains, not meeting anyone, until late one night, on his way to Değirmenoluk, he stops

*at Sarı Ümmet's house. Ümmet hears Memed knocking and gets up quickly to
tell him to return to the Toroslar immediately. Someone must have seen him
because Kara İbrahim's gang is going house to house searching for him.
Ümmet gives Memed a bag of ammunition and some food, and insists that he
not go to Değirmenoluk. Gradually, though, his longing for his village grew.[10]*

A fire of intense yearning for the village had ignited inside and was burning
and consuming him. He knew that he might be going to his death but he
couldn't stop. He needed to see his village. What's happened to the people of
the village? Did they still burn the thistles with the great feast and celebration? Was Durmuş Ali Emmi still lifting his tired old leg in the air and
dancing the halay? Had Hürü Ana's fury waned? What an angry woman she
was. Her rage shook the earth and rocked and rattled the ground and sky.
Were everyone's oxen everyone's, were everyone's cultivated lands theirs?
  ...

He thought about Ali Safa Bey, Arif Saim Bey and the other ağas of
Çukurova ... and couldn't understand why he would be their enemy. Abdi
Ağa was killed, but Abdi Ağa wasn't their relative ... what had Memed done
to them, that just for him they had filled the Toros with the jandarma? He
simply couldn't understand why.
  ... Bu dünya bana dar geldi. There's not enough room in this world for
me. Gene döndüm koca Torosa. Again I returned to the great Toros. Kimse
bilmez nerde kalır ölümüz. Ben Torosa ölmeye geldim. Nobody knows
where our death takes place. I've come to the Toros to die. Baba toprağıma.
To my fatherland. Death smells sweet to me. There once was a man who was
an eşkıya, İnce Memed, the disdainful world of the ağas and beys didn't
accept ... The earth and sky rejected him as well. Where can I go, Ümmet
Ağam? Bir kanadı kırık kuşum ki ... I'm a bird with a broken wing that,
were I even as small as a finger, there's no thicket that would allow me in.

*His mother's face came to his eyes, Hatçe, little Memed, Iraz, Koca
Süleyman. And he thought of Kerimoğlu and Cabbar ... a brave man, a
friend ... he had married and had two children, one girl and one boy. Should
he go to Cabbar? They wouldn't leave Cabbar alone, or Koca Süleyman ...
where to go?[11]*

What if he died without seeing the village? The huge sycamore tree, Kulaksız, Kulaksız's mill, koca çınarın büveti, kınalı yol, çakırdikenli Dikenlidüzü,
the trees, bushes, devedikenleri, the village chickens, the bobbly yellow chicks
that wander around behind the broody hens. He longed for absolutely
everything. For Durmuş Ali, for his warm, tender, friendly eyes, so humane,
full of love, and compassion ... For Hürü Ana more humane, more ...
strong, stubborn, more humane than everyone. She would give her life for

those she loved. One day while he slept, she stroked his hair ... Memed couldn't forget that warm, mother, sister, the warmth of her friendly hands, their friendship, softness, and tenderness ... [12]

****

He could see his house from a gorge near the village, where he used to play as a child. The soil of its earthen roof was a mixture of colors. In the burning white heat of the day it sparkled like broken glass. His father had brought the special soil from far away. It kept the roof from leaking. His lovely, soft, love-full mother came to his eyes, and he felt a loneliness he hadn't felt his entire life.

He couldn't quite see Hatçe's home or the huge tree in front of it where, his heart beating, he had whistled for her like a hoopoe bird and she – a delicate and loving girl – came out to meet him. Something stuck in his throat, teardrops rolled down from his eyes.

Memed looked towards Abdi Ağa's house. A thick plume of smoke rose from the chimney. "Kesemedim dumanı" – "I wasn't able to put out that smoke," he said angrily.

Just as he was about to enter the village, he caught sight of two eyes looking at him from a nearby bush. He smiled as he saw the look of surprise on the face of a çocuk – a child – and remembered hiding there, too, when he was a boy. One time he had even seen a couple kiss from there.[13]

"Çocuk kardaş," he said, speaking in a cheerful, soft, and kind voice. "I'm İnce Memed, whatever you do, don't tell the jandarma that you saw me."

The child was so happy that he had seen him like this that he wasn't even thinking about going somewhere and telling someone. And Memed was feeling such pleasure when he saw the village that he at once forgot everything, his being an eşkıya, his being İnce Memed, that the huge government had filled the mountains with the jandarma to capture him, and the bloody burdens of the hired gun of the ağas, Kara İbrahim. Inside him awoke a childish and beautiful hope, affection, and joy. A subtle warm love filled his heart. Suddenly he had an idea.

"I wouldn't kill a bird," he said, "I wouldn't crush an ant. I wouldn't catch a bee, a butterfly, or a bird and hurt it." At that moment, he was surprised, perhaps more than he had ever been, at the gun in his hand, the dagger on his waist, and the rounds of cartridges wrapped around his body. He took a good look at himself and laughed.

At this point, the boy, who had been freed from Memed's attention, left the bush like a fearful fox. He slid out of the shrubs, sprung to his feet and took off. As he ran, he looked back at Memed. Seeing the child in this mood pleased Memed even more. Who was this child, he wondered? Who did he look like? He wasn't able to get a good look at the boy's face, so he couldn't figure out who he was.

His patience gradually ran out, though somehow the day didn't end. The smoke continued to rise from Abdi Ağa's chimney, the jandarma constantly moved between the houses. There was not a soul outside to be seen, not a woman, not a man, not a single villager. Had they thrown everyone in jail?

His head was fixed on the smoke coming from Abdi Ağa's house. Because of him he wasn't able to enter his own village, he wasn't able to wander around his fatherland at all. He grit his teeth, "I'll put out that smoke," he yelled. "I won't leave a single one, not a single one. Not even a single one ..."

He threw himself quickly to the edge of the rock. His waist hit it with a thud.

Darkness fell, a wind came from the north, and the heavy scent of wild mint, thyme, and peryavsan cooked from the heat of the day blew in the breeze.

He thought about that night. The night Recep Çavuş was going to kill Abdi Ağa's children. Just as he pulled the trigger of his gun and fired, the bullet went in some other direction, and no child was killed. What if they had been? Ne günahı vardı çocukların? What were the sins of the children? When they grew up were they not going torment others as their fathers had? At least let them be, and we'll see. Maybe they won't be like their fathers. Eskiden de kurt eniği kurt olur. The puppies of the wolf will be wolves, too. But there's something seriously wrong in that. He thought more about the past, about Abdi Ağa, about Asım Çavuş, and Yüzbaşı Faruk, the one who killed Hatçe.

When he thought of him, he was filled with an excruciating and bitter sense of enmity. The hair on his skin stood up. He wouldn't leave this world without taking Hatçe's revenge. "Allah," he said, "Great Allah," he said, "don't grant me death before killing this Faruk."

He rose to his feet and started to go down to the village, stumbling from side to side as if he were intoxicated. Suddenly, he felt full of joy again. "This fall I will come to the village," he thought. "I'll come to the village on the day that they toss the hay on the ground, and I'll be the first one to light the thistles during the toy düğün. Together with Hürü Ana ... " He grew restless as he approached the village, and his heart beat faster and faster.

He waited at the door, let out a breath, and then spoke in a crackling voice.

"Hürü Ana, Hürü Ana!"

Inside, Hüru Ana was sleeping alone. She couldn't believe her ears. She thought she was dreaming, opened an eye, and then shut it again.

Memed thought, maybe she thinks I've been killed.

"Hürü Ana, Hürü Ana!"

Again, Hürü Ana thought she was dreaming. She opened her eyes and then, prayerfully, shut them.

"Hürü Ana, Hürü Ana, it's me. I've come."

My god. This is no dream, no way. The voice coming from outside the door sounds like Memed's. But how can this be?

"Hürü Ana, Hürü Ana!"

I should go to see who's at the door, she thought. She rose, half asleep, half awake, grabbed a burning piece of pine kindling, came to the door and spoke in a hesitant voice.

"Who's there?"

Memed, as soon as he heard, softly responded.

"It's me Ana, İnce Memed, Döne's son. Open the door."

Hürü Ana lifted the bolt on the back of the door and opened it. There, standing on the threshold was İnce Memed. She was speechless, unable to say a single word. For a while, they stood there facing each other like that. Then Memed took Hürü Ana by the arm and led her inside. He put the pine kindling in her hand on the wall, and sat her down on the side of the bed. They were quiet together for a long time. Then Hürü Ana gathered herself and spoke very seriously.

"Hoş geldin yavrum, Memedim. It's good that you've come. We thought you had disappeared, that you had vanished. Hoş geldin safalar getirdin yavrum. The village is full with jandarma."

"I know."

"Did anyone see you on your way?"

"A child."

At that very moment shots started to come from the area around uzun kaya.

"The jandarma are shooting at me, Ana. The child saw me over at uzun kaya … "

Hürü Ana smiled.

"Let them keep shooting, this infidel government, let them shoot the bullets of the ağas off in vain, let them fire and we'll see."

Memed smiled, too.

He wanted to ask Hürü Ana a few things, but somehow wasn't able to bring himself to ask. "Where's Durmuş Ali Emmi?" he would have asked. I wonder where he is. Has he died? If he has, why was Hürü Ana not wearing the kara çatkı? Are they burning the thistles every year? Are they working the fields since then without being bothered by anyone? These couldn't be asked. Memed was worried and couldn't ask a single question, so that no more harm would come. He would wait a month, he would gaze like this at Hürü Ana's face with eyes full of questions for an entire month, and still not be able to ask a single question.

Hürü Ana understood his eager eyes full of questions, but she couldn't bring herself to deliver the bad news. The poor boy was broken, crushed and run down, she thought to herself. His mother had been killed, his beloved had been killed, he couldn't hold and love his child whose whereabouts were unknown. What would happen to him if he heard this bad news? What would happen, Hürüce, what, what would happen?

She's looking into his eyes and thinking, he's so down, so sad. İnsan söyleyemezlik de edemez. It also doesn't do not to say. Look at him, for god's sake. Look at him, kurbanınız olayım, for god's sake, look at this face, he looks like a little baby taken from his mother's breast, sniffling and about to cry.

I'll tell you yavrum, I'll tell you. Şu Hürücenin yüreciği taştan demirden oldu. This heart of Hürüce turned to stone and iron. I'll tell you yavrum, I'll tell you. If I had been iron for all that happened, I wouldn't have endured, I would have melted, I would have rotted away. I was stone and I couldn't endure. So many pains, so many troubles, how can you endure them? How can you, how can you? I wish you hadn't come, yavrum. You rightly left all this behind and rode off like a gazelle on a cloud. Why did you come yavru? Some thought that you had joined the Kırklar. Some said that you had become a commander by the side of Mustafa Kemal. Some said you had entered the feather coat of a large bird and that you would come every night and visit Döne's grave until the morning. And Hatçe's too … How could you bear all this Memedim, your mother, sweet Döne, lovely Hatçe? Why did you come yavru? How can I tell you what has happened? Look at my hair, is there one single black strand? Look at my face, is any of it left without wrinkles? Was I like this when you left Memedim?

She fixed her eyes on Memed's face and chattered on inside. It was as if Memed heard what she was saying from within. He sat there gesturing, wrinkling his face, expanding it and then contracting it.

Sooner or later he'll hear, she told herself. One who has born this much will bear this, too. He's no child, he's the great İnce Memed.

When she decided to speak, she began with a dirge that, with difficulty, she had been holding inside within her for a long time. She cried and lamented the dead as she recounted her troubles. She finished every thought with, "if I were iron I would have broken down, I was earth so I endured." Singing the lament, she wept for Döne, she wept for Hatçe, she wept for Durmuş Ali, and she wept for her children.

Memed sat stone-faced and listened to Hürü Ana like a wall, without the slightest expression on his face. Shots of fire rang out outside. Neither seemed to notice them at all.

Hürü Ana finished the dirge. Still weeping, she wiped her nose with her scarf and stood up.

"Damn me," she said. "When I saw you I totally forgot that you had come from far away. Let cursed Hürü be damned. I've left you hungry."

She took out a spread right away and placed it in front of Memed. It was a lovely embroidered spread, woven from cotton. She took out a bowl of yogurt and one of pekmez, and then a bit of honey and cheese.

"Eat yavrum," she said. "Hürü Ana sana kurban olsun. Eee, let's see where you've been since you disappeared? Where did you go?"

Memed didn't respond, he was lost in his thoughts, his face still like stone.

He rolled a bit of yufka bread, dipped it first into the pekmez and then the yogurt, tossed it into his mouth and then chewed and chewed without swallowing. The bread somehow didn't go down. Durmuş Ali didn't just die, he had been killed, but he wasn't able to make out from the dirge how he was killed. The villagers, all of them, had become enemies of Hürüce, and the villagers' homes had been ransacked. This is how Ana told it in the dirge, but who sacked the homes?

Hürü Ana would be deeply saddened about his not being able to eat. He chewed and chewed and forced a swallow but a coughing fit seized him. When he stopped coughing, he held her hand. It was burning like fire.

"Ana," he said. "Tell me what happened. Ne yapalım, whatever happens to us, we go through it. What can we do, başa gelen çekilir, we have to bear what befalls us. It's not going down, kusura kalma. Forgive me. I would eat your food if it were poison, but it's not going down. Kusura kalma, güzel anam, I've been through a lot."

Calm and still, like nothing had happened, Hürü Ana spoke.

"Yavrum Memedim," she began. "When you rode off and left the village ... Köylü sevindi. The people of the village were happy. Later they were scared. They thought Abdi hadn't died. Then we learned that he had, and more so that the domdom bullets had blown his heart to pieces. Köylü çok sevindi. The villagers were very happy. Then the five villages of Dikenlidüzü got together and held a toy düğün like had never been seen before. The young girls wore their best outfits. The older ones wore milk white headscarves, white like sakız. The drums beat in pairs. Even Durmuş Ali ignored his not feeling well and danced. Afterwards, as the morning light shined, the women and men, including those in bad health and their families, went to the thistles and lit the thorns aflame. Real human beings haven't tasted joy like this. It continued like that for one or two years. Everything was plentiful, nothing was missing. On that day, when we lit the thistles, a fireball would burst on the peak of Alidağı at night. It shimmered continuously atop Alidağı for three nights. The peak of Alidağı was like it was in the daytime for three nights. This also made the köylü happy. A year passed like this. In the second year a more beautiful, more celebrative toy düğün took place. The thistles burned even more beautifully, and a ball of fire burst even more beautifully on the peak of the mountain. The third year came. It was even more beautiful than the second year, and more celebrative ... Bir toy düğün ... Durmuş Ali both danced, you know he danced very well, and, with the piece of lit pine kindling in his hand, went to light the thistles. Suddenly, three pistol shots were heard from further on, and we looked in that direction. A rider was galloping at full speed, raising dust. He came and first ran over Durmuş Ali who stood by the side of the pile of thistles.

Durmuş Ali fell to the ground. The rider had his horse stomp all over Durmuş Ali. After that, ten more armed riders rode their horses through and shot at the families. A lot of people were wounded. Five children died, two of them girls. Durmuş Ali Emmin lived only two more days. Sana selam soyledi. Tell my boy, he said, that even though things didn't end well, iyi bir iş yaptı, he did a good thing. He still did a good thing. And that's how that year the thistles didn't burn. And a ball of fire didn't burst atop Alidağı. Durmuş Ali Emmin died. In his last breath he thought all about you. Who was the rider who came, did you guess? Kel Hamza was there for sure, Abdi's brother Bald Hamza. Abdi expelled him from the village, to the mountains, and he wouldn't come while Abdi was alive. Did you know Kel Hamza, Memed?"

"I knew him Ana."

"That Kel Hamza settled in the village."

Without stopping, and looking for a long time in Memed's eyes, Hürü Ana explained the things that the villagers went through because of Kel Hamza.

Kel Hamza was a full brother of Abdi, born of the same mother and father. Abdi didn't care for him at all. That's why he chased him out of Değirmenoluk when he was only fifteen, forbidding him to enter Dikenlidüzü. Kel Hamza came to Dikenlidüzü only one time his entire life, and he was taken and brought to Abdi Ağa, who had his brother beaten for three straight days, loaded half-dead on the back of a horse, and taken and thrown out of Dikenlidüzü like a dead dog. Following this terrible beating, Kel Hamza didn't recover for a long time. After that, he shepherded at the side of the nomads who found him by the road and helped him recover. Then in Çukurova, he remained a laborer at a farm near Telkubbe. He's not short, thin, and ugly like Abdi Ağa, he's tall, broad-shouldered, strong, and powerful. When he heard of his brother's death he was quite happy, happy out of his mind. Not knowing what he would do from the happiness, he staggered around the farm like he was drunk for three days, telling everyone who he met that his brother had been killed. Then he forgot the whole thing and went on with his farm work.

One day Pıtırakoğlu from Dikenlidüzü came to the farm to see him. He was a loudmouth.

He spoke bluntly to Hamza.

"You are quite a foolish man, didn't you hear your brother was killed?"

"I heard, and I was crazy happy about it."

"It's good you were happy. Did you hear the villagers had shared his lands?"

"I heard," said Kel Hamza.

"That every year they go to burn the thistles with a toy düğün?"

"I heard."

"And a ball of light bursts from the peak of Alidağı?"

"I heard."

"Both Abdi Ağa's two wives are widows?"

"I heard ... "

"If so, why are you still doing farm work, you dog?" he hollered. "You're a farmworker here waiting while you could be the ağa of Dikenli, the padişah? You foolish dog."

Pıtırakoğlu was a very old man.

"You're right," said Kel Hamza.

"If I'm right, then you'll give me some fields that I like that have water under them, from some place that I like in Dikenli."

"I will," said Kel Hamza.

And right away, right there, that day, they made their preparations. With all the money Kel Hamza had saved from working, he bought a pair of boots, a nice pair of şalvar, a jacket, a hat, and, with a loan, a beautiful four-year-old, tall, English-bred horse. With a loan, he also bought a German shotgun and a hundred bullets. He found five or ten hardened criminals and, with Pıtırakoğlu ahead and those guys behind, went to Dikenlidüzü. They waited a few weeks outside the village. Kel Hamza carried out everything Pıtırakoğlu had suggested.

When the villagers went out to burn the thistles ... well, they scared the living daylights out of them. And with the government. The government later ...

The people didn't resist or anything. They bowed down like sheep. Most of them even went and apologized. İnce Memede attılar tuttular. Babasının kemiğine sövdüler. They condemned İnce Memed. They cursed the bones of his father.

The same day, Kel Hamza called Göktefikli Hoca and was married to Abdi's two wives. He slept with one in the evening and the other towards morning. The women were quite pleased with Kel Hamza.

After that, Kel Hamza brought the jandarma to the village. Everyday he roasted lamb and served rakı to the officers.

"Kurban olduğum Memedim, yavrum, let me not say what happened next and let you not hear. Kel Hamza sent word to the villagers: you cultivated the land for three years but didn't give the beylik hakkı – the bey's share – or the toprak hakkı – the land's share. I'll take whatever is in your house from these three years. Led by a sergeant, ten soldiers went from house to house in the village and took everything there was – flour, wheat, oil, horses, cows, and donkeys – and piled it into Abdi's barn. The people starved that year. They groaned like hungry wolves. The villages nearby heard about our condition and sent some bread to us. Most of the villagers here went to the villages nearby ... That winter fifteen people ballooned and died from hunger. Did you see anyone outside when you came? You wouldn't see yavru, all of them are yarı çıplak, ruined ... they don't go outside."

"And Topal Ali?" Memed asked, almost without a voice.

"That one, he's Hamza's dog. He carried the villagers' goods to the storehouse ... Didn't I tell you to kill him? Didn't I tell you to take that huge dagger and stab him in the stomach?"

Memed rose to his feet, half dead and swaying. He couldn't stand and clung to a wooden beam. He staggered outside and walked down towards Dikenlidüzü. His teeth were clenched. He shook all over.

Hürü Ana found him the next day standing motionless, erect in the middle of the fields, his teeth still clenched together. "I killed you yavrum," she cried. "Quickly let's go, the jandarma will see you, someone will see you." She took Memed by the arm and led him to a stream nearby where she comforted him. When Memed came to, he spoke.

"Anam," he said, "güzel anam, the bravest of the anas. I've done all of you a great harm."

He reached out took Hürü's hand, pressed it against his lips and kissed it. Then he smiled.

"Ana," he said. "Tell Topal Ali that he should come."

Hürü was going to say something but then let it go.

"Okay yavru," she said dropping her head. "I'll go and send him to you tonight. Kurban olayım Memedim, don't trust that infidel. He'll create troubles for you later. The village is full of jandarma. He's no different than the jandarma or Kel Hamza. Kurban olayım, watch yourself ... There's only you left ... "

Demir olsam çürüdüm, toprak oldum dayandım ... Toprak, toprak, toprak oldum da dayandım. If I had been iron, I would have rotted away. I was earth and so I endured ... Earth, earth, I was earth and I endured.[14]

****

Arif Saim Bey and his land speculator rode into Çukurova in a shiny new automobile to "build the largest and most modern farm" on "the most fertile land." "The best land will be mine," Arif Saim Bey proclaimed. "It's my right." Like the other ağas, he made this claim because he had fought in the War for Independence. "What right," he said concerning one villager at Yumurtalık, "does he have to the land? I shed blood at the front. While I was battling with my body, he was sleeping in his wife's arms."[15]

Arif Saim Bey used every means to aquire Çukurova's most precious lands. He paid those willing to sell and beat and shot those who resisted. Only İdris Bey, a brave young descendant of the Circassians who had settled in the plains, offered hospitality but not servitude. So Arif Saim Bey fabricated an overdue debt, had İdris Bey charged with defaulting, and sent the jandarma to jail him. İdris Bey escaped and vowed to kill Arif Saim Bey.[16]

In Vayvay, news that Memed had been in the village strengthened the will and resolve of some, but the attacks continued. Ferhat Hoca continued to say to those who wanted to leave that they should stay and fight. "Not to oppose injustice is infidelism," he said. "It's infidelism not to protect the livelihood of your children and your fatherland, to abandon them and let them fall into the hands of the foreigners. Not to confront oppression is to share in it. To be afraid, to be intimidated by fear is infidelism."[17]

Zeynel countered, "This is just the beginning of the troubles. Wait till you see what's coming. You say that it's infidelism to fear, then don't fear and let's see what happens, Ferhat Hoca!" Ferhat Hoca didn't respond directly, but he said, "God doesn't leave those in need alone. God always stands together with those who oppose oppression. If not, would the injustice on earth have decreased as much as it has?"[18]

****

Memed gets caught in an ambush but manages to escape when Topal Ali throws the jandarma off track.[19]

He took several deep breaths. Everything was quiet around him. It was pitch black wherever he looked. He took two more steps. He heard a tiny rustling sound. Then something like a cough. A door opened, and Memed's eyes were dazzled by a beam of light. He heard a sound. Someone grabbed his arm and pulled him inside.

A long, white beard flowed like water in front of his eyes:

"What happened to you, yavrum?" asked the white beard.

A woman caressed him. She had a very warm voice. She spoke in a voice like one that sings lullabies. Memed didn't make out what she was saying. He listened instead to the sweetness of her voice, and he drifted away in ecstasy.

"You're covered with blood, yavru," said the woman in her sweet voice. "There's blood on top of your head."

Memed's teeth were clenched shut. He tried to open them but for some reason wasn't able to pry them apart. Having been in such a sad mood, he was stuck like this.

Memed now heard some voices coming from far away.

"Let's lay the boy down."

"Has he been shot?"

"He's not wounded."

"What happened to him?"

"Who knows … "

"Where shall we hide him?"

"Will the jandarma search around here?"

"He's still a child."

138

"He hasn't grown at all."

"Where's the blood from?"

"He's been cut by a rock, or scraped by a bush ... There's no bullet wound."

"At least look him over well."

"There's no wound anywhere."

"How did he find his way here in this condition?"

"How did he find our house?"

"In this shape?"

The sounds were imperceptible. Memed turned a few times from right to left, he moaned, he tried to say a few things, but his teeth were still locked shut. A few moments later, they loosened up. As if talking in his sleep, he said a few words. "Evran," he said. "Black Hamza ... Kel ... What will happen? What will happen Kamer ... Seyro ... "

He went silent. Fell asleep. Slept comfortably. Breathed calmly.

He slept till afternoon. Then he sprang up, grabbed the gun by his side, swung around, and at that moment Süleyman grabbed him. Memed opened his eyes. When he saw Süleyman he smiled, unwound and looked around in total surprise. Süleyman's elderly wife came as well, and, as though nothing had happened, said:

"Welcome yavru."

When Memed heard her lullaby-like, sweet, soft voice, he understood everything.[20]

Before he knew it he was enjoying Kamer Ana's soup again. They all smiled when Süleyman warned him not to eat it too quickly and burn his mouth. Süleyman told him that Topal Ali had thrown the jandarma off Memed's tracks, so he could enjoy the soup.

Süleyman asked Memed what he planned to do.

"I'm going to that village," he said. "I'm going there, and I am going to find that man."

"You think you'll find it, son?"

"I'll find it," Memed said confidently.

Süleyman wondered if he knew about Değirmenoluk?

"Who did you see in Değirmenoluk?"

"No one, I didn't see anyone Emmi, Süleyman Emmi," he said as his eyes teared up.

Süleyman understood that Memed knew everything, so as not to persist he changed the subject.

"İnşallah you'll make it to that village and find that man."

"I'll find him."

Koca Süleyman told himself inside that he won't find that village. O köy bulunmaz. I've been looking for it for seventy years. That man, that village ... Bu dünyada o köy yok, yok yavrum – that village doesn't exist in this world, it doesn't exist yavrum. Ara bakalım. Search and let's see what happens. You search too. Ever since the earth was created everyone has been looking for that village and that man of that village.

"Oooh," Memed said as he finished his soup. "My stomach is as big as a drum."

There was some silence between them. The woman cleared the dishes, the silence continued, their sons and brides came and looked fearfully at Memed. They had heard the clash the evening before. Memed glanced down. And Koca Süleyman waited for him.

After some time, Memed lifted his head. His eyes shone, full of questions. He started talking. Without stopping, he explained everything, what he felt, what he thought, he bluntly and calmly explained everything. He described and spelled out everything, Koca Osman, Vayvaylılar, Seyran, Akmezarlılar, İdris Bey, Ali Safa, Arif Saim Bey, Hürü Ana, Kel Hamza, her şeyi anlattı, boşaldı.

"Abdiyi öldürdük. Zalim, imansız bir adamdı. Anam gitti, Hatçe gitti. Ben de dağlara düştüm. Ölümün ardınca yürüyorum. Ne oldu? Kel Hamza geldi. Hiç aklıma gelmezdi Kel Hamzanın gelip de köye çökeceği ... Toprağı geri alacağı, köylüyü beterin beteri hallere sokacağı. Hiç aklıma gelmezdi ... Şimdi Kel Hamzayı öldüreyim, diyorum; yerine bin beter bir Kel Hamza daha gelecek. Ne diyorsun, Süleyman Emmi, bana bir akıl ver."

"We killed Abdi. A ruthless, cruel man. My mother is gone, Hatçe is gone. I went to the mountains. Ölümün ardınca yürüyorum. I walk in the shadow of death. And what happened? Kel Hamza came. It never occurred to me that he would come and fall upon the village ... that he would take the land back, that he would drive the villagers into the worst condition ... Now I'm thinking that I should kill Kel Hamza; in his place a Kel Hamza a thousand times worse will come. What do you say, Süleyman Emmi, give me some advice."

"Bu dünya böyledir," he said. "Sular hendeğine dolar. İnsanlar doğar ölür, gün doğar batar. Ağaçlar büyür çürür. Sular akar, bulut ağar. Ağayı öld-ürürsün, ağa gelir yerine. Bir daha öldürürsün, bir daha gelir."

"This world is like this," he said. "The river fills the ravine. People are born and die, the sun rises and sets. Trees grow and decay. Water flows, the cloud rises. You kill an ağa and an ağa takes his place. You kill one more, and another one comes."

Memed:

"Bir daha, bir daha öldürürsün, bir daha gelir. Bir daha, bir daha gelir. Abdi gider, Hamza gelir, Hamza gelir, Hamza gelir," diyordu sayıklar gibi. "Hamza gelir, Hamza gelir, Hamza gelir, Hamza gelir ... "

"Another, you kill another, and another comes. Another, another comes. Abdi goes, Hamza comes, Hamza comes, Hamza comes," he said, as if delirious. "Hamza comes, Hamza comes, Hamza comes, Hamza comes ... "

Koca Süleyman:

"Hamza gelir!" he said hollering. "Dinsiz Hamza." Infidel Hamza.

Ayağa fırladı, geri oturdu. He jumped up and sat down again. The hairs of his long white beard shook.[21]

****

Ali Safa Bey persuaded the provincial governor to come to Vayvay to order the villagers out, but the Kaymakam had never been to the villages. He despised villagers. Whenever he saw one, he would wrinkle his face, say a prayer to ward off the devil, and spit on the ground. Deep under his skin, in his heart, he feared them.

It was late morning when they rode together into Vayvay in a car borrowed from Arif Saim Bey. The Kaymakam got all excited when the car reached the market. The chauffeur blew the horn and all the shopkeepers came out and waved. The Kaymakam could have ridden around in the car all day, but he was shocked by the poverty of the villagers. Ali Safa Bey told him that it was the villagers who were ruining him, not the reverse. "I went bankrupt because of them. They neither till my lands nor have them tilled for me. If they would give me my lands, I would put them all to work and look after them like a rose."

The Kaymakam had the clerk read out the names of the villagers against whom Ali Safa Bey had registered a complaint and the names of the places that belonged to him. An argument broke out between supporters of each side. The Kaymakam told everyone to be quiet.[22]

"It is understood from the statements of the authorities that Ali Safa Bey's deed includes Vayvay village. According to the testimony of the authorities, not long ago the villagers of Vayvay came and built seasonal homes from the bushes and reeds from the lands that belong to Ali Safa Bey. It is understood that the villagers of Vayvay wrongly occupied Ali Safa Bey's lands. To lift their occupation, the dismantling of the said flimsy houses of the residents of Vayvay has been decided."

Then he turned to the villagers.

"You are opposing the government. You've wrongly occupied the man's land with the building of these shacks. I can't take the land of anyone and give it to you. I'm giving you a deadline of one month. If you don't pack your things and leave in a month, I'll send the jandarma, and I'll break these reeds on your heads. You've been spoiled, you acknowledge neither the great, nor the government, nor Allah. Neither right nor law, hak hukuk, ne de adalet, nor justice … "

The villagers:

"No one knows for certain when this village was founded. The grandfathers of our grandfathers founded it, way back in the time of the Fırka-i Islahiye."

The Kaymakam spoke at the top of his voice:

"Are you disagreeing with me, are you objecting to me, are you trying to pull one over on me? Is it at all possible that this village is a hundred years old? Didn't you build these homes a few days ago in order to seize Ali Safa Bey's land? Who are you deceiving? Does the village look anything like a hundred years old, or ten years old, or ten days old? Is this a village, this? Liars, frauds, lowlifes, infidels, unbelievers!"

He screamed and yelled. He foamed at the mouth. He got all riled up and lost himself. He rolled his eyes. He stomped his feet. He waved his arms in the air.

"Let's see if you don't leave here within a month. I'll crush you, I'll crush you like an ant ... "

He stomped and kicked up the dirt with all his energy.

"It's like this, like the head of a snake, I'll crush your heads ... crush ... crush ... I'll crush your heads."[23]

****

Topal Ali and Yel Musa join Memed and Süleyman in another discussion.

"You all know what I have been facing," Memed began. "I won't say that the things that have happened to me haven't happened to the kul, the serf, who is worse off. The kul has faced things we can't imagine. But I've faced some unbearable things. You know all of them. In the end, I killed Abdi Ağa to free the wretched of the earth. And they were freed ... After Abdi Ağa the people were happy and joyful, olmaya gitsin. They shared the land. And they thought and I also thought that now it would always continue like this ... Then what happened? Then Kel Hamza came, a thousand times worse than Abdi. Bloodthirsty. He came down hard on the people. So, what will be the end of this? Abdi gitti, Hamza geldi. Abdi went and Hamza came. One Hamza makes a thousand Abdi ... So, what came of my efforts and tribulations, where did they go? You have a lot of wisdom, a lot of skill, and a lot of experience, tell me, show me, what should I do? Give me some advice."

"Ben söyledim sana," dedi sert. "Sular aşağı doğru akar hep. Akçadenize doğru. Suların yukarı doğru aktığını gördün mü hiç?" I've told you, Koca Süleyman said firmly. The water flows downward, always. Towards the sea. Have you ever seen water flowing up?

"Abdi gidip Hamza gelecek hep, öyle mi?" said Memed. Abdi will go and Hamza will always come, is it like that?

"Öyle." That's how it is, said Koca Süleyman angrily, helplessly, hopelessly, his beard shaking.

"Ağa gidecek, ağa gelecek," added Yel Musa. An ağa will go, an ağa will come. "That's how it is everywhere. God created it like this. Birds fly with their wings. The breeze blows without wings. Human beings walk on two legs. Both the moon and the sun rise and set."

Memed, his face completely confused, cut him off:

"Abdi gidecek, Hamza gelecek, öyle mi?"

"Öyle," dedi, bowing his head.

Topal didn't say a word. It was clear that he had thought about this a lot.

"After you left, and after Kel Hamza arrived, I thought about this all the time. I couldn't fall asleep at night. I couldn't figure it out." He took a deep breath: "Çok çok düşündüm, bir yere vardıramadım, bir kazığa bağlayamadım. I thought and thought, but couldn't get anywhere, I couldn't make the connection, I couldn't tie the stake."

"Abdi gidecek, Hamza gelecek, Hamza gidecek, Süleyman gelecek, Ali gidecek, Veli ... "

"That's how it always was," said Süleyman. "Ali gitti, Veli geldi. Grandfather died, father came. Father died, you came. You will die, your son will come ... "

"Öylese niye uğraşıyoruz, canımızı dişimize takmışız sen, ben, Ali, Yel Musa?" If that's how it is, then why do we struggle, why do we sacrifice everything we have, you me, Ali, Yel Musa?

"Uğraşıyoruz," he said confidently. "We struggle." "Uğraşmak haktır." "It's one's right to struggle."[24]

A horse for Memed had been waiting at the door. Memed rose, embraced each, and smiled a kind of painful smile on his face. "Take care," he said as he left and mounted the horse. As he rode off, he repeated Süleyman's words, "Uğraşmak, dövüşmek, canını kanını vermek ... Boş yere ... Uğraşmak haktır ... " To struggle, to fight, to sacrifice ... In vain ... It's one's right to struggle. "Uğraşmak, hiçbir şey değilse uğraşmak, nasıl hak olur?" To struggle, if it doesn't amount to anything at all to struggle, how can it be a right?

He agonized under the weight of these thoughts, feeling them throughout his entire body. The story he had heard of İdris Bey was also on his mind. İdris Bey put his life on the line for his people and now death followed him, too.

He rode to İsmail's mill, where he thought he would be safe.

"Who's there?"

"İsmail Emmi is that you?" Memed asked.

A lifeless, broken, and tired voice spoke.

"It's me," he said. "It's me kardaş, who are you? Did you come to grind some flour? Where on earth did you find wheat? Has Hamza shown some mercy? I'm coming. Wait, I'll put on my şalvar and come."

He came to the door while pulling up his şalvar. The sun forced him to squint ...

"Are you a traveler?" he asked.

"İsmail Emmi, it's me, Memed."

Kulaksız – Earless – İsmail woke up and snapped to.

"Which Memed are you?" he asked softly. "Which Memed?"

"It's me, İsmail Emmi, me. İnce Memed."

"Neeeee." What! "İnce Memed? Which İnce Memed?"

"How many İnce Memeds are there İsmail Ağa?"

Kulaksız gave him a good looking over.

"The İnce Memed that went and became an eşkıya?"

"Yes, that's me."

Kulaksız İsmail paused, looked at him, turned around right away, grabbed a thick stick, came back and started attacking Memed.

"You kafir" – you infidel. "You kafir, son of a kafir! You've ruined everything – you've driven five villages to hunger, and still you wander around here, around here, around here, saying I'm İnce Memed?"

If Memed hadn't grabbed him and taken the stick from his hand, his head would have been split in two.

Kulaksız İsmail, who couldn't free his wrists from Memed's grip, started screaming at the top of his lungs. "İmdaaaat, imdaat," – help, help – "someone save me, İnce Memed has attacked the mill. He's killing me, imdaaat, imdaaat! Someone help … "

Memed held his wrists tightly while İsmail's powerful screams echoed all over, carrying throughout the mountains and bouncing off the cliffs like the sound of a foghorn. With Kulaksız yelling and squirming, Memed tried to calm him down.

"Are you crazy, have you gone mad İsmail Emmi, have you lost your mind?"

"İmdaaat, he's killing me! He's killing me, he's killing … "

Kulaksız threw himself on the ground in a huge fit and shook and thrashed about.

Memed grew angry, lost his temper, and gave a hard kick to Kulaksız lying on the ground. He pulled out his gun and said:

"You, kara dinini imanını … Quiet! Either shut up or I'll shut you up."

Kulaksız İsmail immediately, in the blink of an eye, went mute. He didn't make a sound. He lay there on the ground curled up on top of some hay and dried dung. Weak and exhausted, his neck was wrinkled even fully extended. The bottoms of his bare feet were torn apart with cracks into which one could slide a finger. He was in tatters. He had so many wrinkles all over that he looked like frozen meat. Aged and worn, filthy, his long beard was yellowed with soot.

Memed looked him over and his heart swelled. Something stuck in his throat. He went to him, lifted him off the ground, and took him inside. He grabbed a glass of water and washed his face well. Then he brought his horse that was standing outside and tied the reins.

Kulaksız İsmail leaned against the wall and sobbed. He sobbed more as he spoke.

"Who told you snotty İnce Memed, who told you to kill our ağa and leave us under the cruelty of Kel Hamza? Who asked you … ?"

"Don't cry, İsmail Ağam, don't cry. Listen to what I'll say."

"I don't want to … Not a single piece of grain has entered the mill for two years. No wheat, no corn, no barley, no millet, the mill hasn't ground a thing. This is what you brought us. The villagers of Dikenlidüzü have been begging for two years. All of them are stripped to the bone … you brought this about, like this … "

"Don't cry İsmail Ağam, don't cry! Listen, listen to what I'll say."

"What will you say, kafir, you heathen, bloodthirsty … Our caring, conscientious, brave, and compassionate ağa drowned in his blood up to his wrists, and what will you tell me, kafir? Children withered away, dried up from hunger and died. They got nothing from Kel Hamza's warehouse and well. He took whatever the villagers had, everything. He didn't leave a single piece of grain, not barley, not millet, not corn, he didn't leave a single piece. Everybody died from hunger. Kırfacana döndü millet – The people were ravaged. We gathered and ate herbs from the mountains. We ate bark, madımak, and sorrel. We ate whatever we found. Kel Hamza took everything, whatever cattle, oxen, goats, sheep, horses, donkeys we had in our hands. He took it with the government. One week his men beat the villagers, one after the other, and the next week he had the jandarma beat them. Beating after beating, the backs of the people split open and became calloused Memedim, my eşkıya, eagle of prey of the great mountains! Tell me, if I shouldn't cry then who should! For six months I haven't had an honest meal. And it's all your fault … You ruined us. You destroyed our homes. You ruined our village. You destroyed our family. You ruined us. Who said, who, who, who told you to kill our rose, our ağa, the bebek of our eyes and leave us orphaned like this, who, who who told you?!"

He started to praise Abdi Ağa, sobbing and singing mournful, heartfelt dirges for him, his compassion, and his limitless humanity.

"Don't cry İsmail Ağam, enough," said Memed. "Come and let's have a few bites to eat together."

He took a pouch of food out of his bag and opened it. Inside was some wrapped yufka bread, and a huge roasted chicken.

Kulaksız İsmail threw such a look at the pouch of food. He got up, went to the grinding stone, washed his face and came back.

"Help yourself İsmail Ağam," said Memed.

Kulaksız İsmail attacked the chicken like a hungry wolf. Memed stood and watched him swallow the chicken with a starved appetite. Kulaksız dug in with his two hands, his nose, his chin, and his eyebrows. The chicken was gone in no time. Kulaksız started to lick the bones. He licked one clean then took another and licked it. Whatever was in the food pouch was gone before you knew it. Kulaksız İsmail threw it all down. After he finished, he drank some water and spoke.

"Oooh," he said. "Ooooh! Cana geldim. I've come to life. Praise the souls who have left us ... Ooooh, I'm full. Please excuse me yavrum. I loved your father very much. He was the best person in the world. Etliye sütlüye karışmazdı. He totally avoided getting involved in anyone's business. Eline vur ağzındaki lokmayı al! Don't be so naive! You mustn't be so meek! Memed, you didn't do this well. You made us miserable. Excuse me yavrum. Eeeee, hoş gelmişsin bakalım! If only there were a cigarette now too ... Where have you been kardaş? Eeeeh hoş gelip safalar getirmişsin bakalım. Welcome, welcome, what other pleasures have you brought, let's see."[25]

****

Everyone had a story about İnce Memed. To the ağas and their families, he was a bloodthirsty force for evil, an enemy of civilization and humanity, who kills, rapes, and steals from the villagers.[26]

The villagers said that he is a person as soft as cotton who speaks very little. Out of embarrassment, he always holds his head low in front of him. When he speaks he turns as red as a young girl. When he looks far off, he's like a majestic mountain. Fire radiates from his eyes. When you approach him, if it's a calm time, he's like a small child. And no bullet can penetrate him. Nor can a knife pass through him, fire burn him, or water drown him. He's protected with charms and prayers – muskalıymış, blessed, dualıymış, enchanted, and afsunluymuş. Those who were present when the villagers lit the thistles after Abdi Ağa was killed said that Memed entered and sat down in the middle of the fire. "We swear we saw it with our very eyes." They say that there's only one place a bullet can penetrate him. That is in the eye.[27]

****

Ali Safa Bey stayed inside most of the time. When he went out, he went with six armed guards. He was terrified. One day he had İdris Bey brought to him.

"If you kill İnce Memed, all the ağas and beys of Çukurova as well as the government will be grateful to you. The other day İsmet Pasha said that the head of this snake must be crushed. What won't he do for you when he hears that you've killed İnce Memed. We support you, too. He's a very bad, very despicable man. If you heard the things they say about him in town ... Let them explain to you what he has done! It makes a person's hair stand on end."

"If you don't kill Memed kafir İdris, then you're just like him. Kill him! İnce Memed is an opportunity for you. If you let this opportunity go, the government won't rehabilitate you, İdris Bey."

"At least let me think about it, Safa Bey."

"To kill İnce Memed is easier than drinking water ... For you."

"At least let me think about it, Safa Bey."

"What does it mean to kill İnce Memed! Whoever kills İnce Memed will be a hero!"

"At least let me think about it, Safa Bey."

"The Beys have decided, it's either İnce Memed's head or ... İdris Bey, your situation is not very bright. You're walking on the blade of a sword."

"At least let me think about it, Safa Bey."

İdris Bey mulled it over and weighed things, and understood that it was either the head of İnce Memed or his own ... If he didn't kill İnce Memed he wouldn't be able to live on this plain. If he killed him, his situation would be much better than it had been before. And Memed was such a naive boy. To shoot him wouldn't be that difficult.

"Have you thought about it İdris Bey?"

"I've thought."

"When are you headed to the mountains?"

"Tonight."[28]

****

They met in the deep rock gorges of Tuvara. Memed knew that İdris Bey had come to kill him. Three of Memed's companions hid behind a rock with their hands on the triggers of their guns. Memed and İdris Bey greeted each other without shaking hands.

Memed liked İdris Bey very much. He said to himself that he's quite a handsome man. And innocent as a child. How could he have been an eşkıya for this long! Such innocent men don't last even three days in the mountains. They're killed. Memed knew even the smallest details of what had befallen İdris Bey. His heart burned for İdris Bey, but he didn't forgive the man who had come to kill him. He'd kill him. Memed's usual downcast eyes were even more downcast.

They started to talk. Memed asked İdris Bey why he had come. Somehow, İdris Bey wasn't able to come up with anything. Finally, he said:

"Buradan geçiyordum, şöyle bir İnce Memede uğrayayım dedim. Ne biçim bir yiğitmiş, ben de göreyim dedim," dedi. I was passing through here and I thought I'd come by like this to İnce Memed. I thought I'd also see what kind of brave man he's said to be.

Memed was surprised at his clumsiness and how naive he was.

They spoke about being an eşkıya in the mountains and on the plains. As they spoke, İdris Bey didn't pay much attention. He spoke as if coming from a far-off place, and his hands continually and increasingly shook. Then, the blood drained from his lips. Then his whole face turned white.

147

A falcon in the sky descended to the ground like a bolt of lightning, and then spread its wings as wide as the length of a person and flew up to the cliffs and sky at the same speed. It flew back and forth, without stopping, leaving jet-black streaks between the sky and the cliffs. The falcon's streaks, dizzying with anger, were signs of great danger for Memed.

Memed stopped speaking. İdris Bey didn't even seem to notice. His left cheek twitched. He seemed to lose himself, with his hand and arm flapping about. His forehead wrinkled. His leg started to shake rapidly. His right one bounced up and down. For a while Memed watched the man in front of him experiencing these tremblings and movements. He awaited the end. Suddenly, the man calmed down, his shaking stopped, and blood slowly returned to his face. The falcon in the sky spread its wings, pointed in the direction of the wind coming from the south, glided calmly, and flew peacefully in the sky. Its tiny black silhouette faintly drifted above the red cliffs.

İdris Bey lifted his head. He fixed his eyes on Memed and looked at him for a long time. Then suddenly he rose to his feet. Memed did as well. İdris Bey removed his dagger from his waist and, right away, slit his forefinger. Then he took Memed's hand and cut into it. Memed smiled. İdris Bey licked Memed's blood that had come from the cut and extended his own bloody finger to Memed. Memed dabbed his tongue on İdris's finger.

With the enthusiastic innocence of a child İdris Bey hugged Memed.

"I came here to kill you, kardaş," he said. "And here kardaş olduk." We've become brothers.

"I knew that you came to kill me. I was prepared. But before you killed me, I would have killed you," Memed said as he pointed to the rock. "Look." Three people came out, each one's weapons gleaming.

"How do you like that İdris Bey kardaş?"

"I like it very much," he said. "Yes, I enjoyed this very much. But I want to say to you that one who sees and knows you cannot raise his hand to you, cannot kill you. You don't know me, and I didn't know you. But you knew me. I should have known that a real human being cannot kill you."

Memed extended his hand, slowly grabbed İdris Bey's finger, and held it tightly.

They ate together at the head of the Tuvara spring. İdris Bey told Memed that they would always be blood brothers and that he would return after he took care of some business in Çukurova. When İdris Bey departed, Memed's heart ached for him. He was the most pure, decent, and generous person Memed had ever met.

The hawk gliding in the sky folded its wings and, like a mournful dirge, followed and saw İdris Bey off.[29]

****

In the village those who favored Hamza questioned whether a village without an ağa is possible. They thought they were headless and divided without one. The aftermath of Abdi's killing had been too much to bear. People starved to death, and the villagers of the Toroslar, who were probably the most talkative people in the world, went silent. "It's good that Hamza Ağa came," they said. When Hamza made them worse off, these villagers praised Abdi more than ever, according him features reserved only for the sacred. They blamed Memed for their troubles as Hamza's cruelty grew. He said "work," and they worked. They lost the life and hope that had once been in them.

When word spread of Memed's coming to the village, however, they began to feel alive again. They started to smile and talk and curse and cry and enjoy and become excited. But one afternoon they blew up in a rage that had never been seen before. They got out their sticks, guns, old swords, and baltas and attacked Hürü Ana's house. They didn't find Memed there, but they broke the door and the only window of Hürü Ana's hut. Then they went and ransacked Memed's empty house, leaving it in rubble. They couldn't control their rage and started assaulting each other with rocks and sticks. Some had their arms broken, others their legs, and others were hit and hurt in the head. A ruthless struggle took place. Each attacked the person they met. Companion, friend, mother daughter, father son, it made no difference.

The jandarma hid Hamza out of sight and watched the unbridled anger of the villagers in fear, unable to muster the courage to confront them. By midnight, there was not a thing in the village that hadn't been broken or spilled. Not a person remained who hadn't been injured. No one knows how the fighting stopped. That night the villagers slept unperturbed and at ease in a way they hadn't slept for years.[30]

****

Kara İbrahim's gang and the jandarma surrounded the mill one afternoon. They were sure that they had Memed cornered. "We'll bomb this mill," said Kara İbrahim, "and if he doesn't escape, let the novice deyyus die under the rubble." "Is this what it means to be an eşkıya, to close oneself inside a cage like this and have oneself killed?"

Memed could see Kara İbrahim and heard what he said. Kara İbrahim had been one of the most famous eşkıyas in the Toros for a long time. He had had his way. One day he accepted the amnesty. He now made his living by hunting down enemy eşkıyas for the ağas.

Memed noticed that Kara İbrahim was not being careful. Just as Memed pointed his gun, the others started firing at the mill. Memed pulled the trigger. Kara İbrahim let out a scream and fell. For a moment there wasn't a sound. Memed saw several members of the gang and the jandarma run away. Could he get away now? No way. He'd be shot. It would be dark soon. But Yüzbaşı Faruk and Asım Çavuş would no doubt be here soon, too. His death was near.

"Abdi gitti, Hamza geldi, Abdi gitti, Hamza geldi," he suddenly thought, over and over. He really wanted to understand this. What was this, what did it mean? Will it always be this way? Was everything in vain? Was there no solution?

His hands stopped squeezing the trigger. His mind drifted. The shooting outside stopped as well. He looked at Kara İbrahim's body. It looked as though there was a taunting smile on İbrahim's face. Kulaksız İsmail sat in the dark corner like an owl.

Memed heard Asım Çavuş's voice.

"Hurl two bombs at that door!"

With a boom, the door and the walls of the door collapsed.

"We've surrounded the mill with hundreds of people. There's no way out. Come and turn yourself in! The captain will spare your life. The captain knows the whole situation. We'll crush the mill."

It had become dark. Rain fell, increased steadily and started to flood the area. The horses neighed nonstop. More shooting.

Memed understood that the Çavuş was trying to frighten him. What if Memed were to capture his captain? He'd ask him: Abdi gitti, Hamza geldi. What does it mean? Such a great, three-starred captain. Maybe he would know.

More shooting, the wall of the hut collapsed. Just then a hand grabbed his shoulder, and Memed immediately jumped up.

"Wait a moment and listen to me," said Kulaksız İsmail in a hoarse voice.

"Three months ago Kel Eşkıya left me his gun and a hundred and fifty bullets. He said he'd be back a week later for them but he didn't come. I'm going to get the gun from storage. Don't turn yourself in. You mustn't turn yourself in Memedim. Nothing will come of it. Nothing will come if you die. Take cover over there," he yelled. "Eşek herif – you donkey fool – and he's going to be an eşkıya! If those over there weren't donkeys like you they would have shot you in this mill a long time ago."

Asım Çavuş was shouting something and talking, but with the sound of the rain, the neighing of the horses, and the buzzing of the bullets what he said couldn't be made out.

Kulaksız İsmail returned with a brand new Alaman rifle, loaded it and fired twice into the darkness. He told Memed to get into the water and to let himself float away with the stream. He would make sure no one got close and would surrender once Memed was gone. There was no other way.

As Kulaksız sprayed fire, Memed paused and thought. One moment he was elated and another deeply sad. Kulaksız shouted and pleaded with him to run, but he just stood there in thought.

"My dear son, yavrum, Memedim, the rain is saving you. If it hadn't rained, they would have demolished the mill long ago. N'olur git, let Kulaksız İsmail kurbanlar olsun for you, go! The rain saved you, go. Allahın bu nimetini tepme – Don't ignore this blessing from God, go!"

150

He pleaded and pleaded.

"Go, kardaş, go! The rain has saved you. I'll hold them off till morning. Go you stupid foolish eşkıya, go ... What can I do, he won't go. He's become a stubborn donkey. Hey Ümmeti Muhammed has there ever been a donkey in the world as foolish as this? This is all the manhood that will come from Sefil İbrahim's son!"

Asım Çavuş's voice also called out. Memed didn't hear or understand what Kulaksız was saying. Then a huge bolt of lightning struck. For a moment the area became bright with light, as though the sun were rising. Memed almost collapsed. His entire body started to sweat, he shook with cold, his teeth chattered.

"Yavrum, Memedim, don't let them kill you. Look the rain is stopping. Yürü git! Get going!"

Memed took a few steps towards Kulaksız İsmail, gave him hug, and in a sad, warm voice like those of the dirges spoke.

"Sağ ol, var ol İsmail Emmi, sağlıcakla kal! Gene geleceğim," dedi. "Thank you, may you live long, İsmail Emmi, stay well! I'll be far from here within half an hour. Don't shoot too much. Stop right away. Hide your gun. It's a nice gun. Sağlıcakla kal ... "

He said no more, went straight for the opening and slid into the water. He made no sound whatsoever, not even a splash.

Kulaksız fired until the rain quieted and dawn broke. Deep down he was pleased with Memed's escape.

Asım Çavuş called out to the mill. There was no answer. He suspected some trap and used every weapon he had to attack the mill until it was reduced to a heap of rubble. No sound came from inside.

"We've hit our target," he said. "I feel very sorry for this young man, Yüzbaşım." Two huge tears flowed down his cheeks. "What a shame!"

The captain was surprised.

"You admired him this much?" he asked.

"I don't know," the Çavuş responded.

Asım Çavuş yelled out again. No response. Shaking with dread and sadness, he rose and slowly approached the rubble. He couldn't endure seeing Memed's dead body. He wanted to call "Memed" one more time. He couldn't open his mouth. He grit his teeth. He knew that Memed was alone and there was no chance for escape after the shooting had stopped. If Memed hadn't been killed he would have responded. It means he was hit. "İnşallah he was only wounded," he said to himself.

"What's going on," the captain said from behind, "are you afraid Asım Çavuş? Are we afraid of Memed's death?"

Asım Çavuş looked back at him, then entered the mill, and then, with a cheerful look and a wide smile, spoke: "He's hit, Yüzbaşım, and dead," he said. The captain came running. "But the one who's been shot is not Memed."[31]

****

Memed arrives at Koca Osman's in a nearly unconscious state, clearly shaken and totally unresponsive. Zeynel runs off to report to Ali Safa Bey, but when the bey asks about the noise in the village the night before, Zeynel says it was a wedding and doesn't reveal that Memed has returned. He promises to keep Ali Safa Bey informed.[32]

On his way back to the village, though, Zeynel is stopped on the road by Muslu, Ahmet, and Süleyman from the village. They take Zeynel to the swamp where they shoot him. Then they go to Ali Safa Bey's and set his barns on fire. Winds blow the flames over all of Ali Safa's fields. The villagers see the fire in the distance and Koca Osman is especially happy. Even as Memed sleeps, his shadow has been cast over all of Çukurova. "Let him sleep and snore till the end of time if he wants," he explains to Ferhat Hoca. "It's enough for us that the shadow of a hawk falls over our lands ... It's enough that the people know that he has stepped foot in Çukurova. Enough. Dağları deler yol eyler. If there's a mountain in his way, he'll dig through it. The villagers are as brave as they are scared. It's enough that they know that they have support, even if it's the size of a stem or seed of rye."[33]

****

Ali Safa Bey's father had been the ağa of Çıkçıklar village, where the villagers earn their keep through stealing and banditry. They would do anything for Ali Safa Bey.[34]

"What happened to you Ali? Would we sit here and watch from above as Vayvay village gives you trouble? Why are you so down? I'll sacrifice this entire village on your behalf. Go home and look after yourself. This year the village of Vayvay will leave your land and go. If they don't we'll leave this village to you. We'll not show our faces again. Do you understand what I'm saying, son of our ağa? Go about your business. Leave Vayvay to us. And don't worry."

Choking with tears, Ali Safa Bey said, "thank you Hoca Veli Emmi. You've made me content."

"Stay like that, be calm."[35]

The villagers slaughter a goat in Ali Safa Bey's honor, light a huge fire and cook the meat on the embers. They even find some rakı for Ali Safa to drink. Without wanting to appear nervous, he tries to learn what they think about Memed.

"You know," he said, "a while ago an eşkıya went to the mountains. A boy, what was his name? You know, Abdi Ağa's killer."

152

"İnce Memed," they said.

"I heard he has been seen again in the mountains."

Haci Veli spoke.

"Aslan, o," he said. "A lion, that one. Recently he also shot Kara İbra-him. Fought with an army of jandarma for three days and three nights and in the end broke free and escaped. An able man, that one, very able. And then … "

All faces turned towards Haci Veli with anger … he understood the mistake he had made immediately.

"And then," he said, trying to correct himself. "Then he wired Mustafa Kemal Pasha, 'don't send these poor ones against me. If you're brave, you come for me'."

Ali Safa Bey regretted having asked. Among these villagers, there was deep affection and respect for this eşkıya child. Where did this come from? He couldn't make sense of it.[36]

****

Hamza is terrified, too, so much so that he takes Topal Ali with him to Hürü Ana's to make peace.

"Who's there?" Hürü shouted.

Topal Ali leaned in Hamza's ear. "You talk, and don't mention me at all. Talk."

"I'm Hamza, Hamza Ağa," Hamza said.

"Bastard," she said, "where do you come off being an ağa, hele önce köpek ol da" – see if you can first be a dog – "not a human, be a dog and then be an ağa! What do you want in the middle of the night?"

"I want to talk with you a little, Ana."

"There's no way I've got anything to say to you. A tyrant, smeared with the blood of my husband and sunk in blood up to his hands and arms … Var git kapımdan." Get away from my door.

"Ana, I'm going to say something. It's really necessary."

"Var git kapımdan! I won't look at your vile face. You're the one who's killed the children from hunger. I won't look at the face of such an infidel."

"Ana kurban olayım." I beg you.

"Var git kapımdan dog! You're the one who deprived the villagers of bread."

"Ana I beg you, open the door."

"Var git Kelçe Hamza, var git, I won't open the door. You're the one who has the ten thousand, no the fifteen or sixteen thousand, the thousands and thousands of people, of the Toros laughing at us."

"Look anam at what I'll say, I have news for you … I'll give news to her. When you hear, when you hear you'll be pleased, you'll be so happy, güzel anam. You'll be overjoyed."

"Var git Kelçe Hamza, var git from my door. Your bloody feet, your foul body, won't cross this threshold. Var git on your way, var git Kelçe. You can have your news. Even if it brings me back to life, even if it gives me the whole world, I don't want what you have to say. Even if you killed me, I wouldn't look you in the face, your filthy face ... "

Hamza pleaded, Hürü Ana said nothing other than, "var git." Hamza and Topal Ali remained there till morning. Hürü Ana didn't sleep. She tossed and turned in her bed till morning and continued to talk to herself. When the morning came, she opened the door and, recognizing Topal Ali next to Kel Hamza, shouted:

"It means you're really worried, aren't you, you're scared to death of Memed, aren't you?"

Hamza jumped to his feet and wrapped his hands around hers.

"Ana I've done nothing wrong. Tell Memed that he shouldn't kill me. I'll buy three, no ten new dresses for you. I'll buy a lot. And I'll buy gold earings. I'll by ten, five of them all at once at the same place."

With disgust, Hürü Ana shook her hands and took them from his:

"Var git işine Kelçe," dedi. "Var git! Am I to be a bride, öyle mi, really? You're going to pin these gifts on me and I'll be a bride, öyle mi? She'll be a bride and jump for joy at Durmuş Ali's grave, öyle mi?"

She turned to Topal and laughed:

"You're fearing for your life, aren't you? You're really scared for your life? Memed doesn't belong to me or anyone. And I don't see him. If I do, he doesn't listen to what I say. Topal knows that if he did, that Topal wouldn't be here right now, he'd be rotting in the dark soil. Go about your business yavrucaklar, varın gidin. You'll get no favors from me. I won't save you. Olsa – even if – olsa ... Olsa da olsa ... "

She locked her door and walked into the village. Ali and Hamza remained where they were.

After this, Hürü Ana wandered around the village in a fit of rage. She looked at every person in the village with disgust. Everyone that saw her looked to the ground when they saw her, they couldn't look her in the face.

And the five villages of Dikenlidüzü heard of how Hamza and Topal Ali came to Hürü Ana's door and pleaded till morning. The news, along with fearful whispers, slowly spread throughout the whole Toros –

How Hürü Ana didn't open the door for them, how she said, "Var git from this door you dogs. If that İnce Memed doesn't kill you, I'll kill you. I'll strangle you with these hands. I waited for this day, for this day *yezitler*. For this wonderful day ... do you understand? The tiger of the red rocks, the dragon of Akçasaz, the snakes of the Yılankale, and the ghosts of Kırksuyu may pass across this threshold, but you will not. If Memed doesn't kill you in the near future, I won't give him my blessing ... I won't, I won't, do you understand?"[37]

Fearing for his life, Hamza heads to the hills to hide.

****

The ağas and the Vali, the regional governor, gather to share their concerns about Memed. Arif Saim Bey says there's no reason for concern. Murtaza Ağa of Karadağlıoğlu disagrees. He tells Arif Saim Bey that the villagers are being incited by İnce Memed, that they've learned from his example. "Today it's us and tomorrow it will be you."

The Vali tells the ağas to stop wiring Ankara for help and to take care of İnce Memed themselves. Murtaza Ağa again disagreed. He pointed out that the problem was not İnce Memed but the effect he has had: "Vali Bey, what's happened has happened, whether or not this son of a bitch is captured. Kurdun ağzına kan değdi. The blood has touched the mouth of the wolf. Hem de eşeğin aklına karpuz kabuğu düştü. Moreover, they have this new idea. After this, neither we nor the government will recover," said Murtaza. "The snake must be crushed when it's young. İnce Memed has grown … we'll never kill Memed. İnce Memed will not die."

"Don't exaggerate the size of this zavallı çocuğu," the Vali responded. "This country has lived through Çakırcalı. These Toros have lived through Gizik Duran, Karayılan, Yozcu, Çötdelek, and Kürt Reşit. Soon İnce Memed's corpse will be dragged through the streets of this town."[38]

****

Memed has been recuperating on a small island bostan, an orchard, in the marsh near Vayvay. The watermelons of the village come from the bostan. He is under the care of Köse Halil and Seyran, who finally meets Memed and, to her and everyone else's astonishment, falls head over heels in love. One day, as they all sat together under a willow tree, Seyran began to have feelings she had forgotten long ago. She couldn't keep her eyes off Memed. The more she looked at his face, the more these feelings stirred.

Halil rose and picked two bouquets of velvet roses. He gave one to Seyran and another to Memed. Memed breathed in deeply the scent of the flowers. A wind from the west kicked up long dust columns on the roads in the direction of Anavarza castle. Seyran rose to her feet.[39]

"I'll light a fire and make some warm soup for you."

She gathered some kindling. Halil helped her and the two of them lit a fire. The oil they placed on the pan in the fire sizzled and the smell of the onion in the pan filled the air. Seyran spread a cloth, placed bowls on it and served the soup.

"Buyurun," she said.

Memed and Halil sat down cross-legged and began to eat.

Today, for the first time, Memed ate by savoring the soup, letting it linger and go down with ease. He closed his eyes and, as he placed the spoon in his mouth, experienced total enjoyment, as if he were drawing out every flavor of the soup. Halil didn't fail to notice this.

When Memed finished his soup, he looked around a few times. He was in the kind of unbelievable state of excitement that a person enters when a spell is slowly broken, like waking from an endless sleep and falling from a huge world of dreams into the real world. Finally, his eyes focused and remained fixed on Seyran. For a moment their eyes met. Seyran looked away.

"Eline sağlık bacım," Memed said. "I've never had soup as good as this." His voice made Seyran tingle from head to toe. A sweet flutter that a person can feel only once in a lifetime shot through her entire body. She was swept away and off balance. Memed's voice came from far off, from another world. His voice was so magical.

The shadows of the evening twilight started to fall. She lost Memed's face in the shadows for a moment. She got up, walked around, took a container that was hanging on a branch of the willow, and brought it over.

"Bal," – honey – she said. "Selver Gelin sent it to you. It's good honey. She doesn't give it to anyone. Just to you." She poured it onto Memed's plate that she had cleaned.

"Sağ ol bacı," dedi. Thank you sister. "How quickly you healed my wound."

Seyran blushed.

"In Kamer Ana's lineage, they're all healers," she said, turning red and speaking in a nervous, trembling voice. "They're from up in the mountains, from Sarıtanışmanlı. They know how to heal gunshot wounds really well. I'm also from the mountains. Our people are always getting wounded by gunshots," she said. Then she fell silent. She so regretted having spoken. The whole time her body was weak and shaking all over. She was afraid that Memed and Halil would notice this. Thank heavens the sun was setting and darkness had arrived.

Clouds of mosquitoes swarmed around their ears and over their heads.

Seyran both wanted to escape right away and not to go at all. She had never stayed this late at night before. In the darkness now, she couldn't make out Memed's face very well.

She rose immediately. Memed and Halil rose with her.

"I'm late," she said. "Sağlıcakla kalın."

Memed spoke, too. "At the middle of the night ... All by yourself ... "

Halil laughed.

"Ohhooo, Memed kardaş," he said. "You don't know Seyran Kız. Right now, she'll, in the middle of the night, walk into the middle of an army and nothing will happen to her. She's not afraid of anything, or of anyone ... "

Seyran took off quickly, already appearing to reach the Savrun. There, she slipped her feet out of her shoes and crossed the stream. She crossed the stream at once, slipped her shoes back on and set out along a dirt path. She tingled, pined, and even shivered with a feeling inside that she had forgotten for years.[40]

That night she didn't sleep a wink. Swept away by the anticipation of day-break, she rose early. An early morning breeze blew and a mist rose from the ground. The birds softly chirped. Huge blue, yellow, violet, and red butterflies flew about. The bees, frogs, and insects left their nests or sat atop the moist ground and awaited the new day. The earth, the sky, the trees, streams, flow-ers, animals, birds, and bugs – all restlessly excited and elated for the coming day. Everything beautiful, everything carried away by joy. The sun rose. Seyran had never seen a sunrise like this. The sky opened in a dreamy sweet blue. An immaculate sky, gleaming, crisp and clear as can be, without a cloud. Not even a bird flew across it.

Seyran ran straight to a dammed area of the Savrun, among the willows. In a moment she took off her clothes and threw herself into the water. She swam and floated above the shining pebbles in total delight.

She stepped out of the water and dressed quickly so that no one would see her. She had never experienced such a beautiful sunrise, such a beautiful sky, such joy in the water.

The first person to see Seyran back in the village was Ali Ahmet, a man in his seventies whose back had become hunched when he was young. He stopped and looked at Seyran's face. "What happened to you kız? You're a smiling kız. And you look like an angel. What's happened to you?" Seyran gave him a big hug.

Seyran went home and took her favorite dress from her chest. She had worn it only one other time. She put it on, along with a necklace made of coral, silver, and gold that she had forgotten for years. She slipped a pair of shiny shoes on and wrapped a Lahore shawl around her waist. Then she put on some gold earrings and bracelets and looked in the mirror. She gazed in the mirror for a long time. How pretty she looked. She had become so beautiful. Then she went to the village. The first one to see her like this was Selver Gelin.

"Abooov kız!" dedi. "Bu ne güzellik! Your face is smiling, Seyran, are you aware of it, your face is smiling. When you smile, how beautiful you are! Seyran your face is smiling kızım." Seyran hugged and kissed her.

She had an uncontrollable, bubbling desire to kiss every person, friend or enemy, tree, insect, or bee. If she kissed the entire world it wouldn't be enough. For so many years she tucked these feelings away. Now they were overflowing everywhere.

For a moment, a deep sorrow came across her face. She wiped it off and walked to the neighborhood where her mother and brothers had settled. Her mother heard she was on her way and went outside to meet her. Her brothers, their wives, relatives, children, other women, whoever there was, filled the street to greet her. Smiling, Seyran came up to her mother and embraced her, then she took her hand and kissed it. Her mother wept in joy, kissing her daughter's hair and face and breathing her scent in deeply.

"You've made peace with us, Seyranım. If only your father were alive to see this day. He died longing for you until his last breath. Now he can rest in peace. We've done so much to you kızım. Still, you were humane and forgave us." Her mother wept and wept.

Everyone hugged Seyran. Today the huge wound inside them all was healed. They wondered why, but it wasn't the time to ask.

"Düşünmeyin," exclaimed her mother. Don't think. "It doesn't matter what happens, I will always love you. Let Seyran do what she wishes. Son günlerimde yüzümü güldürdü ya. In my final days she made me smile. My beautiful daughter, my Seyran." Seyran's face had lit up with a smile. She brought everybody back to life.[41]

Seyran next went to Kamer Ana.

Her eyes were fixed on the ground. Then she lifted her head, her face was aglow in a bright red.

"Kamer Ana ... " she said, but she couldn't find the rest of the words. "Kamer Ana ... "

Kamer Ana became impatient.

"Out with it kız, hörtük. What is it? Are you trying to learn my name? Kamer Ana, Kamer Ana!"

Seyran again looked down.

Kamer Ana spoke again, this time softly and compassionately.

"Tell me what's going on kızım. Senin başında bir iyi hal var." There's something good on your mind. "Söyle anana ... "

Seyran again lifted her head, her large black eyes twinkled. She had the look of love all over her.

"Ana," dedi. "Ana, let's go over to the bostan, come let's go together."

Kamer Ana felt happy and smiled.

"Demek öyle ha!" – That's what this is all about! "So the one who's made your face light up ... Deli kız," dedi, and she gave her a warm hug. "Oh my, let no one hear or get word of this. Deli kızım, deli kızım, deli kızım."

As she repeated "deli kızım," Kamer Ana also caressed Seyran's back slowly and kissed her hair.

"Deli kızım if we go over there now, everyone will understand everything. You're the talk of the village after all. They're all saying, what happened to Seyran, she's smiling? We'll find a way and we'll go."

"Duramıyorum ... " I can't stop ... "Ana. I can't stand still. Help me Ana, nothing like this has ever happened to me."

Kamer Ana smiled.

"This is how it always is," she said. "Bu işin sağlamı adamı durdurmaz. This is what always happens. It will set a person's blood on fire."

She took Seyran's hand and held it tight.

"Ana kurban olayım, let's go," Seyran pleaded. "Ana you understand my situation. Ana, Kamer Ana I'm dying. Since the first day I saw him."

Koca Osman entered and, when he saw Seyran, in a loving way asked:

"Kamer Ana, what's happened to this our deli kız, they say she smiled. The whole village is talking about her. They say she smiled and went to her ana and kardeşler. What's happened?"[42]

****

Halil was happy to see Kamer Ana and Seyran. He had just hunted two partridges and was ready to cook one for them and one to take to Koca Osman.

Seyran stared spellbound at Memed, but Memed was totally lost in thought.

"Vay kızım, kınalı kızım," Kamer Ana thought to herself. "He's got no idea! So this is what you're facing ... You're shaking like a leaf in front of him and he's hardly noticing ... Oh kadersizim, my unfortunate one, Seyranım, you're going to get burned again. I had no idea it would be like this ... I thought he knew. Aaah, kınalı kızım aaah! Aaah, the inexperience aaah! What are you going to do now? Even Köse Halil is aware, but he's got no idea, rose kızım, kadersizim."

Memed came out of his trance and asked Kamer Ana if he could ask her something. He recollected all that had happened to him and talked about his mother, Hatçe, their child, Recep Çavuş, Cabbar, Topal Ali, Koca Süleyman, Durmuş Ali, Hürü Ana, Hamza, the current troubles in the village, Kulaksız İsmail – everything that happened to him.[43]

"Ana," he said, "you're an ana who has seen and lived a lifetime with a heart of gold. Tell me, what should I do? Abdi gitti, Hamza geldi. Hamza gidecek Bekir gelecek. Ali Safa Bey gidecek ... "

"Kenan gelecek," Kamer Ana said.

"Vayvay will be an enemy to me, hurl curses at me, and hold a mevlut ceremony every Friday for Ali Safa's soul ... "

Kamer Ana continue to think. She thought long and hard and then spoke:

"Benim buna aklım ermedi Memedim," dedi. I'm not able to understand this. "Kusuruma kalma." Forgive me.

Memed turned to Seyran:

"Bacı," he said, "what do you think about this? Seyran bacı?"

For the first time he noticed Seyran's beauty. He noticed her dress and outfit and said to himself, "Bu kadar da güzel insan olur mu? Bu kadar da, bu kadar da güzel insan olur mu?" Can a person be this beautiful? So beautiful, so beautiful, can a person be this beautiful?

Seyran trembled and was unable to speak. Red as a beet and sweating, her hands went numb and her mouth dry.

"What do you say bacı? Koca Süleyman said that to struggle, to fight, to stand against the oppressor is a right. Sen ne diyorsun? What do you say? Hiçbir sona varmayacaksa, zalimle dövüşmüşsün, onu alt etmişsin kaç para eder? If it comes to no end, and you fight and defeat the oppressor, what's the purpose of it? Sen ne diyorsun bacı?" What do you say sister?

Seyran had a lot to say but she was all choked up and unable to do so. If she spoke, her voice would give her away. And she was scared to death of that. She couldn't, and, so, looking down at the ground, she said slowly:

"Bilemem kardeş, bilemiyorum." I can't know kardeş, I don't know. "Not at all. You know better than us, better than everyone. Sen İnce Memedsin. You're İnce Memed."[44]

"They'll kill him Ana," Seyran said on the way back to the village. "Have you ever heard or seen of an eşkıya who's survived?" Kamer Ana didn't say a word because she, too, believed this. Still, she tried to console her. "Heaven forbid kızım," she said. "But bullets don't pass through him ... He has thunder in his chest, he has a protective prayer on him. The Hızır protects him ... and his eyes ... The Hızır will also protect his eyes ... " Seyran wasn't listening. "They'll kill him. They'll kill him."[45]

****

In Vayvay, Ali Safa Bey tells the villagers that their attacks on him and his property are inhumane, un-Islamic, and against the laws of the nation and state. He accuses them of killing Zeynel and his stableman Adem (who is still searching for Ali Safa's horse), and gives them ten days to clear out of the village. If they don't, blood will flow. "Things you have never imagined will happen. This village will be Kerbela. Listen to me, listen and listen well, this village will be Kerbela. Have you heard of Kerbela, do you know Kerbela? That's how it will be, this village will be Kerbela, exactly like Kerbela. Kerbela ... "[46]

The next day, he notified the authorities of the attacks on him and has a prosecutor frame Yobazoğlu for the murder of Adem and Ferhat Hoca for Zeynel's. The arrests were easy to fix. Yobazoğlu had no relatives in Çukurova, and little was known about Ferhat Hoca's background.

"I came knowing it would be like this," said Yobazoğlu, as the jandarma led him and Ferhat Hoca away. "But believe this, killing a person is evil. No one will believe, at least you should believe, that I didn't kill Adem. See after my children everyone." And, with a painful grin on his face, Ferhat Hoca turned to the tearful villagers. "You know who I am. There's no need for me to say. I won't be returning to the village again. They'll hang me. Hakkınızı helal edin kardeşlerim." The jandarma beat them badly and marched them through the town where people cursed and threw all sorts of dirt and garbage at them. When they reached the jail, they collapsed.

160

That night Ali Safa Bey dined and drank rakı with the town officials at Nazifoğlu's restaurant. During the meal he spoke about Zeynel and Adem as good, friendly, and loyal people. They didn't deserve this vile, contemptible, bestial death. Ali Safa Bey spoke so sincerely and eloquently that he convinced everyone.[47]

****

Koca Osman once told Memed about the gazelles of the plain.

In late winter, the gazelles would come in the thousands to Çukurova from the south and roam around the Anavarza plain. Above them would fly sharp-winged and extremely quick black eagles that could fly faster than the gazelles could run. The eagles would land on the shoulders of the gazelle, thrust their beaks into the gazelle's eyes from behind, rip out their eyeballs and eat them. Koca Osman said his heart ached for the blinded gazelles.

"In our youth, hundreds of helpless blind gazelles roamed throughout the plain of Anavarza. No one captured and slaughtered the blind gazelles and no one shot them. They would end up dying like this."

"I'm a blinded gazelle fallen onto the Anavarza plain," he would say. "I'm a helpless blind gazelle in the clutches of the black eagle … "[48]

****

Seyran explained to Memed and Halil every detail of what had happened to Ferhat Hoca and Yobazoğlu, how their hands were bound in heavy chains and they were humiliated in town. Memed didn't say anything while Seyran spoke, but Halil saw a sudden and total change on Memed's face. It resembled the sharp blade of a knife. A small flash flickered a couple of times in his eyes and then a beam of light shined in his pupils. Seyran noticed, too. Suddenly, she stopped talking and stared strangely at Memed's eyes as if it were the first time she had seen them. He looked like he had returned from the lost. A flash of steel flickered again and again in his eyes.

Inside his head, bright beams of light flashed. Blinding, shining, glistening yellow rays rapidly scattered and spun around. The world turned bright yellow, palpitating with flowing, sparkling yellow light … Memed staggered down to the stream, dunked and lifted his head out of its ice cold waters, dunked it and raised it again, and then started to walk around the bostan. He walked quickly and without knowing where he was going, his feet getting snagged on the shoots of the watermelons. Now everything disappeared. The plants, the trees, the cliffs of Anavarza, the stream, the soil, the thickets of Akçasaz, the surrounding low-lying mountains, everything was wiped out, only Memed remained, in a fit of rage. Halil and Seyran watched him. He went back and forth for a long time. After a while, he stopped and stood straight in the middle of the bostan. Totally erect. Like a sharp sword stuck in the ground.

Halil went to his side.

"Kardeş," he said, "Memed, don't stay here. It's very hot. The sun will knock you out and you'll get sick."

Under the çardak ... Memed looked at Seyran, and she saw him. This time, his face was entirely different. It had a warm, friendly, sweet, and pleasant look. He smiled.

"How about Ferhat Hoca!" Memed said. "He acted like a lion. I've never seen a hoca like this. Halil, do you know what Koca Süleyman said?"

"Yoook," dedi.

"Koca Süleyman bana, 'Abdi gider de yerine Hamza gelirse,' dedi ... İşte öyle dedi. 'Dünyada boş olan, işe yaramaz olan hiçbir şey yok,' dedi. 'Uğraşmak haktır. Savaşmak haktır. Dövüşmek, boş olmaz, haktır,' dedi."

"Koca Süleyman told me, 'if Abdi goes and Hamza comes in his place ... that's how it is,' he said. 'In the world nothing is done in vain, nothing that's of no use,' he said. 'To struggle is one's right. To fight is one's right. To battle is not in vain, it is one's right'."[49]

****

Seyran walked to the bostan in the evenings without anyone noticing and would watch the çardak where Memed slept until the sun rose. Now and then she noticed an armed man wandering around the area till morning. The man stepped on the ground without making a sound. Sometimes he would come close to Memed's çardak, listen closely, and then run away. Seyran couldn't mention this to Memed. Also, she thought that maybe the armed man was one of Memed's own guards. "Let him sleep, my brave one, my lion, I'll guard him," she thought. One night, she approached the man. He was just about to run when Seyran spoke.

"Dur." Stop. "Who are you?"

When the man heard a woman's voice, he stopped. Seyran crossed the stream, approached the shadow, and insisted:

"Who are you? What are you looking for here every night?"

"I'm Adem," the man said. "Ali Safa Bey's head stableman ... A horse ran away and Bey said to me that ... Bey said to me that ... Don't come back without catching that horse. I have no idea how many months it's been."

He got a little closer to Seyran.

"Bacı," he said, "you know, this horse is no ordinary horse ... Yaaa, it's no horse at all. This horse is a jinn ... This horse is something special, a fairy, an unseen ... You see it in front of you, look again and its gone."

Overcoming her surprise, Seyran asked:

"I thought they killed you? They threw Yobazoğlu in jail for killing you."

"Bilmem," dedi Adem. I have no idea. "I don't know anything. This horse is a jinn, a fairy … "

He turned around and started to run straight towards the bed of the stream. Memed, who had awoken from their voices, ran down from the çardak.

"Who's there?" he yelled.

Trembling, Seyran immediately lay down on the ground. She remained there shaking, until the shooting stars could be seen, her body aflame with passion from the sound of Memed's voice.[50]

****

The village was encircled and bursts of gunfire came from every direction … suddenly women's screams filled the night. Horses neighed, dogs howled together, roosters crowed, women shouted, children wept together. Then the gunfire stopped. The horses' neighing diminished and faded.

Towards morning another burst of gunfire came. Again the horses neighed and the dogs howled. Long shrieks filled the village and the plain. The women's screams gradually receded and went silent in the night.

The villagers poured out of their houses. Three daughters of those who had newly arrived in the village had been abducted, dragged by their hair and taken away. The mothers of the girls and other village women gathered under the long branch of the mulberry tree, pulling at their cheeks and pounding their breasts. Frantically beating themselves, they cursed Ali Safa.

Those who had raided the village also drove out whatever cattle were left, and they stole the horses of the villagers who had recently arrived.

That day, the villagers wandered around inside the village with their arms hanging at their sides, without doing or saying a thing.

The second night the riders came again. After shooting up the village, they set three homes on fire.

The girls who had been abducted and raped were left outside the village. Naked, exhausted, bruised, and bleeding from their breasts, they covered themselves with their hands as they slowly returned to the village. Those who met them covered them with sheets and took them in.[51]

****

Sightings of İnce Memed occur throughout Anavarza. It is said that he has over thirty men with him to challenge the ağas, beys, and government. One report tells of how he singlehandedly battled the jandarma at Anavarza. It was really just a gang of thieves.

Yüzbaşı Faruk knew that his running all over the plain only helped make Memed more legendary. Faruk took out his anger on the villagers. He had them beaten to the point where their feet hurt so badly that they couldn't walk for days. In Vayvay, he even beat the women and children, and Koca Osman bled for a full week.[52]

"Either you'll tell me where İnce Memed is or I'll beat all of you to death."

"İnce Memed ne gördük, ne biliriz, ne de adını duyduk." We haven't seen İnce Memed, we don't know where he is, and we haven't heard his name.

The villagers wailed, ached, convulsed, and screamed but said nothing other than this.

"İnce Memed, şahinim." İnce Memed, my hawk.

The villagers wrote and recited türküs and created new stories about Memed's powers. Yüzbaşı Faruk didn't believe the stories about the yıldırım muskası – that Memed had captured the thunder and put it in his sacred charmed necklace, or that a falcon flew above and guarded him – but, still, when he was about to clash with those he thought were Memed, he searched in the skies for a white falcon.[53]

****

Memed had never seen a person with eyes like Seyran's, so warm, friendly, full of love, humane, and pure. Her face, her dimples, her lips, her unbelievably beautiful skin … her tall body, her walk, her sway. She walked as if she never touched the ground. He awoke every night listening for the sound of her footsteps, unable to contain his excitement. He shook with passionate love, and his head spun thinking about her, but he also felt pain and cried for her when he thought about her love for him. Sooner or later, he would either be killed or need to leave.

One night Memed wandered around the area where Adem had been tracking Yobazoğlu's horse. Memed had gotten out of bed early to meet Seyran when she arrived and saw Adem from a distance. Memed sat down on the edge of the stream and placed his feet in the water. The water had cooled a bit from the day. A slight breeze still blew.[54]

Seyran came slowly, crossed the stream, and crouched and sat down in the place she always sat when she arrived. The light from the stars was stronger than the dimmer light from the moon that had just set, but still Memed could only vaguely make out Seyran's silhouette. As soon as Seyran heard the sounds of footsteps her whole body again became undone, and her heart beat fast.

Memed rose several times and tried to approach Seyran but his heart also beat fast and he shook so much that he had to sit back down. A while later he was able to get himself up. He walked towards Seyran. Seyran saw that he was coming straight to her, slid behind the trunk of a tree without getting up, and withdrew slowly back towards the stream.

Memed was going to say something to her, but his voice cracked. He also didn't know what to say, so he stayed quiet. Seyran recognized his sound and stopped. Impassioned, Memed flew to her and grabbed her hand. Seyran's hand burned like red-hot iron. Memed lifted her and brought her to him. Seyran Memede yumuşacık, cansızmışcasına bıraktı, göğsüne doğru sağıldı. Memed embraced her, kissed her neck. His lips burned like fire.

In a moment, they forgot the night, the trees, the horse that had come by their side, and the world. Ne zaman soyundular, iki beden ne zaman bir yalımda biribirine kenetlendi farkında bile olmadılar. Ne yörelerinde vızıldayarak bulut gibi dönen sivrisinekleri işitiyorlar, ne çıplak bedenlerini yolan dikenlerin, pıtırakların acısını duyuyorlardı. Bir sevişmenin değil, iki hasret bedenin bitişmesinin ateşinde, tadında, büyüsündeydiler.

Birkaç kez suya girdiler çıktılar. Bedenleri hiç ayrılmayacakmış gibi sonsuz bir yalımda birleşti. Bir birleşmede toprak gibi, ışık gibi, gelişen büyüyen hayat gibi zengin bir tattaydılar. Alone in the middle of the world, united in unbearable longing and love, they resembled the first woman and man of the species.

Dağların başı ağarırken Memed kendine geldi. Seyran daha soluk soluğa, ağzı yukarı suyun kıyısındaki kumların üstüne serilmiş yatıyor, topuğunu sular yalayıp geçiyordu. Memed onu elinden tutup kaldırmasa böyle delice bir istekte soluyarak gün kızdırıncaya kadar yatıp kalacaktı.

They dove into the stream. Ayrı ayrı yerlerde, biribirlerine kaş altından bakarak aptes alıp, giyitlerine koştular, telaşla hemen giyindiler. Biribirlerinin yüzüne bakmadan suyun kıyısından aşağılara yürüdüler, sonra geriye döndüler. Memed wandered in the orchard, picked a ripe watermelon, kırdılar kemirerek yediler. The karpuz was cool. An early morning breeze blew. Serinlikten, bir de doymuşluktan ürperip usultan titrediler.

When day broke and they looked into each other's eyes, they suddenly laughed together. They gazed and gazed at each other and laughed in wonderstruck amazement, in a spell, in a miracle.

They caught sight of the horse in the place where Adem had seen it many times. Seyran walked straight to the horse. Approaching it like a friend of a thousand years, she caressed its neck, and then took hold of its mane and walked with it. The horse, which had evaded capture and death by Adem for weeks, walked behind her like a lamb.[55]

****

Adem now believed that Memed was hiding in the bostan and went to tell Ali Safa Bey. But when Ali Safa Bey saw Adem, he turned to Dursun Durmuş and said, "son, this one wasn't murdered? Aren't there people lying in prison for this, and even facing execution?" At first he wondered what they should do, and then he thought it was pretty simple. "Dursun Durmuş oğlum, is there that much to think about, hasn't this one not been killed already? We didn't kill him ya. Isn't that right?" He told Dursun Durmuş to grab a shovel and take Adem to Akçasaz. "Make sure nobody sees you."[56]

****

The July heat in Çukurova is the worst. It's as if fire shoots across the earth and sky. The soil of the ground dries and cracks, the plants wither, and the world turns to a scorched yellow. The colors on the insects whiten and glimmer under the heat of the sun, not a bird flies in the afternoon, people sweat all the time, and their sweat dries instantly. Sometimes it gets so hot that the bees in their hives, the baby chicks in their nests, the turtles in their shells, the flowers in their buds, and the ants in their anthills all dry up. And, in July, the swamp of Akçasaz boils. It gets so hot that you can't even dip the tip of your finger into it. The water bubbles and boils just as water boils in a cauldron, breathing in the expanse of the swamp like a mighty giant.

In the late afternoon the white clouds over the Mediterranean thicken and rise to the sky and a cooling western wind begins to blow. First the wind blows, then it stops, then it blows and stops, and then suddenly it breaks loose. Dust tornadoes, high as poplars, spin and travel across the plain, over near the Mediterranean and on the roads and mountain passes. Sprouting up, growing smaller, then larger, then collapsing, then growing again and circling the plain, one bursts over there, another dwindles here. Suddenly all the roads and passes, hills and mounds, earth and sky are buried for a long time in a huge cloud of dust. Other than dust, you can't see a thing, not even the end of your nose.

Memed was experiencing this kind of heat for the first time, and sometimes he nearly suffocated. If there hadn't been a master of these lands like Köse Halil by his side, he would not have survived July in the land of Anavarza and the Akçasaz marsh. "Memed kardaş," Halil would say, "it's not difficult, it's not difficult, you'll get used to it."

One day at the stream, Memed is startled.[57]

"Halil, Halil, Halil," he hollered, "the stream dried up, Halil."

"What's happened?"

"The stream dried up," dedi.

Halil ran and came to look at the stream. There was no water.

"Does it dry up like this all the time?" asked Memed.

"Sometimes, sometimes," Halil said, thinking. "They're sowing the rice paddies. But I've never seen it cut off this drastically."

They sat on the edge of the stream, hanging their legs down from the small bank. They sat there side by side without speaking and thought until the sun rose.

Seyran ran to the bostan in the afternoon. Agitated, completely flushed, and covered from head to toe in dust, only her teeth shined.

"It's been cut," she said. "Now what will we do? Ali Safa cut our water. We've withstood everything, now what will we do?"

Memed didn't understand how a huge stream could be blocked. Seyran explained that years ago a man from Maraş named Pişmanoğlu Mustafa came to the plain. He opened canals to the Savrun and constructed dams to plant rice fields. Ali Safa Bey offered him three years of rent-free land for rice patties if he would cut off the water to force the villagers of Vayvay out.

"Yesterday, three riders came storming into the village with Dursun Durmuş at their head. He gathered the villagers and said he had some news from the Bey: 'Safa Bey sends his regards. He said get off my land, leave my village. If you don't, if you don't stop trusting that snotty İnce Memed and get off my lands, he said, since I wasn't able to discipline you with hunger or rape, I'll teach you with drought. Vayvay will be like Kerbela. And so will the other villages. It's because of them that the others will burn, but what can we do, let them all burn. It's not my fault. It's the village of Vayvay's. Let the other villagers come and share and distribute what they have with those in Vayvay. Get the Vayvaylılar off my land and the water is ready. The Bey said that, let them not be stubborn, everything can be endured except for drought. Let them not make their children drink from the marsh. They'll all break in defeat. This is what I have to say, I'm not at fault.'

"That's what Dursun Durmuş said, and then he got on his horse and rode away."[58]

****

The first, second, and third days, they drank from the ponds. A week later, the ponds also dried up. Then they dug open the springs and waited in line all day for water. In a short time, the springs also dried up.

The hot, yellow July dust poured continuously on the villagers, inside their houses, into every nook and cranny, everywhere, piercing under the skin of their bodies.

In Aşağıçiyanlı a man shot and killed his best friend for a drop of water.

But no one from any of the villages came to Vayvay and said: "Friends leave this village and save us from this disaster." Instead, someone from each of the villages went several times to the Kaymakam and explained how bad things had become and that children were getting sick and dying. The Kaymakam faked concern. "I'm very sorry, I hope this passes, you have my condolences ... this makes me very sad. But what can we do, Pişmanoğlu Mustafa Bey is cultivating the rice paddies ... they're the wealth of the nation, it's not like we can make them dry ... "

"So what should we do?" the villagers asked. "Ali Safa Bey is doing this on purpose to force us out of our land, he's doing it on purpose."

"I won't get involved," said the Kaymakam, "never, especially in Ali Safa Bey's business. Am I his kahya, or am I a man of the law? Go to Ali Safa Bey and come to an understanding, then come to me."

They wired Ankara and Adana but received no response.[59]

****

İdris Bey had been wandering Çukurova at nights like a hunted wolf. The jandarma who knew his courage and his disregard for death rarely got close to him. When they heard İdris Bey was on one side, they went to the other and searched for him over there. Also everyone knew what had happened to him, and for this reason showed him respect.

İdris Bey went to as many esteemed notables as he could to enlist their help in settling the dispute with Arif Saim Bey. Kürt Hurşit Bey of Antep, who fought in the war with Arif Saim Bey, and others, including an educated descendent of the Ottomans, all went to Arif Saim Bey to discuss İdris Bey. Arif Saim Bey turned them all away. All he would say was, "It means this will end badly, so let's see what the end will be." He felt badly for İdris Bey, but what could he do? İdris Bey came from the brave, courageous, pure people who were extinct in this age. Arif Saim Bey was truly proud of İdris Bey's enmity. Having an enemy like him was quite an honor for a person. "Yazık yazık, ama ne kadar yazık, şu dünyada yalnız onunla dost olunabilirdi." It's a shame, a shame, such a shame, in this world one could be friends only with him.

İdris Bey went to see Memed.[60]

"Memed kardaş," he said, "I want to work together with you. I came to make this offer to you. I want to be at your service. Because you are a very respected, very courageous, pure, noble person. It would be an honor for me to battle our enemies under your command."

He spoke at length. He used words that Memed had never even heard before. Memed was flattered and pleased.

Memed was quiet and gave no response. It was towards midnight that, unable to endure his constant insistence, he spoke and explained at length and in the smallest details, the matter of Abdi going and Hamza coming in his place.

"Hatçenin kanı, the death of my mother, and my going to the mountains produced all this," diye bitirdi. "Abdi gitti Hamza geldi."

İdris Bey:

"Then kill Hamza too," dedi.

Memed smiled at İdris Bey's simplicity.

"Hamza will come again. There are many Hamzas in the province. Isn't there a way to do away with Hamza?"

İdris Bey:

"That I don't know," dedi. "I would first do away with Hamza and then think about the next Hamza when he comes."

Koca Osman, Halil, and the other Çerkezler listened to them without interrupting. And they supported Memed. If you kill one of them then a thousand will come in his place. If you kill them all en masse, then in their place still they'll come en masse.

Memed sözünü:

"This is what is holding me back, this is what is killing me. If nothing good comes from my efforts, not no good, but if the end is worse, is the worst of the worst, this is what overwhelms me, this is what keeps me awake. Ben kaş yapayım derken göz çıkardım. I was going for the eyebrow and I took out the eye. And the eye of a huge village. Much worse. It's because of me that my people saw worse oppression, that their stomachs grew and they died from hunger, it's because of me ... It's because of me that their daughters who were like roses were raped. This is what has me all tied up."

İdris Bey didn't seem to understand Memed's troubles at all.

"I'm going to go now," he said as he rose. "I'll come in two days. I have my most important matter to take care of and then I'll come. There's no time now. After I return we'll go up to the mountain and there you'll explain all these things again to me very well. And I'll understand you then, and I'll be the cure for what pains you.

Memed gave no response. İdris Bey hopped on his horse:

"Allahaısmarladık," dedi. "In two days ... "

Memed:

"Güle güle ... " diye söylendi, and he watched him go with a strange sadness.

Koca Osman didn't look at Memed at all. He didn't say şahinim at all. There was a deep pain, a feeling of ill-will in his eyes. Grief settled in and sat like poison on his face. The wrinkles on his face multiplied more, resembling a mass of intertwined spider webs woven one on top of the other.

While leaving the bostan in the morning:

"Memed oğlum," Koca Osman said, "this Safa has finished us off, destroyed us, we haven't been able to do a thing to him." He turned, without looking back, and walked away.[61]

The next day İdris Bey rode to Arif Saim Bey's konak to challenge him to a duel. "I've come to fight you, I've come to settle our accounts. Grab your gun and kindly come down ... " He waited in the courtyard for a long time. As he called to Arif Saim Bey once more, "a bullet came from behind, entered the back of his head, shattered his throat and came out the other side. İdris Bey slipped slowly, lifelessly, to the ground from his horse. His cap to the side, his head fell a bit further on, his blond hair spread across the dirt. A pool of his blood formed next to his shoulders, reaching and mixing with his hair."[62]

"Yazık," Arif Saim Bey said. A shame. "Çok yazık. Onunla dost olunabilirdi." A huge shame. One could have been his friend."[63]

****

The sun had just risen one morning when, on the north side of the Anavarza castle, a large group of people walked east from the plain. No one knew why they walked or where they were going. Villagers from the villages above the Savrun, from Çiyanlı, Narlıkışla, Dedefakılı, emptied like bees gathering around their hives – families, women and men, the sick and the healthy, the young and old all came and joined the crowd. Others heard and saw the crowd in the area of Azaplı village and rushed to join as well. Now it was clear where they were going, and why. A long wide cloud of dust moved in the direction of the town. This long cloud gradually grew longer and wider. The villagers of Vayvay also joined. Women in front, behind them children, and the men further behind.

Half the crowd was caked in mud from head to toe, since when Pişmanoğlu released the water into the plain from the dikes below, a number of villages were flooded. Pişmanoğlu had mocked these villagers for complaining about having too much water in the summertime. The bastards rejected a blessing, he said, as he laughed at them. He made others, including Ali Safa, the Kaymakam, and Yüzbaşı Faruk, laugh as well.

The long, wide crowd, which had been making all sorts of noise, reached the Kubbe, the shrine, of the town and went silent. As though they had all been dipped and pulled from a sea of dust, their entire bodies, their faces, eyes, and hair were covered in dust – creatures literally created out of the dust.

The townspeople were at first shocked in disbelief. They made jokes and laughed. Then they looked and saw the endless, huge crowd coming from the Kubbe. The merchants lowered the shutters of their shops with a clang, and everyone ran to their homes and tightly bolted the doors behind them.

Yüzbaşı Faruk had no idea what to do. The Kaymakam, the other officials, the ağas, and the jandarma commander took cover.

Finally, the Yüzbaşı gave the jandarma a strict order: "Süngü tak." Fix your bayonets.

Was this a rebellion? Most of the ağas were shaking like leaves. All of them had the look of death on their faces. The Kaymakam had collapsed on the floor, taken out his prayer beads, and was blowing prayers to the air with trembling lips.

When the crowd saw the beautiful, large, white stone bridge at the bottom of town, they ran down the hill. The dams that Pişmanoğlu had used to block the water of the Savrun were under this bridge. One after another, they came to the bridge and stood above the dams. It was quiet. Those on the bridge stared at the water that had formed a lake.

Suddenly, as if nothing out of the ordinary was happening, the crowd gradually entered the water. In a moment everything was astir. The water was full of people. They opened the dams so that nothing in the least remained, not a stone, not a piece of wood, not even a shrub.

The water cascaded straight down. A thunder of joy erupted from the crowd. The cheers were so loud that the town shook.

Dipping themselves in and drinking from the frothing water, the villagers floated downstream with the water in a wild drunken victory. They enjoyed themselves so much, making so much noise, no one understood a word anyone else saying. The cascading water flowed downstream for a few kilometers, then it slowed and stopped.

The riverbed had dried with cracks as deep as a person's leg. The water came, filled the cracks, and after that flowed to another place where it would stop and fill the cracks again. The crowd followed it, its eyes glued on the slowly moving, cursed water. From evening till morning it hadn't traveled very far. The water would come and with a hooor hooor hooor slowly fill the cracks.

When the townspeople understood the situation, they ran out of their houses in joy. Like the villagers, they fixed their eyes on the river and waited.

"Every one one of them must be arrested," the Kaymakam shouted. Only Yüzbaşı Faruk disagreed. The people were without water, they came and broke the dam. Bunda ne vardı? What was there in this?

"These ... " Ali Safa Bey responded, "if this movement remains unpunished, if it's not punished to the severest degree, it will cause a lot of troubles. This is a revolt. All the villagers that joined this movement must be arrested."

Ali Safa Bey took the prosecutor to the corner and, holding his arms like a thick envelope, whispered something in his ear. A moment later, the prosecutor spoke:

"I'm writing up an arrest to the court for each of them," he said. "In a short while, the announcement for the arrests will be made."

A division of the jandarma, with Yüzbaşı Faruk at their head, arrived and opened fire on the villagers who stood waiting, with their eyes fixed on the river that had hardly advanced to fill the cracks. The villagers huddled together. The jandarma didn't hear the command to open fire again. They rounded up the villagers. There were so many that they filled the courtyards of the jandarma's headquarters, the mosques and schools, and the remains of the homes of the Armenians. There, they roasted under the sun, hungry and thirsty. No one was able to approach the villagers to give them even a drop of water or a piece of bread.

Ali Safa Bey spoke once more to the Vayvaylılar: "If you leave and go from my village, I'll forgive you, otherwise, those who encouraged you by unfurling the flag of revolt against the government will be hanged, and the others will be thrown in jail for fifteen or twenty years."

The villagers resisted for a few more days. The children and women cried and screamed from hunger. Some of the townspeople gave them water and bread.

Koca Osman said he would die before looking in that herif's slimy face. Others went to Ali Safa's konak to talk with him, the prosecutor and the Kaymakam. The prosecutor told them, "you have done much harm to Ali Safa Bey. You're tyrannizing the man."

"Haşa," said tall Seyfali as he rose to his feet. "Never, God forbid." His head touched the ceiling of the room.

"Sus!" said the prosecutor. "Quiet. Sit in your place. Just last night five young men of yours were caught burning Safa Bey's farm."

Ali Safa Bey interrupted:

"Deli Muslu, and the name of one of the others was Süleyman. Five people," he said. "What do you want from me, friends, what did I do to you?"

Seyfali rose again:

"Leave us alone, we'll leave Vayvay and go. The land of our fathers since the İskan ... What can we do, fate is like this," he said with a deep voice of lament. "Our fathers' lands ... "

"When?" asked Ali Safa Bey, excited.

"Right away," said Seyfali. "As soon as you release us, we'll leave."

"In that case go already, you'll be free tomorrow morning," said the prosecutor.[64]

****

Memed looked at the dry bed of the stream, a tiny amount of water had come and quietly filled the cracks. It meant that the village of Vayvay was finally leaving, he thought. That flash of light came again and sat in his eyes, with his pupils fixed. Koca Osman, Seyran, Tall Seyfali, beautiful-eyed Ferhat Hoca, stubborn Yobazoğlu, Kamer Ana, and Selver Gelin came to his eyes. It meant that all of them were leaving Vayvay now and going away. Or they had already gone for some time and left Vayvay completely empty. Seyran hadn't come for two days. The last time she didn't say a thing, but she looked so hurt that when he looked at her she made Memed shiver to his bones. The mark of defeat and exhaustion was stamped on her forehead. Sooner or later it would kill her.

Topal Ali had been hanging around. His crippled foot under him, he whistled a strange song from the branch of a willow tree. Köse Halil was at the edge of the stream watching the water fill the cracks.

172

For some reason Ali raised his head, looked at Memed and saw the light in his eyes as soon as he did. A mood somewhere between pleasure and pain, laughter and tears passed across his face. Memed got up, walked over and stood in front of Ali. He looked at him with the look of the closest of friends. He put his hand on his shoulder and didn't lift it for a while. Then he went to the çardak and removed his bundle from under the bed. He took out his shirt and trousers and quickly, in no time, got dressed. He fastened his pistol, his dagger, his binoculars, and his cartridge belt. He hung the rifle over his shoulder, and placed his embroidered Maraş cloak on top of it. After flipping his fez in his hand a few times, he didn't put it on but placed it in the pocket of his cloak. He pulled his socks up to his knees. His shoes had dried and were a bit tight, but they loosened up. Now he looked as he had when he came to Çukurova.

He went up to Topal Ali and stood there. The yellow flash in his eyes was beaming even more, flowing and palpitating nonstop in his head, filling every space.

Ali told Memed that Hamza spent his days in such fear that he would never recover. Even if he lived, Ali said, Hamza would only remain half alive. He wanted to forgive Memed and give him two of his villages.

Ali had never seen Memed's face as bitter, as tough as a boulder, as this. He had also never seen that flash of steel stay in his eyes like this.

The afternoon passed. Far off, in the south, the white clouds sailing above the Mediterranean slowly thickened and rose toward the sky. A little later, a strong wave of the western wind blew and cooled the surroundings off a bit. Then it stopped. It stopped for a while, then it blew, it blew and stopped. The sailing clouds then grew very thick and rose up, the higher they rose, the bigger and brighter they became.

At that moment, the western wind started kicking up the dust with all its speed. Dust spirals sprang up on the roads here and there and began to move from the south towards the Toroslar.

Memed took Topal Ali's hand and stared straight at and into his eyes without saying a word.

"İyi," Ali said, as if speaking to himself.

Memed:

"I'm going to go stop by Vayvay … "

"In that case, I'll wait for you outside town," Ali said. "Look, listen to me good, you know the dried creek outside the village."

"Bilirim."

"There, just on the right of the road, when you go down the creek, there's a very old, huge mastic tree. At its base is a single grave. You can see it even when it's pitch dark. I'll wait for you there."

Memed mounted the bare horse. He grabbed and pulled back on the reins that Halil had had woven for days. Köse was still drifting off, watching the water fill the cracks.

"Hakkını helal et Halil," said Memed, and he rode the horse out from inside the bostan. He sailed off in a cloud of dust and, a short while later, tied the head of the horse to the large mulberry tree in the middle of Vayvay village.[65]

There were only a few people left. They had gathered under the mulberry tree, where Koca Osman lay very ill. Kamer Ana and Seyran were with him. Seyfali was laying on another bed nearby. Deli Muslu's mother and Seyran's family were there, too. Seyran's brothers were looking after Ferhat Hoca's wife.

Seyfali had refused to leave. Weeping, he had said, "I'll die on my father's land. I'm afraid to die in another place."

Memed got down from his horse and walked straight to Koca Osman. When he saw Memed, Koca Osman lifted his head slowly from the pillow, looked, and then set his head back down and closed his eyes.

His face had withered, it was more wrinkled than usual. Even his eyes couldn't be seen from under the wrinkles. Memed approached, took his hand and placed it between his palms. Koca Osman opened his eyes with difficulty and looked at Memed. Memed read an unforgiving sense of offense in his eyes.

"Nasılsın Emmi, geçmiş olsun," he said in a broken voice.

Koca Osman didn't respond to him. Memed waited and waited. Koca Osman said nothing.

He tried again:

"Nasılsın diyorum Osman Emmi sana," he said, and when Koca Osman again gave no response, Kamer Ana stepped over.

"Osman, Osman," she said, "look Memed has come to helallaşmaya – to make amends – with you, the boy is going. He's asking how you are."

Koca Osman opened his eyes, looked and stared at Memed's face. Then in a faint voice, he said:

"Kocadım İncem kocadım." I've aged my Memed I've aged. "I've been beaten, son, beaten ... "

He shut his eyes. Memed understood that Koca Osman was pretty angry with him. If not, he would have called him şahinim.

Memed went to Seyfali's side and wished him a recovery as well. Seyfali's long body was even longer, his face and eyes were black and blue, swollen, and filled with cuts and bruises.

Memed rose and looked around the empty, abandoned village. His eyes met Seyran's and stayed there. Then he went back to Koca Osman and again grasped his hand, taking it and caressing and kissing it between his hands. About to cry and in a crackling voice, he spoke.

"Hakkını helal et Osman Emmi."

Koca Osman's lips quivered. Memed took Kamer Ana's hand and kissed it, and Kamer Ana hugged him and kissed his neck. After helallaşing with everyone individually, he came to Seyran and stood by her side. Somehow he couldn't raise his head and look her in the face. He slowly took her right hand hanging by her side and held it tightly. Then, again slowly, as if fearing to hurt her in any way, he hugged Seyran gently, and then, still looking down, mounted his horse and galloped at full speed from the village in a cloud of dust. Seyran couldn't say farewell or wish him luck, she couldn't watch him go, she couldn't cry, and she couldn't smile, she just stood there beside the huge mulberry tree, withering under the sun.

The sun had set for a while when he reached the mastic tree outside town. Ali saw his gliding shadow coming from far off and had gone to the road.

Memed:

"Ali," he said.

Ali:

"It's me."

Memed pulled back on the reins.

Ali:

"We'll go now, the Bey is at home. If he's not at home, you'll go ahead and wait for him. You'll say that Dursun Durmuş sent me from the farm, that's what you'll say. Don't forget, Dursun Durmuş."

Memed:

"I won't forget," dedi.

"They won't suspect you at all. Armed men like you come and go every night."

They passed through the unlit, dark streets of the town, and came before the big, arched gate along the high courtyard wall. Ali got down from his horse and opened the wooden gate. The gate squeaked. Memed rode his horse inside and jumped to the ground.

Ali took the horse's reins and showed Memed the staircase up ahead a bit. Memed ran up the staircase, knocked on the door, and a woman's voice inside answered:

"Who's there?"

Memed calmly replied:

"It's me," dedi. "I've come from the farm. Dursun Durmuş Ağa sent me. Is the Bey at home?"

Kadın:

"A man is here. He says he's from the farm, that Dursun sent him," a voice said to the Bey inside.

Memed heard the Bey say, "Let the man in," and for the first time lost his cool. His heart started to beat fast. The Bey was in bed, holding a

175

newspaper in his hands. As Memed entered, he closed the door slowly behind him. The Bey looked up from the newspaper:

"What is it, what's happened now?" he asked without much concern.

Memed:

"Benim adım İnce Memed," he said at once. My name is İnce Memed. In a full, challenging voice, he asked, "Beni bilebildin mi?" Were you able to recognize me?

The newspaper in Ali Safa Bey's hands fell. He lay there half straightened up, dumbfounded. His face turned totally white, even his black eyes. His lips trembled. He opened and closed his mouth a few times, but no sound came out.

Memed pointed the pistol in his hand at him and fired three times. The light in the room blew out from the wind of the bullets. Right away, at that moment, all hell broke loose in the estate. Memed slowly went down the staircase, took the horse in Ali's hands, jumped on it and left the town at full gallop.

At sunrise, he entered Değirmenoluk village, rode straight to Abdi Ağa's house, and, with his pistol pointed, ordered Hamza to walk in front of him.

"Öldürüyorlar, öldürüyorlar" – they're killing me, they're killing me – Hamza screamed. "İnce Memed beni öldürüyooor" – İnce Memed is killiiing me – "öldürüyooor, öldürüyooor!" He ran from one door to the next begging for help, but no door, not even his own, opened to him. He tried to run away but stumbled and fell on his face several times. Memed rode behind him the entire time, never losing his cool, never losing or gaining distance, speeding up if he sped up, slowing down if he slowed down. Memed led him to the middle of the village.

"Stop here," he shouted.

There was no one around. Not a living thing in sight. Not a cat, not a dog, not one living thing ... Nor was there a single bird flying in the sky.

In one last effort, Hamza again cried out:

"Yetişin" – Help – "öldürüyorlar, öldürüyorlar," and then he collapsed on the ground. He swayed from right to left, shaking like a leaf.

With his teeth chattering, "Don't kill me efendim," he said. "I'll give you a fifth of this village. Allahaşkına."

He wasn't able to finish what he was saying. Memed emptied the bullets in his pistol into Hamza's head. He didn't die right away. He spun around where he was and then clawed at the ground.

Memed slowly took the pistol from his shoulder, pointed it, and emptied another cartridge into Hamza. Hamza hunched over face down where he was and didn't move. On top of his horse, Memed went around Hamza, reloaded his pistol and emptied it into the dark corpse lying hunched over. He rode the horse around the body like mad, going away and coming back, unable to vent his rage, and he empted another cartridge of bullets into Hamza.

Those watching Memed from inside thought he was playing some strange, old horse game.

Memed finally tired and stopped shooting. He sat erect on his horse at the head of the body, lost in thought and not moving at all. His sweat dripped onto the horse's neck. The dark coal-black horse breathed heavily.

The sun rose as high as the poplars and Memed and the horse withdrew into the shade. Fragments of light that fell on the back of the horse made its muted colors sparkle.

No one in the village made a sound. Not even a bird chirped or a bee buzzed. In the distance, on the far side, was the wavy, deep blue plain of Dikenlidüzü.

Memed sat and waited atop the horse, watching the village like a hawk, looking in vain for some movement, some sound. One door, five doors, ten doors would open, all the doors of the village would open, and the people would soon pour outside. Memed had no idea why he waited for this, but he waited. He waited for a long time.

The sound of footsteps coming slowly from a distance startled him. He turned and saw Hürü Ana. They both smiled and watched a pool of blood form in the hollow of a stone next to Hamza's body.

"Ana, Ana," he said, "Hürü Ana, hakkını helal et."

He didn't say anything else. Hürü Ana also didn't speak. He pulled back on the reins of the horse, pointed its head towards Alidağı and took off. The dark horse ran out of the village like lightning …

Hamza's corpse remained where it had fallen on the ground for two days, by the side of the stone with the hollow in it. The villagers didn't leave their houses. Only the most curious stuck their heads out from their doors, took a look at what they could see in the middle of the alan, saw the corpse, and then immediately stuck their heads back inside. On the morning of the third day, Pancar Hösük came out of his house with a rope, went to the center of the alan, and tied the feet of the corpse with the rope. He dragged the corpse out of the village, brought it some distance, and then rolled it over the cliff below Kulaksız's mill.

"You got what you deserved bastard," dedi, smiling from above. "You bald infidel. Here, you got what you were looking for. Get out of here and be prey for the bald vultures."

After this, the villagers – many of them without doing anything, without difficulty, and without talking with each other at all – timidly strolled, wandered around, and idled about inside the village, swinging their arms by their sides …

One day later they went and slowly opened the door of Kel Hamza's warehouses. As they did, Hamza's wives watched without saying a word, as though what was occurring wasn't actually happening. The warehouses were brimming with containers of oil, honey, pekmez, boxes and boxes of dried grapes, almonds, walnuts, figs, dried berries, pears, dried apples, and squash. In front of all the eyes of the village, the villagers handed out and shared the supplies like brothers and sisters, without complaint. They set aside a share for Hamza's wives, "Take this, your share, too," they said.

Afterwards, after the sharing of the warehouse supplies, a long time later, they assembled in front of Hamza's house and asked his wives for their money. One of the women brought a bag filled to the top and handed it to them. They sat together and also shared this as brothers and sisters. And they gave a share to Hamza's wives. Later, everyone went to Hamza's house and brought home the horses, donkeys, goats, oxen, and cows, many of which Kel Hamza wasn't able to sell. Later, for years, they opened the storehouses filled with wheat, barley, and millet and shared them as brothers and sisters. They also gave a share to Hamza's wives.

They did all this very quietly, a bit fearfully, hesitantly, and a bit bashfully, but steadily and çıt çıkarmadan – without making any sound, without a voice of objection.

Autumn arrived, and no one moved at all. The cool breezes blew, the shadows spread and faded, the thistles dried and cracked, and yet there wasn't the slightest movement on anyone's part. It was almost the time of the year to plough the fields and, still, the hands of the villagers were tied behind their backs. They leaned forward and backward, and they continued to wander around inside the village looking each other in the eyes. If not for the calls of Abdaloğlu Bayram's tan davulu, the drum played at dawn.

It was one morning when the sky hadn't yet lit up that the sounds of the tan davulu were heard from the center of the village. The drums beat heavily, steadily, and intensely.

They understood immediately that it was the drummer Abdaloğlu Bayram, and his son Cümek, playing the zurna. They knew of him, too. Because there was no Dervish in the entire Toros who could play like this.

Together, Abdaloğlu Bayram and his son beat the drums, starting low, then rising, then rising even more, and then roaring, crying out, whirling, and dancing. Caught himself in tremendous enthusiasm, Abdaloğlu Bayram soared in a storm of joy in the center of the village. As long as he could remember, he had never fallen into this kind of exuberance.

It was late morning when the villagers came one by one to the alan. They were all fully cleansed, bathed and pure. They wore their best holiday clothes.

The older women wore milk-white headscarves, the young girls colorful silk scarves. They were decorated in red, green, and maroon. Hürü Ana was such a flower today that she could be picked out even from within such a large crowd.

They arrived, gathered and filled the village alan. It was so crowded that if you had dropped a pin in the crowd it wouldn't have hit the ground. A short while later the crowd joined Bayram and Cümek in their dancing. They swirled and swirled in a huge joyful whirling, and then danced as they withdrew towards the thistles.

The villagers in the other villages of Dikenlidüzü heard Bayram's drums, and they beat the drums as well. They also went to the thistles. All five of the five villages came out and met in the east, at the edge of the thistles at the foot of Alidağı. The young men brought scythes and cut the thistles, and the young girls gathered and piled the cut thistles into huge mounds. Bayram leapt on top of one of the mounds with his drum, and began to dance a dance that none of the villagers had ever seen. He stretched, contracted, and whirled around, curling his hands and arms in a dance from the old days. While he danced, on his signal, the villagers lit the mound below him on fire. For a while Bayram danced with and in the middle of the flames. He blew, and he swayed. Then he emerged from the flames standing and mixed with the crowd.

The flames skipped from the mounds of thistles across the plain. The dried thistles quickly burned from one end of the plain to the other. The north wind blew as well. It seized the flames and carried them, scattering, spilling, and blowing them about. Screams coming from inside the crackling flames filled the night as the flames were carried all over the plain. Towards morning, all of Dikenlidüzü was ablaze, tossed about in a flood of fire.

Not a word was heard from İnce Memed again. He dropped out of sight.

O gün bu gündür – Since then, every year – Dikenlidüzü köylüleri her yıl toprağa saban atmazdan önce çakırdikenliğe gelir, büyük bir toy düğünle dikenlere ateş verirler. Before taking the plough to the land, the villagers of Dikenlidüzü first come to the field of thistles and burn the thistles with a huge toy düğün. Yalımlar üç gün üç gece bir sel gibi düzde dolanır, akar durur. The flames fill the plain like a flood for three days and three nights, flowing unceasingly. Ova bir yalım fırtınasında çalkanır, yanan dikenlikten çığlıklar gelir. The plain is whipped up in a storm of fire, screams come from inside the burning thistles.

Bu ateşle birlikte de Alidağının doruğunda bir top ışık patlar. Dağın doruğu üç gece ağarır, apaydınlık, gündüz gibi olur. And together with this blaze, a ball of light bursts atop Alidağı. The mountain's peak turns white for three nights, bright as can be, just like in the daytime.[66]

Notes

1 Y. Kemal, *İM2*.
2 Ibid., 10–15.
3 Ibid., 16–18.

4 Ibid., 20–23.
5 Ibid., 45–54.
6 Ibid., 73–74.
7 Ibid., 78.
8 Ibid., 81–85.
9 Ibid., 127–32.
10 Ibid., 141.
11 Ibid., 142–43.
12 Ibid., 143.
13 Ibid., 144–46.
14 Ibid., 146–55.
15 Ibid., 160–61.
16 Ibid., 163–91.
17 Ibid., 181.
18 Ibid.
19 Ibid., 195–96.
20 Ibid., 204–5.
21 Ibid., 207–8.
22 Ibid., 218–22.
23 Ibid., 223.
24 Ibid., 232–33.
25 Ibid., 235–37.
26 Ibid., 244–47.
27 Ibid., 255–56.
28 Ibid., 261.
29 Ibid., 262–64.
30 Ibid., 270–74.
31 Ibid., 276–82.
32 Ibid., 294–99.
33 Ibid., 310–12.
34 Ibid., 321.
35 Ibid., 319.
36 Ibid., 320–21.
37 Ibid., 327–30.
38 Ibid., 335–40.
39 Ibid., 354.
40 Ibid., 354–56.
41 Ibid., 357–60.
42 Ibid., 358–61.
43 Ibid., 363–64.
44 Ibid., 366–67.
45 Ibid., 367.
46 Ibid., 374–75.
47 Ibid., 381–86.
48 Ibid., 391–92.
49 Ibid., 390–91.
50 Ibid., 402–4.
51 Ibid., 404–5.
52 Ibid., 410–14.
53 Ibid., 413.
54 Ibid., 419–22.
55 Ibid., 422–24.

56 Ibid., 425–27.
57 Ibid., 430–31.
58 Ibid., 432–33.
59 Ibid., 433–35.
60 Ibid., 438–39.
61 Ibid., 440–41.
62 Ibid., 442.
63 Ibid.
64 Ibid., 443–47.
65 Ibid., 448–50.
66 Ibid., 451–59. End, İnce Memed 2.

IV
Sakızlı[1]

Continually passing in front of his eyes was Kel Hamza's elongated, saffron-yellow face, still and frozen with a scream of death, pleading with his huge wide-open mouth and bulging eyes. He hoped for help from the bird that flew above, from a friend, from an enemy, from the ants crawling on the ground. He was half asleep, half in a dream, and for the first time thought about how a person's life can be so fragile, so necessary, that so many people, maybe the vast majority, are able to degrade themselves so much and not give up. Is human life worth this much humiliation? Must life be lived at any cost? The diseases, illnesses, oppressions, tyrannies, hunger, poverty, these things haven't been able to break the vital strength of the human species; even after the cruelty, humiliation, damage, and carnage, human beings live on. What was this amazing strength, this endless resilience, to endure the most miserable conditions of cruelty in order to live, and for what? Kel Hamza, stumbling in the village in front of the horse with fear cutting through his entire body, stopped now and then and looked at him, as if he was begging like a dog, in such a way that the human heart can't endure. He struggled a lot with himself to kill him, and after all was done, thought that it was haram that the life of a person was taken like this from humanity. And when Ali Safa Bey saw him and Memed said, "Benim adım İnce Memed, beni bilebildin mi Ağa?" Ali Safa's face stiffened and his eyes grew big and opened and closed in fear, and in a moment, in the blink of an eye, his eyes were fully fixed on the barrel of the gun with an unbelievable look of pleading. In that momentary appeal, here was perhaps the worst kind of descent, the lowest that the species can fall. Was a life worth this much humiliation? Is life this much more valuable than anything else?[2]

The jandarma followed Memed's trail the whole way and, in a clash in the woods at the base of the mountains, Memed is shot several times in the hip and leg. He survives when his horse carries him to safety.[3]

****

At Ali Safa Bey's funeral, the ağas argued again about İnce Memed. "İnce Memed has taken the Toros Mountains," said Karadağlıoğlu Murtaza Ağa, expressing the fears of many. "The wolf has tasted blood." "Yoktan var etti- ğimiz, düveli muazzamanın o kokmuş ellerinden aldığımız gül gibi vatanımız yok olacak." That which we brought into being from nothing, our perfect country that we took back from the rotten, stinking hands of the powerful, will be destroyed. Arif Saim Bey, one of the most powerful ağas, disagreed. "We saved this nation ... However much land you want, you can take it from the place you like."[4]

Murtaza Ağa seeks protection by taking Topal Ali into his confidence and making him his best friend. He called Ali his dear brother and outfitted him with expensive clothing and weapons.[5]

****

Since the night before, the fourteen-year-old shepherd boy Müslüm sat on the slope, on his own, dosing off now and then, but mostly awake watching over his herd. His carved red dogwood staff in front, and his felt shepherd's cloak embroidered with an orange sun on its front breast to his side and extended to the end of his feet, he stretched out on a patch of thorned keven flowers. And at the foot of the rock by his side slept a huge, yellow shep- herd's dog with its large head extended and resting on its front legs. The spikes on the collar around its neck were as long as daggers. The sheep dosed off in the lush field below that had trees planted here and there. Rose- pink keven covered the slope from here to the top of the hill. The rising sun released its light with all its radiance in the surroundings, filling the orman – the forest – the cliffs, and the sky with a pink light.

The boy shepherd Müslüm wasn't relaxed at all, getting up now and then, going up to the high cliffs on the ridge where the sun set, looking out on the road from where the sun rises, to the small meandering stream, the undu- lating forest filled with a thousand greens down below, and the path that went over to the other side and climbed up the bare slope of the opposite mountain where the sun sets, and then he would come back and stretch out beside his cloak. His face constantly flushed from one color to another. Last night, volleys of gunfire had come from behind the tall cliffs over there, then they stopped. Towards morning an outcry came from the lower side of the plain where the sheep were spread out, and following the cry, three handgun shots were fired.

Çoban Müslüm was from the oba, the camp, of the Sarıkeçilis, established in the large Kızılkartallı valley of the high plateaux of the eastern mountains. Below the end of the huge boulder right on the top of the mountain, a spring with enough frothy water to spin a mill flowed right down the middle of the lush valley.

There was a silence in the oba since last night. Everyone spoke in a whisper, those coming and going from tent to tent did so with some anxiety, a bit of fear, but more sevinç – joy. Çoban Müslüm knew everything, he brought the sheep here and waited since last night. He felt the fear in the oba as well as the sevinç all the way through to his heart. No one said anything to him and, moreover, no one said, hey, Müslum boy, you should do it like this, or do it like that. His green-as-grass eyes were bright with sevinç in the way he tended the herd. Now and then, it's not that he didn't fear or suffer a bit. But he knew what he needed to do. It was to watch on their way whoever came from there below, from Çukurova, who passed on the path from the base of the cliff covered from top to bottom in green moss that wound around that small creek there in the forest and came to the path in the middle of the plain where the sheep were spread out, from there or from the Kızılkartal valley, or whoever was crossing the mountain in the distance. And Çoban Müslüm watched where the roads opened. He breathed quickly and his heart beat steadily with anticipation.

He lay down for a long time next to the keven flowers. Red and black-spotted ladybugs swarmed under the piles of thorns. The thorns on the slope and pink keven flowers shined, sparkled, and erupted like crystal in the bright daylight, and the ladybugs here lit up in a bright red, a rich redness, like a flame.

Çoban Müslüm began to feel impatient. His eyes looked to the farthest shadow, his ears listened for the slightest crackling sound. The sheep in the field below grazed in peace. And the dog slept by his side. Müslüm got a bit hungry, since, because of his impatience, filling his stomach hadn't even come to mind. Finally he took the ladle around his waist and went down alongside the sheep, caught a large dark one and started to milk it. When the scoop was full with warm, frothy milk, he went back by the side of his sun-decorated cloak, took out some bread from his bundle and ate it with the aromatic milk. A white cloud came and rose above the forest. A small breeze blew and then faded. The early autumn sun increased the brightness more and more, and the deep green of the forest and the heavy pink of the pink-thorned keven flowers fused together. From here, from the slope of the mountain all the way to down below, perhaps going all the way down to the edge of Çukurova, the keven flowers spread on the bare slope, from the orman to the top of the mountain, glittering, radiant in silver, pink, and purple. Some humming sounds came from very far off, huge eagles high up in the heights with their wings spread wide, not moving the slightest, soared in place as if they were glued to the sky. A long-stemmed flower with a red cluster extended from the middle of a bush towards the sun. Tiny blue, purple and yellow flowers teemed amidst the kevenler. Thick, dark, powerful bees, buzzing loudly and noisily, flew from flower to flower. Small colorful birds as tiny as a finger alighted from keven to keven. His appetite satisfied, Müslüm grew bored. Though he never got fully bored. In the mix of the life of a small bird, an ant, an insect, the plunging eagle, he forgot himself and drifted off. For him the sky was a strange, huge blue flower, a grand flower with its petals wide open. After satisfying his hunger, he always went to dig up crocus bulbs. In the ground under the çiğdem flowers he would find the largest bulbs and pull them out. The bulbs with faded and dried flowers were large and very milky. With one yank, he could rip the stem out of the soil. He had become very skilled at this. The largest çiğdemler grew among the shrubs under the kevenler on the rocky ground. The deep yellow, short-stemmed flowers dazzled the eyes. So bright, so yellow. While digging the çiğdem roots, the ground smelled of a dewy, fresh scent that he had never known that made his head spin and drunk with pleasure.

Digging the çiğdemler took quite a long time. The sun set and disappeared, and he forgot everything in the excitement of pulling out the bulbs. When his sack was full of bulbs, he turned his slightly aching waist in the direction of the forest below, then above and watched the eagles soaring over the peaks of the mountains. Then he sat down and started to peel the souring çiğdem bulbs. The bulbs were covered with a light brown web, like a membrane. After peeling and taking off the web around the bulb, he took out a bright white bulb a bit larger than a large chickpea. The çiğdem flowers are eaten either raw or cooked in milk. They are considered a remedy for every problem – their scent doesn't leave a person's nasal cavity for a long time.

Müslüm slowly peeled the çiğdemler and, at the same time, chewed and ate them slowly. His face was perspiring, turning pink like the keven çiçekler, his grass-green eyes constantly watching over the area like an eagle's eyes. Suddenly, he saw his dog lift its head and its ears stand straight on end. He immediately got up, tossed a handful of peeled çiğdemler, and searched the forest and the area with his eyes. Then the dog stood up and started barking straight at the forest, then ran barking directly to the sheep. Just at that moment, from inside the forest, the brass crescent moon under the hat of the first jandarma flickered. Behind, Faruk Yüzbaşı, riding a grey horse, emerged as well. There was a fierce look on his face. Following him there appeared many jandarma with their rifles hanging on their shoulders. The Yüzbaşı got off his horse over at the spring on the right side of the plain. At first, the binoculars on his chest stood out. His weapon was strapped just under his cartridge belt. He was wearing boots that shone. His moustache was twisted very sharply, giving him an awe-inspiring appearance. His clothes had been recently pressed, as if he had just put them on a short while ago. The jandarma stacked their rifles at the head of the spring, filled their pinewood canteens, and drank some water. Müslüm flew like lightning to stop the dog from barking at them, he went down to the field, grabbed the dog, and stood there and looked at them with blank eyes, filled with surprise.

Onbaşı Kertiş Ali directed the Yüzbaşı to the boy çoban:

"A shepherd," he said, "for the first time around here we come across a person."

The Yüzbaşı lifted his head to the child before him, and, after playing with the silver ornamented handle of the whip in his hand, lowered his head and slowly spoke:

"Bu bir çocuk." This is a child.

Kertiş Ali was from an impoverished village in the valley of those barren mountains across the way, where the land was poor and nothing grew. When he became a soldier he gave up his discharge and extended his service. After being a commander at several jandarma stations, he was appointed to a post in his own town. He was very proud of this. The stations in these parts were unable to take many bribes, and what he had earned had been enough, though it grew, too. He already had a house built in a large garden left from the Armenians. He wanted to show himself off, to add fame to his fame in the village, and to become famous in all of Çukurova. For him, money meant nothing. According to his humble thinking, fame was necessary for a person. And for this fame, capturing İnce Memed or shooting him was necessary. If İnce could be captured or shot, though all the fame would go to the Yüzbaşı, a share of it would fall on him, even if only a small amount.

As for Asım Çavuş, he wanted neither fame nor glory. In fact he was tired of this life. Moreover, he admired İnce Memed, the bloodthirsty one, who killed our Abdi Ağa, our Hamza Efendi, our Ali Safa Bey. He shot these many precious people of the newly blossomed Republic at point blank without having any mercy, he stabbed babies in their cradles, he cut their tongues out from the roots of those who say I'm an ağa, I'm a bey, and then, after that, he impaled these people. These mountains are filled with eşkıya. Kertiş Ali Onbaşı knew well that many of the eşkıya bands could never be touched ... because most of them were the men of the Çukurova beys and ağas. There were also eşkıyas who were beholden to no one. İnce Memed was famous, and he was supported by the poor and wretched, they protected him like they would their own lives, like he was one of their very own, and the others, they couldn't be friends with anyone ... neither the beys nor the villagers ... They were being wiped out. And there were so many of them that five or ten were killed every month and still they weren't finished off. Kertiş gained fame from killing eşkıyas, from shooting them in the eyes. They already started calling him Allahsız Kertiş Ali, Godless Kertiş Ali, the butcher of the eşkıyas. Among these jandarma there was no one better at beating the villagers than him. Especially the mountain villagers ... In the stations he had become such a beating expert that he could teach them in Ankara for ten years. Not only the village creatures, he could make wolf and bird, snake and centipede, even stone, talk. "I swear by God these villagers were created by great God only to be beaten, to be hit until they piss and shit in their underwear," he'd say. He would resign from being a corporal in a few more years of extended service, and become a farm owner near Akçasaz in the Anavarza plain. He'd already made his path. For this, he also needed to get close to Zülfü Efendi and Arif Saim Bey.

"Children are better for this business," said Kertiş Ali. In front of the Yüzbaşı he stood stiff and erect at attention, chest out, belly in, and head held high. "Learn what you can from the child."

"In that case, call him over ... "

Kertiş Ali ran to Müslüm's side. The boy was over there, holding the collar of the dog and watching the jandarma. When he saw Kertiş Ali coming and running straight towards him he was very glad but tried not to show it.

"Çabuk gel!" Come quickly. "Leave the dog, my Yüzbaşı wants you." His forehead was wrinkled, the veins in his neck stood out. "Shoo that dog away and come quickly."

Müslüm, who had been holding the dog around its neck, sent the dog toward the sheep. The dog listened to his command and walked toward the herd.

With Kertiş in front and Müslüm behind, they approached the Yüzbaşı.

The Yüzbaşı lifted his head, and after looking Müslüm over from head to toe spoke:

"Sen buralarda ne yapıyorsun?" he asked without paying much attention to him.

"I'm a shepherd," said Müslüm, turning completely red and shaking from head to toe.

"Where do you live, which kabile are your from?"

"I'm from the Sarıkeçili oymak."

"Whose oymak is that?"

"Bizim oymağımız." Ours.

The Yüzbaşı smiled.

"How long have you been here?"

"It's been one night and two days."

"Have you seen a rider, a man, an armed man, an injured person pass through here?"

"I haven't seen anyone. No one comes around here ... I don't see any one around here, how many years I shepherd the sheep here. If you're looking for someone, he's somewhere down below."

"I understood, Yüzbaşım, this dog is lying."

The Yüzbaşı lifted the whip in his hand towards him as if to say, be quiet.

"Last night did you hear any sounds of gunfire?"

"I didn't."

"How could that be, how could you not hear, there was a clash and the sound of gunfire spread through the entire forest, how could you not hear?"

"I was sleeping. I sleep deeply."

"What kind of shepherd are you that you sleep, the wolves don't steal the sheep?"

"They aren't able to steal them," said the shepherd boy proudly. "You see that yellow one over there, he'll eat ten wolves. There's no dog like him."

His dog, o sarı tıpkı – that yellow kind – was like a person. He knows, he understands, everything, and he thinks, too. The only thing he doesn't do is speak. If he tried hard, maybe he would speak as well.

"Benim bu sarı var ya – I have that yellow one over there, you know – he can take a herd and shepherd into the mountains without any need for a shepherd for a week, for ten days, for a month. "Benim bu sarı var ya, in the smallest dangers, a snake, a scorpion, a person, even if I'm sleeping, he comes and slowly tugs on my arm and wakes me up."

"Last night he didn't wake you up, he didn't hear the sounds of gunfire?"

"If he had heard them, he would have woken me up."

"He woke him up," shouted Kertiş Ali, "but he's lying when he says he didn't hear."

"He would have woken me up," responded Müslüm. "It means he didn't hear. He knows the sound of gunfire. He can distinguish between the eşkıya, the jandarma, good people, bad people. Once he grabbed a man by the throat and nearly buried him in the forest down there. There was that guy, you know, after he raped the girl, he cut her up into pieces. Yes, my yellow one is that kind of yellow dog. He's the ağa, the pir, of the dogs."

"You love your dog very much?"

"More than others ... O benim arkadaşımdır." He's my friend.

"He's his mother, Yüzbaşım, and his father," ridiculed Kertiş Ali.

Müslüm threw him a sharp look. He knew very well who he was. When he became Onbaşı, he went to his own village with fifteen jandarma and for three days and three nights they beat the entire village with their clubs and batons.

"What were you thinking ... ?"

"He's lying Yüzbaşım. This guy knows which way İnce Memed went. Let me get it out of him."

And in a cold-blooded way, the Yüzbaşı said, "Go ahead."

"Here or in the forest?"

"Here," said the Yüzbaşı. "There down below. Let's see how you'll get this deyyus to speak."

Kertiş approached Müslüm showing kindness and compassion:

"Bak yavrum," he said, look yavrum, "yesterday morning as it got light, you didn't see an armed man riding a dark horse, a horse without a saddle, galloping at full speed in front of you? The man on top of the horse is a bit bigger than you ... Speak yavrum, he left right out of the forest, came towards you, and you awoke from the sound of the horse steps, or your dog woke you up. And when you awoke, you saw the rider at full gallop. Which way did he go, that rider?"

"Görmedim." I didn't see.

"Görmedin mi?" You didn't see?

"Hiç görmedim." I didn't see anything.

"Yavrum, what's your name?"

"Müslüm."

"Müslüm yavrum, if you don't talk, it won't be good for you."

"Hiçbir atlı görmedim." I didn't see any rider.

Four jandarma who had been prepared for a while waited. The half of the largest of them held large bully clubs in their hands.

"Yıkın şunu." Break him down.

Right away they beat him and wacked his feet with the straps of their guns.

"Çıkarın çarıklarını." Take off his sandals.

They quickly took off his sandals and socks, and tossed them on top of the keven shrubs.

"Başla." Get to it.

With all his strength, a huge jandarma soldier struck and beat Müslüm's feet with his club, and the child didn't make any sound. The Yüzbaşı looked on with surprise and wonder.

"Devam, daha sert." Continue. Harder.

Müslüm, whose face and eyes were dripping with sweat, just clenched his teeth firmly, his body tightening and bouncing with every blow, and then he went weak.

Quite a while passed, and not a sound came from Müslüm. The Yüzbaşı looked at him with his eyes wide open in surprise. The less Müslüm made a sound, the more the Yüzbaşı was angered.

"Ali, you take the club," he sternly commanded. "What's going on here!"

Ali took the sopa from the huge jandarma and pounced upon the child with all his strength and expertise. Müslüm still made not a sound.

The dog then came a bit forward, tiptoeing on the end of the spring surrounded on all sides by blue flowered pennyroyal, prostrate with fearful eyes, watching Müslüm on whom the club fell from head to toe, ready to pounce. But no sign, not even the smallest sound, came from Müslüm.

The Yüzbaşı couldn't stand it, rose from his place, went to the head of the child shepherd and stood. Kertiş Ali turned totally black, gritted his teeth, lifted the kaim sopa, and lowered it with all abandon over Müslüm's body, and, other than jerking and tightening, not the slightest response came from the child.

Finally, the child's feet started to bleed.

Yüzbaşı:

"This isn't possible, Ali Onbaşı, not possible. Have you ever encountered a creature like this?" Breathing deeply, sweating all over, Kertiş Ali said, "No," and with all his strength lowering the sopa with a whooshing sound, "No Yüzbaşım, I've never seen such problems in my entire life."

"Söyle oğlum, sen İnce Memedi gördün, değil mi?" Out with it yavrum, you saw İnce Memed, didn't you?

Müslüm's teeth were clenched, they didn't open.

"Tell us my boy, otherwise Ali Onbaşı will kill you. He's killed many men beating them like this."

"Çok öldürdüm, çok öldürdüm," said Kertiş Ali, I've killed many, I've killed many, as his entire body tightened and the veins in his neck swelled, confirming what the Yüzbaşı said. It appeared as if the thick club beating Müslüm's feet had bent. And blood gushed from his feet. The club turned bright red.

Yüzbaşı Faruk for a moment noticed the dog standing up off to the side.

"Wait," he commanded with some pleasure to Kertiş Ali, "wait Ali Onbaşı."

Taking a deep breath, Ali Onbaşı stopped.

"Stand him up."

Kertiş Ali grabbed the boy by the arms and pulled him to his feet. Müslüm was unable to stand and collapsed full length on the ground.

"Bring that dog."

Kertiş Ali lifted the boy from the ground, putting one of his arms around him. Another jandarma lifted him with his other arm. Between them, the boy swayed lifelessly.

Asım Çavuş who had been watching what was going on with blank eyes, then got up and came over to them.

"This boy is dying Yüzbaşım. Look, he's losing consciousness."

"These kind have seven lives, nothing will happen to them," responded the Yüzbaşı sternly.

"Haven't you been watching, he took this much of a beating and didn't even groan."

"They have seven lives," said Kertiş Ali.

"I know how to make him speak," said the Yüzbaşı. He took his gun from his belt and turned toward the dog standing over there. "Open your eyes now peasant boy, open them and you'll see what's about to happen!" His voice was as sharp as a knife, angry, filled with the pleasure of victory.

The boy slowly opened his eyes, and looked at the gun, at the Yüzbaşı, and at the dog.

"Talk now," growled the Yüzbaşı. "If you don't tell the truth right now, right away, I'll kill the dog."

The boy blinked his eyes and looked quickly at the dog, at the Yüzbaşı's pistol that was glistening in the sun, at the trembling edges of the Yüzbaşı's moustache:

"I'll talk," he said. "Don't shoot sarı. I'll tell right away. I saw İnce Memed."

"Ha this is how it is," said the Yüzbaşı proudly. "Bring that … "

They took the child back to where he first was and sat him on the stone.

"Ne bildin İnce Memed olduğunu onun?" How did you know it was İnce Memed?

"Tüfeği vardı." He had his gun.

"Başka?" Anything else?

"Altındaki at yağızdı." The horse he was riding was dark.

"Başka?" What else?

"Altındaki at çıplaktı." The horse had no saddle.

"Başka?" What else.

"Benim kadar bir çocuktu." He was a boy about my size.

"Başka? Hangi yana gitti?" What else? Which way did he go?

"That way ... " he pointed to the west. "And I know the place he went ..."

"Nereye gitti?" Where did he go?

"There's that place called Bakırgediği, you know, in the cave over there is Kel Eşkıya, with nine men. İnce Memed went there to join them."

"Ne biliyorsun bütün bunları?" How do you know all these things?

"Onlar konuştu." They spoke.

"Kim?" Who?

"Yesterday Kel Eşkıya here, while talking at the head of that spring, İnce Memed is coming, he said, the news came from him. We'll wait for him in the cave at Bakırgediği. Then they left. They were wearing red fezes."

"Alright, why didn't you say these things before?"

"I was very afraid."

After rising to his feet, stretching, and then, leaping like an arrow, the Yüzbaşı jumped on his horse that they brought before him and, after giving the order to move out, he turned his horse toward the dog standing erect over there. He took out his gun and without hesitating pointed and pulled the trigger. The dog howled, convulsed, and started spinning in circles. The Yüzbaşı fired all the bullets in his gun one after another into the dog's head. In a moment, the dog spread out lifeless over there on the green grass, drowned in a pool of its own blood. Hearing the shots, Müslüm got up right away and ran to the dog, but the dog was already dead, stretched out like a person among the keven.

As the jandarma withdrew and left, Müslüm held his dog in his arms, holding its bleeding head tightly, slowly swaying the corpse back and forth as if he were singing lullabies for a child ... [6]

****

Word spreads that the jandarma have killed İnce Memed along with several other eşkıyas, mostly young men who had taken to the mountains after resisting tyranny in their villages. Their bodies are brought to town to be identified. When Murtaza hears that İnce Memed is dead, he sheds Topal Ali like an old coat, but when the family of the dead eşkıya everyone thought to be Memed comes to claim his body, everyone learns that the one thought to be Memed wasn't Memed after all. Molla Duran Effendi criticizes Murtaza's treatment of Topal Ali and, having learned of Ali's closeness to Memed, takes Ali into his home for protection.[7]

In Değirmenoluk, the news of İnce Memed's death had been met with complete silence. Even the crying babies stopped crying. When word came that Memed was not the eşkıya killed, a wave of happiness spread through the village. That was quickly replaced by dread and worry, as Memed's horse showed up in the village without its rider. At first, the villagers hesitated to tell Hürü Ana. But soon, she realized something was wrong, and no one was saying why. When she knocked on Hösük's door to find out, at first no one opened the door.[8]

"Something's going on, come on, tell me. Did you kill İnce Memed again? If so, let him die," hollered Hürü. "Let them shoot if they will, when İnce Memed dies, they think the world will stand still. Mothers will give birth to many more İnce Memeds. He – İnce Memed will never die. İnce Memed will die and die and rise again. If he's dead, İnce Memed, we should not worry. If he is dead he'll – I'll prepare a düğün feast in front of his enemies, and I'll jump for joy, do you understand?"

"Come now, Hürüce Bacı, come inside now."

"If İnce Memed has been killed, I'll jump for joy," she said, this time turning the other way and shouting to the entire village. "İnce Memed dies once and will return a thousand times. The analar, the mothers, shouldn't worry. Analaaar, stupid villagers listen to me, analaaar. İnce Memed came from our village, didn't he, he's the son of Sefil İbrahim isn't he, and his mother, poor and meek Döne, wasn't she, why have you closed the doors of your homes like this, like each one is a grave?"

Hösük, lowering his voice more:

"Come bacım" – come my sister – "come in and rest a bit ... "

Hürü freed her arm from his grasp and, hollering and calling out, went towards the center of the village, coming to the small alan, where she stopped. And then she further laid into the villagers, the jandarma, the yüzbaşı, whoever came to mind other than İnce Memed.

She yelled and hollered so much over there that one by one the villagers emerged from their houses to the alan out of curiosity and gathered around her. The more the villagers came, the more she let loose. "You're men aren't you, human beings aren't you, like you, İnce Memed has two eyes, two hands, and two ears ... If he's shot, let him be shot ... "[9]

Every time she said, "let them kill him," she felt an incurable pain, she herself died.

"You won't tell me about İnce Memed's death, isn't it because Hürüce Ana has gotten old, she won't be able to take it, because she won't be able to take it, isn't that it?" But she reminded them as they stood in silence, "I can take it yavrularım, I can endure," she said ... "I can take it yavrularım I can endure. There is no end for the eşkıya, that I know yavrularım, that I know. I know, and still my heart burns, it burns like a blacksmith's bellow." Again she roared: "Stop this and say something," she demanded. "I'm İnce Memed's Hürü Ana, I will endure."

She lowered her voice, now speaking in a fully loving and warm way. "Demir olsaydım çürürdüm, toprak oldum da dayandım, toprak oldum da dayandım, toprak oldum da ... "

Suddenly she bristled. It was as if she wasn't the woman of a moment ago, with the caring and comforting, soft-as-silk voice.

"Tell me and let's see again what happened to İnce Memed?" The crowd stood in front of her, hanging their heads, motionless like stones and silent.

She looked around and saw Kısacık Mahmut – Tiny Mahmut. His mother had died when he was a year old, and she had raised him and married him off. She asked him only once, and he told her about the horse. She went pale when he said the horse was without its rider, and then she had Mahmut take her to the horse.

The dark horse stood right on the peak of a steep rocky crag. It had turned towards the sun, its head held high, its tail slowly swaying from right to left. Its hair sparkled radiantly under the abundant light that brightened the whole world.

Hürü knelt atop a rock, fixed her eyes on the horse, and after taking a short rest, rose again to her feet.

"You wait here, Mahmudum," dedi, as she started to climb the rocks. "I have a few questions for this dark horse, let's see what it will say and what I'll hear."

She found for herself a narrow path that went up to the peak of the cliff. Allalem, she thought to herself, this one must have gone up from here as well. As she ascended, she both listened carefully to and talked with the horse. My apple-eyed beauty, my dark horse with a maiden's face, the leap of a partridge, and the look of a gazelle. My silver mane with a silk tail, you're like Köroğlu's horse Kırat, fix some wings on you and you'll fly to the sky, a seven day's journey, you'll gallop away in the blink of an eye. Hürüce begs you for your rider, what did you do with him, tell me, please? Did you let him get snatched by the birds of prey, the tigers, or the seven-tongued snakes, tell me, I'll do whatever you need, what did you do with your rider? Tell me about the rider, give me something about him, may Hürüce Ana die for you and your beautiful hooves, did you fly off a deep precipice, did you fall into the depths of the sea, did you go and surrender him to the forces of the savage, wolf-fanged jandarma, tell me my apple-eyed, maiden's faced dark horse ... You're like Hazreti Ali's horse Düldül, you slip away from inside a hundred thousand swords. Tell me what did you do with your rider, did the flames seize him from your hands, was he ill or sick, tell me what happened to him? You, you're like Muhammed's beautifully named beautiful Burak, who took off and flew to the sky. You're like the Hızır's Benlibozu, who walked on the seven seas, tell me, did you drop your rider off in these huge purple mountains, in the dark tents and grass-green eyes of the Yörük's, did the good-hearted, impatient villagers take him from your back, I'm begging you as İnce Memed's ana Hürüce. Tell me what did you do with your rider, dark horse whose hide glows so brightly in the daytime?

Talking nonstop like this with the horse, she went up by its side, stopping a few steps away. The horse didn't move at all. It stood there swaying its tail. Emboldened, Hürü came all the way up next to the horse, raised her right hand and touched its back and slowly, very slowly and shyly, caressed it.

"Hürüce begs you silver mane, tell me where did you take your rider, was he healthy or sick, in good condition or poor?"

Just then, the dark horse moved, stood on its back legs, and kicked the air with its front legs. Hürü then saw it suddenly bolting down the cliffs. If she hadn't drawn back from where she was, the dark horse would have sent her tumbling over the rocks in a thousand pieces.[10]

Hürü Ana cursed the horse. "I wish it had fallen down dead ... what do you know of being a horse ... and I compared you with Köroğlu's Kırat and Muhammed's Burak ... " She climbed down the cliffs.

Kısacık Mahmut said that the horse was headed to the village. Hürü Ana held her head low and didn't say a word as they made their way back.

She cooked a meal for Mahmut, and they sat outside Hürü's house. The horse flew by at full speed. "Do what you want," Hürü said angrily, "I won't speak with that pig again ... I won't look in its face another time, I wish it had died." The horse flew by again, and once more at dusk.[11]

"Mahmudum," she said, "you know what, this İnce Memed didn't die, he's still alive. Alive but something has happened to him, that's for sure. If something hadn't happened to him, this horse wouldn't wander around here footloose like this. And if he had been shot, he wouldn't be able to wander around here."

"You're right Ana."

"Now I think I know where he is. This horse came to give us news. If only I hadn't sworn and cursed at him. İnce Memed wants me. Will you come with me?"

"I'll come Ana. I'll go with you of course, if you wanted me to go to hell with you, I'd go. Is İnce Memed's place far or near?"

"Quite far," dedi Hürü Ana.

"Then how will you be able to go that far?"

"I'll go," said Hürü Ana, shooting up. "It's enough that you don't tire."

"I'll take our donkey with me. I've recently remade the packsaddle. And I'll throw a cushion on top, if we get tired, we'll ride. My donkey is like a horse, Ana. Even that horse of İnce Memed's can't walk as far as it can."

"Okay," smiled Hürü Ana. And then she added from behind: "No, it can't. We'll take off tomorrow at midnight, no one should know where or in what direction we're going. Tell your wife that we're going to town, is that okay?"

"Yes, it's okay," Kısacık Mahmut dedi.[12]

Hürü Ana prepared a bundle with figs, pomegranates from Delice's koyak, and beautiful knee-high socks she had knitted for Memed. They left for moonlit Alidağı at midnight. Hürü Ana led with Kısacık Mahmut and his donkey behind. Mahmut saw that Hürü Ana was cold and implored her to ride the donkey. She told him she was okay and would walk until sunrise.

They arrived at the base of Alidağı at daybreak and stopped to admire the small bright blue flowers that painted the mountain the color of the sky from top to bottom. The maroon, misty cliffs of Alidağı appeared and disappeared in the blue.

Mahmut insisted that Hürü Ana ride the donkey. Towards afternoon, they reached the first grove of the orman. The trees were short and spread out. Soon they came upon eleven Yörük women, all of whom were carrying their children on their backs in red knitted pouches. Hürü greeted them warmly and asked if any of them had seen the horse. Strangely, they immediately withdrew into the orman as if they were running away. Hürü Ana took this as a good sign. "Deeeh!" she said with excitement. "Did you see what happened to us, there's something going on, İnce Memedim is alive … otherwise, why would they run off after asking about the horse?"

The same thing happened a second time, and Hürü Ana got a bit angry. "What is going on, don't these Yörüks know how to speak, have they lost their minds?"

The next day, they came across some kadınlar – some women – kneeling along a stream in a ravine along the path to the highlands. The women rose to their feet all at once.[13]

"Selamünaleyküm kadınlar."

"Aleykümselam," said a kadın Hürü's own age.

"Kolay gelsin" – may it come with ease – "are you doing laundry?"

"Laundry," said the old woman.

That these were Yörük women was clear from even a distance. The Yörük women cover their heads with an embroidered silver bowl that they call a tiara, that they decorate with tiny beads, the wealthy with gold and pearl. Their dresses are also different from those of the villagers. Very colorful, very decorative.

"Which oba are you from?"

"Sarıkeçili," said the Yörük kadın.

"I'm Hürü, and this is Kısacık Mahmut. I raised him, that is, he is my son but not by birth."

The women smiled.

"The two of us are from Değirmenoluk köy there down below. I'm going to ask you something but you won't run away. As soon as everyone hears what I ask they take off out of sight ... "

The women smiled again.

The large, older woman who had just spoken responded:

"Maybe we'll run off, too. If you prefer, don't ask us at all."

"I can't not ask."

"Then ask bacı, maybe we won't run away."

"Have you seen a dark horse around here, yesterday or the day before, or maybe in the last ten days. A dark, awesome horse, a bit crazy. No one can catch it, no one can shoot it. Other than one person, no one can mount it. It wanders aimlessly and stops in some places."

The old Yörük woman who had just spoken:

"I'm also going to run off bacı," she said. "Forgive me. Neither you asked us this kind of thing nor did we say anything to you. Sağlıcakla kal."[14]

"Abooov, my mothers, what kind of women are you," Hürü hollered. "If you say we haven't seen the horse, what can happen?" Next she and Mahmut met a small girl, ten or eleven years old, tending a herd of sheep. A young dog guarding the herd barked fiercely as they approached. The girl held the dog, and, in a loving voice, Hürü Ana asked if she was from the Sarıkeçili oymak. Yes, she said, "Biz Sarıkeçiliyiz," dedi. We're Sarıkeçili.

"I'm the daughter of Aslanoğlan," the girl said.

"I know Aslanoğlan."

"Have you seen my father?"

"Could I not have seen him? Never, he comes to our house, he calls me Ana. He's a huge man with grass-green eyes."

"You're making fun, aren't you teyze, my father is tiny." She pointed to Kısacık Mahmut. "As small as this one."

Hürü quickly recovered:

"Ya, ya, I was just kidding."

The embarrassed girl seemed bored, and her face was covered in sweat.

"And what have I brought for my girl, Aslanoğlan's daughter. What was your name hele?"

"Fatmalı."

"Yaaa, and I brought a pomegranate that flows with honey for my lovely Fatmalım ... and I brought figs that I dried with my own hands. Mahmut!"

Mahmut went and brought a huge pomegranate and a handful of figs from the donkey.

"Take them kızım, take them!"

The girl was embarrassed, and she was sweating buckets. Then suddenly she smiled and spoke:

"And you know me, too, teyze," dedi.

"Your teyze would die for your golden hair," Hürü said, caressing the girl's hair slowly. "Have some figs to eat."

The girl looked first at her, then at Mahmut, and then she turned her back to them and ate one of the figs. When she turned back around, her eyes shone.

They went back to the slope of the field and sat down next to each other. To the one side, the girl gobbled down the figs. To the other, she looked at Hürü with affection, her eyes sparkling. And then she ate another fig. After finishing the figs, she asked Hürü Ana a question.

"Teyzem, would it be possible for me to take this pomegranate to the tent and give it to Müslüm? I would rather he eat it than I. He's sick and ... "

"Mahmut, bring another pomegranate."

Mahmut brought another and gave it to the girl. The girl was really happy.

"And can we take this home, split it and eat it? Share it with my Anam and Babam."

"Olur" – "Yes," said Hürü, caressing her hair. "Olur güzel kızım, Fatmalım benim."

The small girl looked at her gratefully, opened the bag on her back, placed the two pomegranates neatly into it, and then tied it closed again.

"Müslüm is not well," she said.

"How is Müslüm related to you?"

"He's my elder," she said. "It's said that they made him ill. What are you looking for around here teyze?"

"I'm looking for a horse," said Hürü Ana. "A horse, black, dark ... I'm looking for a beautiful horse. Have you ever seen such a horse around here?"

"I have," Fatmalı said with excitement, and her face again turning red. "Could I have never seen it, that horse ... It comes flying around here every day, sits down on the peak of that cliff, and stays there without moving at all. Yaaa, and it swishes its tail. Then, when the hawks come, they hover above it a lot and then it takes off in a flash." Suddenly she was uncertain, and her eyes looked into Hürü's eyes for a long time. "Why are you looking for that horse, teyze?"

"The horse is my son's, my son and ... "

"You're lying talking like this, aren't you teyze?" said Fatmalı asking with a smile. She still had her eyes, filled with doubt, trained on Hürü's. "There's no owner of that horse. That horse is said to be a jinn. They say that it's Köroğlu's horse Kırat. My father says that Köroğlu's horse never died. As it aged, it became like this, dark black. My father says that that's Köroğlu's horse that never dies, yaaa ... My father says that that horse keeps itself disguised."

"There is one person who has ridden that horse," said Hürü Ana.

"No, no," said Fatmalı anxiously. "Is that possible? You know that horse, it's been there for many years, before I was born, before my father was born, you know my grandfather, he has a white beard, this long." She opened her arms wide. "It's like a lapful of beard ... They say the horse has been coming to that cliff, standing there like that, even before he was born. The hawks are its enemies, when they arrive, it flees. Yaaa ... " She still looked with doubt at Hürü. Finally, with a smile, "Liar," she said, "you're not looking for that horse. They beat my Ağam Müslüm and he's sick now. And I'm shepherding in his place."

"Who beat him?"

"Who beats, Kertiş Ali Onbaşı ... you know teyze, there's that Kertiş, if he beats you once, he'll break a man's bones. He beat Müslüm up bad ... "

"Why did he beat him?"

Fatmalı leaned her chin on her hand, put her head forward, and after thinking for a while looked at Hürü, and then again put her head down in front of her.

"Why did they beat him?"

Fatmalı again gave no response. It was as if she didn't hear the question. Suddenly she raised her head, made a decision, her eyes sparkling with affection.

"They asked for İnce Memed," she said. "Do you know İnce Memed?"

"Hıııım," Hürü said, putting her hand on her head, "I've heard the name."

"You're lying," said Fatmalı. "But still I'll talk with you."

"May Hürü Ana die for your golden hair."

"Your name is Hürü, isn't it?"

"Hürü ... "

Placing her hand under her chin, Fatmalı thought for a while about this. "What did Müslüm do?"

"Müslüm said he didn't see İnce Memed. Still they beat him. Again he didn't say. He didn't say on purpose, dishonestly, he didn't say. They beat him up badly, broke his bones, and still Müslüm didn't say. Then they were going to kill his dog, and Müslüm this time, and again dishonestly told them İnce Memed's place, where he is. Müslüm İnce Memed's place ... " She bit her lips and went quiet.

"What happened after that Fatmalım?"

"There's that man with the whip, you know, the one who killed İnce Memed's Hatçe ... and İnce Memed is going to kill him ... "

"The one with the whip in his hand?"

"Yes, that one, when Müslüm told them İnce Memed's place, he still killed the dog. Müslüm didn't cry from his wounds or being sick, but he did, night and day, for his dog. Yaaa. Müslüm surprised them. After taking such a beating, Müslüm told them İnce Memed's place ... and they believed him."

Then Fatmalı suddenly grew angry:

"I don't know a thing," she screamed. "What kind of Hürüce are you ... "

She leapt to her feet, went to her leather bag, "here, here take the pomegranates, take them if you want," she said. "That horse is crazy ... There is no İnce Memed. They shot him at Bakırgediği, didn't you hear?"

"No, my pretty kızım, no," said Hürü Ana rising to her feet. She hopped on the donkey right away and rode off.

After some distance, she turned back and said: "Sağlıcakla kal, benim gül yüzlüm," and kicked the donkey. "Since you gave such good news, just wait a bit, I'm going to get you so much." She didn't pay attention to whether or not Fatmalı heard these last words. Fatmalı stood where she was with her small dog and watched as they rode away.[15]

Toward mid-afternoon they reached the highlands and decided to go to Battal Ağa, the leader of the Sarıkeçili. "He's a very good man," said Hürü Ana. "I've known of him a long time."

"Battal Ağa, Battal Ağa take hold of your dogs, tanrı konuğu ... " – a visitor of god ... – hollered Hürü.

A very tall man came outside.

"Buyurun, buyurun," he shouted. What can I do for you, what can I do for you. "Tie up the dogs ... " Several others emerged from the tent to greet them as Battal Ağa invited them inside.

"Hele içeriye buyurun." Come inside please.

"Sen Battal Ağa mısın, Sarıkeçilinin soylu Beyi?" Are you Battal Ağa, the Bey of the Sarıkeçilis?

"I'm Battal."

"Good," dedi Hürü Ana, and she went inside.

The magnificence of the inside of the tent completely took Hürü Ana aback. She had never seen such kilims and cloths. Battal Ağa spread a felt cloth on the ground for her. She gathered herself and sat down.

"Abooov," she said smiling, "it means that the Yörük tents are still like this, ha! I've been told that the Yörükler are finished, worn out, and impoverished. I'm happy to see a tent like this Battal Ağa."

"Sağ ol bacım." Thank you my sister.

"My name is Hürü. Have you ever heard of me Battal Ağa?"

The man was a bit embarrassed, he rubbed his hands against each other, his long thin beard fluttered.

"I haven't heard of you bacı," he finally said.

"They call me Hürü Ana from Değirmenoluk village. İnce Memed's Hürü Ana, that's me."[16]

Battal Ağa was a warm, handsome, and well-dressed man. He wore a gold ring on his finger and had large, grass-green eyes. For Hürü, he looked at the world with such love that anyone who met him felt instantly cleansed of any enmity, grudge, jealously, or trouble. There are such people in the world, she thought, when looking at his dimpled cheeks, the deep lines in his face, his red stringy beard, his prominent, protruding cheekbone, and his long face. One who sees such a face cannot kill another, do any harm, or endure the pain of the needy.

Battal Ağa thought that Hürü Ana had something to say to him. Some of the men who had gathered said goodbye and left the tent. Hürü spoke of the size of the tents and their posts. She asked whether they still had large tents with seven posts.

"Hürü bacım," said Battal Ağa, "we no longer have enough strength. You need four camels to carry them. We have neither camels anymore nor the Arabian horses ... They finished us off Hürü bacım, they've worn us out. The çadır is now down to five direks. Next year, it will be three, then the following years it will go down to one ... "

His face became sad, his beard shook, and his beautiful green eyes clouded over. If he hadn't held himself back he would have broken down in tears in front of this old woman.

Hürü knew what had befallen the Yörükler and spoke of the old days when they settled on the plains at Dikenlidüzü after summers in the highlands. The people were happy, the horses roamed freely, the Dedeler from all over Anatolia played their saz instruments and told great destans, and the people who visited the Yörüks stayed for days and months as their guests. This was before Abdi Ağa took everything the Yörüks had, and from then on they didn't settle in Dikenlidüzü. Hürü Ana felt sad and spoke angrily about the lot of the Yörüks.

Battal Ağa smiled with his handsome, bright, grass-green eyes and pearl-white teeth and asked Hürü if there was something she wanted.[17]

"A wish will be yours, from us, Hürü bacı, tell me your wish, don't be afraid, whatever your wish is, I'll do it with pleasure. I'll do it at once."

Hürü Ana straightened up where she was sitting:

"I am İnce Memed's Hürü Ana. Listen to me well, you Hacıbektaşı Veli imposter Battal Ağa, look here ... " She pointed with her hand to Kısacık Mahmut who was crouched down nearby. "This one here, his mother died when he was a year old, and I took him in and raised him. İnce Memed's mother died but didn't die, I gave so much to him. Because of this, I am Hürü Ana, a real mother to him. I'm begging you, my beautiful eyed, rose-faced Battal Ağam, give me some news about İnce Memedim."

"How can I give you news about him Hürü bacım, he's an eşkıya who roams the mountain."

"Look, don't play with me Battal Ağam, I've followed his trail carefully and it brought me here. He got off the horse down there. Tell me Battal

Ağam, I'm his real mother, or forget motherhood, my heart is aching, give me some news about him, is he dead, did he fall from the horse, or is he alive?"

She looked Battal Ağa straight in the eye, beads of sweat filled her brow, and she waited.

"Is he dead, or is he alive?"

Battal Ağanın yüzünden durmadan ikircik gölgeleri geçiyordu. Shadows of dilemma passed over Battal Ağa's face.

"Söyle ala gözlü Battal Ağam, I'm his mother, is he alive, is he dead?"

"He's alive," said Battal Ağa with a very pensive, hesitant look. "İnce Memed is alive, Hürü Hatun."

"Is he injured?"

Battal Ağa's beautiful eyes became melancholic. In a moment, the joy on his face departed.

"He's injured," he said, "and it's a bad wound bacım." His voice was soft, aching like a lament for the dead.

Hürü straightened up again:

"Don't worry great Battal," she said, "the mothers are giving birth to so many more İnce Memeds, more ... Don't you feel sad for him. This İnce Memed, will die and die, and then will rise again. He is like Hazreti Ali. He's like a Mehdi. Did you bring any doctors or healers?"

"We did," dedi Battal Ağa.

"I need to see him. When he sees me, Hürü Ana, he'll get better."

"It's impossible for you to see him today. They don't even tell me where he is. Only one person knows where he is, and that's our Temir."[18]

They agreed that Temir, Battal Ağa's nephew, would take her to Memed the next day. That night, they ate a hearty meal of lamb stew, rice, and sweet honeycomb, after which Hürü Ana slept on the softest bed she had slept on her entire life. She fell asleep as soon as she laid her head on the pillow.

The next morning Battal Ağa introduced her to Temir and told Hürü to forgive him but that, in the custom of the eşkıyas, Temir would blindfold her along the way to Memed's hiding place.

Temir didn't stop to look back once, nor did he say a word. The further they went, the faster he rode. They entered and left an orman and came to a meadow flat as long as the eye could see. Everything was so green. Even the sky was lit with green. Çayırlığı geçmek epeyi bir zaman aldı. Crossing the meadow took quite a long time, after which they entered a deep cavern and then came to a mountain with very steep, flint cliffs. Temir blindfolded Hürü Ana.

She smiled and let go of the reins as he asked, but she wasn't pleased. I'll let go, she grumbled to herself ... I'll go blindfolded ... Oğlum için – for my son – for my şahin ... whatever they ask of me, I'll do ... but to herself she cursed Temir ... Do you know who I am, who I am, you snotty nomad ... am I a person who gets blindfolded like this … do you think I'll tell the jandarma where İnce Memed is? She so regretted the position she was in that her anger turned on Memed. Nothing good, she said in frustration, has come from this son of Sefil İbrahim. She got so angry that if she hadn't been embarrassed about crying in front of Temir, she would have broken down right there.

The horse frequently lost its footing as rocks tumbled under its feet. Hürü clung tightly to the saddle.

Temir heard all of the old woman's grumbling. Now and then he would turn and see her all worked up, but he couldn't understand why she was so angry.

They arrived at the cave. Temir asked Hürü Ana to remove the blindfold. She did, but out of anger resisted his help getting off the horse. "Don't come near me, take your hand away. I can get down by myself." She got off and rushed passed a huge armed guard at the entrance of the cave, came to a quick stop, and embraced Memed who was lying in front of her.[19]

"Memedim, my hero, my lion, my dear, nasılsın?" How are you?

Memed opened his eyes, fixed them and looked with tenderness in hers, and smiled:

"Thank heavens I saw you before I died, Ana," he said, "after this I won't worry. This was everything I wanted. I begged Allahım, don't take me before I can see the face of my Ana, I said. And here God … " Two tears burst forth from his eyes and flowed down his cheeks.

"Sus, köpek," shouted Hürü. "Be quiet, dog. Your Ana begs you. What kind of thing is that to come from you, suuus! If you don't be quiet, if you whine like a woman, like babies, I'll leave here now and go right away. Show me, show me your wounds my gül yüzlüm."

Memed smiled and showed his wounds, which were thoroughly wrapped. Hürü first noticed his bed, it was like the one she had slept on the night before.

"Do your wounds hurt?"

"A little."

"It means they hurt a lot." She rose, left the cave, and looked for Temir. She asked the man at the entrance, "Where is that Temir, the one who blindfolded me?"

"Inside, Ana," said the huge man with a smile.

Hürü turned towards the cave, Temir stood at the head of the bed, lost in thought.

"Did you bring doctors to my yavrum?"

Temir:

"Three times," he said, and walked outside. Hürü Ana understood, and followed him out. They reached a shelter of a cliff and kneeled down.

"Tell me Temir, my boy is okay, no?"

Temir, in a sad voice:

"He's not well, Ana," dedi.

"What did the doctors say?"

"They couldn't get the bullets out. Two of the doctors were from the Yörüks. One from that village down below."

"That means my yavru is going to die?"

"That's something God knows, Ana."

"My yavru will not die. Even if that's something our great Allah knows, Hürüce's child will not die from the enemy's bullet."

"İnşallah Ana, Allah ağzından duysun Ana ... " God willing, let God hear what you're saying ...

Hürü went inside and sat at Memed's side. She began to stroke his hair, caress his forehead and kiss him. She talked with him warmly, softly, and from the heart. Those who saw her at Memed's side like this, who saw this love flow throughout her body, had a hard time believing that this immensely loving woman was her.

Memed did have a fever, but it wasn't that high. He opened his eyes for a moment. He looked at Hürü and smiled:

"You've come now and I've seen you before I die, now I will get better."

"You will get better," Hürü said firmly, determined. "Not getting better is not possible. I'll make some soup for you now ... "

She went outside to speak with Temir:

"You have supplies to make soup?"

"We have everything, Ana, whatever you want ... But for days he hasn't put a thing in his mouth ... "

"If I cook, he'll do so. Light a fire over there and we'll see. Bring the pot, too. And gather a lot of mint from around there."

"A fire can't be lit here Anam."

"Why not?"

"They'll see the smoke."

"It's also not possible in the cave. The smoke will suffocate my boy."

Temir was thinking.

"Don't think so much, find a place where the smoke won't be seen."

"Over there there's another small cave, will that do Ana?"

"It will do," dedi Hürü. She was pleased. She unwound for the first time, and her face shone. "Mint soup will relieve him."[20]

She rolled up her sleeves and cooked a delicious soup for Memed. Not a speck of smoke left the cave as she cooked. Memed, who hadn't eaten for days, ate a huge bowl. "Didn't I tell you Ana," he said. "When you arrived I would get better ... "

Memed groaned in pain all night long. Worried about his fever, Hürü was unable to sleep. In the morning, she cooked more soup, this time mixing lots of mint and yogurt. Memed ate it all up, but his fever remained. Hürü thought that a doctor was needed ... but not that kind of doctor. She called out for Temir.[21]

"This boy is okay for now, he's holding on, but if this lasts a long time, he'll die."

"What can we do Ana?"

"I'm thinking of something. Is Kırkgöz Ocağı – the Hearth of the Forty-Eyes – very far from here?"

"It's pretty far Ana."

"Have you ever heard of Kırkgöz Ocağı?"

"Who doesn't know Ana ... "

"Isn't the head of the order at Kırkgöz Ocağı now Anacık Sultan?"

"She is."

"You know that that Anacık Sultan saves those whose hearts have been pierced and blown to pieces by burning bullets."

"Everyone knows Ana."

"She saves even those who have been killed and died by being shot. It's an ocak of life, that ocak. It's enough that blood be let out from somewhere, it's never been seen or heard that Kırkgöz Ocağı didn't revive someone."

"We also thought of Kırkgöz Ocağı, so did Battal Ağa ... it's just that we can't take İnce Memed there in this condition ... as for Anacık Sultan, the way of that ocak is apparently such that she never moves anywhere."

"I'll make her move."

"She's very old, maybe a hundred years old, how could we possibly bring her here?"

"You take İnce Memed down below, okay, to the foot of that mountain ... The jandarma are still nervous. Over there, below, there's a Yörük camp ... I'm going to Anacık Sultan. Send me someone from the Sarıkeçilis right away, now ... Battal knows where Memed is, doesn't he?"

"He knows."

"Bring him down, if he is going to die, let him die below, not helpless here on top of the mountain."

She instructed Temir to feed Memed and implored Memed to bear the pain until she returned with Anacık Sultan. "She'll cure your wounds quickly. And I'll have her offer a prayer for you so that no bullet will touch you, and if one does, it won't pass through. A bomb won't work on you after Anacık Sultan ..." As she left, she prayed, "Allahım, great Allahım, for the love of beautifully named Muhammed, for the love of long-sworded Ali, for the love of all the dervishes and saints of Kırkgöz Ocağı, have mercy on my son for me, for the poor and wretched ... "[22]

****

Since the time when the Türkmen from Horasan arrived, Kırkgöz Ocağı stands there, between the flint rock and the white cliffs, next to huge trees whose age is unknown. The old house, wrapped in flint, is entered from three arched gates. The gates are sturdy and made of oak. Carved into them are various verses from the Kuran, and flowers, birds, and insects. The carving on each door contains a secret prayer. Since Horasan, this ocak is the cure for all difficulties, the remedy for all the ill. At the ocak, the poor, the broken, and the oppressed seek out cures for their problems. Under those huge trees there's also a clear white spring. After meandering thunderously with white caps through and over the rocks, it goes at an incredible speed straight down the slope below, sculpting the stones. Some say that they've seen this water flowing at an unstoppable speed like this, suddenly stop in place, and not only stop, but flow at the same speed back toward the spring in the opposite direction. In the Toroslar that this happened was undisputed, for until now no one thought at all to argue lack of faith or unbelief. When spring comes, a crackling sound comes from night till morning, the entire night, from the cliffs to the pure white and sharp, flint mountains of Kırkgöz Ocağı, and that night all the creatures – the birds, the insects, the wolves, the tigers – come alive. And when morning comes, that morning, there's not even a speck of a cloud in the sky, the surroundings are filled with an eye-dazzling brightness, and in this light on all the white cliffs, one understands that the crackling sounds were those of yellow flowers breaking through the rocks as they blossomed at night. The entire world, from the earth to the sky and the thunderous, running water, turns yellow. In the wake of this, the world glistens brightly like a white crystal. When autumn comes and you look, in one night those yellow flowers disappear. The world again turns milk white. The nights and days of the first days of autumn transform into an unbelievable, pure whiteness. The sky, the land, the trees, the plants, all the flowers are completely white. Even the birds that fly in the sky are white. Then, in one night, the world again begins to crackle, the mountains sway, it's morning and when the day breaks one finds oneself astonished again, this time with blue flowers that have broken through the white cliffs, everything turns a still, fuzzy, warm blue, the kind of blue that's so brittle and soft that if you touch it, it will shatter. One who enters that blue just once is freed from all problems, darkness, and pessimism, and filled, like being born from one's mother, with a bright blue. With this glowing inside one's entire life until death, let what comes come, for one's entire life until the end, one is happy with a child's joy that no human being can reach. Before death, one lives the exuberance, radiance, and pleasure of paradise every second of one's entire life. To reach this, to enter this blue, to worship the joy of this blue is not so easy. The tyrants, people who humiliate others, killers, the unjust, the exploiters, those who have done nothing or those who live on their wealth don't come here, and if they come they aren't able to enter the blue, or if they enter they do not achieve joy like this, their hearts do not flutter in the warmth, the ecstasy, in the taste of such joy.[23]

Gazelles arrive at the entrance of the ocak every morning, their antlers glittering in the morning sun, their hides glowing. The sisters of Kırkgöz milk them. *Every month a male deer collapses at the entrance. For three days and nights, it bends its neck, fixes its eyes on the ocak and waits. On the third day, they slaughter it, dry its skin and bring it to Anacık Sultan. She has the skin taken to someone in the world whose impurities and wrongdoings have been cleansed.*

Neither reaching Kırkgöz Ocağı nor paying one's respects to the head of the ocak is so easy. Many beys, shahs, and padişahs came to conquer this area by the sword, waited months or years, and returned without ever seeing the spiritual master. The door would open to the poor but was closed to these tyrannical beys and padişahs.

The saints of Kırkgöz are said to form forty gönül gözleri – forty seeing hearts. One of them sees the west, and one the east. One heaven, the other hell, one is on the good person, another on the tyrant. One of them looks on the past, another on the future. One of them on the ant, another the bird, and so on for the rain, the clouds, the water, the fire, the stars ... and the hearts of humanity. As long as this door has existed, the evil and those who oppress are not able to enter.

With humanity astray and the world sullied now, the door is not easily entered at all.

In her youth, Anacık Sultan was once unable to break the resistance of a handsome young tyrant bey she allowed to cross the threshold. For seven years the gazelles stayed away, the clouds withdrew, the pigeons didn't fly, the water stopped flowing backwards, and the yellow and blue flowers didn't sprout from the cracks in the rocks.

Hürü Ana worried that maybe she would be turned away. Anacık Sultan could know from the outside whether a person was good or evil on the inside. Hürü wondered if she had committed any sins, her whole life passed before her eyes. Sometimes she was hopeful and cheerful, other times she was worried. Were my sins or my good deeds greater? As she thought, she emphasized her good deeds. In her youth, when she had just married Durmuş Ali, and when he was in the army, she was with someone else in the mill. I wonder if Anacık Sultan remembers such an old thing, and whether she won't admit me because of it? It was a long time ago, a long time ago, she thought. Anacık Sultan is also very old.

On the second day of the trip, she turned to her young guide.[24]

"Yavru, when you've come here, have you seen the blue flowers break through those cliffs, splitting and crackling?"

"Not the splitting, but I have seen the flowers. They sprout from the cracks of the rocks, and spread like a blue kilim all over the place."

"Will I see them, too?"

"Why shouldn't you see them Ana?"

"Have you ever committed adultery yavrum?"

The young man looked at her strangely.

"I've never committed adultery because adultery is a sin."

"Have you ever killed a man?"

"I have not."

"Have you ever beaten another?"

He went quiet and didn't respond.

"I'm talking to you," Hürü Ana said, stubbornly. "Have you ever hit a man?"

"I have."

"Have you ever shot dogs?"

"I have."

"Have you ever killed any animal?"

"I have."

"A bird?"

"I've also killed birds."

"In that case, how could you see Kırkgöz's Anacık Sultan?"

"It means that I don't have any sins Hürü Ana."

"Huuuum."

Hürü Ana was pleased, even she herself only vaguely remembered what took place in the mill.[25]

****

The story of the healing powers of Kırkgöz Ocağı went back to the time of Sultan Murad. Sultan Murad was a fearless padişah whose mother called him to her side to give him advice as he planned his conquest of Bağdat. "Those who stand against you are very powerful," she said. "When you go on this campaign, don't go without getting a blessing from Kırkgöz Ocağı. Those who depart from Kırkgöz Ocağı with a blessing leave with their blades sharp and their fortune bright. Don't forget my advice. And don't forget this, you are a great padişah, overwhelmed with pride, when you come to the threshold of the Kırkgöz Ocağı, when you're there, act like you are in the presence of God. While entering the ocak, kiss the ground seven times. There are three thresholds, stop and pray at the third one … "

During his march to Bağdat several months later, however, Sultan Murad got caught up in the fervor of the campaign and forgot everything she had said. He took his army all the way to Diyarbakır and remained there for a long time, thinking that there was something he was forgetting. The army stayed there so long that Murad's men wondered if they had come to conquer Bağdat or to settle in Diyarbakır. The padişah heard what was said but somehow was unable to proceed. He spoke with no one and tried to figure out what he was forgetting.

One day, suddenly he said, "Haaaa, thank God I figured it out," and immediately called his chief commander and vezirs. "Amanın," he said, "For God's sake, find and bring me the pir – the saint – from Kırkgöz Ocağı," he told them. They responded that that's not possible. The pir of Kırkgöz Ocağı doesn't leave and go anywhere to meet anyone. Your father and grandfathers all girded their swords to enter the pir's presence. Sultan Murad still commanded them to go and bring the pir.

The vezirs pleaded to the padişah a few more times, but Murad stood his ground, and so they went to the Kırkgöz Ocağı. A young pir met them at the threshold. "I know why you have come. Sultan Murad, who does he think he is that he turns his back on the ocak from which his father and grandfathers sought blessings?"

When his vezirs returned without the pir, the padişah blew his top and threatened to take his army up to the ocak. The vezirs told him that, as they were departing and performing their prayers, the pir had smiled and said: "Tell Sultan Murad, whatever army he has, bring them upon our ocak. A lot of people have tried that and none of them remained as strong as they had been before."

The padişah growled from the earth to the sky and turned his army towards Kırkgöz Ocağı. That day a storm like the flood that hit Noah's ark burst open from the skies. The more the rain fell, the more the padişah's anger grew. When the rain stopped, the army began its assault on the ocak. Uzun bir ova geçmişler. They crossed a long plain, went up a huge mountain and came to a snow-spotted, pointy-peaked, beautiful mountain. The vezirs were about to say that Kırkgöz Ocağı is on the other side this mountain when the mountain roared and fires began to spread down to the plain.

Seeing this display of power, the padişah kneeled on the ground and begged the pir not to wrong him. At that moment, a white pigeon landed in front of him. When the mountain quieted, the pigeon flew away. Sultan Murad sent his army back to Diyarbakır and went in disguise with his commanders to Kırkgöz Ocağı.

As they approached, the earth crackled and they looked and saw blue flowers cover the landscape. The padişah performed his ablutions and kissed the ground three times. He repeated these seven times on his way to the outer gate. When the gate opened by itself, Murad performed his prayers again, as he did at the second and third gates.[26]

The voice of the pir instructed him to approach alone.

"It's your fate that you will conquer Bağdat Sultan Murad, may joy be upon you."

"Thank you pirim," said Sultan Murad who kissed the ground once more.

"But I have something to say to you, something to say from which you cannot stray. Tonight you'll stay here, and tomorrow morning, you'll set out on the road early. In the village of Karaburçlu down there in Çukurova is the son of a widow, Osman is his name, his moustache hasn't even started to grow. Now you are going to take this Osman and add him to your army. Osman opposes you, he roams in the mountains, he takes from the rich and gives to the poor. He's the remedy for their troubles, for the desperate. Bağdat is in the grip of tyranny. The poor and wretched are suffering deeply. If you don't take Osman and add him to your army, you will not free Bağdat from tyranny."

"Where can I find this Osman rebel roaming in the mountains? Would it be possible for me not to go searching for him?" he asked.

"Don't go," the pir said, "I'll send him to you."

Then the pir stopped and looked straight into the eyes of the padişah. His eyes were so powerful that, if the padişah hadn't turned away, his eyes would have burned and gone blind from his light.

A horned red gazelle flew down from the mountain. The pir said that this was their kismet. Murad would sacrifice the gazelle for his Bağdat campaign. The deer lay down on the ground. When Murad struck its neck with his knife, not a single drop of blood flowed.

The gazelles arrived the next day, like any other day, and the sisters of the ocak milked them and offered the padişah and his vezirs fresh, warm milk. None of them had ever, in their entire lives, tasted such a head-spinning, joy-inspiring drink. The padişah wondered if it might be better to be a servant in this ocak than the sole padişah of these great countries of this world. Tears of blood flowed from his eyes as he accepted his fate and traveled back to Diyarbakır. Osman had arrived three days earlier.[27]

"This is a child, and so young, padişahım," the vezirs said. "How can we take one who can't hold a comb to a moustache into the army and to Bağdat?"

"Hand me a comb," he said. When he took the comb he stuck it on Osman's upper lip.

"He can hold a comb, don't you see," he said smiling.

Right there, the padişah kissed his two eyes.

In this way they arrived at Bağdat. The war started at the gates of Bağdat. Osman's name in the army became Genç Osman, Young Osman. And he fought at the head of the army, like an arrow shot from a bow. He was the first to jump the moat around the walls and the first to open the gates of the castle. Above his grey horse he waved his sword without stopping or tiring. And one afternoon, with the sun burning down on the Bağdat market, and the fighting becoming fierce, when blood was pouring out everywhere, a sword came and cut off the head of Genç Osman. Genç Osman bent down and picked his head up off the ground, and fought for three days while holding his head. Those who saw him like this, friend and foe, ran in fear. Finally Bağdat fell. When the fighting stopped, the padişah who, from the towers of Bağdat castle, watched Genç Osman fight while holding his head for three days, said find Genç Osman for me. They searched and combed the area, but they were unable to find either Genç Osman or his horse. However, in the place where his head had fallen, they saw different kinds of roses every day – roses possessing an aroma that filled the world. Those roses are there today, in the place where Genç Osman's head fell, they blossom every day. And they will blossom in the center of Bağdat until the end of the world.

As soon as Bağdat fell, Genç Osman, holding his head, made his way on the path and came straight to Kırkgöz Ocağı, stopping at the gate like that, completely upright on his horse. He couldn't perform prayers without his head. He stood there like that, in place ... At this moment the pir understood what had happened and came outside:

"Gazan mübarek olsun Genç Osman," the pir is said to have said. Blessed be your mission. "Go now on your way. From now on, in your honor, this ocak will be an ocak that heals. Even when those with lethal wounds and those dying in agony come, they will heal and then depart."

With these words, Genç Osman spurred his horse on and took off from Kırkgöz Ocağı, disappearing in the maroon mist of these majestic mountains. And from that time until today, they say that Genç Osman's grey horse continues to roam in these mountains.[28]

Hürü Ana's horse struggled to climb the sharp cliffs, but what she saw as she made her final approach almost sent her flying with happiness.[29]

"Gördüm, gördüm çocuklar," she shouted. I saw them, I saw them, boys. "Blue autumn crocuses, look, they're stretched out all over the ground like grass."

"I saw," said the young man she had been talking to. The other young man in the lead didn't talk at all, his head lowered in thought.

"It means that they are also on the cliffs."

"Can it be otherwise, there are," said the young man confidently.

Hürü Ana was more pleased when she saw the domed roof above, under the huge trees. She got angry with herself for her disbelief, for her distrust.[30]

****

The entrance of the ocak was in ruins. Chickens roamed around like they do in front of village houses, and a mangy dog slept where the entrance was supposed to be. There were no three gates, not even one. Half of the large arch had collapsed. There was one violet butterfly the size of a bird flying above a pile of ashes. Hürü Ana didn't even notice it. At the door of the ocak, there was only one tiny window, and it was closed.

Hürü Ana got down off the horse, bent down and kissed the fallen arch. The young men with her followed her lead. She walked to the middle of the courtyard and bent down and kissed a large white stone. Cautiously, she looked inside the open gate. It was dark. She took another step and passed the stone threshold. Coming out to greet her was a tall young man who took her through several large rooms with decorated walls to a bright room where Anacık Sultan sat crosslegged on a divan. Hürü Ana came up to her, knelt down prayerfully on her right knee, clutched Anacık Sultan's hand and kissed it. Anacık Sultan held her hand, raised her up and had her sit down next to her. In a loving way, she turned her large, beautiful, grass-green eyes, shining inside with blue sparkles, to Hürü Ana.[31]

"Welcome Hürü Hatun," she said in a warm, soothing, and heartfelt voice. "A pleasant welcome to you from the blessed Kırkgöz Ocağı. Don't be sad at all, your son İnce Memed will not die, he'll recover from those wounds."[32]

Hürü Ana's eyes lit up, but her face showed some confusion. She wanted to talk but at that moment she couldn't. She thought to embrace Anacık Sultan's hands and took one, kissed it and let it fall. Then she took the other, kissed it and let it fall. Her tongue became untied and she spoke.

"Let Hürü sacrifice herself for those, your, miraculous words, let Hürü worship the blessed ground on which you walk."

"Tomorrow morning we'll set out early, I'll send word now to Battal of the Sarıkeçili oba, that they bring İnce Memed down to Kızılkartallı. And I'll look at his wounds."

"Let Hürü kiss the bottom of your blessed soles."

Anacık Sultan smiled modestly and with her right hand gently caressed Hürü's shoulders. And now Hürü Ana fell silent, unable to speak, and with tears in her eyes looked in amazement at Anacık Sultan's snow-white hair, her slender chin, her eyes teeming with sparks of love, her long swan neck, and her high cheek-boned, round, saintly face. If, at that moment, the young man who had brought her hadn't appeared with a silver tray of coffee whose smoky aroma suddenly filled the entire room, Hürü Ana would have remained there like that, gazing and speechless.

Shaking as she brought the coffee to her lips, Hürü looked around the room. A long, white silk banner, perhaps three fathoms wide, hung on the opposite wall. Sewn in the upper corner of the banner was a small taç – a crown – and from under the crown all the way to the other corner was some writing, Arabic writing. To the right of the banner there stood a shiny golden Kuran. And the walls were lined all around with strange, gilded black-framed lines that had never been seen, pearled sazes, ivory, silver, and gold-inlaid tambourines, bowls, and gilded axes. And in the middle of the wall on the other side of the ocak was mounted a single sword adorned with precious stones. The kilims on the floor were very old and their colors stunningly beautiful.

"İnce Memedi gördün mü Hürü Hatun?" Have you seen İnce Memed, Hürü Hatun?

"I've seen him Anacık Sultan. He was burning up. He was unconscious. I swear Anacık Sultan, I made three pairs of socks for him and couldn't give them. I wasn't able to feed him dried figs or a pomegranate that I picked from Delice Koyak."

"You'll feed him soon."

Hürü slowly gathered herself, her face widened, her hands stopped shaking. Now she was able to think and ... Until now Anacık Sultan neither heard of me nor met me, so how did she know who I am? It's impossible that she had heard from anywhere that I had come for İnce Memed, no one knew that ... How did the gate open by itself, as soon as I reached it ... [33]

Anacık Sultan smiled a soft smile filled with good favor. She put her long tespih with ninety-nine inlaid dark gold beads to the side and rose to her feet. While sitting she appeared to be an imposing figure, but when she got up she was a small, slight woman, and Hürü Ana was a bit surprised.

Anacık Sultan led Hürü Ana outside into a large garden where she introduced her to the family that lived and assisted Anacık Sultan. They walked and stopped at the edge of the cliff on which the ocak stood. An autumn breeze whistled through the trees around them, swaying them and their branches. They sat down, face to face, and Anacık Sultan asked Hürü Ana a question.[34]

"Bu akşam geyikleri bekliyorsun, değil mi?" You're expecting the gazelles this evening, aren't you?

"Bekliyorum." I'm expecting them, said Hürü Ana, completely unsurprised.

"The gazelles will come to the gate, and we'll go and milk them. When morning and daybreak comes, the gazelles will withdraw and go back to the mountains. From among them one gazelle will remain at the gate for us to slaughter and eat, isn't that how it will be?"

"One will remain," said Hürü Ana. It wasn't clear why Anacık Sultan was asking, what was so extraordinary in this that ...

"It's been a hundred years since the gazelles last came to this gate."

"Let them not come," said Hürü Ana in anger. "Let them stay away! May Hürüce admire even the stone of your blessed ocak."

Every year, Köroğlu's immortal horse Kırat that disappeared with the Forty would come to the gate on a spring day with its youthful, shining coat. After the gazelles left, Kırat never came again either. They say that Kırat is still fighting for goodness, kardeşlik, equality, and freedom in some corner of the world. Düldül, Hazreti Ali's horse, is apparently fighting somewhere on the other side of the Kafdağlar mountains. Düldül hasn't remembered the gate for a hundred years either. Only Genç Osman's Arabian horse, with its rider holding its head in its hands, roams around here from one mountain to the next. A shepherd is said to have seen him last year at the opening of a cave, a beheaded young man apparently holding a sword that still has blood on it. It's also been a long time since it has come by Kırkgöz Ocağı ...

"Let Hürüce be enchanted by your güzel keramet – your beautiful miraculousness – and your comforting words. It doesn't matter whether they come or not, one day they will tire and come, they'll come again to the ocak."[35]

The sun was setting, darkness fell like a heavy boulder at the bottom of the mountain. On the mountain peak opposite them a bright, blinding light glowed continuously, as if the peak were covered in gold. As Anacık Sultan rose, she pointed to the light.

"That's all that's remained from the old days of this ocak, everything else has finished. There, when darkness falls on the world, the peak of this mountain flickers for a long time like this. The cliffs no longer crackle, the blue flowers no longer bloom, the water no longer flows in the opposite direction," she bemoaned. "I'm unable to make anyone believe, the miraculous powers given by God to this ocak are gone."

Hürü Ana gradually became angry at her. She extended her hand pointedly at the peak that remained lit in a flame of light.

"What are you saying Anacık Sultan, Hürüce gives herself to your divine eyes."

"All that's remained for us is that, Hürü Hatun. From all that had been in this ocak only that remains. In a world that pits one person against another, is the power of this poor Kırkgöz Ocağı enough?"

"A day will come, and it will suffice," said Hürü Ana with all her trust and faith.

They went inside. Anacık Sultan took her to a large room. The room was lit by a blue, globe-shaped gas lamp. In the room small earthen jugs and jars, containers, and unusually colorful bottles were arranged side by side on the shelves. Among these were the medicines that will heal İnce Memed tomorrow. Here in this ocak these medicines had been brewed for exactly a thousand years. All the healing flowers and herbs from the steppes of the Binboğalar, Alidağı, Düldül, Erciye, Hasan, and Çukurova, were brought here and for a thousand years their extracts were removed.

"Let Hürüce sacrifice herself for your miraculous powers."

"Hürü Hatun, Hürü Hatun," said Anacık Sultan placing her hand on Hürü Ana's shoulder, "I have no miraculous powers, nor does the ocak, the powers are in the land, the trees, the water, the people, the insects, the birds ... Take a good look at these ... " She took a red bottle from the shelf, opened its top and smelled it. The place was filled with a fine, smooth and deeply soothing scent that Hürü Ana had never sensed.

"İşte bütün keramet bunda. Kırk yıldır ben bu işi iyi anladım. Keramet sende bende değil, keramet toprakta, insanlıkta." Here, here are all the miracles, in this. I've known this work well for forty years. The power of the miracles is not in you or in me, the miracle is in the earth, in humanity.[36]

They put the bottle back in its place and left there, performed their ablutions, and went to the large room where they did their prayers on the hides of gazelles. Afterwards, they went to the kitchen and Anacık Sultan made some soup. As she did, Hürü noticed how skillful she was and wondered if she had ever married. Who knows how beautiful a woman she was in her youth, even now with a soft, lovely face and a sweet smile filled with love for humanity.

Ever since the saints of Kırkgöz Ocağı went to war and didn't return, this Anacık Sultan boiled the flowers of the mountains in this kitchen, removing their extracts, and all with her own hands. She had only one helper, just that one assistant whose family she had met, Mülayim Baba. And she never took a single kuruş for anything she did, not for the dead she was able to revive, not even for the soup she served.

They took their soup into the large room, ate without talking, and sat quietly next to each other until they performed their evening prayers.

Anacık Sultan led Hürü Ana to her room and wished her a comfortable rest, "Allah rahatlık versin."

As soon as they finished breakfast the next day, Anacık Sultan leapt to her feet.[37]

"Yolcu yolunda gerek," she said as she went to the room where the bottles were last night. It's time to go. Hürü Ana followed her. Anacık Sultan went and opened a hickory nut chest, the top of which was decorated with embossed roses. The chest squeaked as she opened it. Anacık Sultan took out a green silk velvet pouch from the chest. The pouch was frayed in some places, and some threads fell from it. She opened the pleated pouch and, with a large eyepiece, separately examined the small, shiny scissors, knives, a number of other instruments, and some small shiny boxwood rods that were worn out after much use, and then she returned each to the bag. She closed the ruffled part of the bag very tightly. She then took a small box from the shelf. Inside the box there were a number of large and small bottles of many colors, shoe polish containers, and tubes the size of a finger. As a result the room smelled of the scents of thousands of beautiful mountain flowers, so much so that Hürü Ana was gripped by some kind of mountain stupor as soon as she entered.

Anacık Sultan was going to heal İnce Memed. There was no other possible way, she would heal him.

Hürü Ana was ashamed that she wanted one more thing from her. The herbal scents in the room gave her the courage:

"Anacık Sultan," she said, her face yellow and her voice starting to tremble, "I have another request of you. Don't withhold it from me so that I don't leave this troubled world with my eyes open. Let me wish this from you in this sacred ocak and ... "

"Buyur Hatun."

"Enchant him, my İnce Memed, so that no shot can pass through him. Don't withhold that from me either."

Anacık Sultan didn't give any response to her request.

"Haydi," she said, "let's get going," and she walked in front, out to the courtyard.[38]

Outside, the young men waited with the horses. They knelt before Anacık Sultan in respect.

In ancient times, the caravan had passed on the paths on which they now rode. One came from the south and went north, the other from the east and went west. They intersected right here. Caravan riders would not pass without stopping by Kırkgöz Ocağı and making requests. Otherwise, bad luck would fall upon them.

Since the night before, Hürü had to relieve herself and was about to burst. She thought that it would be disrespectful to do so in such a sacred place.[39]

"Wait," she hollered. While one of the young men alongside her held her horse, she flew from the horse and dove into the forest, found a secluded tree, pulled down her clothes and broke loose there on the grass.

Anacık Sultan waited for her in the middle of the path. A short while later, Hürü Ana looking down and tying up her clothes emerged from the orman and came over. Anacık Sultan understood everything. So many people wouldn't take care of their business in that sacred Kırkgöz Ocağı. She should have thought of this. Still, she smiled very sweetly at Hürü Ana, in a little bit of fun. This gave Hürü Ana, who got on her horse, some courage. And she was angry:

"Anacık Sultan," she said in a strong voice, "don't withhold this from me, charm my İnce, my son, so that no bullet will pass through him. Even the yıldırım taşı – the lightning stone – was of no help, look he has died."

"Ben afsun bilmem," said Anacık Sultan. I don't know charms. "Keşki bilsem." If only I knew.

"Nasıl olur da bilmezsin, hay Anacık Sultan? Beni mi kandırıyorsun? Sen Kırkgöz Ocağı olasın da ... Şimdi gidince benim oğlumu kurtarınca da ... " Heybeyi gösterdi. "Ya oradakiler ne?"

"Oh Anacık Sultan, how is it that you don't know? Are you playing with me? You are Kırkgöz Ocağı and ... And now you're going and saving my boy ... " She pointed to her bag. "Then what are those things?"

"I've been gathering them for a thousand years, I've been brewing them for a thousand years and extracting their essences. I've been distributing them to people for a thousand years," she said. Anacık Sultan was calm, confident. "Look over there," she said and pointed to the dağlar, to the mountains. "Everything is there. Everything is in the flower, everything is in the herb. Bütün tılsım şu şırlayarak gelen ışıkta. All the charms are in that light that comes, flowing in torrents. Forgive me bacım, my sister, I can't perform miracles like these. Keramet şu durmadan doğuran toprakta. The miracles are in this boundlessly procreating earth."[40]

****

Mahmut Ağa was from one of the most noble families in the Toroslar. So that he would become a great man his father sent him to the schools in Adana and İstanbul. He also studied law. No one in the town thought that after studying so much and living in the big cities he would ever return to the Toroslar, to this harsh existence. Still, as soon as his father died, he returned, right away, to the village. Before even a week passed, he rode into the village with fifteen riders behind him, all armed to the teeth. On the same day, he apparently trampled his horse over and killed someone in the village, some-one who had cursed the grave of his father, and then rode the horse away and out of town as if nothing had happened. This incident was never for-gotten in the town, and afterwards, it was remembered that Mahmut Ağa was the one who had trampled the man with his horse. Çiçekliedereli Mahmut Ağa who had trampled a man with his horse inherited a lot of money and property from his father and, on top of that, the wealth that his father had accumulated from his grandfather.

For his wealth he was indebted to the economic order that his father and grandfather had passed on. He developed and perpetuated this order further. This order was an order that was not well known on the plains, especially on the shores of the Mediterranean. For example, the ağa would give a young mare to a villager. Before the mother died, she would double through birth. The villager would take care of the mare, feed, and groom it in his barn. Let's say that in time this mare would give birth to six colts, then three of these would be the villagers' and three of them the ağa's. And the mother always belonged to the ağa. If the mother mare died, then the villager was obliged to pay for it. In this way, the ağa spread hundreds, even thousands of mares, cows, sheep and goats to many villages. Ten to fifteen years later the ağa's herds of horses and flocks of sheep, cows, goats, and bullock grew in the villages. The villager wasn't able to sell the share that came to him to anyone other than the ağa, and the villager was obliged to hand over at whatever price the ağa wanted.

Mahmut Ağa, an educated man, developed this order. He thought about the villages, selected where they raised the nicest horses, gave those villages mares, selected the best places to raise goats, sheep, and cows, and gave them the goats, sheep, and cows. The business before him in the age of his father and grandfather was different, and they distributed mares, cows, and goats in a haphazard way. It was like this that Mahmut Ağa had raised noble horses, bulls, cows, and goats. His many herds of horses, sheep, and cows were all over here in the mountains and in Çukurova. And every year these herds were taken and sold in Halep, Adana, and İstanbul, and would return to Mahmut Ağa's vault in gold.

In the plains, he was the one who rode the most noble horses, and he was the most handsome and the most intimidating person. Astığı astık, kestiği de kestikti. He was severe. What he said was done. He made a habit out of trampling men under his horse. As a result, no one could ask him to pay. If he felt like it, he would pay some blood money to the wife, children and relatives of the person he killed.

Later, someone from the Adana Governor's office heard of his renown, and wondering what kind of man he was, called on Mahmut Ağa, who apparently didn't go to the Vali. The Vali renewed his wish several times, and Mahmut Ağa apparently paid no attention. The Vali grew very angry about this and sent a Yüzbaşı of the jandarma command to Çiçeklidere, and he wasn't able to find Mahmut Ağa at home. While returning from the mountains to Adana, the Yüzbaşı found and caught up with Mahmut Ağa in a house, and Mahmut Ağa said, "How can I help you Yüzbaşım, I'm Mahmut Ağa." He kept the Yüzbaşı for a few days, organized banquets for him that had never been seen, and, placing a bit of money in his pocket, sent him off saying, "Say hello to the Vali Bey, I'm no rebel against the state, if he wants, let him come here and be our guest for a few days in these mountains of paradise, we would be honored."

After this, the Vali left his post in Adana, and nothing came of this business. But Mahmut Ağa became suspicious only once, and after that he always remained on guard. He didn't let an officer, a collector, a government man, or suspicious people enter the mountains. Until the First World War he carried on his life simply, in his own mountains and in his own way.

Mahmut Ağa experienced real difficulties in the First World War. In a short while, the mountains were filled with deserters and eşkıyas. They would raid the villages, loot them, and kill those who got in their way. As a result, Mahmut Ağa needed to increase his men. For this, a lot of money was needed. Some of his men split up, and, although he didn't want this at all, unfortunately he had them rob people. He was bored by this business, but what could he do … His men hung around the regions of Maraş, Kayseri, and Çukurova and they brought him lots of loot.

He also encountered troubles with the villagers. Some villagers ate his goats, sheep, and oxen, and then blamed it on soldiers who had deserted – the kaçaklar. Mahmut Ağa had extensive investigations carried out. The eşkıyas and the kaçaklar took some of the animals, but most of those who ate up his stock were his own villagers, who had grown hungry. This meant that these incidents broke the existing order and this made him furious with rage. It was necessary to cut out the roots of the problem.

So one day he got on his horse with his armed men behind him and went to Sakızlı köyü, a village in a dried forested ravine high on the mountain. He entered the village, which seemed to be completely empty. No one came out to meet him, nor was there anyone in the village to be seen. It was as if the village had been abandoned years before. Sakızlı köyü was a village that raised noble goats. Mahmut Ağa had those goats brought here by spending loads of money. Each one of the goats was huge and supplied a lot of milk. Apparently, the villagers had slaughtered and eaten all those valuable goats. These beautiful, gold colored goats, they did away with them.

He got down off his horse under the large kamalak pine tree in the middle of the village, sat at the edge of a spring at the foot of the tree, and took out his gun. His face bore the look of hell.

"Get and bring me Muhtar Musa."

Muhtar Musa came sheepishly between two armed men, his hands folded over his stomach and bent forward. He wasn't able to look the ağa or anyone else in the face. His hand-knitted şalvar were in patches, the hair of his body stuck out from the torn holes in his shirt. As for the çarık on his feet, they were brand new and made of red goatskin.

"Are there any goats left in the village, even just one?"

Crouching, without lifting his head, and in a faint voice, Muhtar Musa said: "None are left."

"Not even one?"

"None are left."

"Did you eat all of them, all of my keçiler?"

"We ate them."

"Eşkıya, kaçak?"

"Thanks to you not one can come to this village."

"Why did you eat them?"

"We tried not to eat them. We were starving. We withstood the urge for one month, two months, three months. Then we slaughtered one of them ..."

"And then?"

"Then we got hungry again."

"Then?"

"And again we slaughtered."

"Then?"

"Then all of the keçiler were finished. We slaughtered that last one three days ago."

"Now?"

"We're hungry."

Mahmut Ağa rose to his feet, the ones standing there thought that he was going to hop on his horse and trample Muhtar Musa to death. But it didn't go like that at all. Mahmut Ağa became compassionate, as compassionate a man like this can be, he became that compassionate. He rose slowly from his place and went up beside Musa.

"Lift your head!" he commanded in a cold voice.

Musa was afraid, and raised his head slowly.

"Today, you are going to leave and go from this village. Not one person will remain. Tomorrow I'll come again, and if there is even one person still remaining, I'll trample this village to death with my horse. Do you understand?"

"Ağam don't destroy us. Don't make us leave our land and homes. We're the ones who raised the keçiler. We'll raise them again, and instead of one keçi we'll give three. Forgive us."

"Tomorrow I won't see anybody in this village."

The order was final.

Mahmut Ağa returned to the village three days later and it was completely empty. He had his men check each house one by one. Hiding in a sheepfold just outside the village, they found an elderly couple, so old that they could hardly stand, with three old dogs. They brought them to the ağa.

"Why didn't you leave?"

Shrunken and disheveled, the couple gave no response.

Mahmut Ağa did not insist. These old people were very hungry, their eyes were bulging.

"Take these, put them on the horses, and take them to our village. Don't even think that I let harm come to the elderly on the road. Take good care of them. And take these dogs, too. I feel bad for the dogs, too. The poor things starved here."

The good will that Mahmut Ağa showed to the elderly couple and the three dogs, his compassionate courage, spread to all the villages in the mountains within a few days, and it was even heard in the town. Everyone spoke words of praise about him.

After the expulsion of Sakızlı village, none of the villages, not even one person, even if they had to die from hunger, slaughtered and ate one more cattle or goat, not even a chicken.

Muhtar Musa led the villagers and took them down, all the way to Çukurova. It was difficult for them to part ways from their village, from the land of the graves of their ancestors. But they had no other hope, they had to go. A few people who tried to resist had their resistance broken by all the other villagers. And so, shouting and screaming they took to the road. The mountains reverberated with dirges.

They were exhausted when they came to the town. They settled under the bridge. Those who heard about their journey helped them by providing whatever flour, oil, and bulgur they could.

They had no idea what they would do. Almost all the young men went to the war. The older ones like Muhtar Musa focused on a way to be saved from this calamity, and they couldn't find a way out.

They could only stay up to ten days among the chaste trees under the bridge. There was no work in the village. Muhtar Musa had gone into

Çukurova in the old days to work as a farmhand. He remembered the village where he worked on the Anavarza plains, so the refugees went to the plain and found that village. The villagers gave them a hayloft. It rained a lot that year. They suffered terrible poverty. And the situation on the plain wasn't very good either. Many children died.

Not far from the village, from there to the Ceyhan River, stretched a piece of land with shrubs, reeds, and thick brush. There, they found an open space and, without Talip Bey taking any money from them, set up huts with reeds and grass that he provided. They sold whatever they had on their backs. They bought digging shovels, sickles, pruning hooks, and axes and started the difficult work. Entire families, young and old, worked tooth and nail. With a massive effort they removed enough shrub for a field to plant that year. And with the help of the villagers they planted and harvested. That year, almost all of them got malaria. This showed that the people of the mountains weren't able to endure the Çukurova heat, so hot that it makes a person melt. A lot of the elderly people died from malaria. But others survived. Every year they continued to yield crops from the shrub, the brush, and the reeds. The people of Çukurova had never, as far as they could remember, seen people as industrious as these. They were totally astonished. The villagers gave their new village the name Yalnızyurt. The villagers of Yalnızyurt, with their swelled, notched, and gashed hands and their torn, dark and lean faces, immediately stood out among the other villagers.

The boron-filled land that had been restored from the shrub yielded for-tyfold. They grew wheat, barley, onion, vegetables, and cotton. Every villa-ger went around like a hero who had won a great victory from this redeemed land. They bought horses, cows, and sheep. There emerged no one in Çukurova better than them at raising horses. They raised noble horses with stallions and fillies brought from Urfa. And they were the first among the villages in the plains to make houses from stone. While the other villages had neither roads nor alans, they made smooth streets and opened an alan in the middle of the village. Almost none of the villages in the plains had a mosque. The villagers of Yalnızyurt not only built a mosque in the center of the alan, but they did so with brick. When the summer came, they started to go to the highlands. At harvest time, they would descend early to Çukurova, the Yal-nızyurtlular worked together to gather their produce early, then left the vil-lage completely empty and went to the slopes of Meryemçil in the highlands. On the other hand, they stayed away from the area of their own village out of fear of Mahmut Ağa. They were afraid he would start something with them. Most of the men didn't return from the war. Those who did came as crippled, disabled, or sick people. There were many dirges for those who didn't return. The women of Yalnızyurt put up a great deal of resistance. They were beautiful women, some of them married those who deserted the army or the young men from the nearby villages or highlands. In a short time, like the people of the plains, they became people of the plains and, like the people of Çukurova, adapted to the rules of the plains.

As for Mahmut Ağa, he flew like the wind in the mountains during all this, and he fought against the French who came to Çukurova and against the Armenians who had joined forces with them. He gathered many men, and many eşkıyas, under him. They went down from the mountains to the plains and inflicted defeat on the forces of the enemies in Mersin and Osmaniye. His fame increasingly grew. One day while retreating to Kozan from battle, after defeating the enemy, he and his men came upon Yalnızyurt village. Well outside the village, he was greeted by Muhtar Musa, entire families, young and old. Wasn't this heroic man their old ağa, weren't the rumors of his taking a division of French soldiers at Karboğazı with forty people true, and wasn't he renowned for this?

Mahmut Ağa felt pride that everyone in a village in Çukurova was coming out to welcome him. He intended to stay and rest a few days in this village, in this lovely place halfway, which even had a mosque. Among his men there were several wounded.

He pulled the reins of his horse back and looked with joy at this crowd of mostly women that came this far out of the village to greet him, and Muhtar Musa approached him.

"Köyümüze hoş geldin Ağamız," dedi. Welcome to our village our ağa.

Mahmut Ağa immediately recognized Musa:

"What is this, Musa," dedi, "what are you doing in this village?"

"This is our village ağamız. Welcome, buyur."

Mahmut Ağa didn't respond, he put his head down, spurred on his horse, and, without even going into the village, rode off in the other direction.

He asked and inquired in the town. He learned how the people who had eaten his goats had founded a village on very fertile land and had become the most hardworking people on the plain.

The French and Armenians left the plain, and the Independence War ended. The young men who had fought against enemies went down into the towns. Now a new state was established. They would be the foundation stone of this new state. They proceeded with dividing up the plains. This division was very easy in some places, harder in others. For a long time, Mahmut Ağa didn't get involved in this business, he remained a spectator. He didn't want many things, he had everything, like the order that had lasted in the mountains from the time of his grandfather, which had, moreover, continued developing. But this couldn't go on like this and ... It became necessary for him to go down to the plain. He could buy whatever land he wanted and establish farms anywhere he wanted. A new world began. Mahmut Ağa perceived this, he was a person who had studied what could be known and learned about the world. One morning he called his men. "Prepare the horses," he said. The men mounted their horses. Their destination was the Anavarza plain. They came to Yalnızyurt village. When the villagers learned he was coming to their village, they gathered in the village alan, in front of the mosque. It was as if they had forgotten entirely that the ağa had expelled them from their village.

With joy and adoration, Muhtar Musa greeted him:

"Buyur Ağa, in, hoş geldin köyümüze." Welcome ağa, come down, welcome to our village.

The other remained on his horse, his cruel expression even more threatening and enraged.

"Buyur, in Ağamız. Hoş geldin." Welcome, come down our Ağa. "Bizi ziyadesiyle sevindirdin köyümüze gelmekle, dünyayı bağışladın." You have pleased us tremendously by coming to our village, you've given us the whole world.

Mahmut Ağa leaned down slightly from his horse.

"Musa," dedi, "tomorrow you will clear out of this village."

The order was final.

"Ağa, Ağamız, Mahmut Ağa ... "

Mahmut Ağa rode his horse and went away.

The next day he sent his men to the village. The villagers hadn't moved at all from where they were. The third day, and then the fourth day ... Mahmut Ağa was patient. His patience lasted for ten days. It meant that these villagers, these stupid lowlifes, reptiles, they were opposing the hero of the National War. He got on his horse and came to Yalnızyurt. There was not a villager around, everyone hid in their homes and waited for what will happen.

Two men brought Muhtar Musa, dragging him from his home, to the presence of the ağa.

"Why didn't you leave my village Musa? I'm taking this village in exchange for my goats that you ate. If you resist, you know what will happen."

"Where should we go ağam? This village, with our teeth and nails ... look at my hands, do they even look like hands? Look at my face, my body, is there anywhere that they resemble the face and body of a human? Look at the villagers, the women, the men, do they resemble a human being in any way? Do you think we've had it easy ağa, making fields out of the shrubs."

Cruel-faced Mahmut Ağa remained on his horse in a majestic posture. He commanded his men:

"Burn down the village."

Mahmut Ağa had waited for a day with the poyraz, the northeast wind. Suddenly, the village erupted in flames from every direction. Crying and beating themselves, the villagers gathered in the alan. It didn't even occur to them to carry their things outside.

"Tomorrow, in this village, I won't see a single living thing here."

Atop his horse, Mahmut Ağa and a section of the men behind him split the crowd and took off from the village.

After he left, a fight began between the villagers and Mahmut Ağa's men. Many of the villagers were injured. They were trampled under the horses' hooves. In the meantime, Kasım who had returned recently armed from the Greek War, shot Mahmut Ağa's younger brother Salih, who fell lifelessly from his horse. If the villagers hadn't stopped him, he would have killed all the men from the ditch where he was hiding.

When Mahmut Ağa returned to Yalnızyurt on the second day neither a living thing nor any home remained standing. A few homes still smoldered, and the brick mosque with its wood minaret in the middle of the plain stood erect in the smoke.

Mahmut Ağa closed all the mountain roads to apprehend and kill Kasım. He sent word to everyone he knew in the mountains, to his men and to the eşkıyas. He wanted them to bring Kasım, dead or alive. Months passed and no one was able to find Kasım or even the slightest trace of him anywhere. And the villagers of Yalnızyurt disappeared from sight, from that day onward, no matter how much you searched, not a word was heard from them again.[41]

****

Inner intrigues among the ağas and beys, including a letter saying Arif Saim was planning to assassinate Mustafa Kemal, led to an interrogation of Muhtar Kenan, one of their own, during which Kertiş Ali tortured the man to death. They fingered İnce Memed for the murder, but the Yuzbaşı, whose conscience was disturbed and who watched the behavior of the ağas and beys closely, doubted it. "Ulan İnce Memed hakkın var oğlum," he said, "yerden göğe kadar hakkın var." Oh İnce Memed you have the right my boy, from the earth to the sky you have the right.[42]

****

With Anacık Sultan's remedies, Memed's fever subsided within a week, and his wounds began to heal. He moved from the cave to a tent in the most obscure parts of the orman. He drank fresh milk and ate fresh butter, honey, meats and other foods brought from the oba, where his improving health unleashed an unending sense of joy.

Hürü Ana and Mahmut traveled back to the village, and Hürü Ana whispered into the ear of Memed's horse, "Listen to me well, İnce Memed is better, he's better, better." The horse showed no sign of understanding. "He's better, he's better, didn't you hear me ... " But again the horse seemed not to care. Hürü Ana became angry. "My God I hope you'll sacrifice yourself for Köroğlu's Kırat, Ali's Düldül, the Prophet's Burak ... My God I hope you will sacrifice yourself for my feet and İnce Memed's ... İnce Memed has gotten better, he's been saved, he's better, he's saved, Anacık Sultan cured him, did you hear?" The horse soon disappeared from the village and wasn't seen again.[43]

With light beaming again in his eyes, Memed went to the oba to bid farewell to the Yörüks.

Battal Ağa needed to pay Molla Duran for use of the winter quarters. He told Memed that they had nothing left to give and that he was preparing to go to Adana the next day to find some money. He said he wouldn't be surprised if Molla Duran were to take full possession of the land. He also told Memed that Kerimoğlu's oba was in the same trouble, that a new upstart ağa, Sabit Bey, had taken possession of their quarters. "He's also supposedly a hero of the Independence War. Like Molla Efendi, he either wants gold coins or to drive us out." Battal Ağa's eyes filled with tears and asked to die soon and be buried at the head of the spring nearby. "Ağa don't," said Memed, his voice trembling.

Just then, the young girls, brides, and old women, glancing briefly at Memed, brought some decorated bundles and placed them in the corner of the tent. A young man also brought several guns and rifles. After that, a pair of binoculars, a Çerkez dagger, and a nagant pistol. Memed didn't understand what these were all for and looked with amazement at everything. Battal Ağa took the first bundle and without opening it, placed it in front of Memed. Then he did the same with the rest. "These are our gifts to you İnce Memed," he said.

Holding back tears, Memed opened the package and found a brand new set of knitted, silk and silver-threaded clothing. He stared at them, excited and unable to speak. Battal Ağa, Kasım, and Temir smiled broadly. Battal Ağa told Memed to go to the side of the tent and change his clothes. Memed wept as he took off his bloody and bullet-riddled clothing. He used a silk handkerchief to wipe away his tears.

Everything fitted perfectly.

"Our Yörük women know this work well, ever since Köroğlu," Battal Ağa explained.

Memed was moved to hear that the women had outfitted Köroğlu before he went to battle. So that no one would see his tears, Memed kept his head down. He accepted the gifts graciously and then spoke, thinking that what he would say would take them by surprise.[44]

"I'm leaving the mountains. I'm going to some unknown, faraway lands. There I'm going to disappear. There's no end to this. The end is that some worthless person kills you for no reason."

He looked in the faces of the others and didn't see even the smallest sign of surprise.

"Or did you know that I would be doing this?" asked Memed, baffled.

"What I know," spoke Battal Ağa with much experience, "what I know is that no eşkıya wants to remain in the mountain forever. There's never been seen an eşkıya who has grown old in the mountain. If the eşkıya in the end doesn't die by being shot, and grows old in the mountain, then he's unable to do the work, unable to be an eşkıya. Therefore my boy Memed, you are acting wisely with this. Yes, you're doing the right thing. It's also never been seen that an eşkıya like you can disappear and remain on the plain forever. Either he's killed for some reason or another on the plain, or he can't stand the slightest injustice and goes up to the mountain. Don't misunderstand me Memed, I'm not saying stay in the mountain, I'm saying the things that I've seen and heard happen over time. It's harder for an eşkıya to disappear on the plains than to live in the mountain. I still haven't seen to this day an eşkıya go onto the plain and meet his end through natural death, or one who didn't return to the mountains. I'm not speaking of the run of the mill eşkıya, I'm talking about a famous eşkıya like you, who's become İnce Memed or Köroğlu."

"There's Bayramoğlu, Bayramoğlu he went back to a village and lives, like a rose ... "

"Bayramoğlu died," said Battal Ağa. "He killed himself. And Kürt Rüstem is in town, with the sherbet kettle on his back. He dies every day from this foolishness. That Kürt Rüstem, he can't even come close to Bayramoğlu in terms of his courage, boldness, or humanity, he doesn't match up to him."

"I'm dying too," said Memed.

"I don't think so, or inşallah you'll get over it," said Battal Ağa. "I've come to know you a bit, senin içindeki bu kurt var iken, böyle de depreşip durur iken, sen mecbursun. Köroğlu da mecburdu. When the kurt – the worm – inside you is there, it haunts you and remains, and you're compelled. Köroğlu was also compelled."

"I know that I am compelled, I know I can't stop, I know that when İnce Memed disappears, I won't be able to endure it. I know myself, I know what it's worth ... I know, I know, I know."

Battal Ağa fixed his grass-green eyes into Memed's. Memed no longer hid his eyes, and Battal Ağa looked at that steel glimmer in his eyes that had returned and remained there. Woe humanity woe, he said to himself, look at this man who was like a dove a short while ago when he saw these clothes, crying like a child from goodness, pleasure, and embarrassment, and look how he's become a lion, a camel with his hair standing on end.

"I know Ağam ... Listen to me well, I'm telling you what's burning inside me. I'm not afraid of death. Death awaits us, if not today, then sooner or later. One who fears that cannot be a human being. I'm not afraid of being shot and killed. My problem is something else ... "

Battal Ağa clearly listened carefully and gave importance to every word, thoughtfully, with his long fingers stroking his chin.

"My problem is a big problem. Let Allah never place such a problem on anyone. Not even on the enemy ... I killed Abdi Ağa, and Kel Hamza came in his place. I killed him too, let's see now who will come ... I killed Ali Safa Bey. And now another one has come in his place, let's say I kill him too, look Sabit Bey has become a burden to Kerimoğlu, and moreover he fell from the sky. As for your burden, there's Molla Duran Efendi … What good has all those I've killed been, tell me this Battal Ağam? If I kill a thousand of them, two thousand of them will come … ”

When Battal Ağa smiled with laughter Memed felt strange.

“Now I've understood your trouble,” said Battal Ağa. “I've understood it very well.” He spoke and smiled at the same time. “And you listen to me well İnce Memed … ” He kneeled on a knee and spoke in a defiant voice. “İnce Memed will die and Ali Memed will come in his place, and he'll also be killed and Hasan Memed will come in his place … And when he is killed Veli Memed will come … And the same will happen, and the same, and the same … What are you thinking, my son Memed, are you thinking that the İnce Memeds will end? Her insanın içinde bir mecbur kurdu, bir İnce Memedlik, bir Köroğluluk kurdu var. There's the kurt, the worm, of an İnce Memed, a Köroğlu, that obligates everyone. Köroğlu went and İnce Memed came. As long as this kurt is inside the human being, no matter what happens, humanity will not be defeated. You are the kurt inside humanity, do whatever you do, go wherever you go. Now if this kurt inside humanity disappears, then the humanity will be taken out of the human being. İnsanoğlu içindeki bu kurdunu yitirmeyecek, ona kıyamete kadar gözü gibi, yüreği gibi bakacak. Humanity will not lose the kurt inside it, it will look after it until judgment day, like its eye, like its heart. O kurt insanoğlunun şahdamarı, atan yüreğidir. That kurt is the lifeline of humanity, its heart that beats. Senin içindeki kurt da, işte insanlığın bu kurdudur. And the kurt that's inside you, it's this kurt of humanity.”

Somehow, that day İnce Memed wasn't able to bid farewell and say goodbye. They debated that night until morning. Battal Ağa knew so much about the world and about humanity. His words that, “Bir İnce Memed giderse bin, on bin, yüz bin İnce Memed gelir, Ağalar biter de İnce Memedler bitmez” – If one İnce Memed goes, a thousand, ten thousand, a hundred thousand İnce Memeds will come, the ağas will come to an end, but the İnce Memeds will never – affected Memed deeply, shook him from head to toe. He somehow wasn't able to free himself from the impact of these words.

Morning came and the day lit up. İnce Memed didn't change his thinking. In fact, his wounds hadn't completely healed. Finally, he said this to Battal Ağa. He let Battal Ağa say whatever he wanted to say, and in the end agreed. He, too, was a human being, he'll have his children, he'll find comfort. He knew this. But he also knew the kurt inside the human being. Bu kurt onu rahat bırakmayacaktı, bunu da çok iyi biliyordu. This kurt would not leave him alone, this he also knew very well.

In the morning, they ate breakfast laughing and with joy. Towards midmorning, İnce Memed rose:

“I must go,” he said, “hakkınızı bana helal edin, perhaps we won't see each other again until judgment day.”

He took his dagger, his binoculars, his gun, and his cartridges and placed them in front of Battal Ağa.

"Let these stay in the oba, maybe one day another İnce Memed will come to this oba. Give this to him saying these were those of the other İnce Memed who disappeared without a trace."[45]

****

İnce Memed arrived in the village about the time of the evening prayers. A cool breeze blew an old, familiar scent. He remembered his mother, Hatçe, and Seyran. He wondered where his child and Iraz Ana were. One day he would find him. He had no doubt that Iraz was taking good care of him. His memories created an emptiness and longing inside. The more he thought of Seyran, the more he missed her. He wondered if she was carrying their child.

At midnight, he knocked quietly on Hürü Ana's door. She welcomed him, fed him and they talked about what had happened since he had been away. Memed asked about Abdi's children. Hürü Ana tells him that they went to town where they opened a small store.[46]

"My heart ached for them. When they left the village, when they left us, the poor ones, I forgot to tell you when you were sick, they cried and cried. And the whole village wept behind them."[47]

Memed describes his plans to take Seyran away, change his name, and raise a family.[48]

"Ana, Abdi Ağa died and Kel Hamza came in his place. Kel Hamza died and in his place ... Ali Safa Bey dies, there are so many ağas."

Hürü listened very quietly.

"When İnce Memed dies Ana, many more İnce Memeds will come in his place. The ağas are few, the İnce Memeds are many. If one İnce Memed dies, a thousand, two thousand, ten thousand, a hundred thousand İnce Memeds will come. And it will happen without me being there."

...

"Sooner or later being an eşkıya ends with a bullet, isn't that right Ana?"
He waited for her to say something, but Hürü Ana was quiet.

...

"I'm going to go and buy some land in a village, I have a bit of money, I'm going to build a house, I'll make my name Kara İbrahim, Sefil İbrahim, it will be good, I'll have children. I've understood that being an eşkıya doesn't suit me, I'm like my father, a soft and meek person. My work is not killing men. I've thought a lot. That which is made by God can only be destroyed by God."

Hürü leaned down in front of him.

"Would you like some water?" she asked him.

"Thank you Ana. Just as your heart aches for the death of Abdi Ağa ... " he looked at Hürü's face, expecting her to say something in response to these words at least. Hürü Ana still paid no attention. "My heart aches too for Abdi Ağa and Ali Safa Bey."

"Quiet, dog," she said opening her eyes wide. "I didn't say that my heart ached for Abdi Ağa. Hamza, and Abdi, and Ali Safa they were not made by God, they were the work of Satan. An insan – a human being – no, an insanoğlu insan – a humanity being, a being of humanity – can ruin Satan's work ... "

"Look Ana, I'm going now from here down below, down to Çukurova, I'll go and take Seyran by my side, to that country whose name is not known, and I'll be Sefil İbrahim."[49]

At first, Hürü Ana gave Memed her blessings. Then she grew angry at his naïveté. She said that giving up eşkıyalık was a mistake and told him that Seyran's home was probably surrounded and that he wouldn't make it there alive. Memed said he understood and immediately changed his mind.

"Ana I won't go to Çukurova. Really, I've understood what you're saying Ana ... "

She had a different idea, though, which Memed accepted. They would send Kısacık Mahmut to get Seyran, and, in the meantime, Memed needed to go to Anacık Sultan and take from her a charm that would keep him from being shot and killed. "If you go there and kiss her hand, she'll give you a charm, and perhaps enchant you ... like Genç Osman, even if they cut off your head you will not die."

"What need do I have for a charm Ana, after this?"

"Every person needs a charm, all the time, from Kırkgöz Ocağı. In this world and in the next ... "

Memed set out for Kırkgöz Ocağı the next day.[50]
One of the informants for the ağas, Tazı Tahsin, meets Memed on the mountain path to Kırkgöz Ocağı and reports to the jandarma.[51]

****

The Yüzbaşı, Asım Çavuş, Kertiş Ali Onbaşı, and Murtaza Ağa exchanged their views on the saints of Kırkgöz Ocağı.

"This ignorant people worships them," said Murtaza. "This obscurantism, these superstitions are worked into the spirit of the people, this herd of sheep. More than, more than a thousand years is needed to liberate this ignorant people from these superstitions. And they exploit the people, they rob them and oppress them, taking as donations one of their chickens, or a single one of their goats or sheep that they happily take and bring to the ocak."

"There's no longer any man at the ocak," said Asım Çavuş. "A woman sits at the head of the order. And they worship her in the entire Toroslar, and the regions of Maraş, Kayseri, and Antep."

"There were many men with them until the Independence War."

"What happened to them?" asked the Yüzbaşı. "I know only a little, so explain some more."

Murtaza Ağa spoke with excitement.

"They were enlisted as volunteers," he said, "sixteen of the sixteen men and they went to the Independence War as volunteers. And all of them fell as martyrs in one day, side by side, at Dumlupınar. The Greeks apparently say that the Turkish Army didn't defeat them, that they were defeated by tall, sworded men, wearing white cloths and green turbans who were out in front of the army. They didn't stand a chance, they say. Superstition … This is what our people believe."

Yüzbaşı:

"Sixteen saints and all went to war, is this true?"

"It's true," said Murtaza Ağa. "In those days the entire town was in the mountains. All of us were deserters, and later I got involved in the Kuvayı Milliye. I saw sixteen of them go to the army together, with their sacks on their backs. While they walked on the road, the entire, this ignorant people kissed the land on which they walked. Superstition … "

"So none of them returned from the war?"

"They didn't return," said Murtaza Ağa.

"So this woman watches over their place?"

"She does," said Asım Çavuş. "An old woman. Very sert – tough – she doesn't speak with anyone."

"It means that these people won't be saved from this obscurantism, from lies, from exploitation for a much longer time," sighed the Yüzbaşı."[52]

****

Memed stopped and rested by a pond near a spring. A sudden, heavy rain fell. The water soaked into, but didn't pass through, the wool-stitched aba on his back.

He thought of Hürü Ana the entire way, and this made him happy. Her love was boundless and inexhaustible. Like the water flowing so clear from this spring, she lit up whoever was around her, be it a person, a wolf or a bird, a friend or an enemy. One who looked into Hürü Ana's face couldn't be unhappy from her warm love and sweetness, couldn't kill a man, couldn't do any evil ... And there were the words of Battal Ağa, reassuring him that from now on if he died, he wouldn't die disappointed ... Ağalar az, fıkaralar çoktu. The ağas are few, the poor many. The more he repeated those words, the more he was lit up inside and filled with love and friendship, and the more he caressed the mountains, the clouds, those wild flowing waters, and the roaring thunder and lightning. He even cared for that little man – Tazı Tahsin – who ran to the town to betray him ... Bad luck waited for him under every stone, in every corner, behind every bush. How could he take Seyran from the village, cross these mountains together with her – onunla birlikte şu dağları nasıl aşacaklar – where would they hide? He had become accustomed to being an eşkıya, after this what other kind of work would he do, and, moreover, what work could he envision? ... Maybe he would go down to Çukurova, to Adana, to the seashore, to Dursun's village, really, what was the name of Dursun's village, and stay as a gardener in the orange groves. I'll build a small house in the orange groves with Seyran for the two of us, then after some years Hürü Ana can come, too, and take care of the children ... Seyran would always smile. When she smiled, she was the dünyalar güzeli – the beauty of all worlds ... He missed her terribly. He had to take her hand, he had to go to Kırkgöz Ocağı and return right away. He had to take Seyran from there, and then to adı şanı bilinmedik eller – unknown faraway lands ... He loved this expression adı şanı bilinmedik eller. Hadn't Karacaoğlan also said that, adı şanı bilinmedik ellere gitmeyince gönül yardan ayrılmaz ... Unless you go to unknown faraway lands, your heart doesn't separate from your lover. And once there, after moving to a house overwhelmed with the scents of orange flowers, Seyran and the children would work, only Hürü Ana would not work. And he would go straight to Anavarza, find Recep Çavuş's grave, and build there a türbe for him. And when İnce Memed would build that türbe for him, everyone would know that he had been an eşkıya, the villagers and the Yörükler would come, and they would make sacrifices on his türbe, and they would tie good luck cloths on the trees.

Sounds of the pebbles carried from the mountains by the falling rain came, lightning struck. When thinking about Seyran his entire body swelled with maddening desire, he shook from head to toe ... İnce Memed smiled with happiness. This eşkıyalık, however, the end will come, his leaving it would be good.[53]

The door opened for him and a tall man greeted Memed at Kırkgöz Ocağı early the next day. The man led him to the salon where Anacık Sultan, dressed in white and sitting on a divan with her ninety-nine-piece tespih, waited. He approached her, took her hand, kissed it, and raised it to his forehead three times. They sat down next to each other. A short while later, a nicely scented coffee was served. Memed's hands shook so much that he wasn't quite able to

229

take the coffee. Anacık Sultan noticed, took a cup from the tray, and handed it to him. This confused him.

"I was waiting for you İnce Memed. Hoş geldin yavrum, are you well?"

"I'm well Anam," said İnce Memed, with a child's bashfulness. His face was totally flushed and glowed red.

He didn't notice anything in the room other than the kılıç – the sword. Since childhood, he had heard so many things about this kılıç. For years, folk poets and storytellers in these mountains had told of the adventures of the kılıç hanging on that wall. Nine hundred and ninety-nine verses and hadiths were inscribed in gold on this kılıç. It was enchanted. None of the sixteen who went from the ocak to the War of Independence had girded this sword, and none of them were able to return. Why hadn't they taken this enchanted kılıç? Perhaps if they had taken the kılıç, none of them would have received a scratch. And all of them would have been able to return to their ocak. There was no man left in the ocak to carry Hasan Bey's sacred kılıç, it remained there like that, languishing and resentful. No matter how good a person İnce Memed was, he wasn't able to carry this kılıç. Even for those from Hasan Bey's lineage, even those who possessed the right, hadn't been able to show the courage to gird the sword and go into battle. Was the ocak so broken down that no man could put on the enchanted and sacred sword, who knows? There, and not a single one was able to return from the War of Independence.

"What are you thinking İnce Memed, yavrum, your eyes are fixed on the kılıç?"

"Why, when they went to war, didn't our saints take this with them and go, I was thinking."

"They didn't have the strength for Hasan Bey's kılıç. My father, my brothers, my uncles, Hasan Bey's kılıç is like that … They say that not everyone has enough strength for that kılıç, they feared that kılıç."

Padişah Eyüboğlu Selahaddin had given Hasan Bey this sacred kılıç as a gift. In his hand, this kılıç protected Kudüs and Şam-ı Şerifi from the iron-clad crusaders with crosses hanging from their necks and martyrs fell in the cause of the sacred places. One morning, Eyüboğlu Selahaddin Padişah, who awoke from sleep tired, called on Hasan Bey and said, in honor of this rising sun, the shimmering light, the spinning wheel of fortune, for sacred Kudüs, its rich land and its green grass, you will fight those ironclad ones from here on with this kılıç in your hand, and surrender to no one. Take the kılıç, take your soldiers, hurry and go to where the sun sets. Hasan Bey took the sacred kılıç in his hand, took it upon himself and said to his comrades, come to holy war, let's go to Anatolia and the lands of the Rum.

On the plain of Konya, they encountered the ones wearing iron with crosses hanging from their necks and long swords. The iron-wearing crowd coming was huge, as big as the sea, sparkling and clanging, while Hasan Bey's army was few. Their army was thirty times bigger than his.

A ruthless battle erupted on the Konya plain. That day ten thousand of Hasan Bey's fifteen thousand men fell. The hawks and ravens on the plains of Konya got full with the meat of the dead. The next day, the rest of Hasan Bey's army also broke, and Hasan Bey and forty of his men took shelter in an awesome mountain behind them. The crowd of the enemy surrounded the tall, jagged, massive mountain on every side. With the mountain surrounded like ants, Hasan Bey fought the iron wearers all day until evening, and when the sun set there were only three men left on the peak of the mountain. They lit a powerful fire and rested. The light of the fire they burned lit up the entire plain. Morning came, Hasan Bey plunged into the army of the enemy like a wolf into a pack of sheep. The enemies wanted to capture him alive. Hasan Bey and his three comrades were martyred at exactly noon. The enemies cheered with joy. Their commander ordered them, "Find his kılıç for me. That kılıç cut out our roots, it wiped us out." They searched and combed the area for the kılıç, but it was nowhere to be found. They went back to the commander and explained the situation. And the commander said, "There's something going on here, amanın if you can't find his kılıç, find Hasan Bey's body and cut off his head." The iron wearers went and there weren't any dead bodies either.

The next day the villagers came and saw that forty dead bodies had been stretched out side by side. On their lips were smiles, nowhere on their bodies was the smallest drop of blood. They lay there, in a deep sleep. The villagers washed them and wrapped and buried them in white shrouds. And they looked, and behold what did they see, Hasan Bey's kılıç had come and stood straight up, erect, at the head of his grave. They wanted to take the sword, and reached out to grab it, and as soon as they extended their hands, the kılıç withdrew and went underground. When they pulled it, it came out from under the ground with difficulty and again stood straight up. As much as the others wanted to take the kılıç from there, the kılıç would not surrender to them. At that moment, a brave man appeared and hollered, "Stop. Stop Muhammed's ümmet, no one can remove and take this kılıç from here. A time will come when a man from Hasan Bey's lineage will come here, will climb this mountain, whose name will also be Hasan, and only he, that man, will take Hasan Bey's sacred kılıç from its place … Until then, no one can or will be able to remove that kılıç from its place."

Years and centuries passed, the sword there watched over the türbe of Hasan Bey and his brave companions until a pir named Hasan came to Kırkgöz Ocağı. That day, the pir, who was a strong young man at the age of seventeen, walked up the mountain, came to the türbe of his grandfather Hasan and saw the kılıç. Trembling, he couldn't approach it. Instead, the sword walked directly towards him and placed its handle in the young man's hand. And he took it and brought it to the ocak.

From that day on, the name of that mountain is Hasan dağı. And since that day till now, the sunrise comes every morning to the peak of Hasan dağı, stays there for a while, and then rises to the sky.

Evening came and after performing her prayers, Anacık Sultan went to the kitchen and made Memed a pleasant-smelling soup. After eating, they sat side by side, and remained like that till the middle of the night, not saying a word.

Finally Anacık Sultan broke the silence.

"You're not saying a word İnce Memed, is there something wrong my son?" she asked.

"I'm going down from the mountains Anacık Sultan," said İnce Memed. "Eşkıyalık isn't for me. I haven't been able to do any good until now. I'm going to kill İnce Memed. I came to ask you about this."

"Whatever it is inside that you want, do that!"

"I'll do it, it's just where should I go, what should I do? And I have this responsibility, my wife, who is waiting for me down below in Vayvay village."

"Is there no place for you to go?"

"No Anacık Sultan. When İnce Memed dies, many more İnce Memeds will come. The wretched of the earth are many, the others few. Where should I go?" They were quiet and lost in thought. İnce Memed's eyes were glued upon and didn't move from the sacred kılıç. This kılıç remained unclaimed, would someone later emerge who was able to take it from there?

"If I don't go, if I remain in these mountains, is that impossible Anacık Sultan, if I live out my life here, even if I die by the bullet ... "

He wanted permission from her, he waited for her to say bluntly, İnce Memed don't go, continue being an eşkıya, this is your destiny, and you can't erase what is written on your forehead. If she said this, this matter would be closed.

"Gönülün istediğini yap." Do what your heart desires.

"Alright Anacık Sultan ... "

Anacık Sultan rose, took a few keys from her pocket, sat in front of a trunk, and opened it with a clink. She removed and brought from there a ring with a seal on it that was wrapped inside velvet.

"This," she said, "is the seal of the ocak. This ocak will die out after me, take this and keep it with you. If you go to Malatya, there is Ağuiçen Ocak, show this to them, they'll hide you. And until you die, don't remove this ring that I'm placing on your finger. Perhaps it will be of some good to you. When this ocak dies out, this ring should be on the finger of a good person."

She took his right hand and slowly, without any difficulty, slid the ring onto his middle finger. It was as if the ring was made for İnce Memed's finger, it fitted perfectly.

"This sword is your right too, in my heart, but I can't give that kılıç to anyone. After I die it will take care of itself."

In her presence İnce Memed performed his prayers and kissed and placed her hand on his forehead three times.

"Give me a blessing Anacık Sultan," he said in joy, as if he was reborn full of light, and with a new power in his body. His inside was purified that much.

"Let me make more soup for you, after that I'll give you to the newly rising day."

Till the day began, they ate the soup together, from the same bowl.[54]

****

Pulsating with a new light, Memed descended from the ocak as if he had wings on his back. From inside the orman, he heard sounds of crying. Salacan village had just been raided. The village girls had been raped and Hasan, a popular young man, killed. When Memed asked what happened, the villagers told him that İnce Memed had attacked them. Hasan's father took the real Memed to be a friend of Hasan's. "Kör olası İnce Memed" – damn İnce Memed – the villagers said.

Memed told them there must be some mistake, that he knows İnce Memed and he wouldn't do these things. An argument broke out and Memed slipped away to the sounds of dirges for Hasan.

Memed couldn't think about or feel a thing. His entire body froze. He walked to the spring on the edge of the orman. The face of the young man who had been killed affected him greatly. He felt that he knew him from some-where, but he couldn't make out where. He started to eat the food that Hürü Ana had packed, but just as he did, a flock of birds flew wildly from the ground to the sky.

Memed watched as a bird of prey flew like an arrow in and out of the rising flock, and he understood everything. The bird wasn't huge but its wings were as sharp as a dagger. Memed watched it carefully.

The confrontation between the flock and the bird didn't last long. The bird flew too close to the ground and clipped its wing on the thorn of a bush. It fell to the ground and thrashed about. Memed ran to it. The bird tried to fly away but couldn't.

As Memed approached it, it tried one last time to fly, but in vain. Memed extended his hand, and the bird, having lost all hope, struck Memed's forefinger with its sharp beak. "I'll catch you," said Memed with a smile. "You're a novice bird."

Though its eyes were full of life, the bird tired and Memed took hold of him. "My novice bird, the beauty of my eyes, this is how the world is. Inexperience won't do. And it won't do to be as greedy and angry as you."

As he caressed the bird, it struck his hand again, puncturing it like a knife. Memed licked his wound and washed it in the spring. He enjoyed this tussle with the bird. He tied its legs together with a small piece of string and placed it by the thorned keven as he finished his meal. When he was done, he untied its legs and thought he would take it to Seyran. She would nurse it back to health and release it to the cliffs of Anavarza.

He went down into a valley and heard the sound of a horse breathing. He stopped in his tracks. The dark horse was about twenty or twenty-five steps ahead and looked at him strangely. Memed placed the bird on the ground and went straight to the horse. He came up to its side, but just as he extended his hand, the horse sprung forth and galloped away. It had become a bit thinner. It went and stood atop a sharp rock, and after neighing several times, turned in the direction of the sun and raised its ears straight up. Memed took the bird from the ground and looked at the horse longingly.[55]

"Learn from this my heart," he said, "if a small amount of humanity has remained in you, learn from this horse, learn from this bird." He caressed the bird in his hand. "And you learn from this too, bird of prey. Look at that horse, even though it's a horse, even though it can't speak a word, it won't surrender to anyone. It will not surrender and … It will die in these mountains, its skeleton may be small but, and it's like Köroğlu's horse and will not surrender. A horse, as a horse, even though it can't speak … Take a lesson my crazy heart, take a lesson from this bird and from this horse."[56]

Memed was on the path to the Sarıkeçili camp, not far from where he had been injured, when a division of jandarma approached him. He went to the side and waited for the jandarma to pass. When the Yüzbaşı came by on a horse, the division halted.

"Come here villager," dedi Yüzbaşı.

And immediately the other officers ran to his side.

Memed's face went yellow for a moment, then it cleared.

"What's this bird in your hand?"

"It's injured," said Memed, "I don't know what bird it is." He briefly explained the story of the bird.

"So it wasn't able to grab even one bird from among all the others?"

"It wasn't."

"What are you going to do with this bird now?"

"I'll take it to the village and look after it, when it's better, I'll release it into the orman."

"Nice. What's your name?"

"İnce Memed."

"Allah Allah" – My God – said the Yüzbaşı with a smile, "and everyone in these mountains is named İnce Memed."

"İnce Memed," said Memed with a smile.

"And there's an eşkıya İnce Memed, have you heard of him, İnce Memed?"

"Who hasn't heard of him?"

"Where is he now, do you know?"

"I know," said Memed tilting his head down humbly. "He's at Akçadağı now."

"He's establishing a çete … "

"He's apparently creating a çete with sixteen people."

"All the villagers know."

"They'll tell me where he is, won't they?"

"They'll tell."

"And in that case, I'll catch him."

"You'll catch him, Faruk Yüzbaşım."

"I'm not Faruk Yüzbaşı. I'm attached to the Maraş Jandarma Kumandanlığı. I'm going to catch İnce Memed before Faruk."

"If you're committed to your goal, you'll eventually carry it out, Yüzbaşım."

"Have you seen İnce Memed?"

"I've seen him Yüzbaşım."

"What kind of person is he?"

Memed leaned his head forward, thought for a moment, and then spoke eye to eye.

"Like you he's a courageous man. He has big eyes like you, big and strong, and long fingers … If you see him, you'll like him very much."

The Yüzbaşı's face softened a bit more.

"Where are you going like this?"

"I'm going to town."

"Won't you show me where he is?"

"I'm from these places nearby Yüzbaşım, I don't know Akçadağı at all."

The Yüzbaşı rode his horse.

"Sağlıcakla kal İnce Memed."

"Güle güle Yüzbaşım."[57]

When the jandarma was out of sight, Memed sprinted down the slope into the shrubs and back towards the Sarıkeçili camp. He spotted a shepherd he recognized and had him bring Kasım and Temir. They took him to Battal Ağa who has been expecting Memed.[58]

"Hoş geldin İnce Memed," Battal Ağa said as he hugged him.

Battal Ağa's hands, eyes, his whole body bore such love that it gave Memed goose bumps. Only Hürü Ana greeted him like this, only Hürü Ana loved him like this.

"I've waited for you since the day you left."

"Why?"

"I know the kurt in you very well."

…

"Did you encounter the Yüzbaşı on the way?"

"I did, he asked my name, and I said İnce Memed. This bird saved me. Has there ever been an eşkıya with a bird in his arms?"

"Never," dedi Battal Ağa.

At the tent, pillows and a table set for a guest waited. First they brought some steaming soup.

"Soup from Anacık Sultan," said Battal Ağa.

"What is it that you know?"

"That the ring on your finger is the ring of the ocak. Other than the members of the ocak, no one else wears it. How did she give it to you? She must consider you a pir. Now don't forget this. While this ring is on your finger, it will protect you from all accidents and troubles."

They sat and began to eat the soup in a large bowl.

At that moment, a lovely young girl brought Memed's rifle, his cartridges, and the rifle and cartridges that were the oba's gifts and placed them beside him.

Memed:

"The kurt," he said, "Whomever it enters, until death ... "

"Until death," said Battal Ağa. "A human may be freed from everything but not from the kurt inside."

After this was said they didn't speak until the food was finished. Then Memed spoke about Hürü Ana and Anacık Sultan.

Battal Ağa:

"Hürü is one of the kurts inside you."

Memed:

"And the other is Anacık Sultan." Then he talked about the horse and the bird of prey.

"The horse is also one of the kurts inside you."

"And the bird," said Memed.

Battal Ağa placed his hand on his shoulder:

"Memedim, my son," he said with eyes full of love, "my brave one, the biggest kurt inside you is you."

"It's the horse," said Memed, and they laughed.[59]

After breakfast the next day, Memed hugged Battal Ağa and kissed and raised his hand to his forehead three times. Memed wanted to form a çete and chose Kasım and Temir. He laid his rifle on a rock. They placed their hands on it and took an oath on all the commandments they would carry out – those of the Holy Kuran, the beautifully named and beautiful Muhammed, Hazreti Ali, Kırkgöz Ocağı, Hasan Bey's kılıç, and Köroğlu who had disappeared with the Forty.

Memed told Kasım and Temir about Hasan, the young man who had been killed. Kasım and Temir knew that this was the work of Sarıçiyan Abdik, and they agreed to catch him.

They found him two days later with his gang and a group of women they had abducted from the village. They waited till night to surround them. Memed didn't want to shoot Sarıçiyan.[60]

"Give up Sarıçiyan, surrender Abdik," shouted Memed in a deep, strong voice that echoed for a long time through the cliffs. "You're surrounded, either give up or we'll kill you all."

"Who are you?" asked Abdik.

"Ben İnce Memedim," said Memed.

"If it's true that you are İnce Memed, I surrender."

"How will you know whether or not it's true?"

"One of the friends among us knows İnce Memed."

"If that's true, then let him out and come."

A short man came out from behind the rocks. His entire body was armed from head to toe. He came close.

"Throw your rifle on the ground. And your pistols, too … "

The man threw his guns and pistols on the ground at once, stripped the cartridges from his body, raised his hands in the air, and stood in a funny way. That he was shaking wildly was obvious even from far away.

"Come here and let's see."

The man came further, saw İnce Memed, froze in place for a moment, and then shouted frantically down below.

"It's İnce Memed, İnce Memed!" and he started to run, escaping by the skin of his teeth and throwing himself next to Sarıçiyan. "İnce Memed, İnce Memed … I saw İnce Memed."

"I give up," Sarıçiyan spoke out. "I promise, don't kill me!"

"I promise, I won't kill you."

They stripped him down, tied up the other members of the gang and brought everyone back to Hasan's village. There, they had Sarıçiyan Abdik identify the real İnce Memed. This stunned the villagers. Memed accepted their gratitude and prepared to leave.

"We can't send you off anywhere İnce Memed without feeding you and serving you tea," they said.

"I was offended by you," said İnce Memed.

"Tell us our fault," said Hasan's father.

"You cursed me."

"The pain of my son … " said the old man.

"Our honor was destroyed," said an old woman.

İnce Memed raised his voice. It was clear he was very mad.

"You hurt me."

"What did we do to you, İnce Memed?"

237

"Would İnce Memed ever kill a lively young man like Hasan, he hadn't even married, isn't that right?"

"He hadn't married ... "

"Would İnce Memed kill such a person?"

They gave no response.

"Would İnce Memed ever rape, why didn't you think this at all? Look İnce Memed is even handing these bloodthirsty enemies of honor, who have made their own names worthless, to you, you take my revenge on them."

The crowd froze in place, no one could offer a word, they couldn't lift their lowered heads.

As they passed, the crowd split into two, they slowly took off from inside the village with İnce Memed in front, followed by Kasım and Temir.

"What is the name of this village?"

"They call this village Çamlıyol."[61]

****

Memed wanted to see Seyran and marry her, but he was warned by his friend Sarı Ümmet not to go into Vayvay. There were people ready to turn him in. Memed insisted, though, and had Sarı Ümmet bring some other trusted men to join them. Memed was so eager to get into town that he went right to Koca Osman's house in the middle of the day. Seyran made her way there the minute she heard Memed had come. She was furious. He, on the other hand, was floating in air at the sight of her.[62]

"Did you come to have yourself killed Memed?"

Seyran's voice was harsh and cold.

Memed came to. He approached her and wanted to embrace. Seyran swept and threw his hand away.

"The jandarma do what they please around here, Çukurova is filled to the brim with soldiers. Every bush, every insect, every tree, every bird is a spy. Did you come to have yourself killed?"

Memed couldn't speak.

"Get on your horse and go back to the mountains right away."

Seyran was like a piece of a stone, her eyes had fire in them.

"I came to be married with you today."

"I won't marry like this, with someone asking for death like you. Get on your horse right away and get out of here!"

"Seyran!"

"Don't talk to me. What has become of me that I can't speak to those whose status has gone to their head. And he's going to be İnce Memed! Tell me everyone, would someone like İnce Memed do something like this?"

She left the crowd and explained to her relatives that Memed was crazy for coming into the village with the jandarma and their spies all around. Feliksiz

SAKIZLI

Fazlı had already gone to report on Memed. Some men had been sent to stop him. Kamer Ana explained to Memed why Seyran acted that way.[63]

"The news of your death came and that just about killed her ... Seyran korkuyor." She's afraid.

"Nothing will happen to me. Look!"

He showed the ring on his finger.

"What's this?"

"The seal of Kırkgöz Ocağı, a charmed amulet. Do you understand?"

"Seyran doesn't know this."

"Anacık Sultan gave this to me. From now on ... "

"I understand," said Kamer Ana happily. "No bullet can pass through you."[64]

When Seyran saw the imam, and behind him Memed and his witnesses Koca Osman and Seyfali, she understood everything. Her anger hadn't passed and she was still afraid, but she married Memed. That night, in Koca Osman's courtyard, the drums beat, the horns blew, and the dancing began. Memed approached Seyran and kissed and hugged her, but she remained stiff, almost lifeless as a log, drained of her blood.[65]

Memed approached, begged and implored, but Seyran's stubbornness didn't crack.

"You've killed me Seyran. Something, say something to me." Seyran fixed her large angry eyes on his surprised, love-filled face for a while, and looking straight into his eyes said:

"Get on your horse and go Memed," dedi. "If you die, I can't live. You go, I'll find you where you are as soon as possible. Get on your horse!"

Her voice was so melancholic that she hurt Memed. "I'll go right away Seyran," dedi. "This moment." They embraced. Seyran slowly kissed him on his cheek, as if she was fearful of hurting him.[66]

But Koca Osman refused to let Memed leave without eating the food prepared for the wedding. It would be bad luck not to celebrate. Seyran felt both love and a terrible fear, until she realized that the ring on Memed's finger was some sort of protective ring.

"Hani ... that on your finger ... "

"The ring? The saint of Kırkgöz Ocağı Anacık Sultan who cured me of my wounds gave it. Only those of the line of the ocak are able to wear this ring, I'm the first to wear it ... From death, from bullets, from sickness, from lightning ... "

"I know Memed. You go on your way. God speed, may Allah forever make you prosper. I'll look for and find you very soon. Now while this ring is on you I'm not afraid at all."

239

"Don't be afraid," dedi Memed. "Look, can I tell you something, when an Abdi dies and in his place Kel Hamza comes, and he dies and in his place come ten Kel Hamzas ... when Ali Safa dies, a hundred Ali Safas come ... If that's all how it is, what is my struggle for?"

"For what," asked Seyran. She had never seen Memed speak this much. He was probably going to say something very important, suddenly, since he was asking these kinds of questions in the middle of the night.

At the center of the courtyard a huge fire burned, and around it the young men danced a difficult halay, calmly like still water.

"When İnce Memed dies ... " Sesi ışık gibi çınlıyordu. His voice radiated like light.

"Allah göstermesin."

"When İnce Memed dies ten thousand, a hundred thousand, a hundred hundred thousand, a thousand thousand, a million İnce Memeds will come. If you ask why, it's because the wretched and poor are the majority, and the rich are the minority ... In the end, they will be finished."

"I understand," said Seyran hugging him. "I understand very well. In the end, their lineage will break and die out. Now you go inside and eat a meal ... Who knows how many days you've been hungry."[67]

Word came that Feliksiz Fazıl had reached the jandarma. Memed calmly rose to his feet as if nothing had happened, smiled and spoke.

"This was good," he said, then he hugged everyone there, went out and approached those who had danced the halay. "Thank you everyone, how beautifully you danced the halay, why did you stop?"

The drums began to beat immediately.

He asked for Seyran, they showed him where she was, his eyes filled when he saw Seyran in the bride's veil:

"Stay well Seyran," he said.

"Go safely."[68]

****

The ağas make an agreement with an old eşkıya, Kuzgun Veli, to kill Memed in return for amnesty. Kuzgun Veli had been in the mountains for at least thirty-five years and had carried out so much violence that he didn't expect to survive much longer. He was looking for a quick way to settle down.

Memed asks Topal Ali to take him to Molla Duran, who welcomes Memed warmly and invites him to say what he has come to say. Memed demands that Molla Duran not charge the Yörüks for their use of the winter lands. "Give the winter homes of the Yörüks to them," İnce Memed says, sharp as a knife.

"Veremem." I can't.

"Vereceksin." You will.

"Even if I die, I won't give a handful of my property, of my registered land, to anyone. Even to my İnce Memed. Do you know how I gained them, for a life, do you think you can scare me and have me give my land to someone İnce Memed?"

"Wait," Topal Ali interrupted. "There must be a mistake here. İnce Memed doesn't want the deeds of your lands. He's saying he wants the Yörüks to remain there like they used to without giving any money. The Yörüks have fallen into tremendous poverty. The lands are theirs ... "

"Allahım," smiled Molla Duran Efendi. "I paid mountains of gold to buy those lands from them. Tell the Yörüks to come and settle. As long as you live, whether you are in the mountain or on the plain, or sick and bedridden, I won't take any money from them for being on the land."

"Thank you Molla Duran Efendi."

"And thank you İnce Memedim, my boy, my brave one. Allah seni dağlarımızdan eksik etmesin – May God not keep you from our mountains – From now on whatever there is in my lifetime may Allah take it from me and give it to you."[69]

When Battal Ağa comes to pay, he removes a red velvet pouch from his pocket and places it near Molla Efendi on the sofa.

"This is as much as we could collect this year."

"Take that from there," Molla Duran Efendi smiling. "Take it and put it back in your breast pocket."

"But ... Why ... This ... money for the kışlak ... "

"Take it and put it in your pocket!"

Battal Ağa was surprised. He couldn't figure out what he should do with the pouch he held in his hand.

"We didn't do anything to you. What happened, Efendi? You are content with us, and we are content with you."

"Take it and put it in your pocket!"

"Without telling me what happened here ... Maybe we offended you. If so, it's human nature, please don't be offended. What happened, let me serve you, tell me?"

"İnce Memed came."

Battal Ağa's face went totally yellow.

"Vallahi we didn't send him to you, Efendi."

"I know you didn't know. Did you do him a favor?"

"He was injured, he fell from his horse next to our oba, his wound was severe, we took him and saved him."

"You did well," said Molla Duran Efendi caressing the other's shoulder. "You did so well that I was pleased from here to the sky. People like him are needed in our world. With this world full of evil, corruption, hypocrisy and even more oppression, such enlightened people, clean as the water from the spring, are necessary for us. Let us take a bit of a breath. You did well saving him, you know, and he was very angry at me. He came here, and he said, for me you'll give the old kışlaks of the Yörüks, they will be theirs."

Molla Duran explained his dealing with Memed in a way that made it appear that he had stood up to the young eşkıya. He told Battal Ağa that the lands would remain the Molla's but the Yörüks could graze on them forever. Molla Duran then tells Battal Ağa about the deal with Kuzgun Veli. Molla Duran says that it would kill him now to see Memed killed, and that someone needed to get word to him. Battal Ağa agrees to do so.

Battal Ağa rose and looked around. "Ali Ağa, where is my heybe?"

"Behind the door, should I bring it?"

"If it's no trouble."

Ali brought the saddlebag from behind the door and placed it in front of him. Battal Ağa took a key from his pocket and opened the saddlebag. The lock clicked three times. He took a large bag out of the saddlebag.

"There's bee milk in this," he said. "It keeps a person young. It's from the beehives on the tallest peak of mountain, from a flint rock cove that's brittle like glass. This honey is from over there." He took out another bag. "And this is pure butter. Both of you know this butter well." A third bag was a bit bigger than the other two. "And this is purple cheese, it's made with herbs. Only our Yörüks know how to make it. When you eat it, its scent doesn't leave the body for ten days. A pleasant, wild, drunken fragrance wanders inside one's body. And it's a remedy for every trouble. Please take these."

With those words, Molla Duran showed him to the door, and they hugged.

"Don't forget to get word to İnce Memed."

"Tonight."[70]

****

Memed and his çete surprise the guards at the jail where Ferhat Hoca and Hasan Yobazoğlu are held. Asım Çavuş arrives before they can all get away.

"Asım Çavuş," yelled Memed, "I've surrounded the town with forty men. And I've sent Faruk Yüzbaşı to Vayvay, I'm not here to do any harm. And you knew that Ferhat Hoca didn't kill anyone. He couldn't even hurt an ant. I'm going to grab him and take him, what is there in this … If you continue to shoot, now I'll also grab you and take you to the mountain. I'm speaking for the souls of my mother and Hatçe and for the head of the Kırkgöz Ocağı that, you know me, I'll grab and take you. And you, a great Çavuş, will be disgraced to friend and enemy alike."

Asım Çavuş stopped firing.

The guard brought Ferhat Hoca and Yobazoğlu from inside and handed them over to İnce Memed.

"My seeing you made me very happy İnce Memed Bey. Seeing you over-whelmed me with bliss. I believe that there were no faults in the respect shown to Hoca Efendi. If I'm not mistaken they themselves were satisfied by us … " He bowed and kissed Ferhat Hoca's hand. "Güle güle – goodbye – Hocam, geçmiş olsun – may you recover soon. Look, how nice that İnce Memed Bey, they justly set you free. Since you fell in here, didn't I tell you that you were not guilty at all, that you would be saved, and here, you've been saved, congratulations. And because of you we met and saw İnce Memed Beyefendi. Güle güle efendim. If we failed somehow, please forgive us, your servants, efendim."[71]

Since they agreed that Ferhat Hoca had not committed any crime, Asım Çavuş and the Yüzbaşı decided to have their man Taşkın Halil Bey explain to the judge that Ferhat Hoca did not escape but was released because of his innocence.

****

"You know Memed, they would have hanged us," said Ferhat Hoca as they climbed to an isolated village reachable by only one path. There was an ancient fortress there, and all the people knew Ferhat Hoca, and loved him. No one would initially say, but Ferhat Hoca had been in the village before, raiding the rich and distributing to the poor.[72]

"God inscribes the path of the human being. God drew my path a long time ago and I wasn't able to understand. I'll, if you leave eşkıyalık and go, then I'll remain in these mountains. I've understood that there's no other possible choice than this. My end will come by the bullet. I've also seen it in my dreams. I saw that I would be freed from jail, and that I would come to the mountains. A person inscribes his own path and God does as well. I did everything I could not to stay in the mountain, but I looked and saw that wasn't the destiny written on my forehead, I can't escape from what fate lies before me. If not one eşkıya remains in the mountain, I'll remain. For me it will be better that way. God did not have our paths cross in that village where I hid for no reason."[73]

Ferhat Hoca was greeted with even more celebration in the next village. They sacrificed an animal for him and hosted the çete for a week. Memed and Ferhat Hoca talked through the nights.[74]

"You've made up your mind Memed, words, advice to you don't have much value. Take Seyran by your side, go to the sea coast, among the orange flowers ... But know that you won't stay there for a long time, you'll return to the mountains. The mountains are in your nature. İnşallah no trouble will come to you in the orange groves ... When a person is İnce Memed, being İnce Memed becomes a heavy burden to carry on a person's back. When a person is İnce Memed nothing else is possible. You'll be able to stay in the orange groves only for a day, two days, or a year. Able for only a year, and most of that in your wife's embrace. After that, even if they tied you down, you won't be able to remain in any place."

"How did Bayramoğlu stay for thirty years?"

Ferhat Hoca laughed.

"I was in his çete," he said, "and for a long time. I get news about his condition. Every day, every morning, he puts on his guns and walks to and from the mountain across the way. Let them take his gun from him one day, and one morning let him be without his gun, then, after that, you'll see Bayramoğlu. Bayramoğlu will again go up the mountain. Maybe it will be with his last breath, but he'll still go. He's not a man who is going to die farting in his bed. After you killed Abdi Ağa, you disappeared, why did you return, who forced you, who spotted you?"

"I returned ... " dedi Memed.

"And you'll return again. Senin de mayanda onların mayasında olandan var. What you have in your being is what they had in theirs. Köroğlu, Pir Sultan Abdal, Sakarya Şeyh ... "

One of them was a minstrel, both a saint and a minstrel. He sang beautiful türküs. Alevi, Kızılbaş, a rebel. A Şah's man, Şah Ali's, you know the horse Düldül's master Hazreti Ali, his man. Therefore he was an enemy of the padişah, a rebel to him.

One morning he called Hıdır, who worked alongside him, and said, I saw a dream last night Hıdır. In my dream, you go to İstanbul, become governor, and then come to Sivas and you hang me here in the market of Sivas. Get going and have a good trip. One cannot escape one's destiny. As for Hıdır, he took the saint's hands, fell to his feet, and pleaded, aman pirim, yaman pirim, how can I hang you, it's enough that I am to become governor. Pir Sultan said, get going Hıdır, it's time for you to go. Hıdır left, years passed, and a governor with the name of Hızır came to Sivas. One day it came to the Vali's mind that the benevolent pir that sent him to İstanbul after seeing him in a dream was in Banaz village in Yıldızeli. He had said that you would be a governor and then come and hang me, so, I'm going to throw him a huge feast never seen before and let him see, he said. It was a three days journey between Sivas and Banaz. They prepared the day of the feast, and he called on the elite of Sivas, the beys, and the ağas, so as to show the saint respect, even though the governor had become governor. The governor's men were sent to bring Pir Sultan Abdal to the palace, when they arrived to the place of the feast, they performed their prayers in his presence. The pir was pleased deeply but he also had some doubt inside. This Hıdır became Hızır

244

and also an Ottoman ... When a person became an Ottoman, it was not possible to trust him. Moreover, the pir had seen the dream. Nonetheless, the feast began. There were various foods on the table that had never been seen or known around here. Sofrada kuş sütü eksik. There was nothing missing. Everyone started to eat the food, but Pir Sultan folded his arms like this and didn't move. Hızır Paşa didn't miss this. Please my saint, eat the food. The pir gave no reply. While everyone was satisfying their appetite, he didn't move even a finger. Aman pirim ... Pir Sultan lifted his head, he looked and scanned the ağas, beys, and high state officials each one by one, and said, I can't eat this food, because in this food is the right of the orphans, the blood of those who work with blood, sweat, and tears, this food is the food of the oppressor, I cannot eat this food, it is forbidden. Not only me, even my dogs won't eat this.

Hızır Paşa grew very angry, tearing out his hair, he went crazy from anger. To save face somewhat, and not to lose face in front of these beys, he said, call your dogs my pir and let's see if they won't eat ... The pir immediately waved for the dogs to be brought from Banaz, and they came. Buyur Paşa, here are the dogs. The food was offered to Pir Sultan's dogs and the dogs, from afar, smelled the food with the tips of their noses, and no matter what the paşa's men did, they wouldn't eat.

In front of so many people, the paşa was very embarrassed. How was he going to swallow this humiliation, it was necessary for him to save his status.

Your dream is coming true, pirim, said Hızır Paşa. It's only that because you're my pir, I'll open up one more door for you. I should have already had you hanged for these things you've done against me. Now, in the presence of these people, you will do three recitations – üç deme – and in none of them will the name of the Şah be stated. If you do like this, I'll forgive you. Otherwise, I'll have you hanged early in the morning from the tallest tree in the middle of the city.

Pir Sultan took his saz in his lap, and sang his first deme. As he began, he said paşa, and everyone there froze. Pir Sultan said Şah once in every line of the song. Those at the feast awaited the second deme. That one also, from beginning to end, was filled with Şahs. The third one was the same.

Hızır Paşa said, pirim, your dream has been realized, and his guards took the pir and hanged him in the square of Sivas. For that reason the name of Sivas remains bloody Sivas. This city will be remembered like this until judgment day.

As soon as the morning came all of Sivas was talking like this about Pir Sultan Abdal's being hanged. One person said that, at dawn I saw Pir Sultan wrapped in white clothing rise and leave from the Kayseri gate. Another said, and I saw him at the Tokat gate. Some saw him at the east gate of the city, others saw him at the west. Some didn't believe the pir had been hanged. Some of them were doubtful. Halep oradaysa arşın buradadır, they say. If Aleppo is there, the yardstick is here – We'll prove it. Let's go to the square and see, if Pir Sultan has been hanged, he'll be there. They came to the center of the city and there was no one around. Only a long, thick robe hung from the branch of a tree ...

In a beautiful voice, Ferhat Hoca sang those three songs, every line with the name of the Şah in them.[75]

****

Müslüm arrives and warns them about Kuzgun Veli. Memed remembers that Müslüm is the one who was beaten badly and whose dog was killed. Before Müslüm leaves to track down Kuzgun Veli for them, he turns to Memed.[76]

"You have that horse, you know, your horse? He's wild, man, Memed Ağa. He's a lot of trouble. I saw him the other day in Karsavuran. I said to myself that this is İnce Memed's horse, so I said let me get close and pet its neck a bit, aman had I gotten closer, the horse would have killed me. The Yüzbaşı also gave the command, that horse, he said, will be shot upon sight, before İnce Memed is. Yaaa, did you hear Memed, there's an order to shoot your horse. That Yüzbaşı also killed my dog. And I'm going to kill him. And if they kill your horse ... The villagers also can't get close to your horse. They say that as soon as you approach that horse, it's gone. If not, let it be, it's that kind of horse, it's not a horse with a good temperament. If they shoot your horse, don't be sad. Aaah, was my dog like that too ..."[77]

****

Memed and his çete came to Sakızlı köyü. This was the village Mahmut Ağa had expelled after the villagers had eaten the animals. It was in ruins. Kasım, a man of very few words, approached what was left of one of the homes, said this was where he was born, and quickly ran away, out of the village. The others followed him. When it started to rain, they suggested going back and taking shelter in Kasım's old house. He said he would never go back.

Müslüm catches up with them with another message. He had talked with Hıdır, the father of the murdered Hasan, and Hıdır said to tell Memed that Kuzgun Veli was in the village. He also said to tell Memed that Mahmut Ağa and his men were hot on his tracks.

They decided to go to Çamlıyol first. The rain continued, and they got very wet and cold, but with Memed's cat-like eyes leading the way, they made it to the village, where Ferhat Hoca was greeted as Hızır and they were given dry clothes and served a delicious meal. As they drank their coffee, Hıdır had Kuzgun Veli brought in.[78]

Two young men brought a man into the room – naked, tall, thin, so thin that his bones stuck out, with burnt skin and no light in his eyes, and his hands tied behind his back. The man looked around with fearful eyes, and leaned forward trying to cover himself.

"They call this one Kuzgun Veli. The head of the çete. He came all the way to our village, to here, in order to kill İnce Memed. Buyurun, on behalf of Çamlıyol village we hand him over to you."

"Thank you," dedi İnce Memed.

"Bring the others."

The young men brought the other naked eşkıyas. All of them had their hands tied behind their backs. All of them leaned forward to try to cover themselves.

"Why were you going to kill me, Kuzgun Veli?"[79]

Kuzgun Veli explained that he wanted a pardon and to live on the plains with his family. He also told Memed that he shouldn't kill him in this state, that if he was going to do so, they should have a legitimate duel. Memed released him, and, as he walked away, Kuzgun Veli took his chance. He turned to shoot Memed. Only a bullet from Ferhat Hoca, who later explained to Memed that he knew Kuzgun Veli very well, saved Memed and killed Kuzgun Veli.

Just then, a shepherd came from down below shouting that the village was surrounded. Ferhat Hoca invited Kuzgun Veli's men to join them. They heard a shout: "Surrender, İnce Memed! There's no way out. You're surrounded on every side." Shots rang out.[80]

There was a steep cliff behind them. Memed suggested that he go down and try to surround them on the other side.

"Abooov, plague on your house Memed," Ferhat Hoca dedi, "I couldn't even look, I couldn't even see the bottom of the cliff! How are you going to go down there? You'll shatter into a thousand pieces."

"I've gone down many cliffs like this. In the old days, while hunting deer."

"You can't make it down this cliff. It can't be done even with the wings of a bird or the body of a snake."

"Either I'll go down, or we'll all be defeated here by the jandarma. If the jandarma captures us do you think they'll let us live?"[81]

Müslüm said that he knew the path very well from his shepherding days and would show Memed the way. He asked for a rifle to join the fight. Ferhat Hoca hesitated, but then gave Müslüm a gun and ammunition. And to Memed he gave a box filled with gold. "One day you'll need money."

Ferhat Hoca joined the others.

Memed, Müslüm and Şahan went into the gulleys between the sharp cliffs. They had to hold on to something as they descended, so they held on to the sharp rocks, the keven thorns, and the bushes. Müslüm told them not to look down or else their heads would spin. Don't step on the land or the small stones, look for a rock to step on. Don't grab the rocks, grab at sturdy branches. When they made it to the bottom, they were exhausted, and their hands, knees and feet were cut to shreds.

To get behind the jandarma, they had to go further – down a creek that led to another creek that went back up the mountain. It was dark. As they walked, shots rang out all around.

Memed heard something and told them to stop. There was someone ahead. It turned out to be Memed's friend Sefil Ali, who had heard they were surrounded, grabbed his gun, and had been shooting at the jandarma from behind. As Ali and Memed discussed a plan, Müslüm jumped in.[82]

"And I'm going to kill a lot of jandarma."

"Eşkıyalar don't kill the jandarma," said Memed reprimanding him.

"But, they kill eşkıyas."

"They kill."

"If eşkıyas don't kill jandarma, then if that's so what do they do?"

"If they really had to do something, they would wound them."

"And what if they didn't?"

"They'd run away."

"And if I see Kertiş Ali?"

"Shoot him," said İnce Memed making his anger clear. "Kill him. He's an oppressor, a torturer ... "

Müslüm fired first at the jandarma. A scream came with the third shot.

"I saw," said Müslüm. "As soon as I saw the flame of his rifle, I took aim. I didn't kill. My bullet passed through the shoulder."

"Sus, don't talk," dedi Memed.

They spread out, and they lit up the area below with heavy fire. It was as though forty men, not four, fired.[83]

Seeing that they were surrounded by skillful fighters who were showing restraint, Mahmut Ağa and the Yüzbaşı decided to withdraw. Müslüm saw which way there were going and told Memed that there were a lot of civilians with the jandarma. Memed was shocked, but Sefil Ali told Memed that those were Mahmut Ağa's men who had made it their duty and şan – glory – to kill him.

They rushed back to the village where they learned Ferhat Hoca had been shot in the arm and that more jandarma were headed to the village. Memed ran to Ferhat Hoca's side and wished him a speedy recovery. He also introduced Ferhat Hoca to Sefil Ali. They needed to leave right away.

Sefil Ali suggested going to his village, Çiçeklidere, which was also Mahmut Ağa's. Ferhat Hoca laughed, but Sefil Ali insisted since it wouldn't occur to anyone that they would hide there. He assured them that no one in Çiçeklidere would turn them in, and that, moreover, there was a doctor there. Ferhat suggested going to Sakızlı, but Kasım said no way. Memed agreed that it was best to go to Çiçeklidere and suggested splitting into two. "Ben, Hoca, Ali, Kasım, and the eşkıya Müslüm will go to Çiçeklidere village. Temir, Şahan, and the others will go to Sakızlı village." If something happened to either, the others would come to their rescue.

They arrived in Çiçeklidere before the roosters began to crow. Sefil Ali entered first and went to the home of his uncle, Sarı Çavuş, to explain the situation. Sarı Çavuş said they should come stay with him, that there were plenty of rooms, and that no one would think they were there. Sefil Ali brought them there. Sarı Çavuş showed them a path of escape if they needed it.

Word quickly spread that İnce Memed's çete had been surrounded in Çamlıyol and that the injured had quietly entered Çiçeklidere. The informant Tazı Tahsin also heard this.

He hid behind some rocks near Sarı Çavuş's house. In the village homes there were no toilets. Everyone did their business outside among the cliffs. The first one Tazı Tahsin saw come out of the house was Kasım, who was fully armed. After Kasım, he saw Sefil Ali, and then Müslüm, who also had his hand on his gun. Müslüm almost saw Tazı Tahsin. They were so close that Müslüm's pee sputtered from the branches and wet Tazı Tahsin's face and eyes. Then İnce Memed led Ferhat Hoca outside. They spoke in whispers. When Tazı Tahsin saw them, his chest beat wildly and he shivered in a cold sweat. He couldn't move. They knelt down and talked for a while, but it seemed like a year for Tazı Tahsin. When they got up, it took a while for him to recover, and even longer to get himself moving. When he did, he went right to the Muhtar's house. The Muhtar was in the yard performing his ablutions.[84]

"What's happening Tahsin?" he asked. He understood immediately why Tahsin had come so early in the morning.

They went inside.

"They're here," dedi Tahsin. "I saw with my own two eyes. İnce Memed, along with a wounded man. And our Sefil Ali, another man, all of them are in Sarı Çavuş's house. I must tell Mahmut Ağa immediately. And he'll give me a lot of money, even more than Murtaza Ağa. Our Mahmut Ağa is richer than everyone, isn't he?"

"He's rich."

"I'm going right away."

"And if İnce Memed escapes, have you thought about your situation if that happens?"

"I'll escape too."

"Everyone knows that you'll have informed on İnce Memed."

"Let them know. I'll escape."

"Then what's going to happen to me?"

"Mahmut Ağa won't let İnce Memed escape."[85]

The Muhtar was a small man. He grew very nervous about what might happen. He walked to Sarı Çavuş's house, waited there, and then returned. Then he went back to Sarı Çavuş's house and, again, returned to his home. He shuttled back and forth between them all afternoon. Late in the day, he ran into Sarı Çavuş under a tree.[86]

"Wait," hollered Sarı Çavuş. "You know who I am. I'm one who prepared for battle with Mustafa Kemal Paşa. With him I made the Sea of Çanakkale reach the skies. What do you want to say, even since before the sun came up you've been going back and forth like a dog with burnt feet in front of my door? Look at me," he said, pointing to his grass-green eyes. "İnce Memed is in this house. If you're wearing underwear over your ass, you go and tell that to that tyrant, lowlife, blood sucking ağa. Let him come and kill İnce Memed in my house. And then I'll, you know this Sarı Çavuş very well, then I'll kill off all your and your ağa's descendants. Don't forget this Muhtar, I fought in Çanakkale, with Mustafa Kemal I rained down from the sky like thunder on the enemy, and sent water to the sky. Go, get on your way. And you imagine the rest."

It was as if the cat had got Muhtar's tongue. He was pushing and pushing himself to say that Tazı Tahsin had gone to Mahmut Ağa, but for some reason he couldn't tell Sarı Çavuş.

"Don't cut me down Çavuşum," the words finally came from his mouth. "I haven't done anything to you."

"You imagine the rest," said the Çavuş turning his back to him and entering his house. He was extremely angry with the Muhtar. His thin beard shaking from anger, he cursed him.

The Muhtar went a few more times to Sarı Çavuş's. He wanted to tell him about Tazı Tahsin, but when he got to the door, he gave up. When evening came, the Muhtar entered his own guesthouse and gave its key to his wife, saying, "Lock this behind me. If I yell and scream till tomorrow morning, if a fire starts in the house, if Mahmut Ağa comes to the door, don't let me out. Swear on it, on beautifully named Muhammed, on the cloud-covered Kırkgöz Ocağı ... " His wife swore and locked the door behind him.[87]

****

A breeze blowing from the cliffs brought the scent of thyme to the village. Under the light of the moon, the cliffs sparkled like crystal. The plain below undulated like a foamy white lake. The shadows of the large poplar trees fell on the earthen huts.

Mahmut and his men returned to the village. Tazı Tahsin greeted them and told them all he had seen and that Sefil Ali was guarding the door.[88]

250

"Sefil Ali? You mean that eşkıya who plays the saz? One of our villagers?"

"If I saw correctly, it's him," dedi Tazı Tahsin.

The Ağa commanded the huge man next to him:

"You're an expert at this business, get Sefil Ali and bring him here. If you let him escape, or you make the slightest sound, know that we're all dead. If you want, take Tazı with you."

The tall, huge man took off his shoes and placed them on a rock to the side, "Let's go Tahsin," dedi, "lead the way."

They slipped away, quiet as a butterfly. The sound of the water flowing from the middle of the village bubbled all the way over here. Other than that and the cracking sound from the cliffs, there wasn't the slightest sound around.

As they entered a sheltered area of Sarı Çavuş's house, they found him with his back to the wall and his head hanging in front of him. They came five steps, four steps, three, then two steps towards him, and Sefil Ali still didn't move. First the huge man jumped Ali, covering his mouth with his arms in a vice-grip. When Ali shook, Tazı Tahsin jumped on him too. They held him very tightly and brought him to Mahmut Ağa's side.

"Tie his hands and feet, let him stay here. One of you wait and watch him."[89]

Mahmut and his men entered Sarı Çavuş's house while everyone was sleeping and easily tied them all up. Mahmut cursed Sarı Çavuş for hiding the enemies of the people, and Sarı Çavuş warned Mahmut to watch his mouth and cursed him as well. Mahmut sent for the Muhtar.

One of Mahmut's men came and said that the Muhtar's wife had locked him in a room, but soon he turned up as well. It was decided that they should take the çete to the Muhtar's home for interrogation.

Mahmut had each one brought to his feet. First he asked the wounded one who he was.

"I'm Ferhat Hoca."

Mahmut was startled, but happy to say that Ferhat would soon hang as a companion of İnce Memed's. Then he asked Memed who he was.

"Ben İnce Memedim."[90]

"Vay anasını, you look like a boy who, you don't look like İnce Memed at all." He turned to the Muhtar. "Let's take a good look at this brave man, at this hero of the Toros mountains that looks like a starving rat! Is this man İnce Memed? Have you met Memed before?"

"Who doesn't know İnce Memed in this village … This is İnce Memed."

"Allah Allah! Allah Allah, this one that I caught, after all this time running after him, at least he could look like a man. If I take this to the town saying this is İnce Memed everyone will make fun of me, they'll put me in a cage and display me all around the country! I'm going to forego my taking such a snotty maggot to the town. I'll release this and, from embarrassment, free him. I told the ağas and beys that I'll go and bring him by his ears. Look at this man that I boast of, I wouldn't even take him in my house as a servant. Look at his foul face, the face of the stinking balls of a fox who killed Abdi Ağa and Ali Safa Bey! Pffff look at your disgusting face ... And I'm standing here talking to this stinking hyena carcass. If I were in the government, I wouldn't even have some like this, someone who doesn't even resemble a human, hanged. I'd throw him into a well of shit. Into a well of shit I'd throw him, a well of shit ... "

Mahmut Ağa was angry, at times he rose to his feet, leaned over and spit in the middle of Memed's face and kicked him, at other times he sat cross-legged and made fun of him, and then started cursing again. Finally he tired, and hardly said a thing. But he still wasn't able to take his revenge on Memed.

"Who are you?" He asked Kasım.

"I'm Hacı Temirim. I'm from the villages of Anavarza. I'm from Kuzgun Veli's çete. When Kuzgun Veli was shot, I joined them. Kader ... "

Mahmut Ağa didn't focus on him.

"Boy, who are you?"

"I'm from the Sarıkeçili oymak. My name is eşkıya Müslüm."

"Whaaaat, you're an eşkıya?"

"Eşkıyayım yup ... "

"For how long?"

"Since two days ago ... " Müslüm wasn't going to say two days, perhaps two years, but that's what came out of his mouth.

Mahmut Ağa:

"Untie those arms," he commanded.

The men untied Müslüm's arms.

"What harm have I done to you ağa that you're releasing me? Am I not an eşkıya?"

"Throw this one out."

Müslüm frowned. They threw him outside.

"You I know, you're our Aşık Sefil Ali. I can't do a thing to you. Your old man was an upstanding man, Allah rahmet eylesin. He went to the Balkan War, I tried to prevent him, don't go to the army, I said, he didn't listen to me, he went, and he never returned. You left being an eşkıya, they told me."

"I had left. When I heard that İnce Memed went up to the mountain again, I also went two days ago and found him."

"It's good that you found him. If you hadn't, he wouldn't have come to this village, and I wouldn't have been able to pick him like a pear from a branch like this. Untie those arms."

They untied Sefil Ali's arms.

"Take the saz and let's see you strum one or two."

Sefil Ali didn't respond, he didn't move at all.

"Take the saz," commanded Mahmut Ağa harshly.

Sefil Ali again paid no attention.

"You won't play the saz for me?"

Sarı Çavuş lifted his head:

"Not for you, my brave son, my dog wouldn't even play the saz for you, Mahmut."

"Is that right?" said Mahmut Ağa mockingly with a smile. "Really, Mustafa Kemal's go-to guy, really you bullshitter who, with one bullet at Çanakkale, blew the sea up to the sky?"

"Dogs like you shouldn't even mention Mustafa Kemal Paşa's name. Bloodthirsty ones like you. People like you who kill men by trampling over them with horses ... "

Mahmut Ağa slowly got up from where he was sitting. His eyes were completely yellow. He came up to Sarı Çavuş. He aimed at his throat and gave the old man a kick. And after that another, then another ... Then, with the whip in his hand, his feet, and his entire body, he let Sarı Çavuş have it. The old man bled red all over, from his mouth and nose, down the hair of his beard, on his shirt and down to his feet. As Mahmut beat him he became furious, he moved around the man on the floor, and beat him more as he got more and more furious. Until wobbling like a drunk, and not able to stand up any longer, he trampled on Çavuş. As for Çavuş, he didn't make even the slightest sound, he didn't even huff.

"If you don't die tonight, before morning, I'll kill you tomorrow morning. Tie this dog's hands again."[91]

Silence had fallen over the village. It was so quiet that Mahmut worried the villagers knew what was happening.

Mahmut and the Muhtar decided that the most secure place to keep "these monsters" before delivering them to the jandarma the next day would be a tower on Mahmut's estate. It was so secure that even if a thousand people attacked, only three people were needed to defend it.

They went to the tower and locked the eşkıyas in a windowless room. Mahmut ordered his men to stand guard all night, not to close their eyes at all. "I'm afraid tonight. If only we could have taken these eşkıyas right away ... " Mahmut himself was tired and went to the Muhtar's house where the Muhtar's wife had prepared a meal and placed a bottle of rakı on the table. She knew that the ağas aren't able to do anything without drinking. "I'm pleased with this Muhtar." Mahmut said. "But this silence makes me shiver."[92]

****

Since the moment İnce Memed and his friends were captured, there was a quiet whisper throughout the village. The women and girls were talking together in their own way – not a single man or boy heard what they were saying, and even if they had heard, they wouldn't have understood.

"They'll hang İnce Memed."
  "What lovely dirges we made for him!"
  "Now he's been caught in our village."
  "Our village will be considered cursed and unfortunate ... "
  "If İnce Memed is hanged ... "
  "If İnce Memed is hanged ... "
  "Stones, fire, snake and centipedes, dragons, and solucans – worms – will rain from the sky upon us ... "
  "If İnce Memed is hanged ... "
  "This village, this world ... "
  "These great Binboğa mountains will be ruined."
  "Instead of water, blood will flow from the ground ... "
  "Until the last day."
With seven young girls behind her, Emiş Hatun went around inside the village, from house to house, talking with the women.
  "Does this befit us?"
  "Our village will be remembered forever as the village where İnce Memed was caught."
  "And because of us İnce Memed will be hanged."
  "And Sarı Çavuş was killed, that infidel."
  "In the old days he had men killed by trampling over them with his horse."
  "Now he crushes them himself."
  "Instead of his horse ... "
  "When we arrive at the other world, how will we look in the faces of the dead?"
  "And those of our children ... ?"
  "And everyone else's?"
  "And those of these great Toros Mountains ... ?"
  "And that of Mediterranean sea where we picked cotton ... ?"
  "How will we look in the face of the land of Çukurova where we planted and harvested ... ?"
  "Won't humanity question us forever for this?"
  "What will we say to humanity?"
The light of daybreak was about to shine. All of the women of the village came quietly, and they stood outside the gate of Mahmut Ağa's estate. Three women had trays in their hands, there was food on the trays. All the women were wrapped in white headscarves.
  "Open the gates yavrular, we brought food for you."
The guard, when he heard the voices of the women, opened the gate, it was strange when he saw the crowd of women.

Emiş Hatun:

"What's that, yavrum?" she said. "Did we frighten you? Don't be afraid, nothing will happen."

The women crowded inside. The guard took them to the center. And then, all of a sudden, the man disappeared from among them without a sound. Some of the women already went up to the estate, surrounded the guards there, and the guards were swallowed up among them, too. With the Muhtar's elderly wife, who had also composed lovely dirges for İnce Memed, Emiş Hatun, and the young girls behind them, they entered the room of the prisoners.

Emiş Hatun:

"Untie their hands," she shouted.

The girls untied their hands in the blink of an eye.

"Get their clothing and get them dressed right away."

The girls also had the weapons of the eşkıyas.

"These are your guns, put them on. There's little time left till morning. The light of the sun is about to shine. Head to the mountain. Leave Sarı Çavuş with us. We'll look after him."

First İnce Memed, then the others, even the wounded Ferhat Hoca, without knowing how they did either, got dressed and girded themselves. "Sağlıcakla kalın, sağ olun, var olun," they said, as they left from among the crowd of women that opened and made way for them. A short while later they made it to the cliffs. As for the women, as though nothing had happened, they put the trays in their hands on the ground, in front of the guards. "Eat, afiyet olsun," they said, and they left as quietly as they had come.[93]

****

Mahmut Ağa had just fallen asleep when the guards ran to wake him. They couldn't. He could only open one eye and they could only say, "İnce Memed escaped Ağa, he escaped." But he paid no attention, closed his eye and fell again into a deep sleep. Morning came and no one was able to wake the ağa. They shouted at him, but he didn't stir.

In the afternoon he awoke, and after eating breakfast by himself and washing, he turned to a worried Muhtar and asked if the jandarma had come. "No, they haven't Ağam … "[94]

"What happened?"

"I mean they haven't come yet … I mean … "

"Tell me, what's under your tongue?"

"I mean to say that … Ağam knows better, last night ya … I mean ya … "

"What is there, what is happening?"

"Last night İnce Memed and … "

"What happened to İnce Memed?"

"They took him ... "

"Who? The jandarma? I'll show them. The eşkıya that I captured ... It's not possible.

I'll take him from their hands. Why didn't you wake me when they came?"

"We did Ağam, you didn't wake up."

"Get on the horses, let's catch up with the jandarma, let's take İnce Memed from them."

At that moment, the huge man entered, wringing his hands.

"Ağam," dedi, "The jandarma didn't take İnce Memed."

"So who took him?"

"Periler, cinler ... " Fairies and jinns.

"What do you mean periler, cinler? I mean did you downright let him escape, is that what happened?"[95]

Everyone thought Mahmut Ağa would fly into a rage, but he remained calm and cold-blooded. He ordered that his horse be brought and, in the tradition of his father and grandfather, called the villagers to the village center. He smiled at them. It was the first time anyone had seen him smile.[96]

"You did well," he began. His voice was cold, direct, certain. Without even the slightest anger, resentment, or sadness. "You did very well and you freed İnce Memed whom I had captured. And our fools, you fooled them and put them to sleep making them think that peris took İnce Memed. What you have done, you have done well. İnce Memed size mübarek olsun. He's yours, do whatever you want, love him, respect him. Now today I am leaving. I'll tell the jandarma that I'll meet on the road not to hit you, not even one blow. You have been my villagers for a thousand years, my clan, you're my blood. As a result, I couldn't stand anyone insulting you. Now I have one request from you, that within ten days you will go and leave this village. From today forward, not a single chicken, goat, bull, or sheep will be slaughtered in this village. You'll give up your animals to the shepherds that I will send. As you know, the houses you live in, the land you walk on, whatever there is in this village and whatever there isn't, even that flowing water, all of it is mine. Even the underwear on your asses is mine. I'll come here in ten days, and if I find one person here, only God knows what will happen."

He rode his horse and left the village, not even turning and looking back.

The crowd got all confused. For a long time whatever was said was incomprehensible. After that, they scattered in groups.

"İnce Memed's feet brought misfortune upon us, may he go down!"

"May he go down below the soil ... "

"May he not exist!"

"He tore our village down."

"He killed us all."

"He wiped us out."

"Actually he didn't have a good nature."

"His eyes were the eyes of a serpent."

"He was also very short."

"To hell with his height … "

A short while later, there was some screaming in the village. They were singing laments of exile and hurling curses upon İnce Memed. Emiş Hatun was standing in front of her home, shrieking like a bird, reminiscing about the beautiful love that she's had in this home, saying at the end of every sentence, how am I going to, how, to separate from my beautiful home … How will I separate from you my poplar tree, how will I separate from you my river, my snowcapped mountain, my valley with winnowing, dried yellow flowers and purple thorns, my forest that lullabies when the summer and autumn months come, my orioles, my doves, my honey-filled figs, my bees that gather a thousand flavors from a thousand flowers?

The villagers of Çiçeklidere cursed Memed over and over, wishing that he hadn't come to Çiçeklidere, hoping for a painful death for him by bullets and hungry dogs and eagles, asking that he suffer, rot in jail, and be denied a grave. Memed and the others heard the sounds from the cliffs.

"Hocam, something is going on in the village. Something's happened to them."

"Something's happened," dedi Ferhat Hoca. "When Mahmut awoke in the morning … "

"What will he do to them Hoca?"

"What he did to Kasım's village, and worse than that, he'll do to them a thousand times worse than he did."

"So what should we do, Hoca?"

Hoca gave no response.

There was a long silence between them. No one said a word …

They noticed that for some reason the sounds in the village stopped.

"What happened, Hocam?"

"Something bad has happened. Everything going quiet like this suddenly is not a good sign."

"This is exactly what happened in our village," dedi Kasım. "Let Allah not make this kind of trouble for the enemy."

At that moment, coming from below among the cliffs, Müslüm's head with a red fez on it was seen.

"Where did you find that fez?" said Ferhat Hoca jokingly.

"Sarı Çavuş gave it."

"How is he?"

"He's in a lot of pain you know, but good."

"How's the village?"

Müslüm explained in detail about the village, the villagers, and the curses at Memed.

"Demek böyle ha!"

"Böyle," dedi Müslüm. That's what it is. "I've never understood this thing, what is there in being forced out that they cry this much, that they ramp and rage? We are forced out every day. To be exiled is better, isn't it?"

The Hoca got close and caressed his shoulder.

"Although settling and migrating is better, these people have long forgotten the taste of that yavrum. Müslüm, your children will forget even more. When they hear the word exile, like those down below they'll throw a fit, too."

"It's as if the world is drowning ... "

Ferhat Hoca took Memed's hand, and led him away.

"Come," dedi, "come and let's talk a bit between us over there." At the base of a boulder, they sat down with their backs against the rock.

"Now I've understood very well, my boy Memed, that this eşkıyalık doesn't suit you. When the sounds came from down below you were so scared that you died, you died and then rose again. If the villager is exiled and, something similar like this, if Çiçeklidere village resembles Sakızlı, you won't be able to endure it, you won't survive. This work is a different kind of work, it doesn't suit someone with the heart of a child like you. Because of you a village cried some and you almost fell down these cliffs and died. If, because of you, tomorrow Faruk Yüzbaşı, the ağas, and the beys have the entire Toroslar suffer beatings, torture, and repression, or tomorrow or the next day the entire Toroslar is turned into shouts and screams, what shape will you be in Memed?"

Memed lowered his head and didn't speak.

"Look yavrum, you can't even endure a crazy horse staying in the mountain by itself. You're almost crippled from sadness. They try to kill you and you can't shoot anyone. I can't understand how you killed Abdi Ağa, Kel Hamza, and Ali Safa. It seems to me that you didn't kill them. But I understand, that you almost killed Yobazoğlu for not going and catching the horse, for taking off and fleeing. Look Memed, in that box around your waist there's a lot of gold that was Kuzgun Veli's, it's enough for you for your entire life. It's good that Mahmut didn't see it. And I am not in these mountains without the name of İnce Memed. I'll have you in my mind, I'll carry you with me until death. As long as I live, no one will know that you went down to the plains. And when I die another İnce Memed will emerge."

"He'll come, you think."

"Yes, he will," said Ferhat Hoca grabbing a fistful of earth. "How did you emerge? From this earth, just how these yellow crocuses shoot through the earth, look, just how they smiled in our faces like sunlight, İnce Memeds will sprout from within people. Don't worry about me. I'll go now to the mountains, and from the orman to my village."

"Go with Sefil Ali."

"Okay."

"And I'll take Kasım and Müslüm. What happened to Temir I wonder?"

"Don't worry about them, I'll find them soon."

"Hakkını helal eyle Hocam."

"May you have many children."

They hugged.

The eşkıyas came to them. Ferhat Hoca's beard shook. He was wringing his hands and blinking his eyes a lot.

"Haydi, you stay well. Me, Kasım, and Müslüm, we're going."

Helallaştılar.

Memed went to the village with his friends. The day was coming to an end, the shadows were extending. The villagers stood and remained in the village alan. They saw İnce Memed coming down from when he was much farther away.

When İnce Memed strode among them they didn't show any response. They didn't turn their heads and look, nor did they talk, nor did they say a bad word to him, they stood and remained there like that, motionless like clay. Only Emiş Hatun turned her back to him. With Kasım and Müslüm by his side, Memed went from here to there in the village ... For a while he wandered around and then stopped. Not a sound came from the village. In the end, he made his way to Sarı Çavuş's house. No one was there. And Sarı Çavuş was stretched out on a mattress next to the hearth, by himself, groaning.

Memed kneeled down next to Sarı Çavuş and wished him a speedy recovery. Sarı Çavuş was in pain and also seething with anger, vowing to take his revenge against Mahmut and confident that the villagers would survive. "We'll go and make fields from the shrubs, the reeds, and the marsh. The young men in our village are very strong." He took Memed's arm. "You look like you're very saddened. Don't pay attention to the things said back and forth about you among our village women. They speak a little painfully because their souls are burning, because they're being forced from their village." They loved him, he said, and would sing dirges more beautiful than had ever been sung if he died. Memed's eyes teared up. "They saved you last night, our fairy girls, a thousand of them, two thousand of them came and saved you. Don't find fault with them. We'll expect you in our village in Çukurova." He took Memed's hand and told him that a doctor was on the way. Memed should keep his sword sharp and go. Memed, Kasım, and Müslüm all bent down and kissed his hand.[97]

****

In town and the village, the intial news of Memed's capture traveled fast. When Tazı Tahsin told Topal Ali, Ali had a fit. "If what you say you did is true, I'll kill you you little shit Tazı."

Yüzbaşı Faruk was upset that Memed had not been caught under his command, and, worse, that he had been caught by a rival, the tyrannical murderer Mahmut. The Yüzbaşı even considered finding a way to drop all charges against Memed, since no one had witnessed him kill Abdi, Ali Safa, or Hamza.

Murtaza Ağa, Zülfü, Taşkın Halil, and the others agreed. They thought that it would have been better for İnce Memed to remain in the mountains than to be caught by Mahmut. Mahmut will now become a national hero. Arif Saim Bey will make him a member of parliament. They'll need to cozy up to him. Legends about his bravery and courage were already being concocted in the market.

The fearful ağas and beys decided to spread a new version of events: Mahmut Ağa had killed Abdi Ağa and Ali Safa Bey.

At this point, news arrived that Memed had escaped.[98]

****

Mahmut Ağa held Anacık Sultan responsible:

"Everyone in the mountains is hiding İnce Memed, because that whore saint of Kırkgöz is protecting him. Mahmut Ağa trapped that bloodsucker a full seven times. It's both that this guy is like mercury and that all the poor people of the Toroslar are with him. And because of that whore Anacık Sultan. She cured his wound, apparently gave the seal of the ocak to him, and, as a result this, this bloody murderer has come to be a saint."[99]

****

Müslüm brought a bundle of food from Topal Ali and found the others waiting in a marsh nearby. He told them that Topal Ali said that the Yüzbaşı had taken the jandarma from town and now was the time. Mahmut Ağa was in Murtaza Ağa's house. They shouldn't let a moment pass. He'd wait with two horses under the Kabasakız tree for them.

"This means I won't see Seyran. Maybe I'll never be able to see her again before I die. If I die, I'm giving this ring to you Müslüm, you'll do whatever it takes to deliver this to Seyran … " He took a deep breath. "If I die here, don't leave my body in the land of Çukurova. Present my body to Hürü Ana, she'll know what to do, she'll know where to bury me. And tell Hürü Ana that … " He couldn't finish his words. "Haydi, let's get going."

260

When they came to the Kabasakız tree they saw Topal Ali's shadow from afar. A man with three horses standing under the tall tree ...

Topal Ali first hugged Memed and then Kasım.

"What can we do Ali," dedi Memed, "destiny is like this."

Topal Ali smiled.

"I didn't want this at all, Ali. Know that I had no other possible solution."

"May God keep your path open and your sword sharp ... "

Then they sat down on the rocks, Ali explained Murtaza Ağa's house to him in great detail, the stairs, and the room.

"I'll open the gate," dedi. "I'll take you all the way to the door of the room. If something happens, the two of us with Kasım ... The three of us, even if the town was filled with jandarma, we'll cover the mountains. Don't worry."

Memed didn't speak. The three men got on their horses, Müslüm remained there.

"You," dedi, "go to Seyran bacı, tell her everything that has happened. And tell her that Memed said, forgive me. Sağlıcakla kal."

They rode their horses. The plain was completely covered in moonlight, light that surrounded the mountains, just as in the daytime. They passed through the town quickly. Their shadows fell on the streets and the alan. They dismounted at Murtaza Ağa's gate. Ali easily opened the gate. The key of the entire house had long been his. At the staircase, he lit a ship's lantern. Ali went in front. He stopped at the landing, "Here, this door," he whispered, and as he went down Memed opened the door of the room. The lamp with the large shade on the side wall was softly lit. As soon as the door opened, Mahmut Ağa woke up, sat up, leaned on his left elbow with his gun in his hand, when he saw Memed he remained like that. At that moment, Murtaza also awoke, and like him stopped and looked at Memed.

"Do you recognize me Mahmut Ağa, my name is İnce Memed."

The gun in Mahmut Ağa's hand rose in a last effort, and at that moment the rifle in İnce Memed's hand popped three times, one after the other. The light on the wall went out from the breeze of the bullets. As soon as the shots were fired, Murtaza Ağa pulled the covers over his head and curled up in bed like a ball. Memed went down the stairs, grabbed and hopped on the horse in Ali's hand, and took off like the wind from inside the town. He rode from the village, and as he went farther away, he heard the sounds of shots behind him.

He rode the horse for an entire day, at night on the side roads, in the forest, in the flood gulleys, and at the edge of daybreak reached Çiçeklidere village. He stopped at the end of the village alan, right next to the tall poplar. The horse frothed, its nostrils opened, and its belly swelled and shrunk like an ironsmith's bellows. The morning broke, a heavy light filled the surroundings. The shadows of the poplar tree and the rider stretched past the rumbling stream to the other side as far as the cliffs where the sun sets. Not a sound came from the village. A few children and a few women stuck their heads outside and then went back inside. The sound of a bird chirping came from the opposite mountain, then stopped. A huge, orange shepherd's dog with a collar around its neck walked slowly, sniffing around at the bottom of the village, then disappeared among the houses. A white cloud that broke away from the peak of the mountain approached and, after hovering above the poplar tree for a while, turned in the direction of the tall mountain where the sun rises, scattering in threads as it ascended. A rooster shining in green and red feathers came out of a hill of ashes and scrambled around some purple hatmi flowers. In the area of the rooster and the huge purple hatmi flowers, a skittish beaded bee, shimmering in a thousand sparkles flashing under the sun, buzzed and spun around. The sun hit the bottom of the stream, the white pebble stones stretched from here to the plain down below like a winding, white road.

Memed sat still on his horse and waited. Light shone in spots on his brown face, highlighting the deep lines on his face. His head was bare. The silver laced guns reflected waves of blue onto the barrel of his rifle.

Late morning came, it was getting close to noon, and there wasn't the slightest movement in the village. Memed had no idea what to do, so he waited there, next to the poplar. The rooster in the ashes still scrambled around, the beaded bee, increasing its speed and buzzing, still flew around and around. At that moment, a girl wearing bright red, with braided hair, and wearing blue beads came out of the house across the way, nervous, tiptoeing, and stopped in front of the horse. Her eyes opened wide with excitement. She stayed there directly facing Memed. After her, another girl came. She was just like the first one. Then one or two girls each came and stood next to the other girls.

Memed smiled at them … After the children came the young girls, and after them came the women wearing white headscarves, all quietly, like they were flowing, and they filled the area. Memed's eyes searched among the crowd for that large woman, Emiş Hatun. He saw Emiş Hatun on the other side of the creek, at the base of the shadow of the poplar tree, standing there erect, next to a white rock. He rode the horse right toward her, the crowd slowly split and let him pass. The rooster among the ashes scrambled no more, and the bee now stopped filling the world with its buzz by spinning around so fast. It flew in wide circles over the heads of the women down in the lower part of the village.

Memed pulled back on the reins a few steps in front of Emiş Hatun.

"Emiş Hatun," dedi, a little tired, a little embarrassed, "Emiş Hatun, from now on, this village will remain in its place forever. Hakkınızı helal edin."

He turned the head of the horse towards Yıldızlı dağ, and rode off, flying in a flash from inside the village. For a while longer, the villagers who remained in the alan couldn't move. They stood and watched him from behind, until he disappeared from sight.

In mid-afternoon, the first heralds arrived, along with the drummer Abdal Bayram and the horn player Cümek. The other villages in the Toros that received the news flowed from the mountains and plains into Çiçeklidere. Çiçeklidere village had never been this crowded.

The cliffs and plains down below overflowed with people. Drums played from night till morning, and the halay was danced. A magnificent festival took place. Until now the Toroslar had never seen such a festival.

Morning came and the day broke. They took Sarı Çavuş from his bed, and led him by the arm to the center of the crowd, where he spoke.

"Young men," dedi, "it's said that when İnce Memed mounts his horse and disappears from sight, the other villagers do something ... "

With this said, the young men went up the bare, immense slope across the way, and in a short time stacked the dried pink, yellow, and red keven thorns in a pile, and, with Sarı Çavuş's lighter, set the center aflame. The villagers filled the hillside, it was so crowded that if you dropped a pin it wouldn't hit the ground. Abdaloğlu Bayram beat the drums playfully, sometimes running in and out of the fire, playing that old game. The women, holding each other's hands, danced a huge halay that to this day hadn't been seen. The flames spread from the center of the pile to the slope, and in a moment the whole mountain was ablaze. The mountain, with the flames spinning around, shook. No news from İnce Memed was ever heard again, he disappeared from sight.

O gün bugündür – Since that time, on the day that İnce Memed rode off, the villagers of Çiçeklidüzü gather with the other villagers on the hillside of the thorned keven and set the keven aflame with a huge toy düğün. The flames spread on the slope like a flood for three days and three nights, burn the entire mountain from top to bottom, the slope shakes with the thunder of flames, and screams come from inside the kevenler. Together with this, a ball of light glows first from the peak of Yıldızlı, then Çakmaklı, and then the Boranlı mountains. The peaks of the mountains whiten for three days, brightening the surroundings, just like in the daytime.[100]

Notes

1 Y. Kemal, *İM3*.
2 Ibid., 15–16.
3 Ibid., 21–22.
4 Ibid., 26–43.
5 Ibid., 49.
6 Ibid., 77–87.
7 Ibid., 168–76, 240.
8 Ibid., 243.
9 Ibid., 245–46.
10 Ibid., 247–50.
11 Ibid., 250–51.
12 Ibid., 250–52.

13 Ibid., 250–57.
14 Ibid., 257–58.
15 Ibid., 258–62.
16 Ibid., 263.
17 Ibid., 264–65.
18 Ibid., 266–67.
19 Ibid., 266–71.
20 Ibid., 271–73.
21 Ibid., 273–74.
22 Ibid., 274–76.
23 Ibid., 277–78.
24 Ibid., 278–80.
25 Ibid., 280–81.
26 Ibid., 282–83.
27 Ibid., 283–84.
28 Ibid., 285–86.
29 Ibid., 286–88.
30 Ibid., 288.
31 Ibid., 288–89.
32 Ibid., 290.
33 Ibid., 290–91.
34 Ibid., 291.
35 Ibid., 292–93.
36 Ibid., 293–94.
37 Ibid., 294–96.
38 Ibid., 296.
39 Ibid.
40 Ibid., 296–97.
41 Ibid., 336–44.
42 Ibid., 381.
43 Ibid., 382–85.
44 Ibid., 388–91.
45 Ibid., 395–99.
46 Ibid., 401–2.
47 Ibid., 403.
48 Ibid., 407.
49 Ibid., 407–8.
50 Ibid., 408–12.
51 Ibid., 430–45.
52 Ibid., 445–46.
53 Ibid., 453–55.
54 Ibid., 456–60.
55 Ibid., 460–64.
56 Ibid., 465.
57 Ibid., 466–67.
58 Ibid., 468–69.
59 Ibid., 470–71.
60 Ibid., 471–73.
61 Ibid., 474–76.
62 Ibid., 491.
63 Ibid., 493–94.
64 Ibid., 492–95.

65 Ibid., 495–96.
66 Ibid., 496–97.
67 Ibid., 498–500.
68 Ibid., 500.
69 Ibid., 503–4.
70 Ibid., 532–36.
71 Ibid., 504–5.
72 Ibid., 542–43.
73 Ibid., 542–43.
74 Ibid., 545–46.
75 Ibid., 546–48.
76 Ibid., 551–52.
77 Ibid., 552.
78 Ibid., 560–69.
79 Ibid., 570.
80 Ibid., 571–73.
81 Ibid., 574.
82 Ibid., 574–78.
83 Ibid., 578.
84 Ibid., 578–83.
85 Ibid., 584.
86 Ibid., 584–85.
87 Ibid., 585.
88 Ibid.
89 Ibid., 586–87.
90 Ibid., 587–89.
91 Ibid., 590–91.
92 Ibid., 591–93.
93 Ibid., 594–95.
94 Ibid., 595.
95 Ibid., 596–97.
96 Ibid., 597–98.
97 Ibid., 598–602.
98 Ibid., 601–15.
99 Ibid., 619.
100 Ibid., 624–29.

CONCLUSION

Perhaps not crossing at all

Every age must strive anew to wrest tradition away from the conformism that is working to overpower it.

Walter Benjamin[1]

A day will come, and it will suffice.

Hürü Ana to Anacık Sultan[2]

Before a single person enters the stories of Yaşar Kemal, the world is a setting of procreating life and wonder, palpitating with the aromas, colors, and sounds of the marshes and thickets, plants and flowers, bugs and birds, running water, twirling dust spirals, and intricate natural nooks and crannies of the Toros mountains cliffs and the Çukurova plains. Where the Roman imperial conquerors placed the border *fatalis*, Yaşar Kemal magically unveils a hidden landscape buzzing and teeming with vibrant life, beauty, and then togetherness, solidarity, and an ardent desire to live beyond precisely the kinds of injustices carried out by the glorious crossers.

The Toroslar created the Çukurova plains. A long long time ago, the Toroslar began at the edge of the Mediterranean Sea. Later, the Ceyhan, the Seyhan, and after them the large and small creeks and rivers, carrying all the fertile minerals and soils of the earth, filled the seacoast, and Çukurova emerged.[3]

Yaşar Kemal's account of the world contrasts starkly with the depiction of the world one receives in the stories of the classical historytellers, whose tales of the triumph and greatness of the empires of antiquity have been inherited as wisdom in "the West" for generations. In them, the world is divided into more or less two spheres: on one side, Europe, and the other, Asia. To move from the former to the latter one crosses the Hellespont and, shortly thereafter, faces the Taurus Mountain range. In the inherited stories of the classics, both boundaries – actual and as metaphors for others – are filled with mythological significance as sites of danger. Thus crossing the boundaries

266

between Europe and Asia requires going with force, and to end the threat posed by the other, the boundaries must be crossed in a way that unites the entire known world under the power and sovereignty of the glorious crosser.

Determined to get to that unknown and unnamed village, Memed goes with Müslüm to the coastal village of Akyalı where, through a friend of Ferhat Hoca's, he buys and settles in a home amidst the orange groves by the sea. He also buys some paintings – of Köroğlu, Hazreti Ali, Adam and Eve – and brings Seyran and Hürü Ana to live with him. And so, as he continues to question what good has come from all the killing, he quits eşkıyalık.[4]

Every crossing runs roughshod over these hidden landscapes of vibrant beauty, meaning, and purpose. The crosser sees these landscapes, if he or she sees them at all, as possessions-in-the-waiting through the violent assertion of unmatched planning and execution and overwhelming force.

Approaching "border(s)" otherwise, a possibility brought to expression in the stories of *İnce Memed* and that my work here purposefully seeks to promote, must begin by seeing the tremendous violence, actual and potential, in the tradition and cultural phenomenon of *crossing over*, and it must include a real conceptual shift in the historytelling of "the West." Is it not time to shed the tradition of *crossing over* as an aspect of our inherited constitutedness (our *being*, in this sense)? Is it not time, perhaps, not *to cross* at all?

As an alternative to *crossing over*, what might *perhaps not crossing at all* mean? There is a danger in not explicating my meaning, for I might be understood as endorsing either nativist isolationism or, worse, empire; that is, either insisting on always remaining within the given "borders" of life, or ignoring existing "borders" to the end of global conquest and *crossing* no more. I am not closed to staying put, as it were, as well as to sublunary mobility, but these are not my primary meanings, or the reasons I believe we need to think from and around borders in a radically different fashion. "Staying put" means living within borders posited by nationalist and imperial power and, as I have suggested in Part One, those borders (political, civilizational, cultural, etc.) are founded upon a representation of life outside of them as unsafe and dangerous. Borders are seen within this nativist framework as necessary and inevitable in order to contain the violence of the world upon which they are premised using various "empire/homeland/civilization/culture-securing" devices – devices that perforce perpetuate that violence.

What I mean by perhaps not crossing at all is that we need radically to revise, shake up, and rattle our conceptions of "borders," "boundaries," "border spaces," and, especially in relation to this study, the modes of life and experience that exist on "the other side" of what we see as such. We need to rethink what Thierry Hentsch has described as our "sense of self-certainty ... about the Other"[5] – other spaces, other forms of life, other ways of being, and so on. As I mentioned earlier in this study, this effort is not new; it participates in several areas of inquiry aiming to rethink the meaning and significance of borders. I am trying to work at the dispositional and philosophical level of inherited conceptual and cultural traditions that constitute what we understand as the given (b)orders of a politically violent world. "To bring into effect the practice of thinking differently, to modify oneself through the movements of thought, we have to detach ourselves from the already given systems, orders, doctrines, and codes of philosophy," avers Arnold I. Davidson in his comments on Foucault's project of "opening a space in thought" for "the transfiguring space of a different attitude, a new *ethos.*"[6]

Perhaps not crossing at all is my attempt to bring to language a new ethos, one that is drawn from this study and the experience that informs it. Personally, I seek, as Davidson describes it, to "lose my way"[7] – or my "footing,"[8] to borrow from Jacques Derrida as well – within the tradition of crossing over, and to encourage a broader losing our way: to destabilize and release ourselves from the grasp of the life-negating dispositions of *crossing over fatal boundaries* central to the inherited wisdom of the classical storytellers and to attempt to live within the life-affirming attitude of the miraculous beauty and unceasing, always uncertain, longing for goodness and justice of the Toroslar central to wisdom of *İnce Memed*. In this study, I have tried to dwell within each of these discursive spaces hermeneutically, the former linked necessarily to war, violence, and the perpetual fear, destruction, and subordination of others; the latter linked to affirming a form of suffering, communal partnership and solidarity-for-living that rejects life as war, violence, and the calculated manipulation and subjugation of others. In saying that we need perhaps not to cross at all, what I am trying to do is effect a movement in my, our, being as a result of the juxtaposition of the wisdom found in these stories. This movement, to be successful, requires considering, approaching, and imagining liminal spaces as something other than sites to be filled by and with a perpetual sense of antagonism.

Flooding near the rice paddies is spreading malaria that is killing the villagers near Akyalı. A friend of Memed's, the teacher and decorated war hero Zeki Nejad, leads a campaign to have the state protect the villages and is murdered. Thinking that Memed doesn't want to be İnce Memed anymore, Müslüm urges Memed to give him permission to kill Şakir Bey, the bey responsible for the suffering of the villagers and the murder of Zeki Nejad. Memed is clearly shaken by the events, but he doesn't respond to Müslüm.[9]

In the mountains, tens of young men seek out Ferhat Hoca, Kasım and Temir to join İnce Memed's çete. Each is named Memed. And not only this, but they all resemble each other and come to struggle for the wretched of the earth. Ferhat Hoca has them all take an oath on the Kuran: "None of you will wrong the wretched of the earth. You will also look towards them with friendliness and you will always speak kindly to them. You will assist in meeting whatever needs they have. If you rob and steal from the rich, you will distribute everything, without spending a cent, first to the most poor. You won't wound anyone's honor. Just as Köroğlu, Ali and İskender Zülkarneyn – Alexander the Great – didn't wound anyone's honor. The people's honor is your honor ... "[10]

The disposition of crossing over with violence in mind and purpose is not the exclusive property of "the West," for crossers come from many directions and their "heroic" feats of conquest, plunder, destruction, subordination, and massacre are celebrated within many traditions. Alexander is the best example of the latter: he is almost unquestionably considered "Great" the world over, including in the lands he conquered. Similarly, as far as global reputation is concerned, the Athenian combination of democracy and empire comes in a close second. It has, in many ways, laid the conceptual groundwork for the democratic and imperial practices of global political modernity. I wish, however, to maintain the focus on the inherited under-standing of the tradition of *crossing over* as it is constitutive of "the West": the glory of the crosser, the individual or collective force that mobilizes each and every human capacity, skill, and technique in a resolute, ambitious, independent, and intrepid fashion in order to transcend the known natural limits of the species, in feat and in scope. This disposition is undoubtedly celebrated and pursued as a quotidian cultural project in "the West" – a cultural project that many outside the conventionally understood geographic boundaries of "the West" participate in and pursue as well.[11] All of what made Athens an "example to others," Alexander "Great," and that dis-tinguished the power of the Roman Empire are sources of pride in "the West," from aspiring to highly disciplined, pragmatic, enduring, and authoritative power to the achievement of equality and liberty for all citizens (along with the subjection of unequal noncitizens, slaves, and colonized). These ideals, this vision of "the West," inherited in large part through the wisdom of the stories of the classics, get passed from one generation to the next. I'm talking about hundreds of generations and the teaching of a set of stories so stable that, as I have shown in Part One, they are often repeated, verbatim, in the scholarly and popular histories of our age.

Importantly, the transfer of this tradition at the present time benefits tre-mendously from political and military conditions that appear to support its essential storyline. At the time of this writing, a global war that many believe is best conceived as a civilizational battle between "East and West," or "the West and Islam," rages on. Never mind the heterogeneities within and or homogeneities across the boundaries that are considered "East" and "West," the gross misrepresentations of both "sides" of the conflict, or the availability of other stories to make sense of what is happening. The classics seem to possess the wisdom of the day. The great dramas of "the West" and "the

269

Persians" (etc.) resonate widely. One can understand the appeal. The old antagonistic stories are there, layered one on top of the other, easily rehabilitated, and the political and military conditions are ripe for their retelling. Recruitment of students, soldiers, and scholars who will be the storytellers in the cause of civilization for the next generation, on all sides, is made much easier. And the incentives – fellowships, government grants, heroic martyrdom/sacrifice, etc. – are great. Indeed, many of the best educated in "the West" actively participate in the current war *as a war for empire*, both overtly as aspiring or actual, government or government-sponsored researchers helping to secure the homeland/empire with up-to-date research on "the enemy," and covertly as enlisted agents of espionage. The latter, often living across the Hellespont and Taurus range, engage in what the American war hero General David Petraeus called "persistent situational awareness" in his (formerly) secret order of September 2010. The order was "focused on intelligence gathering – by American troops, foreign businesspeople, academics or others – to identify militants and provide 'persistent situational awareness,' while forging ties to local indigenous groups."[12] In short, the political ground for the telling and retelling of the old story, as well as for playing out its storyline, is as fertile as the soils of the Çukurova plains. The storybooks have been filling the shelves of bookstores or the "recommended reading lists" of "other customers" on the Internet since shortly after September 2001.

This epic story has come in several versions, but it seems that it is always, as Hamid Dabashi has emphasized, some version of the same story, that of Orientalism:[13] A world carved up by the powerful into two fundamentally different worlds pitted against each other, with the powerful seeing themselves as possessing all of civilization's superior traits – superior historical achievement, humanity, liberty, rationality, progress, social organization, etc., etc. – that the other either lacks or is in short supply of. The former is ready to "defend" itself from every encroachment of the Other, at *every* level of human existence (intimate matters of faith and relations, dress codes and character, cultural practices, institutional ideals, etc.), and to *assert* its superiority through conquest, subordination, and transformation of the Other according to the image of its own liking (either same and made "great," or different and subordinated). Any accent of Otherness of all Others threatens, either out of unfamiliarity or because "they" "lack" and, therefore, threaten the demonstrably most superior traits of humanity. All Otherness must be assimilated and/or eliminated. Others' efforts to resist such subordination, assimilation, or elimination with force are translated into the often depoliticized language of "terror," which is about as far as most "civilized" groups have been able to extend their collective thinking about resistance to their centuries-long unjust usurpations, dismissals, and subjection of Others. Movement, *any* movement, from "civilization" across "the border *fatalis*," any movement *near* the border *fatalis*, requires going well armed in some sense and/or prepared for violence of one sort or another. (Movement from the latter to the former, if one can climb the actual and metaphorical walls, requires a variety of systematically docile and/or humiliating dispositions, creative subversion, and/or counter-violence.) The view is, overall, supremacist, aggressive, and degrading, and it has tremendous staying power. *It* is where the "lack" is to be found: *it lacks* openness to the humanity of Others, hospitality, and a form of mutual regard that would enable social accompaniments and political solidarities of many different kinds. The Orientalist view undergirds the stories about crossing over. In each case, the "border" is a "border" or "boundary" between hierarchicalized, antagonistic worlds. But the problem goes even deeper: Of the Orientalist British Lord Balfour, Edward Said commented that it "didn't occur" to Balfour "to let the Egyptian speak for himself … "[14] Never mind letting the Other "speak," it does not occur to the crossers to let others *be*. It does not occur simply to *let*. Let, letting …

This study has sought to demonstrate beyond question that an equally epic and grand story, and – by implication – many, many equally epic and grand stories, imaginaries, sensibilities, and conceptions of those other spaces and their life-worlds exist. The spaces on the other side of "the borders" are not spaces of certain death and destruction. They are spaces teeming with beauty, hospitality, life, and, against all odds and sociohistorical forces, endless resilience in the quest for justice. These spaces are not, of course, without violence. Indeed, the violence of the ağas and beys in *İnce Memed 1–4* repeats the violence of the crossers.

The ağas see themselves as heroic figures because of their role in liberating Anatolia from French and Italian invaders in the War for Independence following the collapse of the Ottoman Empire. (We might note that the invading armies were seeking, among other things, to restore classical Europe's imperial reach.) However, claiming exclusive property rights over the lands where people have lived for centuries, the ağas have their eyes fixed on Anatolia not to liberate it but to rule it. They directly engage, order, or support more or less the same violence as those who crossed, in either direction, over the Hellespont and the Toroslar seeking immortal fame and glory in stories of the classics. Indeed, very much like the crossers, the ağas are in pursuit of greater glory by bringing the peoples and villages of the Toroslar and the Cilician plains (Çukurova) under their sovereign control. They forge alliances in order to seize and win more and more from those, even their own loyalists, who toil, suffer, and die in great pain. Those who supported Hamza were the victims of his cruelty that seemed to surpass that of Abdi. Adem, who searched for Ali Safa Bey's horse, should have been dead when he showed up to report Memed's whereabouts. So Ali Safa Bey had him secretly killed.

The ağas and beys display insatiable greed in their appetite for land, power, profit, and status. Their wisdom in the face of resistance is that the

271

head of the snake must be cut while young in order to secure and expand their plundered booty, to feed their drunken appetites, and to pursue further fame and glory. The head of the snake is not only Memed's head, but also all those villagers who see hope in İnce Memed. Thus the ağas and beys assault and attack, belittle and burn, and connive and claim ownership of everything (including the running water and "the underwear on the villagers' asses"). They promise to bring calamity ("Kerbela") upon those who resist their power. They demean, deprive, destroy, enslave to a crushing economic order, expel, and inspire enmity and "knee-buckling" fear. They kidnap, kill, and desire to leave not a single living thing alive as they pillage, plunder, rape, rob, starve, threaten, torture (young and old), trample, and wipe out. Again, they plunder and rape and starve and torture. They impose conditions of hunger and starvation by withholding food and water in order to "teach" the villagers a lesson about their power and honor. That is, they take vengeance upon. For them, there is no middle ground; either everything will fall to them or to Memed and the villagers: "You have ten days!" With the jandarma acting on their behalf, they cross the mountain paths and beat, torture, harass, and kill the innocent, producing so much crippling pain that they turn the entire Toroslar, like the crossers of old, into "shouts and screams."

In his search for Memed, Kertiş Ali finds that either all the young men had changed their names to Memed or the villagers had named their children after him. If the Memeds were beaten to death, they died with smiles on their faces.

"Every mountain and every stone, all the earth and trees in these steep, great Toros mountains has become Memed," declares Murtaza Ağa, who devises a new plan. He offers a huge reward for the capture of İnce Memed's horse. The poor and opportunistic alike bring their horses in. Murtaza Aga and the Yüzbaşı inspect each one. None is Memed's horse, of course, but the ağas claim to have captured it, only deepening the love the people had for both Memed and his horse.[15]

The ağas fail because they encounter a different kind of wisdom: nearly inexhaustible and indestructible resilience among the villagers and their leaders in the face of injustice and, especially, the kurt of humanity and the miraculous powers of life in the Toroslar. For as many Hellesponts as there are to cross, there are as many, if not more İnce Memeds, sprouting from out of the many Toroslar.

Memed buys a gun and shoots and kills Şakir Bey. He kills as he had killed Abdi and the others and rejoins Ferhat Hoca in the mountains where they take from the rich and give to the poor. Memed tells Ferhat Hoca about Zeki Bey and the killing of the bey. Ferhat Hoca notices Memed's melancholic mood. "Alışamadın," dedi, "adam öldürmeye." You haven't been able to get used to

*killing, said Ferhat Hoca. "Kim olursa olsun," Memed responded. "Hiçbir
zaman da adam öldürmeye alışamayacağım." No matter who it is, I will never
be able to get used to killing.[16]*

*During one raid, the jandarma almost catch them, but the eşkıyas make it
to higher ground and force Asım Çavuş to surrender. Memed and Asım Çavuş
meet. The Çavuş is upset with eşkıya raids on the town. Memed tells him they
didn't raid the town. He explains that they are taking from the rich to give to
the poor. Memed asks if Asım Çavuş had heard of the killing of the teacher
Zeki Nejad, and he had. Asım Çavuş said that someone named Memed had
killed the murderer. "That Memed was me Çavuşum ... " Asım Çavuş shook
his hand. "You did well like that," his eyes filling with tears.[17]*

The wisdom in the astonishing story of İnce Memed counters the wisdom of
the ağas and the crossers. *Killing* is *not* Memed's desire; subjugation, possession are not what he *wants.* Early in his life, tattered and bleeding from
the thorns and a life of toil under a cruel ağa, he escapes the exploitation to
which he and his people are subjected and, over time, seeks to destroy the
wretched conditions of such exploitation and oppression. Unlike the ağas
(and their mountain bandits), he genuinely wrestles with the actual and
ethical consequences of the violence he undertakes. This is of utmost significance. He does not simply trample over one to trample over the next. He
sees the faces of those he has killed long after their death has taken place at
his hands, and, witnessing as a participant a seemingly endless cycle of hor-
rific oppression, he asks if, and deeply worries that, his own actions have in
fact made matters worse. Abdi gitti, Hamza geldi. What is the good in this?
Struggle for *what*? His deep questioning of the efficacy of killing contrasts
with that of the ağas and crossers. He does not kill to subordinate, to
destroy, to harm, or to gain. Rather, he shoots a single person – *only* the
person who possesses the power to do otherwise, to let, and does not let, and
in that sense is responsible for the violence (he does not shoot to kill the
ağas' loyalists or the poor jandarma soldiers) – *and* feels the moral pain of
that act. He does so *in order to* restore life, to affirm the life of the peoples of
the Toroslar that has been trampled upon by the crossers for glory. Then he
departs. In him is the kurt of humanity that compels and "obligates everyone" to struggle for "humanity." ("A human may be freed from everything
but not from the kurt inside" – Battal Ağa.) No, he does not *simply* "*kill*" or
"*murder.*" He is compelled to be a force for justice in solidarity with the
wretched, tortured, killed, humiliated, starved, and dispossessed of the earth.
He acts against the unjust cruelty of their condition while they are in that
condition. He wants not to kill, to *not* kill, or even inflict pain. He wants
something else: to end the killing, the pain, the suffering; to end the pilla-
ging, plundering, raping, expelling. His killing is a refusal of the violence of
the crosser and an affirmation of the something else. "I didn't want this *at
all*," he tells Topal Ali. At all. I didn't want this at all. "Know that I had *no*

other solution." The kurt is in him, in Hatçe, in Topal Ali, in Hürü Ana, in Ferhat Hoca, in Kasım, in Anacık Sultan, in Müslüm, in Sarı, in Iraz, in the Scythian elder, in Seyran, in Aziz, in Kerimoğlu, in Asım Çavuş, in the Yörük women, and in all the villagers who take a beating for him. And it is in his horse, a horse constituted very differently from the one Napoleon rides in *Victoire* or the one Alexander rides on "Alexander's Sarcophagus." Memed is neither trampling over the bodies of others, nor is he thrusting himself and his forces forward for glorious victory over "the enemy." Memed restores life through pointed acts of violence and then lets those who have suffered *be*. Nor can his horse be touched by those who attack it.

The kurt signifies a collective capacity to *endure* and struggle, because uğraşmak, savaşmak haktır – *to struggle, to fight to end the cruelty of tyranny and oppression is one's right*. It is one's right, it is *right* to struggle for the end of the struggle: to release dreams of how life was without the ağas, as Durmuş Ali says, or to pursue a dream that has yet to be, to live in some as yet unnamed and unknown village. In the Toroslar, certain death does not await; there is life, life after oppression. In this living after, the villagers share everything, with everyone, including the families of the dead ağas. "This is your share." Şu dünyada ne iyi insanlar var. What good people there are on this earth. The families who benefitted from oppression are, without discussion, forgiven. ("Let Allah not make this kind of trouble for the enemy," says Kasım.)

Arif Saim Bey hires Bayramoğlu to capture Memed. Bayramoğlu searches the villages and encounters the same resistance the jandarma had met. Sarı Çavuş tells him, "What, are you going to kill İnce Memed? You're going to kill Bayramoğlu, Köroğlu, Karayılan and Hazreti Ali as well. You're going to kill all the hearts that have risen against tyranny. Sen insanlığı, sen Toros dağlarını öldürmeye gidiyorsun. – You're going to kill humanity, to kill the Toros mountains – These mountains sang songs and created legends for you. They danced the halay for you."[18]

After shooting each ağa, Memed returns to the scenes of *their* crimes and says to their victims, "hakkınızı helal edin" (or, depending on the specifics of the context, "hakkını helal et," "hakkınızı helal et," or "hakkınız helal olsun"). I have left this untranslated, because there is no direct translation into English, and the meanings of this precious expression vary. Most often, "hakkınızı helal edin" is said to a person or persons who have acted on behalf of the person saying it, as the person saying it departs from some form of loving relationship – a daughter or son departing home says this to those who raised her or him, a person facing death says this to her or his loved ones. In saying "hakkınızı helal edin," the person is saying, let all that you have done for me – the good and pleasant as well as the bad and painful – be helal, meaning be permissible in the judgment of God, not haram, forbidden. Saying it is a way of making amends and is undergirded by the concern that even deeds that have caused some pain not be seen as sinful, as haram. What must be understood about Memed's declaration thus requires viewing this very expression, hakkınızı helal edin, as a ritual act of righteousness in the context of gaining permission, ultimately from God, for one's deeds in the world. In this story, the righteous encounter themselves.

The context of Memed's saying hakkınızı helal edin requires elaborating a slightly different interpretation beyond the common meaning of the expression. In my reading, while the villagers have, in suffering and out of love, done so much to protect and nourish Memed that his expression fits with the common meaning, hakkınızı helal edin in this context has an additional meaning because *he* – the Memed we know to feel the pain of doing wrong – has just killed the person responsible for their suffering.

Memed tells the villagers, "hakkınızı helal edin," after doing what he believes to have been a necessary deed, indeed, to have fulfilled an ethical debt to them for sins committed against them. He returns to them before departing, however, not only to ask that what they have done for him be judged as permissible, but also to ask them to forgive him for the sins he has committed – for the moral flaws of his actions – and to pardon him. Memed is asking for forgiveness for having contributed so much to their suffering (a sin, contributing to, or not having protected them from, oppression) *and* for taking the life of another human being to end that suffering. *That* is not (one's) right. The killing that he commits is, paradoxically, *both* a righteous deed in the story *and* a sin, and, I believe, Memed is, unlike the other characters that either kill or support killing, acutely aware of this. (Or, if you like, Yaşar Kemal enables us to be acutely aware of this.) In this story, the righteous person encounters more than only his or her righteousness. In the world of the violence of the crossers, there is no flawless reversal of injustice. Memed wrestles ceaselessly with this.

Hakkınızı helal edin is thus a ritual pronouncement with profound significance. Memed knows *he has done wrong*. He thinks it is haram that a life is taken from humanity. He therefore comes to announce that he has sinned and to ask, with a reciprocal expectation that he can assume in this very declaration, for the villagers to renounce any claims of sin against him. Hakkınızı helal edin is said such that, when everyone stands together in judgment before God, none will possess any claims against another for the wrongs they have committed in this life. They will have forgiven and apologized to each other for all they have done wrong. Harming or killing another is haram. A higher goal is sought: justice – *hak* – living a shared and welcoming existence with each other in the fecund lands of life, and being good. Much is going on, therefore, when he returns to the villages and says, hakkınızı helal edin, and this is the only thing he says before riding off to the mountains and *letting* them *be*, letting them return to living, *letting*. *Letting by leaving*. The language of the story establishes that all of us do wrong and brings to expression a reciprocal capacity for forgiveness and the possibility of restoring and re-storying life in a just fashion. The tyrants, the crossers, are gone. The story no longer belongs to them. The villagers may now, once again, restore and re-story their lives.

There is real and difficult counsel in this astonishing story. The profoundly felt recognition of the wrongness of the suffering to which he has contributed and the killing he has done to end it constitute his shooting the ağas with a significance that contrasts radically with the violent will and purposes of both the ağas and crossers. After his daring acts to save the villagers from calamity, Memed humbles himself before them and before God. Scarred himself by a lifetime of violence, his righteous struggle, his resort to counter-violence only when there was no other way possible, is an act to end the harshest forms of suffering and to affirm and restore life.

Bayramoğlu catches up with Memed in a village, but Topal Ali is there to convince the person who says he can identify Memed to identify someone else. That person takes a beating for Memed and Memed escapes. Bayramoğlu figures this out and speaks with Topal Ali who tells Bayramoğlu that he would have killed him if he had captured Memed.

Bayramoğlu finally tracks Memed and the others down and agrees to meet Memed. When he does, Memed kneels down in respect, kisses his hand, and raises it slowly and warmly to his forehead. They and Ferhat Hoca embrace. In the meantime, the jandarma surrounds them. Bayramoğlu agrees to cover the others as they escape. He is shot and killed by the jandarma while defending Memed's escape.[19]

Indeed, Memed wants get to the unknown and unnamed, faraway place – the place that has been named as an unknown and unnamed, faraway place – the village of the orange groves. He wants to travel to the end of his known world, but not for glory and greater fame, but to escape violence. He travels but does not cross over. When he "crosses" paths – he asks, how can I take Seyran and cross the mountains? – he crosses to end violence and to recreate, restore and re-story life. Among the usages of the idiom of crossing in the story is one where it means crossing for love, forgiveness, and the restoration of beauty. This usage occurs when Seyran slips off her shoes and crosses the stream to return to the village from the island where Memed is recuperating. She is tingling in love, ready to smile again, to reunite in forgiveness with her family, to overcome grief and be beautiful in life once more, to love Memed. In another usage, Ferhat Hoca and Memed discuss how their crossing paths was no accident.[20] There is beauty and the struggle to end oppression when İnce Memed crosses, which I interpret as meaning that relative to the crosser in the stories of the classical narratives, İnce Memed is not *crossing* at all.

In the wisdom of Yaşar Kemal's *İnce Memed*, what is the source of all this beauty, the hospitality, the goodness of the people, their capacity to endure, their willingness to struggle, their ability to recognize and forgive each other's wrongs, their collective longing for a just world? It is not the miraculous powers of a single Great Man. No, it is the Toros Mountains themselves. "The powers" for these life-affirming ways of being "are in the land, the trees, the water, the people, the insects, the birds," explains Anacık Sultan. She works their wonders for a thousand years by extracting the potent healing potions from the natural flora and fauna that grow in the mountains. "Everything is in the flower" – and therefore the sun, the light, the water – "everything is in the herb. All the charms are in the light that comes, flowing in torrents ... The miracles are in this boundlessly creating earth." Similarly, Ferhat Hoca assures Memed, that just as he emerged from this earth, "just how the yellow crocuses shoot through the earth, just how they smiled in our faces, like the sunlight, İnce Memeds will sprout from within the people." What good people there *will be* in this world. Rest assured. More strugglers for goodness and justice will sprout from the Taurus Mountains. In this story, the Toroslar – the many Toroslar of the world, the many Hellesponts not to be crossed – are *the* force for the miraculous abundance of life, goodness, and justice. The beauty of the people comes from the Toroslar, and they know and feel beholden as a result: Before freeing Memed and his çete from Mahmut Ağa's fortress, the women of Çiçeklidere ask what they will say on judgment day about their having allowed Memed to be captured in their village. They ask what their children will say to them, what the faces of the dead will say to them, *and* they ask what "these great Toros Mountains" will say to them. How will they answer to the Toroslar? "What," they quickly add, "will we say to humanity?" In this world, one cannot think of the Toroslar without humanity, and vice versa.

The ağas and beys blame Anacık Sultan for what has happened. Her "superstitious" ocak has become "the nest" of the eşkıyas. They send Kertiş Ali to arrest her. She welcomes him and his men, saying she was expecting them. She willingly extends her hands, with a smile, for the handcuffs, and, in the cold of the winter, they take her down from the mountains. She freezes along the way. İnce Memed surrounds them and forces them to release her. "My rose my son," she says to Memed, "you've freed me from the hands of the jandarma, but where will you take me, are you going to make me an eşkıya at this age?" "Whatever you wish," he responds. She wants to be surrendered to the jandarma. She knows it won't be easy for Memed. They all know she will be tortured to death. "My death lies with God," she says with a smile. She is returned the next morning to the jandarma, but the Yüzbaşı was very upset. He didn't want to be the one to take her into town.[21]

What in the classical narratives of "the West" are the fatal boundaries – the Toroslar, the Hellesponts – where death awaits and one must go prepared for violence to gather riches and glory are the life-worlds of others palpitating with faith, courage, beauty, and an inextinguishable capacity to face and overcome the injustices of the crossers. The good old days of spending summers near the mountain springs, celebrations on the plains in the mild seasons, and a vibrant ocak with redemptive powers are slowly disappearing. The people now face the cruelty of the land-grabbers and the yellow heat of Çukurova, but in the storied Toroslar, the good people forever display a yearning for a just, beautiful and magnificent world at every turn. They display it in their comfortable sleep; in their delicious meals, milk, butter, and honey; in the magical meanings they give to the ethereal blues, pinks, and purples of the landscape; and in their reciprocal relation to the pulsating and procreating wonders of nature, where a gazelle gives itself to the place where the wounded and injured among the good people of the world are healed. Even the shah who went to conquer Baghdad would have preferred to serve the miraculous ocak than return to power.

Power is not what one grasps for in the counsel of *İnce Memed*. Earthly power does not come from the powers that be above. It sprouts from the cracks of the craggy cliffs and the resilience of the villagers down below. The ray of light that glistens in Memed's eyes shines towards the earth in solidarity with, feeling the pain of, the tortured and oppressed. Those sparkling rays of light are like the balls of fire that burn from the peaks of the mountains when the villagers set the thistles ablaze each year. Those fires spread from village to village, in solidarity, making ashes out of their common past suffering and preparing the fields once again to produce more life. The rays of light, the balls of fire, and the burning thistles all burn for life. The screams from inside the flames are perhaps those of the young Memeds, Dönes, and Hatçes who once suffered under the despotic aegis of the Abdis and Hamzas, or the villagers who absorbed the beatings of the jandarma or died from starvation, expulsion, or malaria at the bloodthirsty hands of the Arif Saim Beys and Mahmut Ağas. Such confidence in the indestructible powers of nature abounds in the Toroslar that it comes to Anacık Sultan, as it had to Battal Ağa, to counsel Memed, their hawk, to "Do what your heart desires."

The entire Toroslar hear of Bayramoğlu's bravery and Anacık Sultan's arrest. People fill the town to see her. Arif Saim Bey refers to her as "that whore," "that traitor witch," and accuses her of making miracles. She denies this. He accuses her of spreading lies about the disappearance of the Forty. She says he can think as he wishes. Arif Saim Bey pounds the table with his fist, "When will this nation be saved, when will it be emancipated from you and your lies?" She said no lie was ever said about the ocak and its power to heal. "I have no capacity for miracles. The miracles are in the flowers, the trees, the plants, the birds, the insects, and the human beings." She agrees that her medicines healed Memed and that she had given him a special shirt on which prayers were written to protect him. Arif Saim Bey accuses her of protecting killers. "Whether they are killers only God knows," she said. Arif Saim Bey accuses her of giving them shelter. She denies it. He insists that she admit it, that she did it because the tekkes have been closed by the state. "Say it woman, say it whore, you whore of the Toros mountains." She is silent in the face of more taunts, curses, and the anger that swelled in him, as well as the threats he made by pointing his gun at her.[22]

Arif Saim Bey threatens to use "European techniques" to make Anacık Sultan talk. He orders Kertiş Ali to get her confession, but not to kill her. Ali is from the Toroslar, though, and he has only respect for her. He takes her somewhere to make her comfortable and pleads with her to say something, and to forgive him. He prays, brings food from home, begs her to eat and drink. He says he believes in her and the ocak. But when she stops speaking, he loses himself, calls her a whore and threatens to bring in some men to rape her. "Say something whore." He tells her that the hand that is about to torture her as he had all over the Toroslar is not his, but the state's and Arif Saim Bey's. A slight smile comes across her face as she opens her eyes. He takes some hope from this that she was taking back all she had done. At that moment, Arif Saim and the other ağas, along with the Kaymakam, come and try again to make her talk. They fail as had Ali. He pleads with her. Fearing she is dying, he brings a doctor who says she needs immediate care. Soon she dies, and they pin her death on İnce Memed.

A jandarma officer named Karafırtına leads a vengeful search for İnce Memed. He has the jandarma turn the villages of the Toroslar upside down. They beat people to death and intimidate the villagers so much that the people flee before the jandarma arrived. So much fear spreads that no one knows where everyone went. But no one gives up Memed. More türküs are written for him. It is clear, as Ferhat Hoca had said, that everyone in the Toroslar has a little bit of İnce Memed in their hearts. Memed is embarrassed by this, but he concentrates on what could be done to stop the killing, beating, and exiling of the villagers. The flash of light comes to his eyes.[23]

Everything and everyone *of* the Taurus Mountains has an İnce Memed in them. Everyone has absorbed a blow for justice. Everyone is together in this struggle against unjust cruelty and violence, for justice and restore/ying life. Thus, everyone you meet across the Hellesponts, on what you think of as fatal boundaries, has a bit of İnce Memed in them. Everyone *is* an İnce Memed, a Hatçe, Süleyman, Hürü Ana, Müslüm, Fatmalı, Koca Osman, Emiş Hatun, Battal Ağa, İdris Bey, İsmail Emmi ...

Because the villagers resist every effort to find Memed, Arif Saim Bey decides to cut the water supply to the Toros villages, forcing everyone down

279

into the yellow heat of Çukurova. He is praised by the ağas. They say he is as smart as Napoleon, Alexander, Atilla and Cengiz Khan. When Memed hears of the expulsion, he is incensed and takes his çete to Değirmenoluk. Memed is feeling horrible about all the trouble he has caused. The çete doesn't stay long and clashes with the jandarma as they leave. Asım Çavuş holds his fire to speak with Memed. He knows that Memed never shoots to kill the jandarma. He tells Memed that Karafırtına has been killed by a villager, and that Memed won't be hanged if he gives himself up. Memed tells Asım Çavuş that he knows Memed won't surrender after all the harm that has been done to the country of the Toros (Toros ülkesi), the unconscionable suffering of the people being forced down into the Çukurova swamps. Asım Çavuş tells him that those were Arif Saim Bey's orders, not the jandarma's. Get out of here, says Memed, so that a stray bullet doesn't find you. "I'm not surrendering."

Memed and Müslüm go to Hürü Ana who is preparing to leave to be with Seyran on the coast. Her heart was burning for the other villagers. Hürü finally tells Memed that he has a son – that Seyran gave birth after he returned to the mountains and that they had named the boy İbrahim, after Memed's father. Memed pledges to come as soon as possible. He tells her to go, and he rides with Müslüm to Çukurova.

The stars in the sky were more than there had ever been. They rode down from the peak of the mountain, passing in front of the Gülek Boğazı – the Cicilian Gates, the pass where Alexander had, against all odds, crossed the Taurus Mountains – where they waited at the opening of the Anavarza plain. The peaks of the mountains were covered in snow, and the orman buzzed and hummed. Memed thought of all that was going on. They stopped and rested at Hasan Dede's türbe.[24]

Perhaps not crossing at all means being "at" or "on" the border and receiving the spaces of others *as if* they are the Toroslar: not a line or "border" to be "crossed" (or "defended") but broad, extended, miraculous landscapes of life filled with thousands upon thousands of Memeds and Hürüces, millions of millions of charmed souls with the kurt of humanity in them. What good people there are in this world. Perhaps not crossing at all means eliminating crossing over as a possibility. It means struggling, putting an end to struggles, and not struggling to share the bountiful life of the world, including the life-affirming efforts of each other, in a just manner. It means not allowing the boundaries and hierarchies determined by instrumental state and imperial power to govern our imaginative relations. Reviving our imaginations, differently. It means to attend permanently to our intrinsically reciprocal debt to each other and, if necessary, to attack the crosser within our being(s), traditions, and cultures. Not to let the crosser attack. To receive and be life, life procreating life. In the words of a famous philosopher with the kurt in her, "If a people or nation, or even just some specific human group, which offers a unique view of the world arising from is particular position in the world – a position that, however it came about, cannot readily be duplicated – is annihilated, it is not merely that a people or a nation or a given number of individuals perishes, but rather that a portion of our common world is destroyed."[25] The Hellesponts and Taurus Mountains are not "fatal boundaries." They are spaces and sources of life, beautiful spaces of interconnected living, homes on the coast, plains or up in the mountains with beautiful people in them, people yearning to knit socks for their relatives, cook delicious meals, harvest their crops, care for one another, anticipate a lovely and loving future, rest on a long journey. Their ways may remain incomprehensible, "backward," and "superstitious" to the crossers and ağas, but they possess a nearly equal, incomprehensible capacity to endure violence launched against them, *and* they seek to enliven each other's heartfelt desires. "Do what you heart desires," the healer says as counsel. The Toroslar and the countless recorded and unrecorded life-affirming stories from the many Toroslar at the edge of every one of "the West's" fatal boundaries, are the miraculous remedies for a world antagonistically divided by imperial pursuits.

There is much more meaning to make in conversation with these stories. Questions peculiar to the interpretive aims of this work now come to mind. Can companionship through conversation with the all-powerful stories of others alter the deeply constitutive dispositions of other others? More specifically, can one – in and/or of "the West" – profoundly receive from others a more compelling political vision of spaces on the edges of "the West" than the contemptuous vision inherited from the dominant Orientalist imaginary of Western Antiquity? Can one dwell within the full, heterogeneous violence of the dominant imaginary, and apologize and ask forgiveness for it in order *to let*? Can we purge *crossing over* and its form of "desire fulfillment"[26] from our inherited constitutedness in favor of hospitality, mutual regard, and the multiple and various forms of social and sensual solidarity that a different disposition towards others and their spaces/sources of life may spark? Can we profoundly receive the counsel of *İnce Memed* and effect a true conceptual shift in the history of "the West"? In light of the inexhaustible wisdom of the astonishing stories of İnce Memed, can we provoke for the future of political thoughtfulness a conceptual shift in our understanding of *crossing over the Hellesponts*?

The challenge of the stories of İnce Memed is, to my mind, deeper than inter- and multi-cultural curiosity of Herodotus, Alexander's ruler-centric empathy, the admirable disloyalty of the Medizer, or the ethical act of remembering or paying witness to the violence of crossing over. The challenge is that of righteous encounter: to receive wisdom from and succumb to the force of the omnipotent life-affirming stories of Others and, for the sake of life, to eliminate the inherited violent disposition of crossing over the borders of "the West." The spaces in which we live palpitate with bountiful life, and it is from and within those spaces that the potential life-affirming capacity of humanity is born and nourished. The issue is thus not simply whether or not we can see boundaries differently. The question is, in light of the perpetual violence of the disposition of crossing over, can we rethink the traditionary bases upon which that disposition rests and alter the cultural practices that until now have been constituted by that disposition? Can we lose something within us that inspires fear and coercion across boundaries pre-constituted as "fatal" and constrains our aesthetic appreciation of the world as an integral whole, comprising the differing life-worlds and ways of being of our neighbors, who are also our unexpected guests. "Throw some wood on the fire!" Can we *be* hospitable and *provide* hospitality to those guests, and, really, see beauty *anywhere* and exhibit mutual regard to *anyone*? "No one I recognize as far as I know." Yaşar Kemal makes us see this possibility: There is nothing to conquer, only to let and share, otherwise and "infinitely."[27] To struggle and fight for this is our right.

Topal Ali tells Memed that Arif Saim Bey is in Taşkın Halil Bey's house and that he will lead Memed to the bey's room. They enter the village, tie their horses quietly, and Ali opens the gate with ease. He leads Memed up the stairs and points out the bey's room. Memed opens the door and enters, his hand on the trigger of his gun. "Arif Saim Bey, I'm İnce Memed."

Lying in a gilded bed, Arif Saim Bey appeared to smile as Memed raised the gun. "My son," he mumbled, "what are you doing, what are you doing, is this possible. I ... I ... me ha, I!" Then he covered his face with his hands. Memed fired five times. The wind of the bullets blew out the lamp. Memed took off, hopped on his horse and rode out of town. Towards morning, he went to helallaşmak with Hürü Ana once more.

He finds her among the crowds leaving the mountains. "Hakkınızı helal edin," he says to everyone. "I will come again, I will come again," and then he rides off towards Alidağı.[28]

In this beautiful place, villages exist that are under attack. The goal of the attacker is gain, plunder, dispossession and booty. In the villages, there is resistance and desire to live otherwise. As long as İnce Memed lives, people believe in a different world. They believe this because their world is not a world of plunder. Life is filled with the painful intrusions of all sorts of power (Hatçe's arranged marriage by the powers that be, for example, fuels already existing antipathy between Memed and Abdi Ağa), but its foundations are those of hospitality and humanity. To admire İnce Memed as they do means to admire humanity – İnce Memed sevmek insan sevmek demektir. Thus, these are not killing fields. They are İnce Memeds' fields. They are not fatal. They are alive. Everyone you meet here, on the boundaries across the Hellespont, on the street corner across the street, or right in front of you at your "fatal boundaries," has the kurt of humanity in them, *is* an İnce Memed.

And the crowd did as the others had. They gathered the thorns, shrubs, and keven and lit a huge fire. Abdal Bayram and other drummers and horn players played and the people danced. Then they sang türküs for Memed. The world was engulfed in a storm of joy, and the storm spun round and round. Word was never heard again from İnce Memed, but every year since that day, in the villages of the Toroslar, before they plough the fields, they get all dressed up, go to the plains and the most handsome of the young men and the most lovely of the young women light the thistles aflame in a huge toy düğün. The singing and sounds of joyful türküs spread from one place to another. The fires burn as the fires of the past did and, together with them, as in the past, on the peaks of Alidağı, Düldül dağı, Yıldızdağı and Binboğa, a ball of light shines, whitening and illuminating the peaks for three days, just as in the daytime.[29]

During the early blasts of what in "the West" is known as the "war on terror," I sat in one of my favorite cafés in Istanbul writing an early part of this work. One of my friends there, a retired gentleman from Anatolia who now worked in the café, asked me what I was writing. I told him that I was writing something about the conflict that I was trying to tell people back home – meaning, so to speak, on the other side of the Hellespont. I thought for a moment and then asked him a question: If you were to have me say something to them, what would it be?

In a heartbeat, he answered: "*Merhaba!*" Hello! "*Merhaba söyle!*" Tell them Hello! "*Söyle biz barbar değiliz!*" Tell them we are not barbarians! He could have said, tell them we live according to the example of Abraham, welcoming guests, like me, as if they are guests from God. Tell them we are a hospitable people. He could have also said, as a kardeş from the Toroslar later told me down on the plains of Çukurova, tell them that if they come to attack us as they are attacking Iraq (a concern that spread during the first decade of the twenty-first century), we will fight back. There will always be resistance in the Toroslar against the invasions of the crosser, I understood.

There I am, in conversation and relationships with "the other side." In Part One, I wrote in praise of the Medizer. Am I one, am I a Medizer? To the crossers, yes, that is who I am and have become. A disloyal traitor, who talks about the other horizon to make it seem superior, who has turned his back on all that "I" "am." A post- or ex-Westerner. A traitor to my country and my tradition. Westerners and the Westernizers alike suspect me. That is why the Medizer is a term of derision within the violent grammar of *crossing over*, but this is one of the problems of this grammar. Its language conveys a *particular* orientation towards *action*. It does not exhaust all possibilities for being "at," "on," or "over" significant "borders" of our lives.

Similarly, having experienced an alteration in my being, I would not say that I have *crossed over* crossing over: The constitutive experience of *crossing over* is a particularly violent inheritance that differs fundamentally from the hermeneutical aims of understanding and constituting one's world differently. The former – *crossing over* – involves approaching other spaces to acquire property and glory for a self that is forever constituted by the purposes of *crossing over*. The crosser takes the same horizon everywhere and, thus, everywhere essentially remains the same.

The hermeneutical relation differs because it involves a different *ethos* – specifically, an openness to having one's being transformed through open-ended conversation, even if such transformation occurs only at the very outer limits of one's understanding (because understanding, as emphasized above, is not synonymous with knowing the other). In its disposition to receiving through dialogue the astonishing stories of others, hermeneutical openness requires taking the risk of being dis-placed without crossing, of losing, of having one's constitutive understanding suspended, loosened, and altered by being taken elsewhere in conversation. Thus crossing is not the correct characterization of where this study has taken me. I have not crossed over crossing over, because the hermeneutic "self" is not the same after conversation.

I have departed, in a sense, from (the dominant imaginary of) my first home. I have effected a shift in my consciousness, a change in my constituted being. My "I" has altered. "I" am happily hyphenated, dancing and burning, with "the other side." I have placed myself within the space between different horizons and have no shame. "I" have neither sunk, caught a bad cold, nor "become radicalized," but "I" have learned to despise the crosser. "I" will resist him or her wherever "I" can. "I" live elsewhere, without having settled on the other shore, or needing to. "I" can hope different hopes, cherish, tell and be open to different stories, see, feel, dream, hear, and imagine the world differently. "I" can be otherwise. "I" have rejected the allure of the crossers' sense of risk and the beauty of the crossers' sense of the beautiful. "I" have rejected the crossers' claims of the absolute necessity of fear and danger. "I" condemn the crossers' fearful and proud, protective preparations for violence, massacre, forced exile, and trophy hunting. "I" care little to pursue glory over what they have constructed as "fatal boundaries." To the contrary, beyond their "fatal" boundaries, "I" understand that life is abundant and beautiful, and that relations beyond power, of trust and solidarity, are possible. "I" can live otherwise.

At and on the border, the difference between what happens "inside" and what may happen otherwise has a chance. The unnamable glimmer may be glimpsed, and something different can even happen *to* "the border." When sitting on the edge of the Hellespont, "I" can no longer *cross*. I am resting on the shoreline and cliffs amidst the homes, ancient and contemporary, of others. I am prepared for losing, letting, and living. The wisdom of the old tradition resides somewhere within me – the best evidence being the dialogical grappling between Part One and Part Two that this very work has required. Deep inside, the old wisdom makes a claim upon me. That is how it is with old, life-negating wisdom. Any effort to shed or purge it, any successful effort, demonstrates its lasting grip. However, the old wisdom is no longer in any sense definitive of my being. I have lost that way in the company of others, and, if I must, I can run up the staircase of my formation, take aim where its coercive power haunts me, and watch the wind of my desire to live otherwise burn out the candles that flicker around it. In short, the old wisdom no longer tyrannizes me. What is deep "in my understanding and being," as I sometimes phrase it in conversation, has altered. "I" have lived another day, received another story, and we are living on, differently. The innuendo and charges of Medizing annoy, but they do not stick. In my, in our, shared social universe, the language of my being has been miraculously altered by others' stories and the possible meanings that can be made in and of the world have changed for the better.

Notes

1. W. Benjamin, "Theses VI," in M. Löwy, *Fire Alarm: Reading Walter Benjamin's 'On the Concept of History'*, London: Verso, 2005, 42.
2. Y. Kemal, *İM3*, 293.
3. Y. Kemal, *İM4*, 11.
4. Ibid., 98, 153ff, 227ff.
5. T. Hentsch, *Imagining the Middle East*, Montreal: Black Rose Books, 1992, 83.
6. A. Davidson, "Introduction," in M. Foucault, *The Hermeneutics of the Subject: Lectures at the Collège de France, 1981–1982*, New York: Palgrave MacMillan, 2005, xxviii.
7. Ibid.
8. J. Derrida, *Parages*, Palo Alto, CA: Stanford University Press, 2011, 109.
9. Y. Kemal, *İM4*, 13–36, 152–84, 227–74.
10. Ibid., 276–78.
11. Here I conceptualize "the West" as a cultural phenomenon, not bounded by territory, similar to Dipesh Chakrabarty's idea of a metareal "Europe" in his *Provincializing Europe: Postcolonial Thought and Historical Difference*, Princeton: Princeton University Press, 2000.
12. M. Mazetti, "U.S. is Said to Expand Secret Actions in Mideast," *The New York Times*, www.nytimes.com/2010/05/25/world/25military.html (accessed 24 May 2010).
13. H. Dabashi, *Post-Orientalism: Knowledge and Power in a Time of Terror*, New Brunswick, NJ: Transaction Publishers, 2009, 102.
14. E. Said, *Orientalism*, New York: Vintage Books, 1979, 33.
15. Y. Kemal, *İM4*, 88, 221ff, 287–99.
16. Ibid., 346.
17. Ibid., 376–84.
18. Ibid., 453.
19. Ibid., 492.
20. In others, Seyran crosses to confront Adem, Ali Safa Bey's man sent to kill Yobazoğlu's horse; Temir and Hürü Ana cross the meadow for Hürü Ana to see and heal Memed; Sultan Murad crosses the plain to visit Kırkgöz Ocağı; and early in the story, we learn that those who unintentionally became the settled villagers of Çukurova crossed as part of an özgür bir dünya in which they would live in the mountains in the summer months and on the plains in the winter, reciting, "May the five thousand armed riders not come."

21 Y. Kemal, *İM4*, 495–510.
22 Ibid., 513–16.
23 Ibid., 572–80.
24 Ibid., 625–32.
25 H. Arendt, *The Promise of Politics*, Jerome Kohn (ed.), New York: Schocken Books, 2005, 175.
26 J. Derrida, "*Différance*," in M. Taylor (ed.) *Deconstruction in Context: Literature and Philosophy*, Chicago, IL: University of Chicago Press, 1986, 401.
27 E. Lévinas, "The Fact of Revelation and Human Understanding," in S. Hand (ed.) *The Levinas Reader*, London: Blackwell Publishers, 1989, 206.
28 Y. Kemal, *İM4*, 636–38.
29 Ibid., 638–39.

INDEX

Alcázar (Toledo), ix
Alcibiades, 31–32, 40, 45, 50, 62, 71–73
Alexander, xiii–xiv, 27–29, 37, 39–40,
    44–45, 50–52, 55, 84, 269, 274; and
    Medism, 66–68, 70, 72–77, 281
*Alexander Sarcophagus, circa
    325–311BC*, xiii, 274
Alfonso VII, xi
Algerian Women in their Apartments,
    xi–xii
Amasis, 69
Anacharsis, 75
Anacık Sultan, 266, 274, 278
Aneristus, 64–65
Antiochus, 28–29, 38–39, 44–46, 53–55,
    62, 74, 76, 82, 91
Arc de Triomphe, x, xiv
Aristeus, 64–65
Aristogoras, 25, 54
Arrian, 21, 30
Art of Triumph, xiii–xiv
Artaphrenes, 24, 69
Artayctes, 25–26, 54
Asım Çavuş, 274
Athens, as "school of Hellas," 32, 269
Attalus, 28
Aziz, 274

Balfour, A., 271
Battal Ağa, 273, 278–79
Benjamin, W., 7–12, 20, 266
Bessus, 40, 62
Brasidas, 71
Byron, 3, 24, 81–82

Capilla Real, x
captured Lycian prisoner, 75
Cathedral of Seville, xi
Chios Nautical Museum, xii
Çiçeklidere, women of, 277
Cliesthenes, 24
Columbus, C., xi
Conveying, 10–11
Corbares, 40
Creasy, E., 82
Croesus, 21, 40–41, 47, 70
Curtius Rufus, Q., 20; and Medism,
    69–70, 73, 76
Cybele, 25
Cyrus, 25, 40, 70–71; friend/enemy, 15

Dabashi, H., xvi, 270
Dadaoğlu, 6, 91
Dallmayr, F., 19
Darius, 24–25, 27, 29, 38, 40, 48, 50,
    64, 67, 74–75
Davidson, A., 268
Değirmenoluk, 93–120
Delacroix, E., xi–xii
Derrida, J., 1, 268
Diitrephes, 49
Döne, 278
Durmuş Ali, 274

Emiş Hatun, 279
Eumenes, 33, 74

Farr, J., 16
The Fanatics of Tangiers, xii

Fatmalı, 279
Ferhat Hoca, 274, 276–77
Foucault, M., 22, 268

Gadamer, H.-G., 11
Gylippus, 35

Hannibal, 39, 45
Hatçe, 274, 278–79, 282
Heckel, W., 21
Hentsch, T., 86, 267
hermeneutical interpretation, 10–11,
    18–21, 89, 284
Hermocrates, 39
Hermolaus, 67–68
Hero, 24, 81
Herodotus: fear, 15; as storyteller, 7–9,
    20; and Medism, 68–72, 281; and
    Orientalism, 68–71
Hippias, 24n
Histiaus, 61–62
Holland, T., 22
Homer, 3, 24
Hürü Ana, 266, 274, 279–80

İdris Bey, 279
İnce Memed, 5–7, 11–13, 267–69,
    276–82; see also Memed
Iraz, 274
İsmail Emmi, 279
Istanbul Archaeology Museum, xiii
Istanbul Military Museum, xiii

Karacaoğlan, 6
Kasım, 274
Kemal, Y., 5–11, 266, 275, 277, 282
Kerimoğlu, 274
King of Spain Building, xi
Koca Osman, 279

La Bataille d'Aboukir, viii
Leander, 24, 81
Lejeune, L.-F., viii, x
Livy, T., 20
Lucius Scipio, 33

Mahan, A. T., 86
Manlius, 91–92
Mardonius, 49, 54, 69
Massacre at Chios, xii
Medizer, 57, 63–77, 81, 83–89, 281,
    283–85

Mehmet (Sultan), 82
Memed, 272–82
Murat, J., x
Museo de Bellas Artes, xii
Museo del Ejército, ix
Musée de l'Armée, ix
Müslüm, 274, 279

Napoleon, ix, xiii–xiv, 274
Nandy, A., 1
Nicias, 62, 72–75
Nicolaus, 64–65

Ovid, 3, 24
Oxantes, 51

Pagden, A., 16, 21–22, 88
Pausanias, 63, 66, 75
Pericles, 31–32, 38, 45, 49, 71
Phillip II, 27
Phillip V, 28, 33, 39, 43, 45, 52–53, 67
Philotas, 75
Phrynichus, 71
Pir Sultan Abdal, 91
polis to empire, movement from, 2–3,
    16–18, 20, 22, 27–29, 56, 81–82,
    85–88
Pollis, 64–65
Persepolis, 35, 50, 55
Porus, 52, 55
Protesilaus, 26
Protodamus, 64–65

Roxanne, 67

Sadocus, 65
Said, E., 271
Sakızlı, 179–263
Sambus, 52
Sarı, 274
Scythian elder, 72–73, 274
Scythians, 76
Seurre, B. G., x
Seyran, 274, 276
Sibylline verses, 92
Sicily, 46–47, 62, 73, 75
Sidonians at Tyre, 74
Sisigambis, 66–67, 78
Sitacles, 65
storyteller, 7–12
Strassler, R., 21, 27, 82
Süleyman, 279

Süleyman (Sultan), 82
Syracuse, 62

Taylor, C., 19
Theophilos Museum, xii
Themistocles, 63, 66, 75
Thucydides, 20; and Medism, 72
Tiberius Gracchus, 33
Timagoras, 64–65
Tissaphernes, 26, 50
Topal Ali, 273–74
translation, as conveying, 10

unnamed second city: Alexander and, 70

Vayvay, 120–79
Victoire d'Aboukir, viii–x, xiv–xv
Western Political Thought, 16–17;
  see also polis to empire
White, J.B., 19
Wittgenstein, L., vii
Wolin, S., 16–17

Xanthippus, 26
Xerxes, 22, 25–26, 29, 31–35, 38, 40,
  45, 47–48, 56, 63, 69–70; and enmity,
  15

Yörük women, 274